AYAHUASCA READER

AYAHUASCA READER
Encounters with the Amazon's Sacred Vine

Luis Eduardo Luna

&

Steven F. White

EDITORS

sʄ

SYNERGETIC PRESS
Santa Fe, New Mexico

ACKNOWLEDGMENTS

The editors would like to express their deep gratitude to Faye Martin, Jesse Lichtenstein, John Bursnall, Cathy Shrady, Deborah Parrish Snyder, Nancy Pierce, Gary Fisketjon, Cathy Tedford of The Richard F. Brush Art Gallery at St. Lawrence University, Mary Lloyd, St. Lawrence University's Faculty Development Fund, and The Department of Modern Languages and Communication, Swedish School of Economics and Business Administration, Helsinki, Finland, for support during the preparation of the manuscript.

The editors also wish to thank the following contributors, literary executors and publishers for their permission to include in this volume previously unpublished and published material in English or in English translation: Françoise Barbira-Freedman, Mengatue Caiga, Oscar Calavia Saez, Francisca Campos do Nascimento, Jean-Pierre Chaumeil, Ohue Coba, Alfonso Domingo, Maria Domingo, Roberto Echevarren, CEFLURIS, Elsje Maria Lagrou, Milton Maia, E. Jean Matteson Langdon, Dennis J. McKenna, Ib Michael, Jonathon S. Miller-Weisberger, Hugo Niño, Huepe Orengo Coba, Alfredo Payaguaje, Dale Pendell, Hilario Peña, Alex Polari de Alverga, Alberto Prohaño, Scott S. Robinson, William Torres C., and Mario Villafranca Saravia.

Excerpt from *The Three Halves of Ino Moxo: Teachings of the the Wizard of the Upper Amazon* by César Calvo, translated by Kenneth A. Symington, published by Inner Traditions International, Rochester, VT 05767. Translation copyright © by César Calvo.

Excerpt reprinted with the permission of Simon & Schuster from *One River* by Wade Davis, copyright © 1996 by Wade Davis. Excerpt also published in Great Britain by Simon & Schuster, London, 1997.

Excerpt from *The Spears of Twilight: Life and Death in the Amazon Jungle* by Philippe Descola, translated by Janet Lloyd, copyright © 1996 by Philippe Descola. Reprinted by permission of The New Press in the United States and HarperCollins Publishers, Ltd. in London.

Excerpt from "The Geometric Designs of the Shipibo-Conibo in Ritual Context" by Angelika Gebhart-Sayer, *Journal of Latin American Lore* 11:2 (1985), pp. 143–176. Reproduced with permission of The Regents of the University of California.

Excerpt from *The Yagé Letters,* copyright © 1963, 1975 by Allen Ginsberg. Reprinted by Permission of CITY LIGHTS BOOKS.

Excerpt from *The Way of the Shaman* by Michael Harner, copyright © 1980 by Michael Harner. Reprinted by permission of HarperCollins Publishers, Inc.

Excerpt from *Rio Tigre and Beyond: The Amazon Jungle Medicine of Manuel Córdova* by F. Bruce Lamb, copyright © 1985. Reprinted with permission of North Atlantic Books, Berkeley, California, USA.

Excerpt from *At Play in the Fields of the Lord* by Peter Matthiessen, copyright © 1966 by Peter Matthiessen. Reprinted by permission of Random House, Inc. Extract from *At Play in the Fields of the Lord* by Peter Matthiessen. First published in Great Britain in 1966 by William Heinemann Ltd. First published by Harvill in 1988. Reproduced by permission of The Harvill Press.

"The Real World of Manuel Córdova" from *Travels* by W. S. Merwin, copyright © 1992 by W. S. Merwin. Reprinted by permission of Alfred A. Knopf, Inc.

Excerpts from *Amazonian Cosmos: The Sexual and Religious Symbolism of the Tukano Indians* by Gerardo Reichel-Dolmatoff, copyright © 1971 by Gerardo Reichel-Dolmatoff. Reprinted by permission of The University of Chicago Press.

Excerpts from *The Shaman and the Jaguar: A Study of Narcotic Drugs among the Indians of Colombia* by Gerardo Reichel-Dolmatoff, Temple University Press, copyright © 1975 by Gerardo Reichel-Dolmatoff. Reprinted by permission of Alicia Dussan de Reichel.

Excerpt from *Shamanism, Colonialism, and the Wild Man: A Study in Terror and Healing* by Michael Taussig, copyright © 1987 by Michael Taussig. Reprinted by permission of The University of Chicago Press.

Excerpt from *The Storyteller* by Mario Vargas Llosa, translated by Helen Lane. Translation copyright © 1989 by Farrar, Straus and Giroux, Inc. Reprinted by permission of Farrar, Straus and Giroux, LLC. Excerpt from *The Storyteller* by Mario Vargas Llosa in Great Britain reprinted by permission of Faber and Faber, Ltd.

COVER PAINTING: Pablo Amaringo

COVER, INTERIOR DESIGN, AND PRODUCTION: V. S. Elliott, SunFlower Designs

For you,
the ayahuasca reader,
whoever you are,
however you enter these pages,
and wherever they may lead you.

TABLE OF CONTENTS

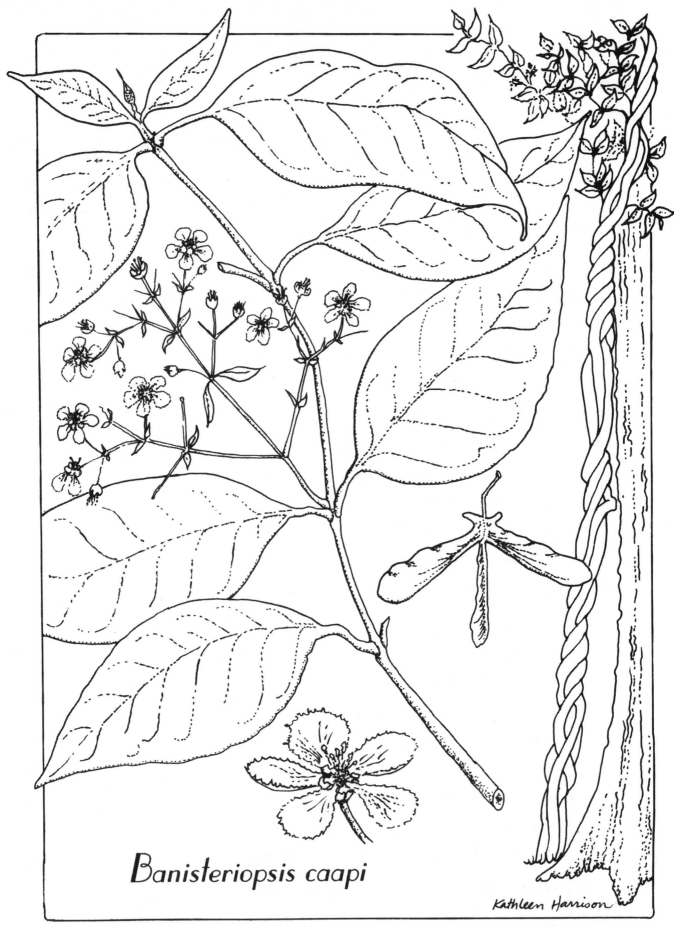

Banisteriopsis caapi

Botanical illustration, ink on paper, © Kathleen Harrison.

INTRODUCTION

We began contemplating the scope of this collection as the result of extended conversations at a 1996 conference sponsored by the Botanical Preservation Corps on Ethnobotany and Shamanism at the Mayan ruins of Palenque. Given our shared interest in anthropology, literature and the dynamics of *ayahuasca,* a sacred drink that has been used for millennia by at least seventy indigenous groups primarily in the Upper Amazon and Orinoco basins for adivination, healing and other cosmogonic/shamanic purposes, it became clear to us that there was the potential for a very exciting project on which we could collaborate. The general objective of this anthology is to provide the reader with a panorama of texts from nearly a dozen languages that, collectively, treat the *ayahuasca* experience from what might be called an "anthropoliterary" perspective. These include indigenous mythic narratives and testimonies (from a number of ethnic groups who use the drink, including the Siona, Cashinahua, Huaorani, Desana, Witoto, Yagua, Inga and Secoya) as well as narratives related by western travelers, scientists and writers who have had contact with *ayahuasca* in different contexts. The anthology also contains *ayahuasca*-inspired lyrics of hymns received by members of Brazilian religious organizations that incorporate the drink in their ceremonies. In some cases, the material included has been published previously, often in difficult to find journals and books in a variety of languages. In other cases, the authors have produced their contributions expressly for this anthology.

In order to organize what eventually grew into an almost unwieldy amount of material, we divided the book into four sections, while recognizing that these categories overlap a great deal in terms of their content: I. *Ayahuasca* Myths and Testimonies; II. *Ayahuasca* Cultural Encounters; III. New Religions: *Santo Daime, Barquinha* and *União do Vegetal* (UDV); and IV. Writing *Ayahuasca.* We realize, of course, that there are inherent dangers in attempting to compartmentalize the (dis)ordering and all-embracing principle of *ayahuasca* itself in that it rejects such mutually-exclusive boundaries.

Ayahuasca (also known as *yagé, natem, caapi, nishi,* and by dozens of other vernacular names) is merely one of many psychotropic decoctions derived by humans throughout the ages based on a profound knowledge of the plant world. As a means of defining with greater clarity the diverse roles of sacred plants in both ancient and contemporary societies, Michael Winkelman proposes the name "psychointegrator plants." In summarizing some of the cross-cultural commonalities with regard to the use of these plants, Winkelman says that "the induced experiences have effects upon personality in: entering into a personal relationship with a reality established in a mythical time; developing relationships with an animal spiritual realm which is the source of power and self identification; the dissolution or death of the ego and its resurrection and transformation; and social rituals to enhance social identity formation, group integration and cohesion, and to reaffirm cultural values and beliefs." He continues by saying that "the ubiquitous simultaneous therapeutic, religious, spiritual and medicinal roles of these plants have implications for understanding the nature of human consciousness and the spiritual."[1] Consequently, efforts to understand the material presented in this anthology necessarily entail a broader than usual interdisciplinary perspective. In this spirit, we have attempted to bridge traditional disciplinary gaps in order to enrich and expand critical vocabularies and approaches to cultural studies. Even so, our whole is limited in scope and seeks to complement itself by means of a bibliography more extensive in disciplinary terms.

The first section opens with a series of mythopoetic narratives in which *ayahuasca* is a protagonist.[2] The *ayahuasca* plant has its otherworldly origin in mythic time: either it comes from the incestuous union of the Sun Father and his Daughter, or the secret knowledge from the subaquatic realm, or the cadaver of a shaman, or the tail of a giant serpent joining heaven and earth. These diverse indigenous groups all believe that the visionary vine is a vehicle which makes the primordial accessible to humanity. According to Stephen Crites, the narrative forms of sacred stories "orient the life of people through time, their life-time, their individual and corporate experience."[3]

Anthropologists make a distinction between the *emic* (the declarations of "natives") and the *etic* (the interpretations of the observer-analyst).[4] For the first section of this anthology, we have preferred methodologies that either emphasize the *emic* or blur the distinctions between the *emic* and the *etic*. Gatherers and interpreters of mythic narratives included in the *Ayahuasca Reader* such as E. Jean Matteson Langdon, Elsje Maria Lagrou, and Jonathon S. Miller-Weisberger[5] mention the names of the indigenous storytellers whose words they transcribe and translate as a way of highlighting the emic perspective as well as the individual stamp on an evolving narrative's latest flowering. The ever-changing new story is, as Stephen Crites puts it, "superimposed on the image-stream of the original chronicle."[6] One example of this phenomenon is the Desana myth (transcribed by Gerardo Reichel-Dolmatoff) of the Snake-Canoe descending from the Milky Way with the first inhabitants of the world, which is transformed into the High River Fire Canoe carrying *yagé* (ayahuasca) people and the white caciques in the narrative recorded by Langdon, the dragon/boat and singing spirits of Harner's account of his *ayahuasca* experience among the Conibo, and the silver canoe with a Lady in the bow coming down from the sky in the hymn received by Mestre Irineu. In the second and third of these narratives, the figures within the canoe invite the narrators to join them on a revelatory journey, an offer that is accepted. Crites sustains that the form of consciousness is narrative and that "consciousness is molded by the sacred story to which it awakens."[7] For Claudio Naranjo, the *ayahuasca* experience provides a unique opportunity "to observe the mind engaged in mythopoetic activity, to interrogate it on its products, and even interact with archetypal productions in their nascent state."[8] The act of concentrating on a particular myth under the effects of *ayahuasca*, according to Osmani/Lagrou, enables the individual to live in it and to understand its meaning. In "Mythologies of the Vine," Oscar Calavia Sáez provides a fascinating analysis of how the archetypes of *ayahuasca* mythology, which he divides into aquatic and chthonic narratives, reflect a particular indigenous group's relationship with its environment (riverine vs. high rain forest) and its ancestors.

Langdon's contribution "A Visit to the Second Heaven: A Siona Narrative of the *yagé* Experience," opens with a fundamental Siona conception that also characterizes other indigenous groups of the Upper Amazon: the assumption that the universe is composed of two superimposed realities and that the *other* is eventually accessible by means of *ayahuasca*. The narrative describes a failure to know the domains or *designs (toya)* of the high river which, as Langdon points out, "runs through the *second heaven,* the heavenly level above the earth that begins at the point where you can see no farther with the naked eye." The fear of being vanquished upon entering the dimensions of the mind is a recurring theme in the narratives throughout the *Ayahuasca Reader*. Langdon's text also highlights the problematic issue of translation with regard to representation. Her more literal, line-by-line rendering of the narrative told by Ricardo Yaiguaje is an attempt not to take the teller's language toward that of the reader, but to bring the reader closer to the teller's words. Her refusal to retell or rewrite a narrative based on an anonymous informant then present it in a monolingual format (a technique related to the important, pioneering work of Gerardo Reichel-Dolmatoff among the Tukano Indians) is, perhaps, more ethical than that of Hugo Niño in that Langdon does not create the false impression that the indigenous text somehow mimics or conforms to western narrative techniques.[9]

Langdon's analytical approach, which she has defined as "symbolic anthropology,"[10] provides an interesting contrast to Hugo Niño's Marxist methodology in "Unámarai, Father of *yagé*," which evolved over a seven-year period beginning in 1967. According to the introduction to his collection *Primitivos relatos contados otra vez: héroes y mitos amazónicos* (Primitive Tales Retold: Amazonian Heroes and Myths), Niño initially believes that a mythology should be preserved just as he collected it so that it can serve him as a document to corroborate scientific principles. Later, he reconceives the ethnoliterary process as one of rewriting. He comes to the conclusion that it is important to take into account the magical qualities of the voice as it shapes myth and ritual poetry and feels that he cannot ignore the aesthetic and culturally creative purposes of this communication as well. In his introduction, Niño compares himself (presumptuously) to Homer in that he believes he is shaping an aesthetically pleasing written form from an oral tradition. For him, his "retold" myth is an unproblematic "faithful restoration" that is the product not of a flight of the imagination, but rather something that is based on his research, his experience and his observations in that part of America.

In many ways, the content of the first section illustrates the current intradisciplinary debate with regard to what Janet M. Chernela calls "the anthropological word, its purpose and its power."[11] According to Chernela, there are two basic positions:

> *The so-called scientific (or "scientistic") extreme holds that objective assessment of an external reality is the realizable goal of anthropology, made possible through disinterested observation and methodological rigor. In contrast, the postmodern humanistic critique asserts that ethnography is a literary creation whose false "scientism" obfuscates underlying interest in both ethnographer and native. At its extreme, the interpretive-humanistic perspective holds to an epistemological relativism in which ethnography is a "literature of observational fact" no more authoritative than any other fictive work whose coherence and orderliness result from rhetorical devices. Proponents of this position claim to be "modern," suggesting a paradigm shift in anthropology away from traditional ethnographic description and explanation and toward an interactive and interpretive ethnographic process in which goals of objectivity are unattainable and misapplied. Postmodernists also criticize the "scientific approaches" for neglecting the role played by anthropology in the service of hegemonic powers. These critics call for a thorough recognition and critique of colonial and neocolonial influences in shaping what anthropologists have misrepresented as isolated "peoples without histories."[12]*

While recognizing the problematic nature of the reproduction of the "native" voice by means of translations that are sometimes translations of translations (a situation that recalls the debate generated by *I, Rigoberta Menchú: An Indian Woman in Guatemala* and "testimonial" literature[13]), we sought texts for the first section of this anthology that approximate the emic, such as the first person narratives of Ricardo Yaiguaje, Alberto Prohaño, Hilario Peña and Fernando Payaguaje that relate individual stories of lives, struggles, journeys to other realms and vast knowledge of botany, emperiled, of course, by ecological destruction and a lack of shamanic successors among today's younger generations. In these four instances, the ethnographer is a *listener*, though no doubt shapes the autobiographical discourse to varying degrees through transcription, editing and translation.

Perhaps one of the most interesting characteristics of the narrative by Prohaño as told to French anthropologist Jean-Pierre Chaumeil is the emphasis on ritual itself and the actual songs used to invoke the different plant-spirits. The individual performance of the shaman facilitates a social function in connection with the mythic presences invoked through the act of singing. This text also exemplifies the role of *ayahuasca* as a milestone in the path of knowledge, following other sacred plants such as *piripiri (Cyperaceous* sp.) and tobacco and preceding others, such as *Brugmansia* sp.

What gives the *Ayahuasca Reader* a circular quality is a link between "*Ayahuasca* Myths and Testimonies" of Section I and the literary selections of Section IV, "Writing *Ayahuasca*," based on the important relationships between psychointegrators and a creative therapeutic culture that joins language, music, art and performance.[14] The idea of performance is a critical concept underlying Jerome Rothenberg's work on "primitive poetry" in *Technicians of the Sacred*: "Our ideas of poetry — including, significantly, our idea of the poet — began to look back *consciously* to the early & late shamans of those other worlds: not as a title to be seized but as a model for the shaping of meanings & intensities through language. As the reflection of our yearning to create a meaningful ritual life, a life lived at the level of poetry — that looking-back related to the emergence of a new poetry & art rooted in performance & in the oldest, most universal of human traditions."[15] Shamanism, then, as a series of individual performances in a dynamic complex across space and time, is a simultaneous process of mediation and domestication.

If the shaman, by definition, is one who goes beyond, he (or she) is also one who crosses ethnic boundaries in consulting with shamans from other groups, generally providing the technology for adapting to an environment that, historically, is characterized not by isolation but by great intercultural penetration over long periods of time. This process also involves the shamanic appropriation of any and all power-metaphors, including received books, radios, magic matches, white pills, drugstores, contemporary weapons of war, and UFOs. Future shamans will no doubt be opening spiritual windows on the Internet. This is entirely in keeping with what Josep M. Fericgla has called the "adaptogenic function" of *ayahuasca* in terms of being something that one incorporates in order to modify oneself or one's external reality.[16]

Fericgla also proposes that "ayahuasca consumption induces a dialogic consciousness" that facilitates "auto-reflexion as an essential strategy in avoiding egocentrism (the starting point of radical ethnocentrism)."[17] Fericgla, in other words, envisions *ayahuasca*-solutions to interethnic conflict, ideas which may or may not be in keeping with shamanic practices in terms of embedding knowledge in the *ayahuasca* experience, seeking power over one's enemies and preserving at all costs a particular, threatened ethnic identity, examples of which can be found in the testimonies of Alberto Prohaño and Fernando Payaguaje. With regard to *ayahuasca* as a human construct, Oscar Calavia Sáez distinguishes between a contemporary pacified *ayahuasca* and an older, more bellicose, conception of the sacred drink.

Janet M. Chernela sustains that western historians highlight "the significance of the speaker as an individual, whose subjective meanings, intentions, perceptions, interests, goals, interpretations and representations must all be taken into account." She goes on to say, however, that "while social historians rely on data derived from the written manuscripts of individuals, ethnographers transcribe audio recordings of naturally occurring speech in which individual contribution is often obscured."[18] Focusing on the individual and speech as the locus of cultural change (as is the case in several instances in "*Ayahuasca* Myths and Testimonies"), new approaches to anthropology no longer treat indigenous people as atemporal members of a static culture outside the vicissitudes of history, but rather as producers of history.[19] This anthology facilitates a kind of "mythistoric" understanding (in keeping with the ideas expressed by Dennis Tedlock in his introduction to the *Popol Vuh*). *Ayahuasca* is a means of transport into an ancestral state, a way of passing into myth itself as a protagonist, which is one way of understanding César Calvo's *The Three Halves of Ino Moxo* (a fragment of which appears in Section IV). The natural world as invoked by Ino Moxo is a living memory of creation. Nevertheless, Calvo's narrative world is not divorced from historical time: the tragedy of the rubber boom (1880–1914) and its disastrous effects on the Amazonian indigenous population periodically emerges from the consciousness of the literary protagonist indirectly allied with the author himself. The adaptive ability of the spirits reflects the changes in human history. This is especially true in the paintings by Peruvian Pablo Amaringo in which an eclectic array of spiritual beings from past and present joins forces in kinetic, visionary panoramas.[20]

The second section, "*Ayahuasca* Cultural Encounters," contains ethnographic methodologies that are characterized by the absence of a so-called objective, *etic* distance in that the anthropologists/ethnobotanists (Richard Spruce, Gerardo Reichel-Dolmatoff, Scott S. Robinson, Michael Harner, Philippe Descola, Wade Davis, William Torres C., Françoise Barbira Freedman, Michael Taussig, and Angelika Gebhart Sayer) all demonstrate varying degrees of interactive participation in *ayahuasca* rituals among indigenous and mestizo populations. A future historian putting together the western chronicle of *ayahuasca* would almost certainly recognize the importance of taking into account the texts we have selected for this section.

"*Ayahuasca* Cultural Encounters" opens with two classic pieces — Spruce's 1852 description of his botanical identification and ingestion of *caapi* among the Tukano Indians of the Vaupés, and Reichel-Dolmatoff's meticulously-documented account more than a century later of his participation in a *yajé* ceremony among the Barasana Indians of the Pira-Paraná.[21] In both cases, the authors manifest a truly scientific urge to document not only the externalities of the decoction (plant identification, methods of preparation and ritual procedures), but also its *internal* function in the human mind. This approach set the standards that would be followed by botanists such as Richard Evans Schultes (as well as his disciples that include Wade Davis) and anthropologists working in the Amazon, some of whom are represented in this collection. Spruce and Reichel-Dolmatoff were truly remarkable scientists. Richard Evans Schultes has characterized Spruce's work, undertaken from 1851–1855, as the most complete phytogeographic labor ever carried out in the Amazonia.[22] Reichel-Dolmatoff, born in Austria in 1912,[23] was the founder of Colombian archeology and anthropology. He was certainly the first anthropologist to fully recognize and document in a human group the omnipresence of the states of consciousness produced by sacred South American plants. Using the categories by which western thought compartmentalizes cultural reality, Reichel-Dolmatoff analyzed the indigenous group's mythopoeia, religion, ecological awareness, music, dance, visual arts and philosophy.

In terms of other contributors to this section, it is important to remember that Michael Harner's well known discovery of the way of the shaman has its origin in his pioneering research among the Shuar and Conibo of Ecuador and Peru. The piece we have included describes his first *ayahuasca* experience with a compelling mixture of drama and humor. Scott Robinson's contribution (written for this anthology) is a remembrance of journeys within journeys by means of *ayahuasca*-driven memories. Robinson personalizes ethnobotanical history by mentioning figures such as Richard Evans Schultes, Schultes's protégées Homer Pinkley and Timothy Plowman, as well as Allen Ginsberg and Claudio Naranjo. Robinson also laments the devastating consequences of oil exploration on traditional cultures of the Ecuadorean Amazon. As he says at the end of his piece, "I'm almost afraid to go back."

From Descola's *The Spears of Twilight: Life and Death in the Amazon Jungle,* a companion to his impressive ethnographic study of the Achuar (a Jibaroan indigenous group of the Peruvian Amazon) *La nature doméstique: symbolisme et praxis dans l'écologie des Achuar,* we have included the author's reflective description of his first experience with *ayahuasca* and how it relates to his theoretical knowledge of shamanism. We also have selected an excerpt from Wade Davis's *One River: Explorations and Discoveries in the Amazon Rain Forest* that is a verbalization of the writer's encounter with *ayahuasca,* treating the terror of dissolution into another dimension and the transformation of thought into vision.

The complexities of the critical model used perhaps too extensively by Torres in "Jaguar-Becoming," could have the unfortunate effect of alienating readers, who may perceive in it an unnecessary, even suffocating, application of the thoroughly "foreign" theories of Deleuze and Guattari. Nevertheless, these authors raise fascinating questions about the difficulty of conceiving a specific causality of drugs in which, according to Deleuze, "desire *directly charges the perception-system.*" Deleuze understands perception in this sense as internal and external and is especially attentive to space-time perceptions. What most interests Deleuze is "how drugs concern above all, velocities, the modifications of velocity, the thresholds of perception, shapes and movements, micro-perceptions, the perception that becomes molecular, superhuman or subhuman times, etc."[24] This new landscape is a potential source of astonishing beauty for Deleuze and, no doubt, Torres. For this reason, we urge the reader to be patient with the experimental and hermetic qualities of Torres's contribution to this reader. In addition to the theoretical complications, there are inter-linguistic and morphological difficulties in the creation of new shamanic chants in the article as well. Sometimes it seems as if it were the Chilean avant-garde poet Vicente Huidobro of *Altazor* fame who drank *ayahuasca* and parachuted into the Amazon of William Torres.

Françoise Barbira Freedman, in her contribution to this section, examines the female principles of Jaguar-Becoming in the context of the interacting polarities of Amazonian religious and ethnic diversity. She describes how indigenous and mestizo healing and symbolic systems coexist and how outsiders, like herself, might have very ambivalent reactions to shamanic power-appropriations from Catholicism.

Michael Taussig's account of *yagé* nights, in "Montage," is punctuated by the contemporary political violence of Colombia, in the context of which, shamanic curers and their assistants are hardly exempt from the government repression unleashed against an armed leftist opposition. Fundamental to Taussig's approach is the concept of montage, which, in Taussig's words, provokes "sudden and infinite connections between dissimilars in an endless, or almost endless, process of connection-making and connection breaking." Taussig prefers to link the *yagé* experience with Antonin Artaud's ideas regarding anarchy, disorder, chaos and the "infinite perspective of conflicts" that the French author proposes as part of his aesthetic of a Theater of Cruelty. Taussig rejects the idea of ritual linked to order as well as the Romantic concept of the Symbol which forms the basis, in his opinion, of the anthropological models defined by, among others, Victor Turner. For Taussig, the notion of the mystical "trip," the ritual leader and the absorption of the individual in the tribe are all elements of an overly male, fascist fascination. Taussig believes that the shaman as Wild Man and Possessor of Magic is a colonial construct. He characterizes the shaman's song as "ordered disorder" and "continuous discontinuity." For him, truth is a shifting, multiple concept of coexisting opposites linked to a series of incomplete representations in the theatrical sense. He prefers to emphasize the *social* function of the cure.

As a kind of prelude to some of the issues raised in the final part of the anthology, we also have included in Section II an excerpt from "The Geometric Designs of the Shipibo-Conibo in Ritual Context" by Angelika Gebhart Sayer. In this article, the author maintains that the visionary design art of this indigenous group from eastern Peru, while not a "veritable writing system . . . may well have constituted a graphic device comprising symbolic, semantic units, in perhaps a mnemotechnical arrangement." Gebhard-Sayer goes on to say that the shamanic act of invisibly marking or writing on the skin of individuals by means of spiritual projection is part of an ongoing therapeutic treatment and that "every person feels spiritually permeated and saturated with designs."[25] She refers to this process in the fragment we have included in this anthology as "design therapy." It may be illuminating to consider this body art a proto-text, a pre-history of writing in what José Sánchez-Parga has defined as "a process of progressive textual separations."[26] In other words, the history of writing can be understood as the gradual de-anatomization of the text as it is lifted from the body and shifted to textiles, stones, ceramics, monuments and other materially-objective surfaces.

Section III, "New Religions: *Santo Daime, Barquinha,* and *União do Vegetal* (UDV)" treats the three primary Brazilian religious groups (all of which have an underlying Christian orientation) that use *Daime/Vegetal (ayahuasca)* as a sacred drink and sacrament in their ceremonies. These syncretic religions were created in the Amazon region by three visionaries: Raimundo Irineu Serra (1892–1971), Daniel Pereira de Matos (1904–1958), and José Gabriel da Costa (1922–1971). The first two (both of African Brazilian descent) were born in the northeastern Brazilian state of Maranhão and established themselves in Rio Branco, the capital of the state of Acre in the 1930s and '40s, respectively. Although Daniel Pereira de Matos learned about *Daime* from Raimundo Irineu Serra, he soon developed his own particular religious offshoot known now as *Barquinha* (the boat), in which there are marked Afro-Brazilian elements. José Gabriel da Costa, born in Feira de Santana (Bahia), arrived in the Amazon in 1943 as a *soldado da borracha* as part of an army of rubber tappers sent by the Brazilian government, which participated in World War II on the side of the Allies: once the Japanese troops were occupying the rubber plantations in Southeast Asia, the idea was to reopen the rubber trade established in Brazil in the previous century. Mestre Gabriel, as he is called by his followers, created the UDV in 1961 in Porto Velho (Rondônia). It is now a religious organization with more than 5,000 members in urban centers throughout Brazil and has achieved a modest expansion outside the country as well.

A fourth religious leader, the *padrinho* Sebastião Mota de Melo (1920–1990), initiated by Mestre Irineu Serra, created the *Centro Ecléctico de Fluente Luz Universal Raimundo Irineu Serra* (Eclectic Center of Fluid Universal Light Raimundo Irineu Serra, or CEFLURIS) in 1974, which was independent from those who succeeded his teacher. His is the branch of *Daime*[27] that has spread outside Brazil, particularly to Spain, Holland, certain Latin American countries and Japan.

These four religious leaders derived their particular doctrinal corpus from European (Catholicism and Kardecism[28]), African and Amerindian traditions. Taken as a whole, it is a religious phenomenon of great importance and probable future impact. It may be seen as a spreading South American counterpart to the Bwiti religion in Gabon and neighboring countries (which incorporates *Tabernanthae iboga* in its ceremonies) and the Native American Church of the United States (which uses *peyotl* as a sacrament).

The section opens with a number of hymns, the sung prayers that form the basis of the religious doctrines of Raimundo Irineu Serra and Daniel Pereira de Matos. Scrupulous attention has been paid to the translation process in an attempt to preserve in English the rhyme and the rhythm of the originals in Portuguese. For these translations to be judged entirely successful, however, they would have to be singable versions that could be integrated into a religious ceremony with the identical music used currently by these groups.

The hymns are said to be *received,* not composed, and are viewed as divine gifts. Although, naturally, it is the *hinários,* or hymn collections of the spiritual leaders that make up the core of the religious ceremonies, many followers of *Santo Daime* and *Barquinha* keep their own collections of hymns they have received as well, and, on certain occasions, these hymns are also sung ceremonially. For this anthology, we have included hymns by Raimundo Irineu Serra, Daniel Pereira de Matos, Sebastião Mota de Melo and his son Alfredo Gregório de Melo as well as a *hino* by *madrinha* Francisca Campos do Nascimento, leader of one of the *Barquinha* churches.

As charged parables of power, the hymns contain the simple enigmas of, for example, a little bird, a gardener, and flowers that become landmarks for a journey toward spiritual fulfillment. These sung texts often have a strong narrative thread. In other words, they tell a story in a highly-ordered pattern of repetitions and refrains that lend themselves to memorization. The constant mention in the hymns of father, mother, brothers and sisters provides a sense of familial peace, unity and consolation to the singers moving in unison in the temple from sunset to sunrise. The hymns also refer to elements of the natural world and its harmonious beauty, which underlie the visionary experience. The continuous movement reinforces this regimented sense of order super-imposed on chaos.

We have chosen to represent the writings of Alex Polari de Alverga by choosing an excerpt from *O livro das mirações: viagem ao Santo Daime* (The Book of Visions: Journey to *Santo Daime)* because of its frank depiction of the author's conversion from a militant Marxist participant in the armed struggle against Brazil's military dictatorship of the 1960s and '70s (activities that resulted in the imprisonment of Polari, whose case as a political prisoner was taken up by Brazilian human rights organizations) to a follower and, later, a leading figure in the *Santo Daime* religious group. Especially revealing in Polari's narrative are the initial doubts and irritations in this evolution. Given the inclusion of numerous *Santo Daime* hymns in this anthology, it is important to note how, in Polari's writing, the hymns gradually permeate his consciousness as he begins to understand and accept their teachings. Another theme in his writing is the nostalgia for an idealized, vanished indigenous culture in the "Journey of the Inca" section as well as the respect for the living incarnation of the past in the myths of a contemporary indigenous group. Polari cites a study by Jean Monod on the Piaroa culture (an indigenous group that incorporates sacred plants in their religious ceremonies) and speaks of his appreciation of indigenous knowledge as a way of combating what Monod calls the "sterilizing influence" of western culture.[29]

In addition to a number of *chamadas* (received songs), the UDV possesses a rich oral tradition, a series of *histórias* told by José Gabriel da Costa to his disciples during sessions in which the *vegetal* was taken. These stories are now either heard on tape recordings of the UDV founder's voice or recited on special occasions by one of the *mestres* leading the session. These narratives are generally kept secret from non-members, and their memorization is an essential requirement in the development of the member along a four-stage hierarchical ladder, the highest category of which *(mestre)* can only be attained by men. For doctrinal reasons, therefore, we are unable to present narratives in this compilation.[30]

As a kind of substitute, we offer here Dennis McKenna's brilliant interdisciplinary contribution with regard to his lived experience of photosynthesis during a *União do Vegetal* (UDV) ceremony which shares a great deal with the ideas expressed in "Natural Science and the Mystical World View" by Albert Hofmann, the discoverer of LSD: "Light is the original cosmic energy source. All life, the life of plants, animals and human beings, is formed and sustained by light. Even the thought process of the human brain is fed by this energy source. Therefore the human mind, our consciousness, represents the highest, most sublime energetic transformation of light. We are light beings; that is not only a mystical experience but scientific knowledge as well."[31]

We have arranged the contributions in Section IV, "Writing *Ayahuasca*," in a rough chronological order based on the date of their publication.[32] The first of these, *Yagé Letters,* is a book billed on its back cover as "an epistolary novel," constructed from an exchange of letters in the late 1950s and early '60s between Allen Ginsberg and William S. Burroughs, two writers who helped found the literary movement now known as the Beat Generation. We have chosen the letter by Ginsberg dated June 10, 1960 (five years after the composition of *Howl)* from Pucallpa, Peru, since it is the missive most closely related to one of the purposes of this anthology, namely to establish interdisciplinary links between indigenous Amazonian mythology, first person testimony, anthropology, religion and literature regarding the visionary experience of *ayahuasca.* In his own way, Ginsberg is engaged on a scientific foray. In his letter, he mentions his contact with the great ethnobotanist from Harvard University Richard Evans Schultes, whose life has been chronicled so ably by Wade Davis in *One River: Explorations and Discoveries in the Amazon Rain Forest.* Ginsberg makes reference to collecting plant samples *(Banisteriopsis caapi* and *Psychotria viridis)* that he will "bring back to Lima Natural History Museum to identify." The intensity of the *ayahuasca* experience with its "wave after wave of death-fear," and the conversion of Ginsberg's body into a "Snake Seraph" are all part of an epistemological and ontological crisis: "I wish I knew who, if anyone, there is to work with that knows, if anyone *knows,* who I am or what I am."

The literary selection that perhaps most clearly illuminates the ideas that Michael Winkelman proposes with regard to the role of sacred or "psychointegrator" plants is the chapter we have included from Peter Matthiessen's novel *At Play in the Fields of the Lord.* The chapter is a compressed, kaleidoscopic version of the life of the novel's protagonist Meriweather Lewis Moon, a Native American (Cheyenne) who drinks *ayahuasca* alone on the edge of the jungle in South America. The *ayahuasca* induces deep emotional reactions, repressed memories from his childhood related to racism in the United States and the loss of his Native American identity: "He spoke American and raised the American flag at school." The multiple voices juxtaposed in the chapter also include the first person narrative of Moon himself as he maintains an inner dialogue with the past and its performers in the *ayahuasca* trance. The sense of extreme isolation that he suffers is a prelude to an opposite integrative impulse: the next day he parachutes from his plane as it runs out of gas over the green jungle canopy and joins the same indigenous Amazonian community that a local politician had hired him to destroy. The figurative death at the end of the chapter in which Moon's eyes are "wide like the bald eyes of a corpse" and "his mind like a lone comet, wandering far out across the long night of the universe" precedes the rebirth of the novel's next chapter.

◆ ◆ ◆

The ordering principle of many of the literary selections is the Journey by River, often toward an indigenous propitiator of knowledge as in the texts by César Calvo and Mario Villafranca Saravia. In the case of Dale Pendell's poem, Ecuador's Rio Napo functions as a lifegiving, land-defining presence invoked throughout the poem as the refrain of rushing water in an engaged, ethnobotanical song. One way of understanding this phenomenon is by means of a Jungian simile that describes a relationship between "universal" forms of thought and the movement of water as current: "An archetype to a certain extent resembles an ancient river gorge through which the waters of life have flowed for a very long time."[33] In an Amazonian context, this analogy is particularly rich in terms of how one might interpret dangerous torrents, vast floods, rivers that suddenly change their course, recapitulations of mythic journeys such as the one undertaken in the anaconda-canoe, sacred petroglyphs at water's edge, and celestial-terrestrial riverine correspondences in indigenous conceptions of the cosmos. This is especially true in Luis Eduardo Luna's series "Ten Poems on a Sunday Afternoon," whose narrator begins "on the lost waters/downriver,/ tired and thirsty/traveler of plants." In these poems, the narrator describes visits of apprenticeship to aerial, subterranean and aquatic worlds that are reminiscent of the places described by Peña and Payaguaje in section I of this anthology. The invocation of the mother of *ayahuasca* as defined by Prohaño also resonates with Luna's female personification of *ayahuasca/yagé* as a goddess dancing naked around a bonfire. The form of this long poem is as fluid as a river and possesses a breathless quality that is the result of a single day's unrepeatable (and perhaps inexplicable) creative surge.

It may seem surprising that we have chosen as many as three texts that revolve around the figure of Manuel Córdova Ríos, a Peruvian *ayahuasquero* and healer who, despite his death years ago, continues to be revered in Iquitos to this day. The first of these is a fragment from F. Bruce Lamb's second book, *Río Tigre and Beyond: The Amazon Jungle Medicine of Manuel Córdova-Ríos,* in which Lamb creates a first-person narrative that enables Manuel Córdova to tell how he came to master *ayahuasca* and how he learned to manipulate the visions of others. Lamb's first work, *Wizard of the Upper Amazon: The Story of Manuel Córdova-Ríos,* was attacked as a hoax for its apparent lack of ethnographic verisimilitude. According to Robert L. Carneiro, the indigenous group that allegedly kidnapped Córdova-Ríos when he was a boy could not possibly have been Amahuaca given the specific customs that Córdova-Ríos attributes to them in his narrative as told by Lamb.[34] Jonathan Ott, using a western dichotomy, urges readers to consider Lamb's work "fiction" and not "ethnography" in the strict, scientific sense of the word.[35] Ultimately, we decided to move Lamb from section II of this anthology to section IV as a way of recognizing Lamb's literary additions to the story of Córdova-Ríos and also to create a block of three related texts that would facilitate a comparative reading. Nevertheless, we would like to vindicate Lamb's rendering of this shamanic narrative, which, in its description of the acquisition of knowledge, is fundamentally a "power story." Córdova-Ríos's narrative may be considered a construction intended to establish the charismatic aura around his person, an element that makes healing and other shamanic practices possible in much the same way that shamans from indigenous cultural groups say that they receive their powers from an eagle or an ant spirit. In this case, as well as in the creation of myths and poems, the role of the imagination must be considered in a positive light. With regard to the particular criticism leveled at Córdova-Ríos, one could say that trying to establish the true identity of the Indians described by Córdova-Ríos (Amahuaca, Boras or Witoto) would be as useful as attempting to identify the correct species of the huge snake at the bottom of a lake that another shaman might claim as a teacher. Although it is crucial, of course, to possess an accurate understanding of plant materials and chemical agents, as well as to undertake sophisticated pharmacological and neurophysiological studies according to the precepts of contemporary science, it is more difficult to apply these procedures to comprehend a phenomenon such as shamanic healing, which is largely the result of a pact between healer and patient, a work of the imagination in its broadest and most powerful sense. In the case of Córdova-Ríos, an "inaccurate" discourse may prove extremely effective due to its beauty or its mysteriousness. The stories of Córdova-Ríos as narrated by Lamb (and also, in different ways, by Calvo and Merwin) reveal the work of an *ayahuasquero* who uses his experience and knowledge (however he acquired it) in the rich *vegetalista* tradition of the Peruvian Amazon.[36]

Although it recounts the life of Manuel Córdova-Ríos, César Calvo's extended chronicle of a hallucination in *The Three Halves of Ino Moxo* might also be considered a radical continuation of Pigafetta, the chronicler who accompanied Magellan on his voyages of discovery and was cited by Gabriel García Márquez in the opening of his acceptance speech for the Nobel Prize for Literature. If it is true, as Eduardo Galeano has suggested, that what the conquistadors did was transport then plant the seeds of Hieronymus Bosch's nightmares in the soil of the so-called New World, and if it is also true that for the Europeans, the American continent represented a place devoid of mythic and historic content, a blankness with vague contours that resembled their evolving maps, an empty space to fill with their own imaginations, it is only because of the unprecedented violent cultural erasure that Europe inflicted on a people (with highly-sophisticated cosmogonies) who used a wide range of psychointegrator plants in their religious ceremonies.[37] One could argue that a map of these sacred plants and their places of growth and use and the routes of their trade would be an illuminating, even comprehensive, way of understanding Pre-Columbian cultures throughout the American continent.

The opening excerpt from Calvo's novel entitled "As a Preface, Ino Moxo Enumerates the Attributes of the Air," contains a preponderance of foreignness (for most readers) that forms the basis of Ino Moxo's intimate relationship with the natural world, namely, the Spanish and Quechua names of the flora and fauna of the Amazon jungle, complete with an encapsulated description of their magic and enigmatic qualities. This enumeration of unimaginable abundance and diversity produces an effect that might be characterized as the other-worldliness of *this* world. We are related to it, whether we know it or not, according to Ino Moxo as he addresses his attentive listener: "You hear the sound of steps of animals one has been before being human, the steps of stones and vegetables and the things every human being has previously been."

The breakdown of linear time in the novel retains an acute, even heightened, sense of lived history especially in the form of the recollection of interethnic warfare during the years of the rubber boom. Even so, some readers may find the passages in which the narrator becomes the mythic character Narowé moving through the jungle over rocks and tree trunks equally shocking in that here is the mind engaged in mythopoetic creation; here is what Stephen Crites has called the *symbolic,* the "luminous moment, in which sacred, mundane and personal are inseparably conjoined."[38] The fragment from Calvo's novel that describes the multiple meanings of *oni xuma,* the Amahuaca name for *ayahuasca,* has a brilliant poetic complexity that calls attention to the need for an increased awareness of translation. The shifting meaning of *oni xuma* may very well reflect an indigenous scientific world in which taxonomy depends on the interaction of the individual with a particular plant species.

Merwin's treatment of Manuel Córdova is based entirely on the work done by F. Bruce Lamb in *The Wizard of the Upper Amazon.* Manuel Córdova/Ino Moxo, who appears in the selections in this anthology by Lamb, Calvo and Merwin, is a kind of repository for the western imagination in that this figure recasts the well-known story of the white person who adopts native ways and becomes a powerful figure within the indigenous group. The "real world" referred to in the title of Merwin's poem is the *visionary* one to which the protagonist has access by means of the "bitter juices" of *ayahuasca* which precipitate a sudden breakthrough of language barriers on the part of the kidnapped boy "who understood every word they/were telling him while they/travelled." Later, it is the *ayahuasca* that facilitates a collective dream-journey and transformation: "dreaming/together flowing/among the trees entering/cat fur monkey voice owl wing." The lack of punctuation, the gerunds at the end of each line, and the word "wing" produce an effect of fluidity and harmonious rhyme in keeping with the *ayahuasca* experience that the author describes. The poem also contains a powerful visionary sequence in which the protagonist experiences the Ovidian-ophidian forms of existence, a characteristic shared by so many of the works included in this anthology:

and the visions rose
out of the darkening voice
out of the night voice the secret voice
the rain voice the root voice
through the chant he saw his
blood in the veins of trees
he appeared in the green of his eyes

he felt the snake that was
his skin and the monkeys
of his hands he saw his faces
in all the leaves and could recognize
those that were poison and those
that could save

As a way of explaining the snake-motifs that are so prevalent in *ayahuasca* visions, Jeremy Narby speculates that *ayahuasca* facilitates consciousness at a level that is simultaneously mythic and molecular: "To sum up, DNA is a snake-shaped master of transformation that lives in water and is both extremely long and small, single and double. Just like the cosmic serpent." Later, Narby links the densely interwined metaphorical logic of shamanic perception induced by *ayahuasca* with the serpentine form of liana, snake, DNA and a linguistic system that establishes new relationships between seemingly disparate objects: "As far as its material aspect or its form is concerned, DNA is a doubly double text that wraps around itself, in other words, it is a language-twisting-twisting."[39]

Mario Vargas Llosa's formidable challenge in *The Storyteller* is the juxtaposition of two narrative voices in alternating chapters of his novel: a western narrative voice subject to the ordering principles of linear time and a voice that mimics indigenous narrative structures dominated by the cyclical temporality of myth.[40] Vargas Llosa attempts to erase the boundaries between literature and orature by embedding a major European twentieth-century narrative — Franz Kafka's "The Metamorphosis" — in a shamanistic sequence of transformation. The resulting hybrid figure, Gregor-Tasurinchi, is a Euro-Amazonian construct that joins Kafka's transformed protagonist Gregor Samsa with a divinity from the pantheon of the Matsigenka, an indigenous group from eastern Peru.

Ayahuasca, for many of the collaborators in this anthology, is a restoration of a lost dialogue in the form of an apprenticeship with the natural world and the possibilities it provides for an infinite variety of metamorphoses. In his landmark work *After Babel: Aspects of Language and Translation*, George Steiner speaks of the evolution of language and the advantages and disadvantages of shared speech-forms among human beings. Citing William James (the nineteenth-century American philosopher who incorporated in some of his writings the use of ether and chloroform as a means of inducing mystical states of consciousness), Steiner delineates the cost of natural selection for efficient communication. The price paid "would have included not only the ideal of a totally personal voice, of a unique 'fit' between an individual's expressive means and his world-image, pursued by the poets. It meant also that the 'bright buzz' of non-verbal articulate codes, the sensory modes of smell, gesture, and pure tone developed by animals, and perhaps extra-sensory forms of communication (these are specifically adduced by James) all but vanished from the human repertoire."[41] Virtually all the contributions to this anthology make reference to these transformations, whether it is in the simple form of a *Santo Daime* hymn[42] or the complex violent mutations in "Jaguar-Becoming" by William Torres C., the piece by Françoise Barbira Freedman and "Returning" by Ib Michael. In the selection we have included from *The Storyteller*, the narrator is transformed into an insect, which in turn is eaten by a lizard. In this moment, the shifting narrative voice in Vargas Llosa's novel perceives the world through the lizard's bulging eyes: "everything was green."

The poetry of Argentine Néstor Perlongher presents a liturgical convergence of the radical Christianity syncretized with Amazonian indigenous ritual that one finds in the *Santo Daime* religious group in Brazil. In his book *Aguas aéreas* (Aerial Waters), Perlongher includes a special note of thanks to the *Santo Daime* Church for providing access to the sacred drink (*daime*, or *ayahuasca*) that is consumed by the men and women who participate in the ceremonies by dancing and singing the received hymns (some of which appear in section III of this reader) of the spiritual leaders of the group. The neo-Baroque poetry of Perlongher, who was widely considered one of the most important younger poets in Latin America at the time of his death from AIDS in 1992, is extremely demanding in Spanish and nearly impossible to translate into English given its Gongorine syntax and hermetic, erudite Latinate vocabulary. The *daimista* ritual with its return to the shamanic origins of religion (in this case, a *democratic* shamanism in which men and women participate collectively) is an underlying presence throughout this particular work by Perlongher. From the "harsh embarcation" of the initial consumption of the sacred drink to the "fringed convulsions" to the "nebulous incense of flowers" to "Elysian helixes" to "the liquid divinity" to the "foot's coming and going" to the "great Lake of Beings" to the "syncopated catalepsies" to "THE THOUSAND CRYSTAL FACETS/ THE RHYTHMIC SHINING/THE CELEBRATORY/ HYMNS OF AN/ ANNUNCI-ATION/ KALEIDOSCOPE/ENAMELED FRENZY" to "the translucent step of the serpent," Néstor Perlongher's poetry pursues the ecstatic, visionary experience at the limits of human consciousness outside the confines of the body: "Where do you go when you aren't there?" asks the lyrical voice, "Where are you when you go out of yourself?"

In an article entitled "Droga e êxtase" (Drugs and Ecstasy), Perlongher cites Luiz Eduardo Soares who affirms that "the liberation announced by *Daime* promises the dissipation of sensual torments, the exorcizing of the impulses of the body, the neutralization of the desire that enslaves us to the century, its fetishes and its illusions."[43] Finally, says Perlongher, the visionary ceremony means "a reconciliation with the divine essence."[44] In "O desaparecimento da homosexualidade" (The Disappearance of Homosexuality), Perlongher speaks of three different ways of dissolving what Georges Bataille calls the "individualizing monad" and thereby recovering a certain original indistinction of fusion: the orgy, love, and the sacred. Perlongher focuses on the first and third of these (the second seems outside the poet's personal purview): for him, the ecstasy of sexuality in the time of AIDS becomes (to use the Nietzschean terminology for the Dionysus/Apollo duality) completely "descending," whereas the "ascending" ecstasy of mysticism facilitates the "dissolution of the body in the cosmic (in other words, the sacred)" in a total, definitive ecstasy. At the end of the article, Perlongher exhorts the reader to abandon the personal body because, as he says, "now it's all about leaving oneself."[45] *Aerial Waters* is also an exhortation, an attempt to create a divine poetics of the extra-bodily experience. *Ayahuasca* manifests itself in Perlongher's poetry as part of what Enrique Ocaña has called a "Dionysian pharmacy," "consecrated to the realization of another utopian goal . . . an *ars moriendi,* an art that helps the human animal accept the transitory nature of our *topos* as living beings."[46]

In most of the selections in Section IV, "Writing *Ayahuasca,*" a protagonist undertakes a journey toward an aboriginal source of wisdom. The movement through space from center to periphery[47] is also equated with a double temporal dislocation: contact with an archaic culture and also with a personal past, akin to Wordsworth's "spots of time," those moments of intense experience, especially, as we mentioned, in Matthiessen's *At Play in the Fields of the Lord,* but also in *La madre de la voz en el oído* (The Mother of the Voice in the Ear) by Alfonso Domingo. In the case of the latter work, the narrator claims a fundamental right to humanity as defined by his indigenous hosts: "After that first night, I'm considered a 'human being' by the Yacarunas. *Ayahuasca* has given me the gift of the first vision, which for them is sufficient. . . *Ayahuasca* is wise and powerful and has taken me to another lost city, another territory, another time. It has taken me to the most important moment of my childhood."

In many ways, *ayahuasca* resembles the trickster-messenger of Yoruban mythology Exu: being in a constant state of metamorphosis, transgressing boundaries, making connections or blocking them at the crossroads of consciousness. In this sense, it facilitates an awareness of Inter-ness: *interdisciplinary* concerns, for example, or, in the case of the literary selections in Section IV, *intertextuality,* (Vargas Llosa and Kafka, Rimbaud's "Le bateau ivre" and White's "Last River" or Neruda's "Galope muerto" and White's "Mariri"). The links between the psychointegrator and the text that it helps generate is repeated in the relationship between two or more texts generated by psychointegrators that coexist in the continuum of literature. In *El texto drogado: dos siglos de droga y literatura* (The Drugged Text: Two Centuries of Drugs and Literature), Alberto Castoldi says that "the original 'drugged' text becomes in turn a drug for subsequent texts."[48]

In her insightful critique of Néstor García Canclini's model of hybrid cultures and, as Canclini phrases it, "the inherent multi-temporal heterogeneity" in Latin America, Marcy Schwartz wonders why Canclini overlooks aesthetics in his analyses. For Schwartz, "the simultaneous presence of the traditional and the modern is also evident in literature and art through textual strategies such as juxtaposed images, fragmentation, and the manipulation of space."[49] These are precisely the qualities that best describe the contemporary texts produced under the *ayahuasca* aegis. In fact, much of the material in this anthology corroborates the idea that *ayahuasca* provides access to the Benjaminian notion of simultaneity-across-time. The "anthropoliterary" panorama of the *Ayahuasca Reader* may serve to open conceptions of hybrid cultures to a fuller appreciation of modern life.

The texts we have gathered are twentieth-century reformulations of an archaic pharmacognostical discovery.

The technicians of the sacred, in their search for power, achieved, through the use of psychointegrator plants, a means to adapt to the hazards of prolonged cultural hybridization. The new shamans, anthropologists, spiritual leaders and writers whose lives and works are imbued with the *ayahuasca* spirit in a time that Terence McKenna has called an "archaic revival"[50] coexist with the globalization of culture and the fluid movement of capital between powerful transnational corporations, a phenomenon that has produced an ecological crisis on a planetary scale, threatening the very existence of the ethnobotanical cultures that could provide solutions more lasting than those generated by political models based on nationalism.

On the other hand, *ayahuasca* is quickly being integrated into western consumer patterns and economic laws. Marlene Dobkin de Ríos and Jonathan Ott have written about the dangers of drug tourism in the Amazon and the potentially disastrous effects of the massive influx of foreign tourists on the indigenous populations that provide *ayahuasca* experiences for them.[51] Is *ayahuasca* destined to become yet another mass marketed item divorced from its traditional origins in a submerged economy subject to northern hemisphere demand and southern hemisphere supply?[52]

It may be, as Enrique Ocaña has suggested, that "modern consciousness has ceased being a stage open to epiphanies."[53] For this reason the aesthetic and ethical possibilities reflected in the *Ayahuasca Reader* are so important. With regard to creativity, as Michael Winkelman has pointed out, "psychointegrator-induced experiences may ritualistically guide creative potentials into traditional patterns, or, conversely, free the artist from traditional constraints."[54] Although the imaginary of psychointegrators is subject to the same cultural conditionings as any other human manifestation, creativity and enhanced artistic freedom are more than the compendium of extraordinary images that may ultimately become tedious in their repetition. In the selection of texts, we have attempted to avoid what Henri Michaux has called "a banality of the visionary world" in terms of the repetitive, interchangeable descriptions of it.[55] If they are successful, these texts (by means of their artifice, their "artificial" nature by definition as human constructs) will approximate the ineffable by means of the word transfigured by *ayahuasca*, and impart a state of grace that in some way resembles the one that lingers and resonates long after the visionary experience itself.

NOTES

1. Michael Winkelman. "Psychointegrator Plants: Their Roles in Human Culture, Consciousness and Health," *Yearbook of Cross-Cultural Medicine and Psychotherapy* (1995): p. 20.

2. Despite our extensive research for this section, there seems to remain a significant absence of narrative treatment of *Psychotria viridis* or *Diplopterus cabrerana* (the two most commonly-used plants in the preparation of the *ayahuasca* decoction either one of which is combined with *Banisteriopsis caapi)* in favor of the *Banisteriopsis* vine that generates the serpent-river-umbilical cord-jaguar complex.

3. Stephen Crites. "The Narrative Quality of Experience," *Journal of the American Academy of Religion* 39.3 (September 1971): p. 295.

4. Current use of these terms seems quite removed from their linguistic source in the words *phonemic* and *phonetic* as investigated by Kenneth Pike in *Language in Relation to a Unified Theory of the Structure of Human Behavior,* a work published in 1954 by the Summer Institute of Linguistics.

5. Miller-Weisberger's contribution "A Huaorani Myth of the First *Miiyabu*" is unique in that it contains the first recorded mythological reference to the plant species *Banisteriopsis muricata,* which complements the ethnobotanical reference by Wade E. Davis and James A. Yost in "The Ethnobotany of the Waorani of Eastern Ecuador," *Botanical Museum Leaflets Harvard University,* Vol. No. 3 (1983).

6. Crites, p. 301.

7. Crites, p. 297.

8. See Claudio Naranjo. *"Ayahuasca* Imagery and the Therapeutic Property of the Harmala Alkaloids," *Journal of Mental Imagery* 11.2 (1987): pp. 131–136. Although this article has many insights, unfortunately it perpetuates a fundamental confusion regarding *ayahuasca* pharmacology and the role of harmaline. See Jonathan Ott. *Pharmacotheon: Entheogenic Drugs, Their Plant Sources and History.* Kennewick, WA: Natural Products Co., 1994, p. 237.

9. See Gerardo Reichel-Dolmatoff. *Desana Texts and Contexts.* Wien-Föhrenau: Engelbert Stiglmayr, editor. Acta Ethnologica et Linguistica Nr. 62, 1989.

10. See E. Jean Matteson Langdon and Gerhard Baer, eds. *Portals of Power: Shamanism in South America.* Albuquerque: University of New Mexico Press, 1992. In their introduction to this work, Langdon and Baer, citing antecendents in the work of Clifford Geertz and Victor Turner, define their perspective as one that "requires symbolic analysis, native interpretation of events and rituals, and the logic of belief systems within their cultural context" (p. 12).

11. Janet M. Chernela. "Death, Memory and Language: New Approaches to History in Lowland South American Anthropology," *Latin American Research Review* 33.1 (1998): p. 168.

12. Chernela, p. 168.

13. See John Beverley and Hugo Achugar, eds. *La voz del otro: testimonio, subalternidad, y verdad narrativa.* Lima and Pittsburgh: Latinoamericana, 1992.

14. See Angelika Gebhart-Sayer, "Una terapia estética. Los diseños visionarios del *ayahuasca* entre los Shipibo-Conibo," *América Indígena* 46 (1) (1986): pp. 189–218. In this article, Gebhart- Sayer speaks of "design-song medicine which is consequently projected onto the body of the patient" (p. 127).

15. Jerome Rothenberg. *Technicians of the Sacred.* Berkeley: University of California Press, 1985. pp. xviii-xix.

16. Josep M. Fericgla. "Theory and Application of *Ayahuasca*-Generated Imagery," *Eleusis* 5 (August 1996): p. 5.

17. Fericgla, pp. 11–12.

18. Chernela, p. 182.

19. Chernela, p. 183.

20. See Luis Eduardo Luna and Pablo Amaringo. *Ayahuasca Visions: The Religious Iconography of a Peruvian Shaman.* Berkeley: North Atlantic Books, 1991.

21. This indigenous group is closely-related, linguistically and geographically, to the Amerindians that Spruce describes.

22. See Richard Evans Schultes, "Richard Spruce, the Man," in M. R. D. Seaward and S. M. D. Fitzgerald, eds. *Richard Spruce (1817–1893): Botanist and Explorer.* London: The Royal Botanic Gardens, Kew, 1996. pp. 16–25.

23. Reichel-Dolmatoff was granted Colombian citizenship in 1942 as a result of his exceptional work in his adopted country.

24. Gilles Deleuze. "Dos cuestiones sobre el uso de la droga," *Archipiélago* 28 (primavera 1997): p. 74.

25. Angelika Gebhart Sayer. "The Geometric Designs of the Shipibo-Conibo in Ritual Context," *Journal of Latin American Lore* 11:2 (1985), pp. 143–145.

26. José Sánchez-Parga. *Textos textiles en la tradición cultural andina.* Quito: Instituto Andino de Artes Populares del Convenio Andrés Bello (IADAP), 1995. p. 9.

27. *Daime* is the name given to the sacred drink by Irineu Serra and Daniel Pereira de Matos, which means "Grant Me" in Portuguese Biblical diction.

28. Kardecism has its origins in the work of Leon Denizarth Hippolyte Rivail (1804–1869), who was born in Lyon, France. A professional educator, he became interested in the phenomenon of the "turning tables," which attained great popularity at French upper class parties of the time. After careful observation of the possible action of thought on material objects, or the possible manifestation of a natural force of unknown character, he came to the conclusion that every intelligent phenomenon must have a corresponding intelligent cause. In this case, he inferred that the intelligence manifested by objects should be external to them. Under the name Allen Kardec, he published a series of books, including *The Book of Spirits* and *The Book of Mediums*, which form the doctrinal basis of this Christian religion. Kardecism implies a permanent and highly-sophisticated interchange, an uninterrupted continuum within the spirit-realm itself, the development of an efficient means to deal with malefactors, as well as the need to seek the help of higher spirits for diagnostic and therapeutic ends. Kardecism, now nearly forgotten in its country of origin, continues to flourish in Brazil (where several million people practice this religion), although, according to Diana Brown in *Umbanda: Religion and Politics in Urban Brazil* (New York: Columbia UP, 1994), it is currently losing ground in relation to the practitioners of Umbanda, a syncretic Brazilian religion that incorporates African elements.

29. Jean Monod. "Os Piaroa e o invisível." In Vera Penteado Coelho, ed. *Os alucinógenos e o mundo simbólico: o uso dos alucinógenos entre os índios da América do sul.* São Paulo: EPU, 1976. p. 27.

30. A partial version of the so-called *História da Hoasca,* which deals with the mythological origin of the two plants from which the *vegetal* is made in this area *(mariri/Banisteriopsis caapi* and *chacrona/Psychotria viridis)* was published in Vera

Fróes, *Santo Daime. Cultura Amazônica. História do Povo Juramidam.* Manaus: Suframa, 1983. It closely resembles similar myths found among the indigenous groups of the upper Amazon (See Luis Eduardo Luna and Pablo Amaringo. *Ayahuasca Visions: The Religious Iconography of a Peruvian Shaman.* Berkeley: North Atlantic Books, 1991, p. 50). Some of these myths are included in this anthology.

31. Albert Hofmann. "Natural Science and the Mystical World View." In Robert Forte, ed. *Entheogens and the Future of Religion.* San Francisco: Council on Spiritual Practices, 1997, p. 51.

32. We are still hoping that, with further research and better evidence, it will someday be possible to consider Horacio Quiroga's short story "Juan Darién" an antecedent to the material in this section. See Horacio Quiroga. *Cuentos.* México: Porrúa, 1978. pp. 74–80; Horacio Quiroga. *The Decapitated Chicken and Other Stories.* Selected and translated by Margaret Sayers Peden. Austin: University of Texas Press, 1976, p. 87–99. See also Emir Rodríguez Monegal. *Genio y figura de Horacio Quiroga.* Buenos Aires: Editorial Universitaria de Buenos Aries, 1967.

33. Ignacio Malaxecheverria. *Bestiario Medieval.* Madrid: Sirucla, 1999.

34. See Robert L. Carneiro. "Chimera of the Upper Amazon." In Richard De Mille (ed.). *The Don Juan Papers. Further Castaneda Controversies.* Santa Barbara:Ross-Erikson Publishers, 1980, pp.94–98.

35. See Jonathan Ott. *Pharmacotheon: Entheogenic Drugs, Their Plant Sources and History.* Kennewick, WA: Natural Products Co., 1994, pp. 234–237.

36. See Luis Eduardo Luna. *Vegetalismo: Shamanism among the Mestizo Population of the Peruvian Amazon.* Stockholm: Almquist and Wiksell International, 1986.

37. On the use of psychointegrator plants among the Taínos as a source of spiritual and political counsel in the genocidal time of Columbus, see José Barreiro. *The Indian Chronicles.* Houston: Arte Público Press, 1993. See also Constantino Manuel Torres, "The Role of Cohoba in Taino Shamanism," *Eleusis,* n. s. 1, 1998; pp. 38–50.

38. Crites, pp. 305–306.

39. Jeremy Narby. *The Cosmic Serpent: DNA and the Origins of Knowledge.* New York: Tarcher/Putnam, 1998, pp. 93, 100.

40. At the end of *The Storyteller,* Vargas Llosa expresses his appreciation to the Dominican missionary Joaquín Barriales, whose work on Matsigenka mythology forms the basis of the indigenous voice in the Peruvian author's novel. From an anthropological perspective, there are certain misconceptions with regard to the ritual use of *ayahuasca* that bespeak Vargas Llosa's lack of direct knowledge of the sacred drink that generates the indigenous cosmogonic speech-forms at the heart of the novel.

41. George Steiner. *After Babel: Aspects of Language and Translation.* London: Oxford University Press, 1975, p. 48.

42. The following hymn received by Sebastião Mota de Melo is a marvelous expression of the sense of awe and bewildering beauty of losing oneself as one knows oneself and finding oneself in another form:

Ai meu Deus, ai meu Deus	(Oh my God, oh my God
Meu Deus aonde estou?	My God, where am I?
Ai meu Deus, ai meu Deus	Oh, my God, Oh, my God
Eu sou um beija-flor	I'm a hummingbird)

43. Luiz Eduardo Soares *"O Santo Daime* no contexto da nova consciência religiosa" in Landim (ed.) *Sinais dos tempos: diversidade religiosa no Brasil.* RJ: ISER. 1990, p. 271.

44. Néstor Perlongher. "Droga e êxtase," *SaudeLoucura* (São Paulo, HUCITEC/USP 3 (1991): p. 89.

45. See Néstor Perlongher. "O desaparecimento da homosexualidade," *SaudeLoucura* (São Paulo, HUCITEC/USP) 3 (1991): pp. 39–45.

46. Enrique Ocaña. *El Dionisio moderno y la farmacia utópica.* Barcelona: Anagrama, 1993, p. 155.

47. The process is simultaneously a transformation of the periphery into a new center as the spiritual destination of a pilgrimage.

48. Alberto Castoldi. *El texto drogado: dos siglos de droga y literatura.* Trans. by Francisco Martín. Madrid: Anaya & Mario Muchnik, 1997, p. 14.

49. Marcy Schwartz, "Is There an Aesthetic in This Hybrid? Literary Absences in García Canclini's Globalization of Culture," Paper presented at the 1997 Modern Language Association Convention, p. 2.

50. Terence McKenna. *The Archaic Revival: Speculations on Psychedelic Mushrooms, the Amazon, Virtual Reality, UFOs, Evolution, Shamanism, the Rebirth of the Goddess and the End of History.* San Francisco: Harper, 1992.

51. See Marlene Dobkin de Ríos. "Drug Tourism in the Amazon," *Yearbook for Ethnomedicine and the Study of Consciousness* 3 (1994): pp. 307–314. See also Jonathan Ott. *Ayahuasca Analogues: Pangaean Entheogens.* Kennewick, Washington: Natural Products Co., 1994. Although, of course, we sympathize with the concerns of these authors, we also feel it is important to point out that most of the so called *ayahuasca* tourism is restricted to the urban areas of the Peruvian Amazon, the mestizo population of which exists in a markedly different historical and geographical context in comparison to groups such as the Huichol and Mazatec Indians, who live in isolated mountain areas, and who use, respectively, peyotl *(Lophophora williamsii)* and Psylocibe mushrooms. In other words, while certain indigenous cultures (in Mexico for example) have suffered a great deal due to the sudden intrusion of newcomers seeking their sacred plants, much of the Amazon, because of its intricate river system, has been open for centuries to outsiders that include traders, naturalists, anthropologists, extractors of gold, hunters of tropical fauna and Amazonian products, guerrillas, drug dealers, smugglers of weapons, developers, rubber tappers, missionaries and oil company employees. With the notable exception of these last three groups whose presence has been devastating, Amazonian indigenous people have shown themselves to be experts in the art of adjusting to non-indigenous peoples. They have survived and define their lives as best they can, absorbing in their own world view what they find useful, and temporarily accepting whatever demands are imposed on them by the outsiders, only to return to their own evolving ways when the pressure no longer remains. Today, *ayahuasca* ceremonies are advertised in Iquitos as one more item on a list of attractions that include jungle lodges, birdwatching and piranha fishing. We are not overly worried by this particular new phenomenon. On the contrary, we have met individuals from diverse countries who have become genuinely interested in the vegetalista traditions and have undergone the hardships of the diet, sexual deprivation and other requirements that are said to be necessary in order to learn from the plants.

52. See Ignacio Castro and Jorge Alemán, "Fin de un viaje," *Archipiélago* 28 (primavera 1997): pp. 67–72.

53. Enrique Ocaña. "Topografía del mal viaje: Prolegómenos a una crítica de la conciencia psiquedélica," *Archipiélago* 28 (primavera 1997): p. 80.

54. Winkelman, p. 13.

55. Henri Michaux. "Volver en sí: conciencia asolada de sí," *Archipiélago* 28 (primavera 1997): p. 14.

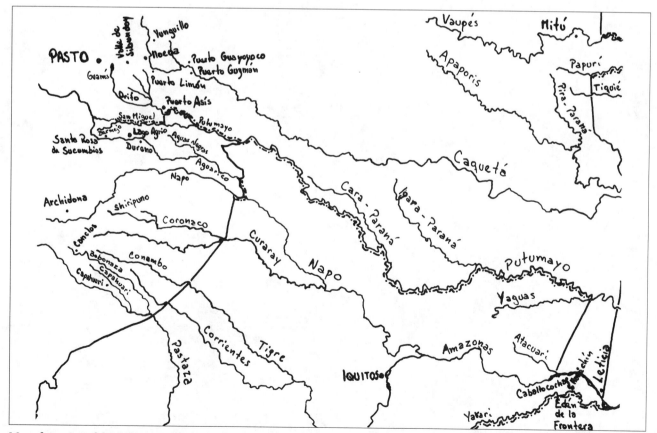

Map of a section of the Amazon region (Colombia, Ecuador, Peru, and Brazil), highlighting some of the places and rivers that are mentioned in the "Amazonian Cartography" section of the General Index.

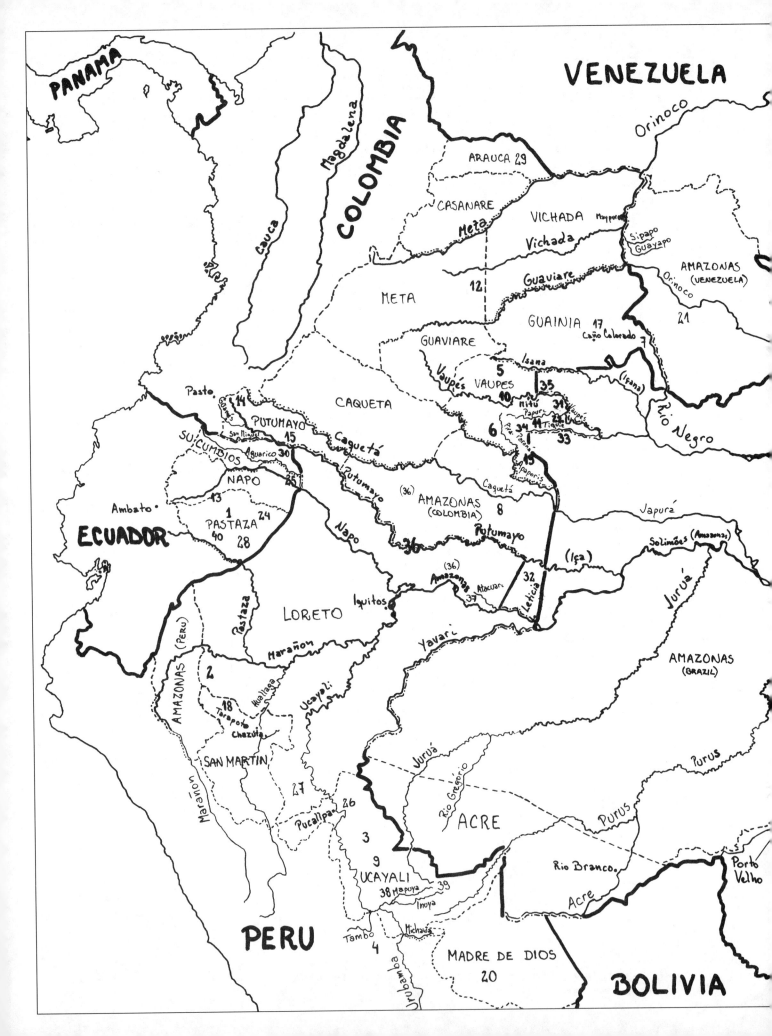

INDIGENOUS GROUPS KEY

1. Achuar
2. Aguaruna
3. Amahuaca (Amawaka)
4. Ashanínka (Campa)
5. Banihuas
6. Barasana
7. Barrés
8. Boras
9. Cashinahua
10. Cubeo
11. Desana
12. Guahibos
13. Huaorani
14. Inga (Ingano)
15. Kofan
16. Kogi
17. Kuripáko
18. Lamista
19. Makú
20. Matsigenka

21. Piaroa
22. Pira-Tapuya
23. Piro
24. Quichua
25. Secoya
26. Shipibo
27. Shipibo-Conibo
28. Shuar (Jívaro)
29. Sikuani
30. Siona
31. Tarianas
32. Ticuna
33. Tukano
34. Tuyuka
35. Uanano
36. Witoto
37. Yagua
38. Yaminahua
39. Yawanahua
40. Zaparos

Map of the Upper Amazon, indicating indigenous groups, and many of the places and rivers that are mentioned in the *Ayahuasca Reader*.

Don Ignacio, Shipibo shaman, Ucayali River. Photograph © Angelika Gebhart-Sayer.

I

AYAHUASCA MYTHS AND TESTIMONIES

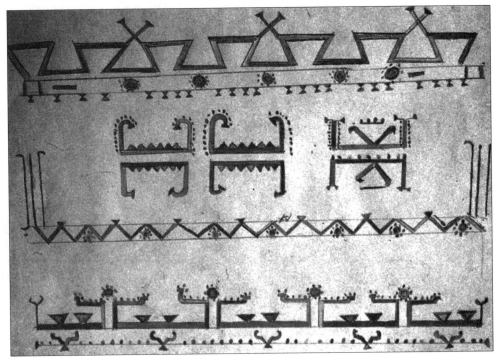

Estanislao Yaiguaje (Siona, Colombia), "Yagé." Collection of E. Jean Matteson Langdon.

Untitled, gouache on paper, © Marlene Lopes Mateus, (Cashinahua, Brazil). Collection of Elsje Maria Lagrou.

Untitled, gouache on paper, © Alcina Pinheiro Feitosa, (Cashinahua, Brazil). Collection of Elsje Maria Lagrou.

A VISIT TO THE SECOND HEAVEN:
A Siona Narrative of the Yagé Experience

E. Jean Matteson Langdon

The Siona Indians of Colombia's Northwest Amazonia are highly motivated to drink *Banisteriopsis* sp., known in the region as *yagé*. Yagé empowers them to know their universe, which is characterized by two superimposed realities. The first, which they call "this side," is that which is normally visible, the everyday reality. The second, designated as "the other side," is normally hidden. It is composed of five disks arranged hierarchically beginning with the level under the earth and extending up to the end of the heavens. Numerous entities inhabit the universe, each one living in its own domain. Through the *yagé* ritual, the Siona travel to these remarkable and beautiful domains. Each domain is characterized by its particular sounds, rhythms, music, smells, and colors. However, adventures in the other side can also be full of dangers that plunge a novice into the "evil spirit domain," a dark and rotten realm full of frightening and evil beings and monotonous zinging sounds, far different from the beauty and colors of the heaven realms. If not brought back by the master shaman, the inexperienced may never return to "this side."

In past articles, I have described the Siona "shamanic cosmology" and their rituals, in an attempt to point out the centrality of *yagé* and its rituals to their notions of well being and health, as well as for their acquisition of knowledge about the occult reality. I have also discussed the efforts which the Siona make to ensure a successful outcome to their journeys into the "other side" and to prevent fearful experiences which can cause severe illnesses, if not death, and destroy all the knowledge the victim has previously gained in his shamanic apprenticeship. The kind of brew prepared for the ritual and the master shaman's guidance through gestures and songs are important mechanisms that help the participants collectively journey with him.[1]

My goal here is different. Rather than describing how the anthropologist observes shamanic activities associated with *yagé* rituals, I wish to let the Siona speak for themselves about their experiences on the "other side" when ingesting *yagé*. Since they have developed a sophisticated oral art form which entertains as well as instructs others as to what happened when taking *yagé*, it is not difficult to give the Siona a voice. They are experts in telling about their dreams and shamanic flights. After a brief introduction to their narrative tradition and to shamanic apprenticeship, I will present a narrative told by Ricardo Yaiguaje about one of his experiences as a shamanic apprentice.

Most Siona narratives can be characterized as shamanic, in the sense that they deal with shamans and/or with experiences in the occult world when dreaming or taking *yagé*. Siona myths tell how the primordial shamans established the order we find today. Historical narratives tell how the shamans defended Siona territory from invasions by other Indigenous groups and from the Spanish who attempted to establish themselves in the Putumayo in the 17th and 18th centuries. Those which relate events of this century include descriptions of battles between the last Siona master shamans, epidemics that plagued the communities, and shamanic journeys to the various realms of the universe. Besides traditional narratives that are part of the public repertoire, they also tell personal narratives about *yagé* experiences, dreams, sicknesses, and other important events in their lives. These personal narratives contain structures and symbols similar to public or "shared narratives."

The term "traditional" is not used to refer to a fixed corpus of narratives shared by all. Indeed, there are vast differences in the narratives that a particular individual may tell, depending upon age, sex, and shamanic status. There is, however, a narrative tradition held in common, which is characterized by certain underlying structural, symbolic and poetic aspects, as well as common themes. It is this tradition that aids in understanding experience and the generation of new narratives. They follow the structure and codes common in the "traditional" narratives and may become incorporated into the public repertoire with time. The corpus of Siona oral literature should be conceived of as a dynamic and fluid body of texts that is created and recreated through time.

Perhaps one of the most important factors in preparation for shamanic apprenticeship is the Siona narrative tradition. People enjoy telling about their experiences with *yagé*, and others take delight in hearing about these strange and dangerous adventures. As mentioned above, drinking *yagé* is not without its dangers, and in order to accompany the master shaman on his journey and also personally experience what he is seeing and hearing, the novice must be prepared. The goal is to travel with the shaman, to know the *yagé* people, also known as the tender *(hwîha)* people, and to learn their songs in order to visit them again. After meeting the *yagé* people, they serve as guides in subsequent journeys. Shamanic apprenticeship consists of repeatedly taking *yagé* with a master shaman to learn the "designs" *(pinta* in Spanish, *toya* in Siona) of the realms and their entities that populate the universe. To know the designs implies that the apprentice has left his body and traveled with the shaman to the domain he is "showing" and that he has learned its songs. There are hundreds of domains to know in the Siona's complex universe, and each time a person knows a "design," he acquires more shamanic power. If all proceeds well in his apprenticeship, he should accumulate enough power to become a master shaman, called "one who sees" /'ïyagï/ or jaguar /yai/. This status is granted to those who have sufficient power to lead the others in these ritual experiences, guiding them and protecting them against possible mishaps.

As part of the transition from only a man to one who has left his body and knows at least some shamanic songs, the novice must pass through a set of initiatory experiences which threaten his life and serve as a test to see if he is strong enough to travel on the other side. This experience, which culminates in leaving the body and knowing the *yagé* people, marks the passage from only a man, *do 'ïmïgï,* to "one who has left," *sa'isigï.* The shaman initiate first passes through a period of "drunkenness," designated by the verb *gwebe-,* which the Siona translate as to be drunk or dizzy, as if having had too much *chicha* or cane liquor. It is marked by disorientation, dizziness, falling down and/or rolling about. It is an altered state without meaning. This drunkenness is followed by dark visions, full of frightening snakes, fires, black monsters and grinding machines which threaten the very existence of the novice. If he remains strong in the face of this fearful experience, the scenes become full of light and the *yagé* people descend to show the novice the way. The action of the *yagé* in this second phase, the revelation of the different realms of the universe in constant transformation which are permeated by constantly moving iridescent design-patterns, changing scenes, surging rhythms and heavenly music, is described by the verb *suña-.* It is extremely difficult to find an adequate translation for this concept, since it refers to the content of the visions as well as the simultaneous experience of emotional, physical, auditory, olfactory, and visual sensations. In the following narrative I have translated it generally as "shining." It should be kept in mind that it contrasts with drunkenness *(gwebe-)* in that *suña-* refers to the imagery experience which takes on form and meaning, and not one of a mere floundering about without consciousness and lacking meaning.

Ricardo Yaiguaje, (1900–1985) was the son of Leonides Yaiguaje, one of the last great Siona master shamans on the Putumayo River in Southern Colombia. His brother, Arsenio, was the last master shaman of the Buena Vista community. Ricardo attempted to follow in the footsteps of his father and brother, dedicating his life to acquiring shamanic knowledge. Unfortunately, he never fully attained their knowledge and power. This was in part due to attacks by other shamans, who repeatedly disrupted his *yagé* experiences through evil entities sent to destroy his shamanic knowledge. In the following translation, Ricardo tells us of his experience during three nightly sessions of *yagé* in which he attempted to know the domains, or "designs" /toya/ of the High River, which runs through the "second heaven," the heavenly level above the earth that begins at the point where you can see no farther with the naked eye.

Ricardo often repeated to me that it generally takes three nights, or houses, as they express each night of ritual in Siona, in order to master the "designs" of a particular domain. Each night the novice goes a bit further, drawing nearer to the goal of the journey. In the following narrative, Ricardo details carefully the preparation of the *yagé* ritual, which is set in motion when the shaman Ignacio tells the others that they will drink *yagé.* The three assistants, the cook (Arsenio), the fire tender (unidentified) and the water carrier (Ricardo), prepare the *yagé* in a secluded place in the forest. The participants gather at sunset to drink. The shaman distributes it, first to the elders present, and then to the youths. He "arranges" it each time he serves it, invoking the beings and domains that he wants the others to see. Ricardo, seeking to know the visions shown by Ignacio, tells of his own desires, motivations, and feelings as he journeyed to the High River. He describes how Ignacio's songs take him to visit the communities along the river and to know the beautiful people and their music. He also tells of the last night, the night in which he expected to go even further along this heavenly river, but in which he became lost in a dark and frightening place, barely escaping back into this side thanks to his brother, who noticed he was in danger.

hâ'â mâkâra ba'igï "yahe 'ûkuñu." At that time he (shaman) was there, "Let's drink *yagé*."

yahe 'ûku wïowï.[2] *yagé* drinking they began.

'ûkurena, "hâ'âka ba'ito, zî dawï, yahe yo'ohi'ï, 'ûkwa sayi mi'ïsa rowïte" kagï bâ'hi bagï. They drank, "Since young ones have come, prepare *yagé* and I will serve it to you," he said.

"ûkuto toya so'o beohi" kabi. "When you drink the visions will not be far," he said.

kagïna, 'ira ko'a kani, hâ'âribi, yahe kwa'ku birabi. He said, and my brother spoke to the elders and began to cook *yagé*.

kwa'kuni, hâ'âgï yi'ï ha'yï 'ïsï wari, 'ïsï wari we'ebi bagï, That was my older brother, Summer Breeze, Summer Breeze he was called,

hwîha mami his *yagé* name.[3]

we'egïna, nakoni yi'ï yahe kôgï ba'ï. He was called, and with him I was a *yagé* assistant.

'oko 'eagï ba'ï. The water carrier I was.

ba'igïna bagi yi'ï nakoni mì'ini, yahe kwa'kubi, I was, with me he ascended and cooked *yagé*,

kwa'kuni hâ'â makara wi'e yahe, 'ïo yahe ne'ebi. He cooked that first house of *yagé*, "burned *yagé*" he began to prepare.

kani, kwa'kuwï. They went on cooking.

kwa'kuni, 'ûkwabi. When it was cooked, Shaman served it.

'ûkwani de'oye 'ûkwabi, hâ'â wi'e'ga. He served very good *yagé*, at that first house.

hâ'â ko'a gwebewï de'oye. Those ones were nicely drunk.

'ûkuni hâ'âribi "mi'ï sako'a, zî ko'a, 'ûkuni 'ïyahi'ï. Shaman drank, then "You, young ones, drink and see."

mi'ï sako'a hâ'hî gânîwite ba'iyï. Your bodies are prepared for easy progress.

'ûkuni kerï, mi'ï sako'abi, te'e du'iñe ro'tato yi'ï 'ûkwayï kabi bagï. "Drink rapidly, all of you, thinking correctly as I serve," he said.

Kagïna, yi'ï do 'achawï yi'ï. He spoke, I just listened.

kani, "mi'ï sako'a yito?" bagï, hâ'âribi dìho kago. He asked, "Do you want?" Then his wife said,

"'ûkwahi'ï yi'ï bâî wagire mi'ï 'ïyayeru ba'iye, toya 'ïyagï." "Serve my relative to see like you, the designs you see.

keaka mi'ïbi dau hû'îtoka? keaka mi'ïre dau sikogi ba'igine bagï? kago dìho. "If not, when you are sick? how will he cure your illness?" said his wife.

kagona, "hâ'âka ba'ito 'ûkwa zan'iyi, yi'ï wagïte siani" kabi bagï. She said, "That being so, I will serve my in-law," he said.

kani, hâ'âribi, somu wi'eña ba'hi'i. He said, then it was the second house.

ba'igina, hâ'ârì kwa'kurena, 'ûkwabi bagï, It was and that time they cooked, and he served;

'ïo yahe bahi'i. burned *yagé* it was.

'ûkwani hâ'â mâkârì 'ûkwarì te'e rïobï ba'iye 'ûkwabi. He served, that first time he served, only a mouthful he served.

'ûkwani yi'ïre "'ûkuma'ihi'ï, kanaye 'ûkuni ba'ihi'ï" kabi. As he served me, "Don't drink more, wait after drinking," he said.

kagïna, hâ'âribi ñami hobo ba'ihi, yua. He said, and by then it was already mid-night.

ba'igina, hâ'âribi yahe re'wabi bagï, It was, then he arranged the *yagé*

'ira ko'are 'ûkwaye. to serve to the elders.

de'wani 'ûkwabi ira ko'are, He arranged and served to the elders,

yi'ï ha'yire, to my big brother,

hâ'ârïra ha'yï watibi 'ûkubi. first my deceased big brother drank.

'ûkugïna hâ'âribi gwina ba'iye yo'he, He drank, then afterwards in the same way

de'wani yi'ï wagï câbo watire 'ûkwabi. Shaman arranged and served to my deceased in-law Canbo

'ûkwagïna hâ'âru yekï ba'ihi. He served and there was another person there.

hâ'âgïga 'ûkubi. This person drank.

yi'ï wagï, dìtu watï ba'ihi. My deceased in-law Dìtu[4] was there.

hâ'âgïga 'ûkubi. That one drank.

'ûkugïna, hâ'âribi, yi'ïre de'wabi bagï. He drank and then Shaman arranged *yagé* for me.

Re'wani, kagï yahe hetubï huigï, He arranged, singing , playing *yagé* flutes,

yahe dekona huigï, playing music on the *yagé* liquid,

re'wagï bagï, he arranged.[5]

de'wani, tuhini, sïkoni, hâ'âribi. He finished arranging, blew, then

"'ì zî wagï, dani 'ûkuhi'ï" kabi. "This, little in-law, come and drink," he said.

kagïna yi'ï sai'ï. He said and I went.

sani, yi'ï 'ûkuwï. I went and drank.

'ûkuni dani hâôrïna hîâôwï. I drank and went and lay in the hammock.

hîâôni ba'irïra yahe dabi yi'ïre. I lay down and shortly the *yagé* came to me.

ah hâ'âka dani hâ'âribi yua bagï hwîha wiabi bagï. Ah thus it came, for already Shaman raised the chants.

hwîhi 'ai kagï ba'ihi'i. He chanted a lot.

kagïna yahega 'aito da'bi yi'ïrega. As he chanted oh how the *yagé* came to me.

daigïna, 'ïyagï gwebegï we'ewï yi'ï. As it came, a seeing and drunken one I lay.[6]

we'egï ba'irïra ba'igï hwîha kabi dani, hwîha kagï, kagï wi'wïni ganogï hwîha kagï bagï. I was lying, and shortly Shaman came chanting, *yagé* chants he sang, singing, running around chanting.

hetubi huigï, kagï bahi'ï. Playing the flute, he was singing.

kagïna, 'achagï we'eyï. As he sang, I listened while I lay.

we'ena ba'irïra hâ'ârura yahe te'e duîye dani, yahe suñabi. I was lying and shortly, in that place, the *yagé* came directly, the *yagé* shined.

suñagïna, hâ'âribi, bagï 'ïmï ziaya toa yogu bâîre. It shined, then to the people of the High River fire canoe

hwîha koka kagï ba'ihi bagï. their chants he was singing.

kagïna yi'ïga yua barure yi'ïga ba'ï'ï. As he sang, I was immediately at that place.

hâ'âru'gata'a 'ai bâî ba'ï, hwîha bâî. At that special place so many people were there, *yagé* people.

ba ko'a kuya wa'i nakoni, Whites were with them,

ba'i ko'abi kuya wa'i azuru kâya huihi, those ones, the whites, were wearing blue clothing.

i azuru tuibïâre tuihi And blue caps they wore.

ba ko'aga 'azuru zapato hui bâîira, kuya hiha bâî ba'ï. Those ones had on blue shoes; white caciques they were.

ba ko'abi "yikïna 'ïho'ore ba'iyi, hijo. mi'ï, keaka ro'tagi dakine?" We in this place live, son. What are you thinking as you come?

yi'ï yikïna ñaka ba'iruâ" kahì bako'a kuya wa'i kawï yi'ïre. "This is how our place is," they said, the whites said to me.

kahìna, 'achawï yi'ï. They said and I listened.

'achagïna, hâ'âribi bagï hwîha koka kagïna. I listened, then Shaman intoned the chants,

"yuaga hâ'â bagï toa yogu 'ïmï ziaya toa yogubi daihi" kagï bagï kwîha koka kabi. "Now his fire canoe, High River fire canoe is coming," he sang; *yagé* chants he sang.

kagïna yi'ïga yua 'ïho'o gwebegïta'a, yua barure 'ïyawï yi'ïga. As he sang, already on this side I was very drunk and that place I was now seeing

'ïyagïna, 'ïme ziaya toa yogu 'ai ba'igubi dahi'ï. I was seeing as the High River fire canoe, a very large canoe, came.

i dani da'kïna, yi'ï baguna, ka'kawï yi'ï. And it came and came, that canoe I entered.

ka'kani, "'ïho'ona, ka'kahï'ï zî wagi, 'ïho'oraru" kabi bagï. I entered, "In here, enter, little one, in this place," Shaman said.

kagïna yi'ï ka'kawï. He said and I entered.

ka'kani, 'ïyatota'â 'ai de'ogu ba'ihi, toa yogu. I entered and saw what a good canoe it was, the fire canoe

ba'igïna hâ'âru bâîgi ba'iko'a yikïnaru ba'i. It was; the people of that place were like us.

ma sai'wa tui ba'ira bâî ba'ï'ï, hwîha bâî. They were people[7] wearing crowns of red macaw feathers, the *yagé* people.

ba'ihïna kuya bâîre gwinaru ba'i bâîra kuya hiha bâî ba'ï'ï. They were, and people like the white caciques were there.

ba'iko'abi bako'a'ga ñaka ba'iye, gïna saiwï bako'a siya saiwïâ, ñu'i bâîra ba'ï. Those ones, as if here, on their metal benches, their chairs,[8] sitting people they were.

ba'ihì hâ'âruna musicabiä bawï ba ko'a. They were, in that place music boxes they had.

musicabiâ'gato 'ai musica kâye 'ai yo'oyï bako'a. Those boxes playing much music, much music they made.

yo'ohì paidahì yo'owï bako'a. Thus they played and danced, those whites.

"ñaka yikïna yo'ohì ba'i ko'a'ì 'ime ziaya toa yugu kuya wa'i" kawï ba ko'a. "This is how we live, the whites of the High River fire canoe we are," they said.

kani, gìna hetubabi, hu'ihì bako'a paidawï⁹ ba ko'a. They spoke, they played long metal flutes and danced, those ones.

paidarena, hâ'âribi bagi yï'ï wagï si'da yai kagï hâ'âki sitahai'ì. They danced, then my brother in-law, Si'da Jaguar,¹⁰ wanted to take me further.

"dani, wagï 'iho'o dani 'ïyahï'ì. 'iho'ore bâî domi ba'iyï, wa'i domi" kabi. "Come, in-law, come and see this place. Here there are women, women of the animals," he said.

kagïna sai'ì. He said and I went.

sani, 'ïyato hâ'âruta'â 'ai bâî domi ba'ï'ì. I went and when seeing that place, so many women there were!

ba'ihìna, bagi "gaheni 'ïyahï'ì" kabi. They were, "descend and see," he said.

kagïna toa yogu sa'nawïna yakawïna gahewï. As he spoke, into the interior of the fire canoe I descended.

gaheni, 'ïyagïna, hâ'âruta'â bâî domi, sêsê domi, ba'ï'ì. I descended and saw, in that place there were women, white lipped peccary women they were.

ba'ihìna, "ah mï'ibi daigï yikïnate, yâka yikïna ba'i ko'a'ì" ba ko'a bâî domi kawï. They were, "Ah, you have come to us, this is how we are," those women spoke.

"keaka ro'tagï mï'ï dakine?" kahìna. "What are you thinking as you come?" they asked.

"bâhi, da'ña 'umu makabi 'ûkwagïna yï'ï daï'ï." "Nothing, the iridescent oriole of hunting he served, and I came."¹¹

"hâ'âka ba'ito, mï'ï yikïna, da'ña domi zî ma'ya dû'hì bâî wa'nâ (mï'ï daï'ï¹²) 'iho'o" kago bago. "That being so, to you we are the iridescent girls, we transform to fragrant people in this place," she said.¹³

kahì, gonogure 'ai ba ko'a sê'sêru siani toawï, 'ai da'ña domi zî siani¹⁴ toahìna, 'ïyawï At the chicha canoe, many peccary-like ones were grinding corn, I saw many iridescent girls grinding.

'ïyagïna hâ'âribi "yurega yekï ziayana saina'a" kani "miaye 'ume ziaya toa yoguwïna saina'a" kani, hâ'âruna ba ko'a da'wï. I saw and then "Now let's go to another river," the *yagé* people said, "upstream in the High river fire canoe let's go." They said and to that place they came.

dahìna, 'ïyagï daï'ì. They came, and I was seeing as I came.

dani, hâ'âruna tî'â dani, yekï yana bako'a sawï yï'ïre. We came, then to a different place we came, to another river they took me.

"'ïyahï'ì wêka ziaya" kawï ba ko'a. "Look at the Bamboo River," they said.

kani saihì, ba ko'a wêka, sieko ba'iyete wêka hetu hu'ihì bawï ba ko'a. They said and went, their bamboo, in strands, bamboo flutes they played, those ones.

"huuuu sêêêêê sêêêêê brêêêê brêêêêê" hu'ihì bawï ba ko'a "huuuu sêêêêê sêêêêê brêêêê brêêêêê," those ones were playing.

hu'ini, hâ'â'ribi "yikïna ñaka yo'oko'a'ì" kahì bawï bâî. They played and then "In this way we play music," said the people.

kani hâ'âribi yekï hobona sani, hâ'âruna tî'âni 'ïyato 'ai de'o hobo bahi hâ'âru, bâî wï'e hobo. They said and then to another town went, and we arrived at that place to see what a pretty town that place was, a people's town.

"*ïho'o yikïna ba'iru 'ïko de'owï bâî yikïna, yekï ko'a'ï" kawï ba ko'a.* "Here is our place, we are the people of the remedy domain, others we are," they said.

"*yikïna 'ïya yikïna 'ume ziaya toagu ñaka yikïna ganihì ba'i ko'a'ï" bâî kahì bawï.* "We, on this river, this way in our High River fire canoe we travel," they were saying.

kani, hâ'âribi mìawï yi'ïre. They said and then sent me up the river bank.

mìini ïyato 'ai de'o hobo wï'e hobo bahi'ï. When I arrived I saw what a nice town it was.

hâ'ârute 'ai bâî bai'ï. At that place there were many people.

kuya wa'i nakoni bai'ï. White people were with them.

hâ'ârute po nukasê'êñâ hu'iko'abi, 'azuru tu'ibiâ tu'i ba'ira, kuya hiha bâîru ba'iko'ara bâî ba'ï. At that place ones wearing white pants, blue caps on their heads, like the white caciques they were.

bï'he wa'nâ ba'i ba ko'a'ga. They were very short, those ones.

ba'ihì "ah, mï'ï daigï amigu" kawi yi'ïre. They were "Ah, you have come, friend," they said to me.

*kahìna "uhuh dayï yi'ïga do paseagï dayï yi'ïga mï'ï sako'a 'ïyahaza," they said. Yes, I just came to visit, I came to see you.

keaka ba'iruâre kayene, kagï 'ïyaza kagï, yi'ï daiyi yi'ï mï'ï sako'are. "I wanted to see this place they talk about, I came to you."

"*uh, de'ohi, hâ'âka ba'ito yurega 'ïyahi'ï ñaka yikïna ba'iko'a'ï" bâi kahì bawï.* "Good, then now come and see. We are like this," the people spoke.

"*mï'ibi gare hâ'â se'e 'ûkuni mï'ï gare hâ'âsikï dûîhagi'ï" kahì bawï.* "Drinking again, you will become fully transformed," they said.

"*hai'ï de'oye" do'tayï do'tagi bohowï yi'ï dekoyo.* "Okay, that is good," I thought and thinking my heart was happy.

bohoni hâ'âribi mi'ato yekï wï'e kwa'kuto, 'ûkuni, ñatawï. I was happy about tomorrow when we would cook another house, and I drank and dawned.

ñatani hâ'âribi na'igïna, kâî'ï'ï. I dawned, then it grew dark and I slept.

kâîni ñatani hâ'âribi yekï wï'e kwa'kuwï. I slept and dawned and then they cooked another house of *yagé*.

kwa'kurena yi'ïre "ì wi'ena mï'ïsako'are 'etohaihagi'ï" kabi bagï. They cooked, "In this house you will take off," Shaman said to me.

"*hâ'âka ba'ito de'ohi, 'ïyahagi'ï yi'ï" ro'tagi 'achawi yi'ï.* "Thus it is good. I am going to see," I was thinking as I listened.

"*gaña wï'e mï'ïsako'a gaña wï'e 'ûkwani tôye 'ì wi'ena mï'ï sako'a hu'ihako'a'ï" kabi.* "This last house, I will show you all with this last house and you will play the flutes," he said.

kagïna, yi'ï bohowï yi'ï dekoyo. He said, and my heart was happy.

bohogï 'achawï. A happy man I listened.

'achani hâ'âribi mì'ini yekï wï'ë kwa'kuwï. I listened, then we went up and another house we cooked.

gwinaru 'ïo yahe kwa'kuwï. Likewise burned *yagé* we cooked.

kwa'kuni na'ito gachawï. We cooked and when it was dark we descended (to the *yagé* house).

gachani, gwinaru te'e dìôbï ba'iye hâ'ârì 'ûkwabi. We descended, likewise one mouthful that time he served me.

'ûkwani, hâ'âribi bagï 'ira ko'are yahe de'wani, 'ûkwabi. He served and first for the elders he arranged and served.

'ûkwagï karahaini, hâ'âribi yi'ïre 'ûkwabi. He finished serving and then served me.

"uh, wagï 'ûku daihi'ì" kabi. "Okay, in-law come to drink," he said.

kagïna, sani 'ûkuwï. He said and I went and drank.

'ûkuni, ba'igïna yahe 'ïo gare daimaha'i. I drank and waited but the *yagé* dream didn't come at all.

damakïna 'ai ba'irì hïhowï. It didn't come and much time I waited.

hïhogï baírìra hâ'âribi yahe dabi. I was waiting a long time and then the *yagé* came.

hâ'ârì mia saiwïra[15] ba'ira yahe dabi. That time a brilliant and clear image came.

"de'oye suñyahi" ro'tagï, "ïyagï we'eyï." "It is shining well" thinking and seeing I lay.

we'egï ba'irìra hâ'âribi ho ba'irìbi'gato yahe'gato zigi kabï se'ega beoru, na'iseru ba'ibireba (ba'ibïra?) yahe dabi yi'ïre. Laying for a while, then right in the middle, suddenly, only black winged creatures everywhere! Everything in darkness, the *yagé* came to me.

dagïna, "gere yo'ogï hâ'âka daigïne?" ro'tagï yi'ï 'ïyagï we'eyï. As it came, "What is happening to me," thinking and seeing I lay.

we'egïna hâ'âribi na'i zi'hei bâî kato "zi'eeeee zi'eeeeezi'eeeee ti ti ti ti ti ti" kahì bawï yi'ïre. I was reclining and when pitch black people said to me, *"zi'eeeee zi'eeeeezi'eeeee ti ti ti ti ti ti,"*

kahì beoru yi'ï gâhogo beoru ta'pigï bahi'i. their noise plugged up my ears.

ta'piyeta'â yi'ï gare kayï be'oye, 'ïyagï ba wesi wagi sïani 'ïyagï we'egï bawï. All plugged up I couldn't speak at all, seeing I was a lost person, as I was seeing and laying.

we'egïna "gare keakara hâ'âka yahe dagïna suñagïne." As I lay, "Why has the *yagé* come shining in this way?"[16]

gebi ba'igï hâ'âka zigi kabïra suñegïne? "Why is it shining those black winged creatures?"

kagi 'ïyagï ba'irìra' hâ'âribi negro wa'i zihe'ina mâî 'ïyama'sako'abi, negro wa'i dahì bawï. I said, looking, and, shortly, black creatures such that I had never seen approached.

dani, gìnameâbi sêhâni yo wêñu kahì. They came and cast out metal chains trying to tackle me.

hâ'âribi yiïbi, yiîñi witomearu, bâîmeabi, Then cotton, like a cotton fishing line, a people-catching line,

sêhâni yo'oni gato zihei mêabi, sêhâni yo wêñu kahìna yi'ï wa'gï, they were casting, a black line they hurled out trying to tackle me

yekï kâ'ko yekï kâ'ko hihagï bawï yi'ï wa'gï. On the other side, on the other side, I remained strong.

hihagïna, hâ'âribi se'e sêhâni gwinaru hâ'âka diâgï, diâgï, 'etahaigï yo'ogïna ba ko'a yi'ïre sêho bawï. I was strong, then again they cast and likewise, ducking and ducking, I tried to escape as they threw the line at me.

sêhoni, yo'omaihì bawï. They threw but didn't catch me.

"mi'ïre yo'oni hâ'âruna" bâî kahì bawï. "They are doing evil to you in that place," the *yagé* people were saying.

"mi'ini sêhoni. mi'ire yo'oni hâ'â zihei wi'ena mi'ire gu'ani wesoha'ko'a'i" kahì bawi yi'ire." They are trying to catch you. That black house is bad for you and they are trying to make you lost forever," they were saying to me.

kato 'aibe wi'e ba'igì bahì, ba ko'a ba wi'e. What a large house it was, their house.

ba wi'e zihei ñaka wi'ereba ba'igïya. That house had a black emptiness inside, a black house!

hâ'âribi 'iyagïna, domiru bâîruko'a si'si kâya, ya'oye ne'eseru ba'i kâya, hu'i bâî domi daihì bawï. Then as I saw, women-like creatures in dirty clothing, people dressed in clothing like it was rubbed in mud, these women approached.

dani gato 'ah mâî 'iyarama'iyi ba ko'a gato, pana zo'aseru ba'iko'areba daihì bawï. They came, I have never seen such ones, those mud-covered ones that were coming.

daihìna, 'iyagi we'egi bawï. As they came, I was seeing and laying.

we'egïna, hâ'âribi yekì ko'a'ga, gwebe wati wa'i kato, As I was reclining, then others, the drunken spirits!

beoru zêmêñoâ ru'tani, to'ini, pulling their tongues way out, dropping down,

hâ'âribi kwaruhì'i, yihana tâ'tani 'ûîhì dahì bawï ba ko'a, then growling and rolling and wallowing on the ground they came.

dahìna 'iyagì we'egì bawï. As they came I was seeing and laying.

we'egïna "ah mi'ire gu'ahi" bâî ka bawi yi'ire. Laying, "Oh it is very bad for you," the *yagé* people were saying to me.

"mi'ire hâ'âka yo'ogï mi'ì hû'îhagi'i" kahí bawi gwebe bâî. "We are going to make you die," they said, the drunken people.

kayeta'â do 'iyagï bawï. Even though they spoke, I could only watch.

'iyagì ba'igì hâ'âribi, bagi yi'ì ha'yï sêhi'ì. Just watching, then my older brother asked,

"yua mi'ire yahe de'oye suñagï, mami" kabi. "Now did the *yagé* shine well for you, child?" he said.

kagïna, "bâhi, yi'ì de'oye suñamaihi" kawï. He said, "No, it isn't shining well for me," I said.

"keaka suñagïne?" kabi. "What is it shining?" he said.

kani, "beoru zigi kabï se'ega na'iseru ba'igì, yi'ire yahe suñahi. gare yahe toya 'iyomaihi yi'ire" kawï. "Only all black creatures, like night the *yagé* shines for me. No designs does it show at all to me," I said.

"gere hâ'âkata'â mi'ì kiama'igïne? kiatoka ba'bo re'awi" kagi bahi. "Then why didn't you tell me? If you had told, I would have cleansed you," he said.

kani, hâ'âribi wìni 'okona tani, yi'ire ba'bokaigï bahi'i yi'ire bagi. He spoke and then got up and fetched water and was purifying me.

"yurega keaka duigïne tuni siki?" "Now has it transformed and has the evil left?"

"tuni sahi" kawï. "The bad is passing," I said.

"de'ohi, hâ'âka ba'ito mi'ì kiama'kine? mi'ì hû'î 'iaye yo'ogïne?" kabi bagï. "That is good, but why didn't you tell? Do you want to die?" he asked.

"keaka suñagi hâ'âka suñagïne?" "Why did it shine in that way?"

"wesïyi yi'ì ba suñaye'ga hâ'âka sïani kiama'ï" kawï. "I was lost, with it shining that way I couldn't speak," I said.

"yure'ga yua mi'i'ga 'etahaigï. ûh yua de'werï suñani beoru sahi'i" *bagïga kawï.* "Now you will come out. Did it shine briefly and now it is gone?" he asked.

"yua wahïyi" kawï. "Now I am well," I said.

"hâ'âka ba'ito de'ohi" kawï. "That being so, very good," he said.

gañañe'ï. I have spoken.[17]

NOTES

1. For a very similar explanation of the *yagé* experience, see Fernando Payaguaje's description in this book. The Secoya are closely related to the Siona in language and culture, and his description fits well what the Siona have told me.

2. Siona vowels /a, e, ï, i, o, u/ are also nasalized and are represented here as /â,ê,ì, î, ô, and û/.

3. When the Siona apprentice first leaves his body and begins to travel in the other realms, he is given a *yagé* name which captures some aspect of his behavior or of his experience. These names are highly metaphorical and extremely difficult to translate.

4. *dìtu* is his in-law's *yagé* name, *dìtu* is the name of a plant whose leaves are particularly fragrant and which are worn attached to the upper arm as adornment; the *yagé* people also wear fragrant leaves and flowers.

5. To arrange *(re'wa-)* the *yagé* is a part of the ritual where the shaman sings, invoking the beings he wants to see, as well as "plays" or whistles over the *yagé* in the cup as if it were flutes. See also Fernando Payaguaje, this volume.

6. Ricardo repeats throughout the narrative that he is lying in the hammock seeing what is happening on the other side, where he is also present. This repetition emphasizes how Fernando Payaguaje (this volume) describes the experience: "You're sitting in the hammock, but at the same time, you're in another world, . . ."

7. This should be interpreted as their identity as Indians and allies, which is the meaning of *bâî.*

8. In Siona, Ricardo used the Spanish word *silla* to refer to the whites' "metal benches."

9. *paida* — from Spanish, *bailar,* to dance.

10. Si'da Jaguar is the Shaman's *yagé* name. *si'da* is the name of a palm tree whose nuts the peccaries eat and which can represent the peccaries on the other side. Ricardo probably identified him by his *yagé* name, since the next line refers to the peccary women that Ignacio showed him, identifying Ignacio as a shaman specialist in seeing peccaries when drinking *yagé* and negotiating with them for hunting. Also, women's souls may be represented as orioles.

11. Ignacio belonged to the Makaguaje group. Ricardo's son-in-law, a Makaguaje, said that their shamans drank oriole remedy *('umu 'ïko)* before drinking *yagé* in order to see the oriole people. This phrase may refer to what was taken before drinking the *yagé.*

12. Ricardo added when revising. This phrase is difficult, because I think that he is trying to produce part of the chants that are sung in the *yagé* ceremony.

13. The peccary women transform into iridescent and fragrant people there in the sky.

14. In revisions he inserted here /'ai toawï/.

15. Ricardo used the word *saiwïra,* which specifically suggests the idea of a design motif that they attempt to capture in their art (Langdon 1992a).

16. I have translated suña-as "shine" here, but in this case it is not bright or full of light. Ricardo feels a loss of consciousness. He is not seeing what the shaman intended him to see.

17. EDITOR'S NOTE: I wish to thank Dr. Gordon Brotherston, author of *Book of the Fourth World: Reading the Native Americas through their Literature* (Cambridge University Press), for his comments on the translation of this text, although I assume total responsibility for the translation. I also wish to thank the Conselho Nacional de Desenvolvimento e Pesquisa (CNPq) of Brazil for the research grant sponsoring my translations.

TWO AYAHUASCA MYTHS
FROM THE CASHINAHUA
OF NORTHWESTERN BRAZIL

Elsje Maria Lagrou

The Cashinahua of Northwestern Brazil (as well as their kin, the Cashinahua of Eastern Peru) use *ayahuasca* ritually as an important element of cultural praxis. The active vision quest and visionary experience resulting from the frequent (twice-monthly) use of this potent psychotropic decoction by the majority of the adult male population have profound consequences for the Cashinahua cosmovision. The transformative character of the Amerindian universe, known by specialists through myths and shamanistic séances, becomes an existential given for people who have gone through the experience of initiation into the visionary world revealed through *ayahuasca*, which the Cashinahua call *nixi pae*.

Transformations similar to those undergone by mythical beings in primordial times when difference and identity were assigned, and when humans as well as animals acquired their definitive shapes, are also experienced by the individual during a lifetime. These transformations of identity are a "change of skin (body)," referred to in mythic and ritual language as "changing one's clothes." The changing of skin is a symbolic death of the same order as the changing of clothes in ritual language. For this reason, during Cashinahua funerals a ritual song is directed to the dead soul to encourage him to put on the "yellow clothes of the Inca" (God of the dead) *(Inkan tadi sauwe, paxin tadi sauwe)*. This means that he must become the Incan God himself, assuming the body of an Inca.

Similarly, in an *ayahuasca* song, the listener is told to put on "vine clothes" *(nixi pae tadi)*, the clothes of a peccary *(yawa tadi)* and those of a squirrel *(paka tadi)*. In this way, in the visionary experience, the person is temporarily transformed into a peccary or a squirrel for as long as he is wearing their clothes.

The snake is one of those paradigmatic animals that changes skin and is therefore thought to possess eternal life as well as the secrets of healing. It is also the master of all liquids, from rain to menstrual blood to *ayahuasca*, the brew of transformation. In Cashinahua mythology, the cosmic snake Yube has mastered all possible appearances of form, color and design that can be perceived by human eyes. All the phenomena of this world are said to be inscribed in the designs of its skin and can be visualized through the (metaphoric) ingestion of his blood *(nawa himi)* or his urine *(dunuc isun)*, which are the names of *ayahuasca* in ritual songs. The eternal renewal or novelty of skin is the eschatological image used by the Cashinahua to visualize eternal life and youth.

The first *ayahuasca* myth I will present is not the myth of the origin of the brew (which is the theme of the second narrative I treat), but a myth linked to the separation of heaven and earth. If the myth of origin, linked to the snake beings, describes the relation between the earth and the water world, the first myth I present shows how *ayahuasca* plays a role in the communication between the earth and the sky world. In mythic times, say the Cashinahua, people knew a special kind of *ayahuasca* vine called *xanka huni*, vine of lightness. This vine enabled them to ascend into the sky, following the example and path traced for them by the sky people when they decided to go and live far away from the earth.

The Myth of Xanka Huni, the Vine of Lightness
(Told by Milton Maia, Village of Nova Aliança, Purus River, 1995)

Well, this is the way our ancestors did it. They wanted to ascend into the sky (the whole village at the same time, taking their house and gardens with them). So they decided to drink *xanka huni*, the vine of lightness. They went to get the vine and beat it into pieces to boil it. After the vine had been cooking, they took it from the fire to let it cool down. Then, when the *xanka huni* was cold, they drank the brew. (They also sprinkled the brew all along the edges of their gardens to ensure that the whole piece of land would levitate with them in their ascension.) They finished it all, and they knew that the vine-drunkenness had begun to manifest itself when their bodies started trembling. With the first signs of the arrival of the brew's effects, they sent someone off to inform the other village.

"Go and tell them! Run! Take the main path and come back quickly!" the people told him. "Go and let them know that we took the vine of lightness. Tell them we are already seeing 'those things you see when it is beginning to arrive' *(betsa betsa watanikiki).* Tell them the effect of the brew has started already. Quickly! Run! Go quickly!" they told him.

The messenger went, but he did not want to notify anybody. He hid himself instead at the edges of the village to try to make love to the women. Hidden, he called out, "Come here, beautiful woman, come!"

"Where is he?" his people asked. "When are they going to arrive? (The earth) is already trembling. What if they do not come? Maybe they're not coming, so let's ascend. We're already going up."

And so they went shouting *hi hi hi hi* and trumpeting (with a trumpet made of clay) *pudi pudi pudi.* They trumpeted on the armadillo's tail *txc txc txc* and drummed on the wooden "canoe" used for grinding *tinki tinki.* Doing this, making a lot of noise, they (the people of the other village) started to notice something strange. They stopped to listen and wondered, "What is happening to our kinsmen? Let's go see what they're doing. Let's go see why they are making all this *purin purin* noise."

They were running, moving rapidly up the path: "We're going to have a look at the other village that's making so much noise."

From the other side on the same path, they saw *Duxau* (also the name of the bird into which the man would be transformed later on, while trying to follow his people) arriving, the man who had been sent to inform them. But this man did not notify anybody. All he wanted was to make love to the women. When he heard the sounds of crying *sai sai* and trumpeting *purin purin,* he left his hiding place and came running in the direction of the villagers, who were coming from the opposite direction.

"Why are our kin making all this *purin purin* noise?" they asked him. "What is happening?"

"Nothing is happening," he answered. "They took the vine of lightness and are already seeing 'those things you see when it is beginning to arrive.' 'Tell our kin so that they can come with us!' they said. And so I came. They're already making a lot of noise. They're going."

"Why did you come so late? Why didn't you come immediately?" they asked.

"I was just arriving," he answered. "Let's go! They took the vine of lightness. They're already ascending. Let's go with them!"

And so they went, running on the path to the other village. When they saw them, they had already levitated up to here (narrator shows the level with his arm above his head). By they time they had actually arrived, however, they had already ascended much more. Seeing them, they cried, "Take me with you!" (narrator reaches out his arms).

"I sent a man to inform you. Why didn't you come immediately?" they replied (from the levitating platform).

"Take me with you! Take me with you! Don't leave me behind!" he (the messenger) cried.

"Come on then!" they said.

But (the platform) was too high. He could not touch the edge with his hand anymore.

And so they went higher and higher, shouting *sai sai,* trumpeting *purin purin,* and blowing on the armadillo tail *txc txc.* Ascending like this, they left the earth. This is as far as my words go.

(end of narration)

This myth is a clear statement on the mediating nature of the *ayahuasca* brew. *Ayahuasca* is a means of transport and of transformation, a means of reconnecting with invisible layers of the cosmos, as well as a way of making present the world and stories told in myth through imaginary experience.

"If you want to learn about the world of the ancestors," Osmani, who is from the village of Moema, told me, "you have to remember a myth before you drink the brew. If you concentrate well on the story, the story and its beings will appear to you in vision and you will understand the meaning this story has for your own life and experience. You will feel the story. You will live it."

In the same way, every initiate in the art of the vision quest has a mental image of the myth of origin of the brew, in which the ancestor named Yube enters the water world of his spiritual kin, the snakes, to marry the beautifully-painted snake woman whose vision had seduced him. The myth recounts his initiation into the taking of *ayahuasca*, as well as his failure to resist the fear induced by the visions. He cries out, offending his snake kin, owners of the brew, and escapes, only to be found and wounded by his angry kin a year later. Before he dies, he transmits to his people his knowledge of the brew's preparation and its songs.

The initiate, while thinking of this myth and under the brew's influence, will live the same primordial conflict of affinity and strangeness in a world where he does not know the rules and habits, an adventure which gives knowledge and power but involves the symbolic death of being caught and broken in the anacondas' grip.

In Cashinahua ritual life, myths are not only told and heard but are also actualized on a strongly existential, experiential level in the vivid and visceral imagery induced by drug ingestion. In the myth of origin of the brew, the contact with the world of the invisible is dealt with in terms of seduction, affinity and potential enmity, while in the myth of ascension one person misses the "flight" because of his obsession with sex. In this sense, his attitude contrasts with that of the discoverer of the brew. While the hunter of the origin myth is seduced and fascinated, ready to risk his life in order to know the secrets of the beauty that was hidden from him, the messenger in the myth about those who took the vine of lightness only seeks easy pleasure, calling any female passerby into his hiding place. The hunter is fascinated by the unknown and returns from his journey with a knowledge that will be dear to his people, whereas the messenger, obstinately repeating well-known pleasures, fails to transmit knowledge, thereby provoking the ultimate separation between his kin and their neighbors.

The Myth of Origin of Nixi Pae

(Told by Milton Maia and Maria Domingo, Village of Cana Recreio, Purus River, 1989)

A man went hunting. He arrived at a lake and, not far from a genipap tree, he built a little hut where he could hide and wait for his game. That day he had decided to kill a tapir. The tapir arrived and took a genipap fruit in his mouth. But instead of eating it, he threw the genipap in the lake, *txibun*. Afterwards, he took another and threw it in the lake and then another, *txibun txibun*. An anaconda rose from the lake and, as she left the water, she turned into an extremely beautiful woman, her whole body covered in exquisitely elaborate genipap design. The woman looked for the tapir who was hidden behind a tree. She found the tapir and he made love with her.

The hunter, hidden, watched them.

"What a beautiful woman!" he said to himself. "I want this woman. Tomorrow I will do the same as the tapir did."

The anaconda went back into the lake and the tapir disappeared in the forest. The man returned home. There, he was unable to forget what he had seen. His wife gave him manioc to eat and banana brew to drink, but he did not touch it.

"I am not hungry," he said.

When she asked him what had happened, he told her it was nothing. He withdrew to his hammock but did not sleep a wink all night. The next morning, at dawn, he left for the lake. When he reached the genipap tree, he took three pieces of fruit and threw them in the water, *txibun txibun txibun*. The snake left the water to meet the tapir. It was the same beautiful woman from the day before, coming toward the tree. There she met the man. He embraced her with force, trying to lay her down, but she resisted. Suddenly, she became a snake, coiling her body around his, almost suffocating him. She asked, "What are you doing here?"

And the man, in a panic, replied, "Well I was here yesterday and saw the tapir making love with you. I wanted to do the same."

"You see?" she said. "We are like this as well. If you really want to make love with me, we will have to talk first."

"Sure!" replied the man, relieved.

The snake loosened her grip and became a woman again.

"Do you have a family?" she asked.

"No, I don't. I'm single," the man lied.

"That's good," she said. "I'm single, too. I'm looking for a husband to take home with me to help my parents. I will make love with you only if you promise that you will come to live with me in the lake."

And the man replied avidly, "Yes. That's exactly what I wanted. I want to marry you."

The man possessed her, and after the act she squeezed the sap of a leaf in his eyes.

"This is so you will not be afraid," she said.

But he was afraid. Even so, without further delay, she had him climb on her back and jumped with him into the water. When they arrived at her village, the snake woman made him wait in the gardens and went to inform her parents. She quickly returned, took him by his arm and guided him into the house to greet her parents who received him well with banana brew and manioc. The man got used to the life in the village of the anacondas, made his own garden, hunted with his father-in-law, and made three children with his wife.

One day, his wife told him that the snake people were going to take *nixi pae (ayahuasca)*. But she warned him, "Don't take it! You will be scared. You won't be able to stand it, and you will call out the name of my people. If you do this, they will kill you."

But the man, obstinate as always, wanted to drink. He went out with his father-in-law to cut the vine and find the leaves, and at night he sat down with the whole village. They served him a cup full of *nixi pae* and he drank it all at once. The vision came, and the man cried in anguish, "The snakes are swallowing me!"[1] Everybody heard him, and the snake people were offended.

The next morning, nobody would say a word to him, nor would anybody invite him to eat. He decided to go to the forest and see whether he could catch some game. On his way, he met the little bods fish who said to him:

"My brother, you are in danger. The snakes are going to kill you. Follow me. I will take you to the stream where I heard your wife cry for you. She misses you. It has been three years since you have failed to return home, and there is no one who hunts for her. I saw her in that stream. She almost tore off my tail, but I escaped alive. She is hungry for meat."

The man remembered his family, and he missed them. The little bods fish put the juice of a leaf in the man's eyes and took him to the stream where he had seen his wife. When she saw her husband approaching her, the woman was scared because she thought he was dead. But when she saw it was really him, alive, she was happy and took her man back home. She gave him manioc soup to drink and boiled bananas to eat. He ate and went to sleep. He tied his hammock very high, close to the roof, so that the anacondas would not find him. He stayed hidden in his hammock like this for a whole year, until finally his child was born.

The man left the house to find genipap fruit to paint his newborn child. On his way, however, it started to rain and the rivers began to rise. The man slipped into a stream and in no time a snake, his youngest son, got hold of his big toe. Soon after him came his oldest daughter who swallowed his whole foot, and when his wife arrived, she gulped down his whole body up to his armpits. She did not manage to swallow him completely because he was holding on to the branch of a tree with both arms. The man cried for help, and his kin came running to save him. They managed to disentangle him from the snakes' grip, but his bones were broken and his body was weak. They carried him home, and when he was lying down in his hammock, he told his people he wanted to know when he would die. So he asked them to find the vine and leaves of *nixi pae*. After bringing him and showing him all the possible kinds of vines, they finally found the right one. The same happened with *kawa*, the leaf of *nixi pae*. Our ancestor then prepared and cooked the brew, and his people stayed at his side to learn. When the night fell and the *nixi pae* was cool enough to drink, our ancestor gathered the men of the village around him and gave them all a cup to drink. The whole night he sang the songs he had learned from the snake people. He sang one whole night, another day, the next night and still another day. At the end of the third night he died.

His body was buried, and after a while the *kawa* leaves grew from his eyes, while four kinds of vines grew from his limbs: *xane huni* (people of the little blue bird) sprung from his right arm, and *baka huni* (fish people) from his left, while from his right leg sprung *xawan huni* (macaw people) and from his left *ni huni* (ant people).

People cut the vine and leaves and made the brew to remember their dead ancestor. When the drunkenness arrived, however, no one could remember the songs. The leader asked every man present at the ritual, "Do you remember?"

"I don't," each one answered.

Finally, a young boy, with his hammock tied high, who had not drunk the brew but had listened carefully during those three long days and nights, started to sing the songs of nixi pae. This is why our people still remember them today. Small boys learn quickly.

(end of narration)

The myth mentions four kind of vines (all *Banisteriopsis caapi*) that are supposed to induce different kinds of visions. The visions vary in intensity and predominant color. They are called 'tapes' (an analogy made by an informant familiar with video tapes). One 'tape' gives blue visions, the other very clear or pastel, almost white, visions, a third produces red visions (one sees a lot of blood), and the last one gives predominantly black, dark visions. The colored ones (blue and red) are considered the most beautiful, while the extremes (white and black) are thought to be dangerous and frightening. When I asked my informants about a possible variety in species of vine and whether one can define by means of botanical identification which vine produces blue, red, white or black visions, I received the following answer: "They are not really different in kind because they come from the same body, the body of our ancestor Yube. Each of these vines will show you a different part of his life, a different part of his thoughts. The white one comes from his bones, the red one from his blood, the blue one from his bile, the black one from his intestines. *Nixi pae* is Yube's body. It is the way he comes back to us when we miss him. No one can ever consume his whole body at once. That would be too much to drink and to face. Every time we drink from the brew, its owner shows us just a little piece of all there is to know about his and our own life."

---

1. EDITOR'S NOTE: A fascinating variant of this part of the myth appears in *Estórias de hoje e de antigamente dos Índios do Acre:*

> Some time later, the snakes and serpents of the lake decided to drink *ayahuasca.* Yo Buié asked his wife if she, too, was going to drink *ayahuasca.*
>
> "Of course I am," she said.
>
> "And what about me? Can I do it, too?"
>
> "No, because you'd be really scared. You'll see snakes and serpents and you'll think that they want to devour you. Then you'll scream like a crazy person. Don't get involved with that kind of stuff. They're our customs, not yours."
>
> But Yo Buié insisted so much that they ended up accepting him in the circle of snakes to drink *ayahuasca.*
>
> As soon as the first visions came, Yo Buié began to scream, "Help! The snakes want to swallow me!"
>
> During that same hour, his wife turned into a snake, coiled herself lovingly around him, and began singing sweetly in his right ear. His mother-in-law did the same thing, singing in his left ear. Finally, his father-in-law coiled himself around the three of them and, balancing his face against Yo Buié's forehead, accompanied the song as well.

MYTHOLOGIES OF THE VINE

Oscar Calavia Sáez

The Cashinahua myths reproduced in the article by Elsje Maria Lagrou for this volume (see "Two Ayahuasca Myths from the Cashinahua of Northwestern Brazil") can be found among other indigenous groups of the region, for example the Yaminahua and Yawanahua, both of which are speakers of the Pano languages.[1] Although the differences between the three versions may seem minimal, they are, in fact, significant in terms of the selection and order of the episodes.

The Yawanahua myth speaks of an epoch in which death does not exist. The tribal chief, hiding at the edge of a lake in hopes of hunting some game, sees the surface of the waters fill with water animals (turtles and snakes) who cast a spell on him. Very ill, he returns home where he dies that same night. His relatives, even they do not know what death means, proceed with his burial in keeping with the instructions received from the moribund chief. Shortly thereafter, they see an *ayahuasca* plant growing from the tomb together with other shamanic plants (tobacco, pepper and datura). The narrative then tells of the ascent of the tribal dwelling into the sky, an event (which is the result of a messenger's carelessness) that separates those who live in the sky from those who reside on earth.

The Yaminahua narrate the origin of *ayahuasca* and the man who falls in love with a snake-woman in several myths. But the episode of the bewitched hunter from whose body the vine grows is shifted to the myth about rising into the sky, analogous to the Yawanahua myth. It is in the Yaminahua versions that one discovers an unusual absence in terms of the episodes in their entirety. Together with the two long narratives (which are equivalent to the two Cashinahua myths though lack any etiological interest) they include a shorter third myth about a snake devouring a man that is meant to explain the origins of *ayahuasca* use. The Yaminahua also have another myth, called Kukushdawa (The Firefly People), which coincides with the previous myths on only one point: a boy plants the three shamanic plants (vine, tobacco and pepper) on the tomb of his grandfather, who is a powerful sorcerer. The sorcerer is reborn in the form of a boa constrictor and takes his grandson on a war expedition alone against the firefly people, transforming him into an adult warrior.

With the exception of this coming-of-age-initiation myth, the other narratives about the vine can be reduced to two: one concerning the descent to an underwater world, the other about the ascent into the sky. The episode about the enchanting of the waters and the germination of the cadaver (which currently forms part of another narrative) indicates how easy it would be to join both narratives in a single myth that embraces the entire Pano cosmology.

Although this unified myth does not currently exist, it seems reasonable to hypothesize that the two present myths were originally from a previous narrative, now fragmented. There is a certain tension between a "jungle" (or, chthonic) version of *ayahuasca* and a "water" version. For the Pano, the high rain forest and the river environment form a very significant binomial that is echoed by the fluvial/interfluvial dichotomy discussed by Amazonist anthropologists and archeologists. In regional terms, this tension defines the relationship between those who live by large rivers (Shipibo, Conibo, Piro, and whites as well) and those who dwell in the rain forest (all the -nahua). An ethnohistorical interpretation might suggest that these water snakes acting as controllers of *ayahuasca* are a construct of the indigenous groups that live next to rivers: in other Yaminahua narratives, the same water snakes appear as fluvial pirates who attack a river boat on a great distant river and engage in commerce with their indigenous relatives in the interior of the rain forest (Calavia Sáez 1995, pp. 211–214). *Ayahuasca,* in this case, could be seen to have its origin in an environment associated with those who live near rivers. In an opposite sense, Tastevin (1926) collects the Cashinahua doctrine according to which the Yaminahua were the inventors of *ayahuasca* and other shamanic arts. If identifying the anacondas with the Shipibo-Conibo has its risks, it is equally imprudent to identify the Yaminahua with any specific ethnic group. Even though the name has been associated with indigenous groups who have had recent non-indigenous contact, Yaminahua is, to a large extent, a topological category, and represents extreme jungle-orientation. The Cashinahua, who occupy an intermediary position in the continuum that joins the two extremes of the riverbank and the high rain forest, are sensitive to two different exotic realms. Here, geography illuminates symbolism. The water versions of *ayahuasca* narrate primarily the origin of the vine-drink and its practice. The jungle versions, including Kukushdawa, treat the germination of the vine-plant by means of a cadaver, not individually, but through the use of a group of shamanic plants with very different personalities.

The *ayahuasca* that comes from the water is the absolute protagonist of a social practice: it is the axis of encounters, the motif of a banquet of sorts. It is also the result of marriage, which generally includes difficult experiences such as uneasiness, fear, contamination, nightmares, the scorn and the susceptibility of the brothers- and sisters-in-law. One could say that marriage is the uxirolocal sadness that always provokes a painful outcome, an appropriate vision for a group that is so concerned about the alliance of marriage (with its potentials and its dangers) as a basis of social life. The Cashinahua have become famous among ethnologists for the importance they attribute to this particular relationship in their sociological elaborations.

The *ayahuasca* that lifts one into the sky, on the other hand, deals with the theme of separation. For the Yaminahua, the sky is an ethnically "purified" habitat in which the diverse family "branches" live separated and incest is the norm.

It is in the Yawanahua version that *ayahuasca* is closest to becoming a complete cosmological axis: the magical power that proceeds from the bottom of the water (in the Yaminahua version the turtle appears on the surface as a kind of emissary from the snakes in the depths) makes the land fertile as plants that are born from the body of the first human to die, and facilitates the ascent into the sky. *Ayahuasca* is the key that enables one to cross a universe infected with hostilities and insurmountable distances: Pano myths frequently narrate the difficulty of any undertaking beyond the earthly realm. But there is a paradox similar to one that appears in many complex religions: *ayahuasca* is both the result of death and also the overcoming of death (albeit a restricted victory limited to a single blessed family). In the chthonic or jungle versions, *ayahuasca* is portrayed as simply one plant among other shamanic plants, all of which seem to be related to death.

It could be said that the Yawanahua version and the Cashinahua version expand in complementary directions. The former orders the great planes of the universe in a vertical sense; the latter limits the vertical reach of the narrative but increases its horizontal dimension: *ayahuasca* is a fortuitous acquisition that occurs during the course of a marriage relationship.

And the Yaminahua? Compared to the narratives of their Pano relatives, the narratives of the Yaminahua seem fragmentary and/or inadequate for constructing a cosmology. But the fragmentation is not necessarily a loss: it, too, transforms the substance of that which is narrated and makes it coherent with the characteristics that the other Pano attribute to the Yaminahua. Neither the fragmented Yaminahua narratives nor the political instability that seems to accompany them are appreciated by the other indigenous groups from Acre, who nevertheless do admire the Yaminahua for the individual and passionate tone of their songs. Something of this lyricism runs through myths that have been considered to be somewhat lacking in ideological content.[2] In the Cashi myth, ones sees how the underwater adventure serves humanity in terms of obtaining *ayahuasca*; in the Yaminahua narrative, on the other hand, *ayahuasca* provokes the loss of the underwater family. For the Yawanahua, death and the ascent of the dwelling seem to be means of illustrating the virtualities and the rules of *ayahuasca*; in the Yaminahua case, this is a miraculous instrument in the hands of a people visibly moved by their chief, and whose origin is explained by myths in a condensed form. In summary, the Yaminahua detach *ayahuasca* from the politics of alliance (like the Yawa, unlike the Cashi) and weaken the role of *ayahuasca* in the earth/sky relationship (like the Cashi, unlike the Yawa). But one should proceed with caution: by explaining things this way, one runs the risk of making the common mistake of describing the Yaminahua as impoverished versions of their neighbors. The fact is that the Yaminahua reveal something that is unheard of or has almost vanished among other indigenous groups: the link between *ayahuasca* and war. The fear of being murdered during an *ayahuasca* session, the anger of suspicious targets that actually begin to plan the crime, the enmity of the kinspeople barely moderated by the father-in-law and the wife, are all exact transcriptions of Yaminahua attitudes with regard to their past wars. Neither the political ramifications of the vine nor its eschatological aspect are absent from Yaminahua memories.[3] Both take on a negative quality in that it was war, according to their recollections, that seemed to be the most significant product of these gatherings to drink *ayahuasca* together; furthermore, the deceased relatives had the habit of taking advantage of their visits to ask for revenge. Consequently, it is not difficult to understand the relationship between the lyricism of Yaminahua songs and violence: the lyrics lament the consequences of war or express an erotic desire capable of provoking one of those wars.[4]

The history of the expedition against the Kukushdawa, which in several ways is the most shamanic of the Yaminahua myths, basically describes a rite of initiation. The dead shaman, however, initiates his grandson not in any therapeutic or divinatory art but rather in the rules of a war that seems more akin to a hunt in that the enemies bear the names of animals and act accordingly. That equation has an interesting correlative: the long process of Yaminahua shaman apprenticeship summarizes and preserves a joining of practices that in other Pano groups corresponds to the training of the hunter.[5] Observing the Cashinahua and Yawanahua versions of the myth of Kukushdawa, the systematic contrast previously mentioned is perpetuated. Although the narrative framework remains basically the same (the predatory expedition of the young man oriented by a guide who shows him the tricks and the abstinences necessary for an honorable outcome), the point of departure is different. In the Yawanahua case, the myth presents a father-in-law who tests the capacity of someone who aspires to be a son-in-law. In the Cashinahua case (which demonstrates the Yaminahua characteristic of misusing the ideological potential of the myth) everything is reduced to the story of a marvelous boy, who is guided by a snake and becomes a hunter and a precocious warrior, who matures so quickly that his mother no longer recognizes him when he returns from the hunt: in both cases there is no relation whatsoever with shamanism, and *ayahuasca* does not even appear.[6]

This is another way of saying that Yaminahua myths, supported by Yaminahua memories of life before the pax branca (the peace imposed by whites), suggest a conception of *ayahuasca* that might seem strange or perhaps even scandalous in another context: the plant-substance is a bloodthirsty agent associated with war and vengeance that eventually is tempered by the blood of a dead relative. It is also the instrument of an aggressive shamanism in which therapy is defense and counter-attack.

Reflecting on the loss of ancient knowledge and the disappearance of the figure of the shaman, the elder Yaminahua are clear: the old shamanism is no longer possible in the current world, especially with regard to hunting and erotic needs. Nowadays, everything favors a (new?) shamanism that is 1) restricted to the few people willing to undergo a long, hard initiation process; 2) devoted to healing (especially diseases new to the Yaminahua); and 3) "moralized." Nothing keeps this pacified *ayahuasca* from being an integral part of a contemporary plant-ecumenism that is highly visible in Acre.

It is enough to suggest here that the symbolic meaning of *ayahuasca* shows a variability that can be appreciated when one compares three peoples who are neighbors in geographic or linguistic terms, or the experiences of two generations. A comparison of two versions of the same Cashinahua myth separated by more than sixty years[7] demonstrates how the narrators tend to unite the plurality of myths that accompany a generalized practice. On the other hand, it also clearly shows their points of divergence, a function of the structural differences between the groups that create these narratives.

There is a great deal to explore in the symbolism of *ayahuasca* that cannot be fully explained based on its pharmacological/entheogenic functions or reduced to "priestly" interpretations (currently in vogue among researchers). I would like to summarize now some lines of reflection that strike me as important with regard to these matters:

A.

Ayahuasca is not an exclusively shamanic phenomenon, unless one is referring to a shamanism co-extensive to the symbolic culture of these peoples, a shamanism that is relevant yet different from the shamanism of the shamans. The values of *ayahuasca* change from people to people and from generation to generation, and there is a considerable distance between a "priestly"/therapeutic use (which corresponds to the current Yaminahua shamanic practice) and an ancient use, more extensive and "democratic," associated with war and hunting. Shamanism reelaborates *ayahuasca's* cultural data and frequently presents greater links with the shamanic doctrines of other ethnic groups (including practicing whites) than with doctrines held by drinkers of the vine decoction from their own people.[8]

B.

In several narratives, *ayahuasca* offers a life after death, or at the margin of death in keeping with very different models: the "reincarnation" of the old sorcerer reborn as a serpent and the aerial transposition of the domestic group of the first human to die. *Ayahuasca*, as I mentioned previously, is nourished on death and overcomes it. It is interesting to consider the resulting ambiguity of the Yaminahua versions in which the vine is either planted on the cadaver or offered on the burial mound in a vessel: does *ayahuasca* feed the recently-dead person or does it draw nourishment from him? The system of food and/or sexual restrictions (and in some cases painful tests) that accompany the apprenticeship of the vine form the most complex and extensive Pano initiation rite. In definitive terms, it reproduces the adventure of the dead shaman-grandfather in the myth: maturing as a snake, ingesting toxic substances, resuscitating outside of humanity, though close to it.

In the Amazonian context, *ayahuasca* values are clearest when they are associated with the separation of the living and the dead. The Yaminahua, in general, fear and scorn the dead, whom they consider dangerous, bloodthirsty, and as incestuous "as dogs". The *ayahuasca* myths, however, suggest a different relationship, an afterlife free of doubt: a powerful sorcerer becomes a snake, a dwelling ascends into the sky, and nothing indicates that those events should become widespread. In any case, it bespeaks a connection with what lies beyond that adorns the everyday avoidance of death.

C.

Things are never what they seem, according to the teachings of the vine. Honoring this teaching, we might ask ourselves, finally, if this same vine really can be called a plant substance. Together with the vine itself, the snake is the common denominator of the myths treated here. In them, the snake appears either as an antagonist or as a subject of the adventure, a successive or simultaneous double of the human being. This has been the case ever since the eye has received the help of the appropriate remedy or the body has experienced its final transformation supported by the same medicines. The ethnology of the Pano groups is characterized by the central role of the snake known as Ronoá: the water anaconda and the land boa constrictor are united by a single term in the common lexicon and clearly differentiated from other ophidians; in addition, the sign of both assimilation and difference can be found in the design of the snake's skin. Beyond the ophidian form of the vine, what unites both elements is precisely that design that offers itself on the surface of the snake and awaits in the interior of the vine; the snake and the vine embody each other as well as the entire animal world of the rain forest. The visions most coveted by *ayahuasca* drinkers are those in which animals that are going to be hunted appear. Tastevin describes the curious magical powers of the Cashinahua hunter who points at details in the skin of a captured Ronoá, thereby facilitating the hunting of the animals identified in the design. It is paradoxical that groups and ideologies involved with "plant substances" (it is difficult to dissociate current *ayahuasca* groups and environmental concerns) have found inspiration in cultures much more interested in animals than in plants. Compared to the oaks and olive trees of the old world, or the cosmic trees of other regions of the Americas, the gigantic trees of the nahua lands have a very low symbolic yield: in any case, they exist as dwelling places for deadly spirits. The Pano do not think of themselves or the world in terms of plants. In other words, they do not symbolize by means of plants in their world of humans, animals and spirits. The more vegetal aspects of Pano mythology no doubt have become increasingly pronounced only in recent times. Even if some Cashinahua myths still speak of a tree that supports the heavens, it is clear that ascents into the sky reject such an obvious means of movement and make use of the vine's action. I suspect that the vine has functioned as a transformer of Nahua mythologies, neutralizing plant symbols with regard to spiritual contents, converting them somehow into animal symbols. The jungle where the vine reigns is a realm that enjoys no peace: everything speaks, everything moves, transforming itself and waging war.

TRANSLATED FROM the Portuguese by Steven F. White

NOTES

1. The Yaminahua were the topic of my doctoral thesis (Calavia Sáez, 1995). The field work was done in six months between 1992–93 in the indigenous area Cabeceiras do Rio Acre in Assis, Brazil. In May, 1998 I made a brief visit to Yawanahua indigenous lands in Rio Gregório during which time I gathered the materials related to this group. I would like to thank the marvelous storyteller Clementino Yaminahua, Juarez Yaminahua, a great host and storyteller as well, and his brother Alfredo, who offered me his reflections on ancient shamanism. This article, although it does not quote them directly, owes a great deal to what I heard from them. I would also like to express my gratitude to Tatazinho, shaman from the Yawanahua village on the Rio Gregório, who narrated the Yawanahua myth of the origin of *ayahuasca* and to village leader Biracie Brasil, who translated it for me.

2. It would be difficult to imagine in the Yaminahua narrators the didacticism that seems to inspire the Yawanahua narrators for whom the content or moral is what justifies the narrative. It depends, of course, on the idiosyncrasies of the narrator, but, even so, the fact remains that the two ethnic groups designate as the best narrators individuals with very different characteristics.

3. Drinking *ayahuasca* was the essential ritual in the meeting of two groups in the rain forest; during the visions, it was very common to receive the visit of some deceased relative.

4. EDITOR'S NOTE: See Aurelio Chumap Lucía and Manuel García-Rendueles. *Duik múun: universo mítico de los Aguaruna*. 2 vols. Lima: Centro Amazónico de Antropología y Aplicación Práctica, 1979. In this model collection of Aguaruna narratives, *ayahuasca* is a significant ritual precursor to warfare between humans and mythic beings.

5. For more on the role of magic in Amahuaca and Cashinahua hunting, see (Carneiro 1970) and (Lagrou 1991: 177).

6. The Cashinahua version in published in the book *Shenipabu Miyui. História dos Antigos* (CPI–Acre 1995).

7. Cf. the Cashinahua versions that Tastevin gathers (1926; pp. 172–3): the first is a short version of the underwater marriage. The second is the "linking" episode (the spell of the waters/germination of the cadaver) that is missing in the current Cashinahua version.

8. On Yaminahua shamanism, see the brilliant article by G. Townsley (1993).

A HUAORANI MYTH OF THE FIRST MIIYABU
(Ayahuasca Vine)

Jonathon S. Miller-Weisberger

The Huaorani are an ethnic minority living in the central region of the Ecuadorian Amazon. They are a proud and independent people who have accepted contact with the "outside" world only in the past forty years. They number 1200 individuals whose homeland is threatened by the activities of several transnational oil companies. Some Huaorani clans to this very day remain uncontacted and will spear anyone who comes into their lands. Traditionally, the Huaorani did not use any consciousness-altering substances. They do not smoke tobacco or drink fermented beverages. They also do not use *Brugmansia* or *Brunfelsia* as do the neighboring tribes, nor do they use *Banisteriopsis* as a strong, thickly-prepared hallucinogenic beverage combined with a DMT-containing admixture plant. Their use of *Banisteriopsis sp.* vines is unique. It is used primarily in order to enhance hunting skills. A mild leaf decoction is administered by a master hunter to a young initiate; it is passed from mouth to mouth through the esophagus of a toucan. This is followed by a severe two-year diet. The first two months consist only of the pulp of the *petohue* palm *(Jessenia bataua)* that is obtained from the stomachs of toucans and spider monkeys (the meat of which is eaten by other community members). Upon completion of the diet, they become master hunters with an ability to locate and call animals with surprising accuracy. In certain Huaorani families, *miiyabu* leaves are lightly boiled with those of *wiyagen (Mansoa alliacea)* and used to wash the freshly cut umbilical cord of a newborn child. Once, an old Huaorani Iroinga (shaman) told me that in the past during times of war, the Iroinga would dry leaves of the *miiyabu* and burn them in the fire. He would be able to see the enemy in the smoke. When he blew away the image in the smoke, that enemy person would die. He added, however, that this was rarely practiced, for the Huaorani do not believe in witchcraft. When an enemy is to be killed, they prefer to settle the matter with a ten-foot barbed palm wood spear. *Miiyabu* has been taxonomically identified as *Banisteriopsis muricata*. Although they have recently acquired cultivated species of *B. caapi* from neighboring Quichua people, the Huaorani attribute the same name and qualities to it. The Huaorani use several names for these plants: some say *mii, miiyeca* and *miiyai*, but Mengatue and Huepe, the elders who tell this creation myth, call it *miiyabu*.

The following narration is written as told by Shaman Grandfather Mengatue Baihua on February 29, 1992 at a small hunting camp on the banks of the Gueyemonpare creek, in the headwaters of the Shiripuno River, Napo province, Amazonian Ecuador. It was translated from Huaorani to Spanish by Jonas Kahuitipe Cohue. The same myth was also told by Grandfather Huepe Orengo Coba at the Huaorani village of Quihuaro in Pastaza province of the Ecuadorian Amazon on April 6, 1993. Another aspect of this myth was told by Ohue Coba on May 3, 1995 in Quehueiriono, a village at the headwaters of the Shiripuno River. These recordings were translated from Huaorani to Spanish by Namonka, Nihua and Nenquerei Enomenga. The accounts were recorded on audio cassette and translated from Spanish to English by Jonathon S. Miller-Weisberger.

◆ ◆ ◆

Long, long ago when the sky was still close to the earth and the stars glistened just above the treetops, this is how the first *miiyabu*[1] vine was born.

There was a huge *degihue* tree.[2] It rose high into the sky and its trunk glistened golden in the afternoon sun. Up in the branches of this towering tree hung many nests of the *menka* bird.[3]

A group of Huaorani[4] walking through the forest came upon the tree, and, being that it was the season that the *menka* raise their young, they said, "Let us climb into the tree and take home the young birds to raise." Now the question was: Just how were they to climb the tree? The trunk was so wide and it rose so high, straight into the sky.

Next to the *degihue* tree was a *tepahue* palm,[5] and one Huaorani climbed up first and laid a pole across from the crown of the palm to the lowest branch of the tree making a bridge to cross. Then the others climbed up, too, but to their surprise, once they were up in the crown of this tree, it was clear that most of the nests were too far out on the branches and impossible to reach. Only some of the Huaorani who climbed up got a bird to raise. The others got none.

The Huaorani all climbed down, and one of the last to descend became angry that he wasn't able to get a bird. Out of spite and jealousy, as soon as he crossed the bridge, he kicked the pole off the branch, making it fall to the forest floor below. Now it was impossible for the last Huaorani up in the tree to climb down, and there he was, stuck high in the crown of this giant *degihue* tree.

When everyone climbed back down, the brother-in-law of the man stuck up in the tree said to the others, "In vain you have done this to my brother-in-law. You all go back to the village now. I'm going to stay here for a little while to feed this little bird I got. I'll be there soon." The other Huaorani all left for the village.

Then the man who stayed behind, who was a powerful *Iroinga*[6] by the name of Inuito, climbed up the palm to try to make a new bridge. When Inuito was up in the crown of the palm, he came up with a much better idea. He told his brother-in-law, "No need to worry or be afraid. A flash of light will fill the sky, but there is no need to be afraid. A large serpent will appear. Its head will be firmly rooted in the clouds and its tail will touch the earth. Its skin will be multicolored like the rainbow. I'm telling you, though, there's no need to be afraid. Now listen carefully. You hug this boa tight and come sliding down to the ground."

"Okay, okay," the man in the tree said, nodding his head quickly.

Inuito slid down the palm trunk back to the forest floor. After a moment, he raised his hands and looked up to the sky. There he stood, in silence, looking deeply into the sky and then . . . he winked. And when he winked, a tremendous flash of light illuminated the forest and the heavens for an instant. The light that flashed was brilliant beyond description, and it was accompanied by no thunder whatsoever, only silence, only a silent flash of light. Then, as soon as the flash of light was gone, there it was, a giant rainbow serpent, its head firmly rooted in the clouds, its tail hanging all the way to the ground. Its smooth shining skin was glistening with beautiful colors like the rainbow, and there it was. There it was, uniting the sky and the ground, like an umbilical cord between heaven and earth. There it was.

"How am I going to get down?" cried the anguished man in the tree.

"No need to be afraid!" Inuito yelled up to him. "Just grab on tight and slide down quickly. It won't fall. Its head is firmly rooted in the clouds. I'm telling you, there's no need to be afraid."

So the man slowly reached out and touched the boa. Its skin was smooth. He reached out and hugged it tight, without fear, and then down he slid, so fast that all his hair blew off!

As soon as he got to the ground, Inuito handed him a palm wood machete and told him, "Quick, quick, cut off the tip of the tail, but do it quickly."

So he quickly cut off the tip of the boa's tail, and, in the blink of an eye, it disappeared, slithering back up into the clouds.

There on the ground was a small pool of blood, and they both stood there looking at it for a while. Inuito then looked at his brother-in-law, and his brother looked up at him.

"Shhhh!" Inuito said with his finger to his mouth. "Nothing is to be said of this. You do not know my name. Within the duration of two full moons, return to this spot. A plant will be growing here where this blood spilled on the earth. This plant is *miiyabu*. Take a branch and plant it somewhere else. Once this plant grows up into the trees, then you can tell the people what happened to you today. You can tell them what you have seen and of your experience, and then you can tell them my name."

His brother-in-law listened attentively and, in almost unbelievable awe, he nodded in agreement. Then they went back to the village.

Two full moons had passed, and Inuito's brother-in-law went into the forest to the place where the blood of the rainbow boa had spilled onto the earth. To his amazement, there it was. The *miiyabu* was growing right from the spot where the blood had spilled. As instructed, he broke off a branch and brought it to another place where he planted it at the base of an *aunghue* tree.[7]

Soon the branch took root and began to sprout leaves.[8] After a few days, the man returned. The plant was growing well, with several clusters of fresh lime-green leaf growth, and there, to his amazement, was a small jaguar the size of a mouse. He saw the mouse-jaguar, but it ran quickly into the forest. Bewildered by this tiny jaguar he had never seen before, he left.

When he returned after a few days, the vine had grown significantly. To his amazement, there at its base were two small jaguars, male and female, but this time the size of a house cat, one on each side of the vine. They, too, darted, almost instantly, into the woods. He ran after them to get a better look, for he had never seen jaguars that small, but they were much too fast and hardly left even a track. So he left to return a few days later.

The vine was growing well, wrapping its way around the tree and full of fresh leaves, buds and shoots. There, to his bewilderment, at the base of the vine, were two jaguars, larger than the last two, now the size of a dog, and they had a small cub with them as well. There they were, nonchalantly resting at the base of the vine. When he approached, they looked at him. He stopped. The jaguars walked away slowly at first, then they ran, stopping some twenty yards from the vine to look back at the man. They growled a bit and then slowly walked off into the forest. The man left in complete bewilderment.

"Where are these jaguars coming from?" he thought to himself. "Is the *miiyabu* attracting the jaguars, or are they coming out of the plant itself?"

A few days later, he returned again. The vine was now wrapping itself around the first branches of the tree and it was covered in fresh new growth. There at the base of the vine was a female jaguar, this one the size of a deer, and at its side it had two beautiful cubs. Just as the man approached, the female jaguar noticed him and growled. She walked back a few yards, held her cubs near and again growled, this time clearly showing her teeth to the intruder. The man stood frozen for just a moment, then slowly began to tiptoe backwards, looking eye to eye into the jaguar's face. Then he turned around and ran off into the forest as fast as he could. Now the man was more bewildered than before and even slightly frightened. He wondered what he was to do now.

Again the man returned after a few days, approaching the place slowly. There by the vine were two large fully-grown jaguars, male and female. The vine, too, was even bigger now and thicker at its base. He did not dare get too close. He only watched from a distance for a while and then he left.

Again he returned a few days later, approaching the place cautiously and without snapping even a single twig, as if he were stalking game. He peeked into the clearing where the vine was growing, and, unbelievably enough, there were many, many jaguars. The vine now was well up into the canopy of the tree, full of fresh green leaf growth and loaded with bright flowers. There, up in the tree, rolling around as if inebriated, were two tremendous fully-gown jaguars, male and female. Other jaguars were playing, running from branch to branch. Just the sight of all this almost made the man dizzy. At the base of the vine were other large jaguars, and still others of smaller and different sizes. Some had cubs, which were nonchalantly rolling around playing with each other. All the jaguars were rejoicing with the leaves of the first *miiyabu*.

There, where the vine grew, was a large colony of jaguars, and the man wondered, "How am I ever going to look at this plant up close?"

Then he thought, "I'll catch some game and leave it nearby. When the jaguars smell the meat, they'll go to eat. Then I'll run up and grab some leaves."

So he proceeded to hunt a *bogee*,[9] a *koogeenkoo*,[10] an *enkara*,[11] and an *ihua*,[12] all with his *omena*[13] and his finely made palm wood darts dipped in curare.[14] He left the game nearby. As soon as the jaguars caught wind of it and all went to rejoice in the feast, he swiftly ran up to the vine, grabbed a branch full of leaves, and ran off.

When he was clearly out of reach of the jaguars, he stopped to observe the leaves of this peculiar vine. He thought, "What is it about this plant? Did the jaguars come out of the plant, or are they just attracted to it?"

He rubbed the leaves together with the palms of his hands and then slowly yet deeply inhaled the smell of the *miiyabu*. The fragrance entered his nose, then his head, throat, chest, and then his body, arms and legs. Soon his whole body was the fragrance of the *miiyabu*. He looked up into the forest. He felt nothing, but was very alert as to what the effects might be. He began walking through the forest slowly, but noticed nothing in particular, so he thought he'd see if he could catch some game for his family. Suddenly, a large troop of monkeys appeared. They came right to him, as if they didn't even see him. He caught several with his *omena*. A little farther into the forest, a group of game birds flew right by where he was and began squawking loudly, as if they didn't even see him. He shot several with his omena, and was now loaded with meat. He returned to his house to smoke the meat: he had more meat than he ever had hunted before.

"This plant is an attractor plant," he thought. "Indeed, this is what must be going on. That's why all the jaguars were attracted to the plant."

Then he thought, "If this really is an attractor plant, then why wouldn't it attract the opposite gender as well?"

It just so happened that there was a festival coming up soon, so he thought he would try it then to see if this really was an attractor plant. At the festival, he lay there in his hammock. He had the *miiyabu* leaves wrapped in a little bundle. He opened the bundle and mashed the leaves a bit. Soon the smell filled the entire house. Suddenly, one young lady caught wind of the smell. She looked over at him laying there in the hammock, arms behind his head. She ran over to him, as if possessed, jumped onto him and started fondling his sexual parts. Meanwhile, other women had gotten a whiff of the miiyabu and, within no time at all, had run over to the hammock. The women were piling onto him, grabbing at his sexual parts and trying to have sex with him. They were fighting amongst themselves, all trying to get at him. He lay there beneath them all, haphazardly thrashing around and screaming in agony. Even an old woman, so old she had to crawl over on all fours, came crying, "I want some, too! I want some, too!"

The man managed to grab the bundle and closed it up. He tried to push off the ladies but couldn't, and was in complete agony. Soon, though, the smell of the *miiyabu* dissipated, and, as suddenly as they had jumped onto him, they jumped off. When they realized what had happened, they scolded him in embarrassment as he ran off into the forest back to his house.

TRANSCRIBER'S NOTE: Mengatue, who recounted this myth, went on to say, "This is how the first *miiyabu* came to be. This story teaches us about the powers of this plant. *Miiyabu* is an attractor plant and its spirit is very strong. Many people are not strong or wise enough to use it in benefit of the people, and carelessly they ruin their lives and the lives of many others. This is why whenever you touch this plant you must be aware of what you are thinking, because whatever you are thinking is what you will attract to your life when you touch this plant. This is why the Huaorani seldom use this plant. When you touch this plant, the spirits come to your side as if they were your children. If you get angry at someone, they go and kill that person. It is very dangerous. This is why it is very dangerous to touch this plant. If you are touching this plant, you must never get angry no matter what the reason may be. This way no one will be harmed and your life will not be ruined. This is how it has always been."

NOTES

1. *Banisteriopsis sp.* — Malpighiaceae
2. *Tabebuia sp.* — Bignoneaceae
3. Olive Oropendula: *Gymnostinops yuracares*. The olive colored menka has always been a favorite Huaorani house pet, and there was much excitement amongst the mythic group on account of this rare find.
4. "Huaorani" in the Huaorani people's language (Huaorani Terero) means "people." This word is used to refer to a person or a group of people who are bloodline relatives of the Huaorani tribe.
5. *Iriartea deltoidea* — Arecaceae
6. The Huaorani elders say that an *Iroinga* is someone who embodies all experiences. It is someone who has sovereignty over nature, a communion with the realms of the spirit, and, consequently, is able to divine and heal with fluent ease. Traditionally, the *Iroinani* (plural) served as communication mediums transmitting messages to other *Iroinani* in other villages, thus passing on news about all aspects of village life and occurrences to distant relatives. The *Iroinani* also have been notorious in instigating spearing raids since they were able to detect the presence of invading colonists on the other side of their territory.
7. *Inga sp.* — Fabaceae. Species of the genera *Inga* are commonly-cultivated fruit trees among Amazonian forest peoples.

8. Mengatue, in another account, informed us that the first *miiyabu* was different from the way it is today. Then it had small leaves that were very fragrant. Today, it is the same plant with the same powers but its leaves are bigger and not as fragrant.

9. capuchin monkey — *Cebus sp.*

10. saki monkey — *Pithecia sp.*

11. two toed sloth — *choloepus didactylus*

12. howler monkey — *Alouatta fusca*

13. An *omena* is the Huaorani blowpipe used with poison-tipped darts for hunting.

14. Curare is the famous South American dart poison. The Huaorani call it *oomae.*

YAJÉ: MYTH AND RITUAL

Gerardo Reichel-Dolmatoff

The following text is a translation of a Desana myth:

"It was a woman. Her name was *gahpí mahsó*/*Yajé*-woman. It happened in the beginning of time. In the beginning of time, when the Anaconda-Canoe was ascending the rivers to settle mankind all over the land, there appeared the *Yajé* Woman. the canoe had arrived at a place called dia vii, the House of the Waters, and the men were sitting in the first maloca when the *Yajé* Woman arrived. She stood in front of the maloca, and there she gave birth to her child; yes, that was where she gave birth.

"The *Yajé* Woman took a *tooka* plant and cleaned herself and the child. This is a plant the leaves of which are red as blood on the underside, and she took these leaves and with them she cleaned the child. The leaves were shiny red, brilliant red, and so was the umbilical cord. It was red and yellow and white, shining brightly. It was a long umbilical cord, a large piece of it. She is the mother of the *Yajé* vine.

"Inside the maloca the men were sitting, the ancestors of mankind, the ancestors of all Tukano groups. The Desana were there, and the Tukano proper, the Pira-Tapuya, and the Uanano; they were all there. They had come to receive the *Yajé* vine. To each one the *Yajé* vine was to be given, and they had gathered to receive it.

"Then the woman walked toward the maloca where the men were sitting and entered through the door, with the child in her arms. When the men saw the woman with her child they became benumbed and bewildered. It was as if they were drowning as they watched the woman and her child.

"She walked to the center of the maloca and, standing there, she asked: 'Who is the father of this child?'

"The men were sitting, and they felt nauseated and benumbed; they could not think anymore. The monkeys too, yes, the monkeys were sitting and were chewing herbs; they were *bayapia* leaves. The monkeys could not stand the sight either. They began to eat their tails. The tapirs, too, were eating their tails which, at that time, were quite long. The squirrels, too were eating their tails and were chewing herbs. The squirrel made a little noise — *kiu-kiu-kiu* — as it was chewing. 'I am in a bad way,' the squirrel said; 'I am eating my tail.' 'What is going on?' the monkeys said and touched their tails, but the tails were gone. 'We are in a bad way,' the monkeys said; 'Poor me!' said one of the monkeys; 'I shall go mad eating my tail! Poor me!'

"The *Yajé* Woman stood in the center of the maloca and asked: 'Who is the father of this child?'

"There was a man sitting in a corner and saliva was dripping from his mouth. He rose and, seizing the child's right leg, he said: 'I am his father!' 'No!' said another man; 'I am his father!' 'No!' said the others; 'We are the child's fathers!' And then all the men turned upon the child and tore it to pieces. They tore off the umbilical cord and the fingers, the arms, and the legs. They tore the child to bits. Each one took a part, the part that corresponds to him, to his people. And ever since each group of men has had its own kind of *Yajé*."

At this point the tale was interrupted and the question was asked how the woman had become pregnant.

"It was the old man, the Sun Father; he was the phallus. She looked at him and from his appearance, from the way he looked, the seed was made because he was the *Yajé* person. The Sun Father was the Master of *Yajé*, the master of the sex act. In the House of the Waters she was impregnated through the eye. By looking at the Sun Father she became pregnant. Everything happened through the eye.

"The *Yajé* Woman had come with the men. While the men were preparing cashirí the woman left the maloca and gave birth to the *Yajé* vine in the form of a child. It was night. The men were trying to find a way to get drunk. The *Yajé* Child was born while the men were trying to find a way to become intoxicated. They were just beginning to sing; their song rejected the child. They rejected it with a stick rattle of *sëmé* wood. The animals that were eating their tails were cohabiting because they had become intoxicated. The *Yajé* should have produced only pleasant visions, but some became nauseated and so they rejected it.

"The woman had walked to the center of the maloca. There was a box of feather headdresses; and there was a hearth. When she walked in, only one of the men had kept a clear head and had not become dizzy. The men were drinking when she had her child, and at once they became dizzy. first they became dizzy; then came the red light and they saw red colors, the blood of the childbirth. Then she entered with her child, and when she stepped through the door they all lost their senses. Only one of them resisted and took hold of the first branch of *Yajé*. It was then that our ancestor acted like a thief; he took off one of his copper earrings and broke it in half, and with the sharp edge he cut the umbilical cord. He cut off a large piece. This is why *Yajé* comes in the shape of a vine. They all tore off bits and pieces of the child. The other men had already taken their parts of the child's body when at last our ancestor, *boréka*, took the part corresponding to him. Our ancestor did not know how to take advantage of *Yajé*; he became too much intoxicated."

◆ ◆ ◆

Now the problem remained of why the Sun Father should have created *Yajé*, and of his intentions when he gave this drug to mankind. Here follow the words of a Desana payé, in answer to this inquiry:

"It was the yellow light. People were like animals; they did not know how to use the yellow light. The Sun Father had to teach them how to use it. He acted in the form of an oropendola bird when he created *Yajé*. He took the great heat of the Universe and put it into the *Yajé* Woman. the oropendola bird traveled upriver and during four days he created *Yajé*. The Sun Father was traveling in his canoe, alone, at the beginning of time, ascending the river. Sometimes he stopped and took his stick rattle and pointed it here and there, trying to find the exact spot where the power of *Yajé* might be located. Mankind needed a means of communication; it was for this reason that the Sun Father was searching for *Yajé*. He thrust his stick in the ground, in the riverbank, wherever he stopped at a rapid. But the stick did not stand erect; it stood inclined. So he went on and tried again. But once more it stood inclined. he went on and on, and at last it stood straight, it stood upright; this was the spot. This happened at the Ipanoré Falls, and at the Rock of Nyí. It happened there where the Sun Father, in his form of an oropendola bird, was trying to find the spot for *Yajé*. When he had found the spot, the Sun Father returned to the House of the Waters. He returned out of shame, because of the purity of the color, the yellow color of the sun, the power of the sun. The color was ashamed. Now he sat for three days thinking and thinking of how to use the color in the right way, without doing harm. First he thought that the color of the heat of the Universe was similar to the color of the caimo fruit; but this was not true. No, it was a different color. He thought and thought until he found the right color which the people should use when they chose their women. He gave the color to the people; he gave them the yellow light. He gave them *Yajé*. And by giving them *Yajé*, he gave them their life; he gave them the rules by which they should live. Once they had *Yajé*, they had found their fields, their conversations. Now they had *Yajé*, and so many other things besides with which to reciprocate: conversations, songs, food, and also evil things. Now they had found their place, even if it was in the midst of troubles and errors. Sitting there, in the House of the Waters, they had found their way of life."

(EXCERPT FROM: Gerardo Reichel-Dolmatoff. *The Shaman and the Jaguar: A Study of Narcotic Drugs among the Indians of Colombia*. Philadelphia: Temple UP, 1975, pp. 134–136.)

THE CREATION MYTH

Gerardo Reichel-Dolmatoff

In the beginning there were the Sun and the Moon. They were twin brothers.[1] At first they lived alone, but then the Sun had a daughter, and he lived with her as if she were his wife. The Moon brother did not have a wife and became jealous. He tried to make love to the wife of the Sun, but the Sun heard about it. There was a dance up in the sky, in the house of the Sun, and when the Moon brother came to dance, the Sun took from him, as a punishment, the large feather crown he wore that was like the crown of the sun. He left the Moon brother with a small feather crown and with a pair of copper earrings.[2] From that time on the Sun and the Moon have been separate, and they are always far apart in the sky as a result of the punishment that the Moon brother received for his wrong-doing.

The Sun created the Universe and for this reason he is called Sun Father *(pagë abé)*. He is the father of all the Desana. The Sun created the Universe with the power of his yellow light and gave it life and stability.[3] From his dwelling place, bathed in yellow reflections, the Sun made the earth, with its forests and rivers, with its animals and plants. The Sun planned his creation very well, and it was perfect.

The world we live in has the shape of a large disk, an immense round plate. It is the world of men and animals, the world of life. While the dwelling place of the Sun has a yellow color, the color of the power of the Sun, the dwelling place of men and animals is of a red color, the color of fecundity and of the blood of living beings. Our earth is maria turí *(mari/our, turí/level)*, and is called "the upper level" *(vehkámaha turí)* because below is another world, the "lower level"/*dohkámaha turí*. This world below is called *Ahpikondiá*, Paradise. Its color is green, and the souls of those who were good Desana throughout their lifetime go there. On the side where the sun rises, in *Ahpikondiá*, there is a large lake, and the rivers of the earth pour into it because all flow toward the east.[4] Thus, *Ahpikondiá* is connected to our earth by the water of the rivers. On the side where the sun sets, in *Ahpikondiá*, lies the Dark Region. This is the region of night and is an evil place.

Seen from below, from *Ahpikondiá*, our earth looks like a large cobweb. It is transparent, and the Sun shines through it. The threads of this web are like the rules that men should live by, and they are guided by these threads, seeking to live well, and the Sun sees them.

Above our earth, the Sun created the Milky Way. The Milky Way emerges as a large, foaming current from *Ahpikondiá* and runs from east to west. Strong winds rush through the Milky Way, and it is blue in color. It is the intermediate region between the yellow power of the Sun and the red color of the earth. For this reason, it is a dangerous region because it is there people establish contact with the invisible world and with the spirits.

The Sun created the animals and the plants. To each one he assigned the place he should live. He made all of the animals at once, except the fish and the snakes; these he made afterward. Also, together with the animals, the Sun made the spirits and demons of the forest and the waters.

The Sun created all of this when he had the yellow intention — when he caused the power of his yellow light to penetrate, in order to form the world from it.

II

The Sun had created the earth with its animals and plants, but there were still no people. Now he decided to people the earth, and for this he made a man of each tribe of the Vaupés; he made a Desana and a Pira-Tapuya, a Uanano, a Tuyuka, and others, one from each tribe.[5] Then, to send the people to the earth, the Sun made use of a being called *Pamurí-mahsë*. He was a man, a creator of people, whom the Sun sent to people the earth. *Pamurí-mahsë* was in *Ahpikondiá*, and he set forth from there in a large canoe. It was a live canoe, in reality a large snake that swam on the bottom of the river. This Snake-Canoe was called *pamurí-gahsíru*, and its skin was painted yellow and had stripes with black diamonds. On the inside, which was red, sat the people: a Desana, a Pira-Tapuya, a Uanano, one from each tribe. Together with the Snake-Canoe came the fish; but they were not in the inside but outside, in the gills; the crabs also came, attached to the rear.[6] It was a very long journey, and the Snake-Canoe was going up the river because *Pamurí- mahsë* was going to establish mankind at the head-waters. Whenever they arrived at a large rapids, the Snake-Canoe made the waters rise in order to pass by and caused the torrent to be calm. Thus they went on for a long time, and the people became very tired.

At that time night did not yet exist, and so they traveled in the light, always under the yellow light of the Sun. When the first men set forth, the Sun had given each one something, some object, for him to carry carefully. To one of them he had given a small, black purse, closed tightly, and now, with the journey being so long, the man looked inside the purse. He did not know what was inside. He opened it, and suddenly a multitude of black ants came out of the purse, so many that they covered the light, making everything dark. This was the First Night. *Pamurí-mahsë* gave to each man a firefly in order to light his way, but the light was very weak. The ants multiplied, and the men tried to invoke them to return to the purse, but at that time they did not know about invocations. Then the Sun Father himself descended and with a stick beat the purse and made the ants enter it again. But those which did not obey remained in the forest and made their anthills. From that time on there have been ants. Once the ants were inside the purse, the light returned; but since then night has come into existence. This was the First Night, *nyamí mengá*, the Night of the Ant, and the man who had opened the purse was called *nyamíri mahsë*, Man of Night.[7]

So they continued on in the Snake-Canoe, but when they arrived at *Ipanoré*, on the Vaupés River, they struck against a large rock near the bank. The people went ashore because they were tired of the long journey and thought that they had already reached their destination. They left by way of an opening at the prow of the canoe. *Pamurí-mahsë* did not want them to disembark there because he was thinking of taking them to the headwaters of the rivers, and therefore he stopped up the opening with his foot. But the people had already got out, having rushed from the Snake-Canoe; they were dispersing throughout the rivers and the forests. But before they got away, *Pamurí-mahsë* gave each one of them the objects they had brought from *Ahpikondiá* and that, from then on, were going to indicate the future activities of each tribe. He gave a bow and arrow to the Desana; to the Tukano, the Pira-Tapuya, Vaiyára, and the Neéroa he gave a fishing rod; to the Kuripáko he gave the manioc grater; he gave a blowgun and a basket to the Makú and a mask of barkcloth to the Cubeo. He gave a loincloth to each one, but to the Desana he gave only a piece of string. He pointed out the places where each tribe should live, but when he was about to indicate the future home of the Desana, this one had fled to seek refuge at the headwaters. The Uanano had also gone and went up to the clouds in the sky. Then *Pamurí- mahsë* entered the Snake-Canoe again and returned to *Ahpikondiá*.

(. . .)

XIII

The same Sun Father was a payé, and *Pamurí-mahsë* was also a payé. The Sun established the functions of the payé, the invocations he should use, and the uses that tobacco was to have and also the hallucinogenic plants. The Sun already had his bench, his shield, and his stick-rattle. He had his gourd rattle, and over his left shoulder he carried his hoe. The Sun had everything that the payés have now, and he established the custom of using them. The Sun showed how the dances should be done and how people ought to talk when they got together for feasts.

The Sun had *vihó* powder in his naval, but a daughter of *Vaí-mahsé* owned the Yajé plant. She was pregnant and with the pain of childbirth she went to the beach and, lying down, twisted in pain. An old Desana woman wanted to help her and took hold of her hand, but the daughter of *Vaí-mahsïe* twisted so hard that she broke her finger, and the old woman kept it. She kept the finger in her maloca, but a young man stole it and planted it. The Yajé plant originated from this finger. The same thing happened with another daughter of *Vaí-mahsë*. When she had the pains of childbirth, she was lying twisting on the beach, and an old woman came to help her. She seized hold of her hand and broke off one of the girl's fingers and buried it. The coca plant[8] originated from this finger.

Curare poison was invented by the Sun Father himself. The Daughter of the Sun was in love with a man, and the Sun became jealous and wanted to kill him. Then he invented the poison and shot the man with a dart from his blowgun.

Thus it was that the earth was created. It was the Sun, the Daughter of the Sun, and the Daughter of Aracú who created things and taught people how to live well. There were *Emëkóri-mahsá* and *Diroá-mahsá;* they were the Beings of Day and of Night who are now in charge of the world. But the Sun is above all these, with his yellow power; the yellow power of the Sun Father who takes care of his creation and covers it with his yellow light.

(EXCERPT FROM: Gerardo Reichel-Dolmatoff. *Amazonian Cosmos: The Sexual and Religious Symbolism of the Tukano Indians*. Chicago: University of Chicago Press, 1971. pp. 24–27, 36–37.)

NOTES

1. The informant is not completely sure if they were twins or if the Sun was the older brother and the Moon the younger. Perhaps we are dealing here with one single androgynous being.
2. It is curious to observe that there should exist a tradition concerning the introduction of metallurgy. The ornaments of small triangles of hammered silver ("butterflies") are rather characteristic of the Arawakan tribes of the Isana River.
3. The words "stability," "to stabilize," and "to establish" occur frequently in the vocabulary of the informant who uses them to express a state of biotic equilibrium.
4. The Papurí and Tiquié rivers, which form the principal habitat of the Desana, run from west to east.
5. No myth refers directly to the creation of human beings. It seems that this theme is repressed because of its sexual and social connotations.
6. Probably this refers to certain small crabs that live as parasites in the anal region of large aquatic snakes.
7. Concerning some aspects of the myth of the Origin of Night see Lévi-Strauss, 1966, p. 358.
8. The informant mentions that the hallucinogenic drugs were stolen in the form of a finger or a phallus by the eagles who carried them to the Milky Way, but he does not remember further details of this myth.

UNÁMARAI, FATHER OF YAJÉ

Hugo Niño

Introduction

What follows is the legend of the first hero, wise man, and organizer of the clans of the Witoto nation, whose name is Unámarai, father of *Yajé*. He was the first person to receive revelation and to experience the delirium of the beyond.

The legend speaks of how Unámarai, the great chief, chose his successors for leading the tribes, how he established the ranks of his followers and his descendants according to his wisdom so that successive generations might know why the tribes developed different dialects in spite of belonging to the same nation. By dialects, I mean the small languages that have something in common with each other. The legend also tells how, from the very beginning, it was established that the clans would not intermingle in marriage. This differs from other nations, perhaps, because, in speaking different dialects, husband and wife would not be able to understand each other.

The truth is that many nations of indigenous groups are divided into family-like clans of those who claim to possess the same origin, the same totem held as a common direct ancestor or only as a symbol in the case of the Witoto totems. Each clan forms its tribe that lives in its own village. The legend teaches about marriage within the same clan as well as laws concerning living in the same village or moving several times (which explains why the name of the dwelling describes not the people who live there but the fact that, when they move, they continue to use the same name that the place had before). That said, here, then, is the legend just as the wise men of the *jeíyai* clan know it, those who dwell in Monochoa and who belong to the Witoto nation.

Unámarai, Father of Yajé

When Jitoma illuminated the world, his light divided beings into people (those who were shaped) and animals (those who, because of the light's arrival, were unable to be transformed). This caused great envy among animals toward people because they couldn't talk like them. They just screeched, howled and whistled. What happened then was that after the ordering and naming of the tribes, Jóriai, the evil spirit of the tiger, the deer, the tapir, and the *caballuno* bear, moved by this anger, devoted himself to pursuing the chiefs, harassing and doing them harm, trying to get revenge on them for not having had the animal-bodies where he dwelled transformed. The humans got sick, died suddenly and no one knew why. Everyone was alarmed and asked, "Why is this happening? Who will find a solution to this mystery that is annihilating us?"

It just so happened that one of the men of the Witoto nation had devoted himself to the study of all the plants of nature in order to obtain medicines from them, and he came to possess a great wisdom. One day, investigating the secrets of the vines, he found one named *Yajé*, the verifier, the revealer of knowledge. He took the vine by its tip, which is nothing less than the forefinger of Unámara. He took in the sap, the forefinger of the *Yajé* spirit, and he had a revelatory vision: the cause of so many evils was Jóriai, the spirit of the tiger, who was angry with humans.

For having discovered so many secrets, so much wisdom, he was called from then on Unámarai, the father, the guardian of *Yajé*.

Unámarai placed his wisdom at the service of the Witotos. He devoted himself to protecting them and was their first great chief.

Knower of the revelation's secret, Unámarai went to look for the tiger, and no longer felt any fear because, having discovered it, just because he knew it, thanks to the magic power of the revealed word, it had lost its spirit. It simply meant going after it, and that is what he did.

He found the tiger and killed it with an arrow. He carried it back to his people and told them, "Here it is. I've killed it. You can eat its meat without fear because its spirit is already dead and no longer exists."

They cooked the tiger and went back to offer him meat, but he gave them a new teaching.

"You should know that we wise men and wizards cannot eat the meat of the tiger, our enemy, because Jóriai pursues us wizards and wise men above all with a special anger. We should not eat it so that the force of its demon does not take control over us. That is why we cannot. That is why we only eat the meat of the good animals, so that we do not cloud our virtue, our wisdom."

"And doesn't he pursue us?" they asked him.

"You, those who follow my orders, have your spirits less threatened. Like the old tree that dries out from its bark inward, so, too, do your bodies dry out. Like the tree that dies because of its sick limb, so, too, do you die."

They continued asking questions: "Tell us, Oh, Unámarai. Are we allowed to face the tiger and kill it in our jungles?"

"Yes, you can. If you find it while you are hunting, you can kill it. If it attacks your dwelling, you can kill it. But you should throw away the bow you have used to kill it so that its spirit does not reach you through the arrow's trajectory, so that it does not cause you sickness, so that it does not strip the bark from the tree of life. And you should rub your hands with leaves to protect yourselves well. Learn this lesson."

"We have learned," they answered, in awe of his venerable wisdom.

The Witotos advanced in many ways during the long reign of Unámarai, the wise man, the first great chief. Through his teachings, they learned the secrets of nature, the arts of medicine, the defense against spells of enemy spirits, the technique of cultivating and the laws of governing. Unámarai, the great, ruled for a long time.

At the end, feeling that his body was drying out after having lived for so much time, that his body could no longer carry his spirit, he gathered his chosen ones, those he had taught primarily himself, to be the new leaders of the Witotos.

They gathered in the *raátírako*, the *maloka* designed for counsel, just them, the chosen ones, who were only men. On wooden benches placed in a circle, they sat beneath the direction of Unámarai. There the first great chief and the chosen ones were gathered to relive the teachings in the so-called *bambeadero*, the temple of wisdom, the place where coca leaves are chewed.

He distributed the coca leaves and invited the chosen ones to chew *(bambear)* them. Then he spoke:

"My body is coming to an end. My wisdom will no longer be with you. I have gathered you, those I have chosen myself on account of your merits, to whom I have transmitted my knowledge, to tell you that leading the Witoto tribes from now on will be your responsibility, in keeping with your counsel and the intelligence of your decisions."

"Will you abandon us, master? How can we be good chiefs without your protection?" they asked him with anguish in their voices.

"Only my body is abandoning you. You should not allow sadness to invade you. My spirit will be protecting the Witoto people always, taking care that there is never a lack of *Yajé* and coca," he reassured his disciples.

Then the great wise man began to ask questions of his chosen ones, the apprentices, so that they could answer and show what they knew in front of everyone.

"What is the secret of the life of our people?" he asked one of them.

"The life of the Witotos is long and, before, it was even longer. During the exploration of the world, our people lived almost two hundred years, until their flesh dried out, master."

"What happens after death?"

"The Witotos do not die, master. The spirit of the dead man is passed on to his son."

"And how does he receive the spirit if the father has not died?"

"As long as the two are alive, the son does not have a spirit. He is only protected by the father's, just as the woman is protected by the spirit of her father first and by her husband's later, since women have no spirit."

"Then, is the spirit of the man who dies without sons lost?"

"It is not lost, master. If a man dies without children, his spirit is passed on to the wise man of the tribe to enrich him."

Everyone paid close attention to the test. Their heads nodded with approval when the answers were given.

"In truth, you have responded successfully, showing that you have learned my teachings. You are worthy of being Nejmáirama. I designate you wise man of your tribe. That is your rank. You will be the one in charge of leading minds, knowing history and transmitting it to your youngest son, since you will be able to shape him the best. You will concentrate your experience on him. When your son is born, you will give him water of *nejmaira* to drink, the herb of wisdom, and he will inherit the responsibility of caring for it from you."

"Thank you, master. I will do this," answered the chosen one, happily as he received the backing of the others and a smile from Unámarai, who told him:

"Hold this recently-cut vine. Take in the essence of *Yajé*. It will reach you through Unámarai. His forefinger will come down through the vine and you will feel the contact from its tip, Unati, the son, so that you receive the most recent revelations."

The chosen one did what he was told and felt how his mind was being invaded by strange sensations, dizzying shapes, multiple colors and voices . . .

"When can a man get married?" asked Unámarai again, addressing another of his apprentices among his disciples.

"When he knows how to hunt the tapir and the *borugo,* when he knows how to fish for the *bagre,* how to extract rubber, how to farm."

"And women?"

"The woman that the man chooses should know how to cook, weave hammocks, help plant the crops. She should be good, faithful and obey her husband. If this is not the case, he can repudiate her or give her back to her parents."

"Where should Witoto men look for a wife? How is the union made?"

"Witoto men should look for wives within their tribe and should take only one. He can replace her if she dies or if he repudiates her if she has turned out bad. Everything will be done simply, with no celebrations, only with their consent and the approval of ranking leaders."

"Very good. How is the land worked?"

"This is how the land is worked at harvest time: everyone works on the farm of one person, then on someone else's and someone else's until the last person's farm is done so that there is harmony and greater efficiency."

"Who restores harmony when it is lost? When faults are committed, who imposes punishments?"

"The difficult task of maintaining harmony, of resolving problems, of deciding on punishments corresponds to the chief, oh, Unámarai."

"Your answers are well given. You are worthy of being chief. I designate you Iyakma, tribal chief, with the task of watching over those you govern until your death. Your eldest son should be your successor. But if he dies, the next son will succeed you, or if not, the son of your brother, in this manner. Remember this, as you have remembered my teachings."

"I will remember, master."

"Hold this and take in the spirit of *Yajé.*"

The chosen chief, *kuraka,* received *Yajé* and also experienced revelation, communion.

Again, Unámarai asked:

"What is our ritual, our ceremony for the dead?"

"When a Witoto dies, his body will be buried beneath the *maloka* where he lived. The *maloka* will be burned and abandoned, because sickness has penetrated it, the tragedy of death. In the same way, the farm of the dead person will be abandoned. No one should cultivate it or pick fruit from it even if it is abundant, but it should not be burned."

"Why?"

"Because this is what you have taught us. When a branch dies, it should be isolated, otherwise the whole tree dies. And you have said that the dead person is the branch and his brothers are the rest of the tree."

"Well answered. Tell me now: if the person who dies is the chief, what should be done?"

"Ah! If the person who dies is a chief, it is necessary to communicate the mourning to all the tribes, who will send people to be with him. His body dressed with *guayuco* will be rocked in a hammock inside the *maloka* so that everyone can cry for him. Then, right there, a grave of four meters will be dug and there his body will be deposited. And, next to the body of the dead chief, a gourd of *ambil,* tobacco juice, will be deposited to kill the sickness, to trap the malignant spirit that killed him forever and never let it escape. Planted upon his grave should be the tree from which he took his leaves in the beginning, during the assigning of names. Then the village will be burned and the tribe will seek its place elsewhere, because he was a dignitary."

"Who, then, should cure the bodies of the living and take care of the spirits of the dead?"

"When you are gone, that mission corresponds to the doctor, the wizard, as you have taught us."

"Let that be your mission. I designate you Jorérajma, the doctor, the wizard of your tribe, and upon your death, your eldest son will succeed you, and if not, the following one, or if not him, then your brother's or if not, your sister's, since, given the delicate nature of your rank and the knowledge it requires, it is necessary that your descendance be clearly marked. You will teach your successor beforehand and you will put him to the test, in the rite of knowledge, here in the *bambeadero.*"

"So be it, venerable master."

"Drink this."

Then the one chosen wizard, wise man, shaman of the tribe, knew the delirium as the others had, the revelation of the *Yajé* spirit.

Throughout the night, Unámarai was testing his disciples, the chosen ones, until he had designated the wise men, the wizards, the chiefs of all the tribes. When he had designated the last one, he stood up on his aged feet, which produced a reverent silence. Then he spoke for the last time:

"My disciples, my chosen ones: we have relived the teachings, the laws of our people. The designation of those who will succeed me is done. Each tribe has its leaders, its dignitaries, whatever it needed. You can go now and disperse the tribes, live where you will and develop your dialects, your particular language, in keeping with the ways that speaking has differentiated itself from the times of the great forays to the corners of the earth.

You will maintain the teachings so that the Witoto nation is great and respected. Now my spirit is leaving this exhausted body, but it will take care of you."

Very gently, amidst the affliction of his chosen ones, the new chiefs, he sat down on the bench and through his thin lips he took in *Yajé* for the last time.

Unámarai, father-guardian of *Yajé,* who, from the moment of his passing is also called Moórama, the great grandfather, the protector, breathed no more.

TRANSLATED FROM the Spanish by Steven F. White

(EXCERPT FROM: Hugo Niño. *Primitivos relatos contados otra vez: héroes y mitos amazónicos.* Bogotá: Editorial Andes/Instituto Colombiano de Cultura, 1977, pp. 111–122.)

INITIATION EXPERIENCE[1]

Jean-Pierre Chaumeil
(as told by Alberto Prohaño)

At that time, my father was a great healer. They often called him *sándatia* (he who knows), since he saved many "souls" during his life. Everyone held him in high esteem and respect, and his name was known beyond the Atacuari and Amazon rivers.

He was already old when we moved to the Yacarité, to a place that was a day's trip upstream from its mouth. It is there that he passed on to me the transmissible part of his knowledge.

"Pwí (son), I want you to know," he announced to me one day. "I'm going to teach you *ndatara* (knowledge, science). With it, you will attend to and guide whoever needs your help, just like I have always done . . ."

He paused.

The truth is that I myself had decided to undertake the search for powers in spite of the dangers that I would have to face, knowing that no one else in the village was more predisposed than I to achieve this goal . . .

. . . I had already had a dream.

"First of all," he continued, "you should drink *piripiri* to initiate the cycle: it's the FIRST PLANT. Then you will drink others, progressively. Everything, as you will soon realize, is in the spirit of the plants: their essence, *hamwo*. It's the only road of knowledge."

The night of the new moon, I was ready to drink the decoction of *piripiri*. My deceased father had grated the bulbs and prepared the brew. Before passing me the *kuwise*, the small receptacle, he warned me about the sometimes terrifying visions that the spirit of the plant might bring, while he sang the song for "drinking the purge."

súñoha hatónu ramëra
súñoha hatónu embeyá

yeee yeee yeee yeeee
yeee yeee yeee yeeee

yáti huñahatándi súñoha

I sing to drink the essence of the plants
now I'm singing

yeee yeee yeee yeeee

Come! We are going to drink your essence

In one gulp I drank it all down. At first, the bitter liquid made me vomit. Afterwards, it made me see strange things at first, but I got used to them to the point of being able to control them.

Then my deceased father handed me a lit cigar and sang the "song for smoking":

ndianemátí nëmase súñohahamwo
huñanëma hatara
teetáu súndehi ariara
hate npënanu ramúco waréndia
súndehihamwo rátí waréndia

yeee yeee yeee yeeeeeeeeeee
yeee yeee yeee yeeeeeeeeeee
ndia sëndatiti súndehi waréndia
hatónëmu huñasëndatiti ware
ne huñahatiara riru
súndehiru súndehiru súndehiru
huñaramacu
ne huñatóci waréndia

yeee yeee yeee yeeeeeeeeeee

The mother of the essence of the plants arrives
we drink (together) the essence mixed with tobacco to get well
and also so that it remains (in the body)
the mother of the tobacco is going to come, too.

(calling) *yeee yeee yeee*

she is going to offer us tobacco since it is smoked while the essence is drunk without letting the ash fall, the ash of the tobacco . . . (several times)
let us swallow it without spitting it out or vomiting it *yeee yeee yeee yeeeeeeeeeee*

The first or second cup, the second, really, provokes the first sensations:
. . . a strange drunkenness takes possession of my body and modifies my behavior. There's vomiting and defecating and urinating . . . I feel like the extremities of my body shrink on me . . . fear conquers me, slowly envelops me . . . things are transformed before my eyes, colors change: blue-green, then black, then red . . . It's frightening. Someone stops me from moving. A voice comes closer to me (my father's): "What do you see?" I can't answer. The colors change but the background remains blue-green. The images are defined. At first, a great candle. It gets closer then disappears when I want to hold it, tchac! Then it turns into a legless person.

Then comes a burning coal. It changes into a worm when I get closer . . . an enormous worm several meters in length . . .

Finally, what emerges is an immense jergón snake. Its scales shine like thousands of lights. From far away, the murmur of a voice reaches me, at first barely audible, then stronger, like the noise of a huge crowd yeeeeeeEEEEEEEE!

This is what I saw the first time, at the beginning of everything . . .

The next day, when the images had ceased, my father asked me, "What did you see?"

I remember that I didn't answer him at all. He made me fast for a whole week: I only ate a plantain and one fish (boca chico) and chapu from a ripe banana. At the end of the fast I had become very weak.

On the second moon, *hánuhú wánditu*, my deceased father called me: *"Pwí,* this is the new drink (decoction of piripiri with tobacco juice). Finally, you're going to know tobacco, which is the "road of the souls," mbayátu rëpwiñu, the nourishment of the spirits. That's why you must never throw away the seeds. Instead, you should pick them up and keep them for planting when the time comes before the plants are used up. And for that reason, too, tobacco should penetrate your body. You should turn it into your ally, since it will lead you wherever you want. It will make you see."

That night, he passed me the kuwise several times. My body couldn't resist the first cup: I started vomiting and defecating. With the second cup, everything was in good order. The effects were immediate. At first they were fuzzy, but then the images became more precise. Once again I see the lit candle. Behind it, animals parade past, some with horns, others without heads, transforming themselves for an instant into human beings.

The colors are alive and changing: blue-green, red, white, black . . . I can hear screams coming from all directions: *AAA! AAA! AAA! AAA!* aaa! aaa! aaa! aaa! They partially drown out the continuous buzzing of a motor rrrrrrrr rrrrrrrrrrrr . . .

Two creatures (twins) appear there, pó. I hear them whispering. I'm scared . . .

"Don't be frightened. We won't do you any harm. On the contrary, we're here to teach you. We are the mother of tobacco."

Then they lift their songs, sharply and slowly . . . *iiiiiiiiiiiiiiiuuuuuuuuuuuuu.*

Little by little, the images are erased, but the songs remain . . . first, the song of tobacco:

súndehihamwo ranatutéhi
yééééé yééééé yééééé!!
yééééé yééééé yééééé!!
súndehihamwo súndehihamwo
. . . hanatutéhi
súndanuhu hanatutéhi
hamëriónëmaheta hinijó
anihamwo ramëra
amane awüéhatahatéhi
anihamwo awüéhata ríta hiwa
hamëriónëmaheta súndehihamwo ta
amane hañatutéhi huñanucëra súndehi
hamëriónëmaheta ta wucinanëmaheta

I'm going to call the mother of tobacco
(call) *yééééé yééééé* . . .
mother of tobacco (bis) . . .
I'm calling you! . . . .
we're going to smoke, I'm calling you
I dream for you (I sing so you'll come)
for my people (allies) I sing
that's why I want (you to come)
I'm asking you that my people come
I dream about you, mother of tobacco
that's why I'm calling on you to light my cigar
I dream about you, we smoke together

Then the song to light the magic cigars:

súndehi mbayátu rëpanëmahetánda ramëra hánijú
súndehi mbayátu rëpanu
súndehihamwo súndehihamwo súndehihamwo
hate mbayátu súndehi awasara
huñareriu watia awasara
hañambarié rëwatia awasara
súndehi rëpacara
oso! oso! oso! oso! oso!
oso! oso! oso! oso! oso!
osohamwo yánrëpa súndehi mbayátu
yanuca ríca
sëndatérió nëmaheta sëdanu súndehi mbayátu ra
wiúrdi powitia awasara
hañatuté nëmaheta mbayátu súndehi rimujú ndaria
hámbiayánëmaheta anejú
hañuca nëmaheta ndaria mbayátu súndehi
hacina nëmaheta mbayátu súndehi

I sing to light the soul-cigar (magic cigar)
I'm ready to light the soul-cigar
mother of tobacco . . . (three times)
this is what the soul-cigar is like
it never goes out
it never is consumed
once the cigar is lit
I call the magic matches, oso oso . . .
the mother of the magic matches is going to light the soul-cigar
light the tip for me!!
you're going to teach me how to smoke the soul-cigars
because they smell good (they're perfumed)
I call the soul-cigar so that it comes
I sing for it
I'm lighting the soul-cigar
I smoke the magic tobacco

As far as the mother of piripiri is concerned, she appeared to me much later. She appeared at the beginning of one of my dreams.

"What do you want?" she asked me.

"I want you to teach me."

She gave me a white pill:

"Here. Take this. You will take it four times (four pills) and you will dream four times. Then you will fast for a week, without leaving your hammock. Don't move at all . . . When I tell you to stop fasting, go into the jungle immediately. There, I will teach you better. I can appear anywhere at any time. But remember the place well."

On the designated day, I went alone to the jungle. I had just passed the last farm when tcha! a giant, threatening demon with horns appeared before me.

I always remember the words of my deceased father: "Don't be scared. Don't run. Instead, take out your cigar and blow the smoke over the earth, slowly, *fuuuuuuuuuuuuuu* . . . , then in the air, very slowly, *fuuuuuuuu-uuuuuuuuuuuuuu.*"

I quickly lit my cigar and blew. The demon calmed down. I saw the mother of piripiri for the first time. She asked me what I needed.

"I want you to teach me everything and give me magic clothing so I can defend myself. In exchange, here is some tobacco."

And I gave her a bundle of tobacco, just as my father had indicated. She accepted it with pleasure.

"In exchange, take this cigar and this pill. Swallow it. You'll have the gift of curing."

Then she blew into my mouth and deposited a virote (invisible dart) in my stomach so that I will be able to resist illnesses.

She taught me the song of piripiri:

híseñuhamwo ranatutéhi
yé yé yé yé yé yé yé yé
yé yé yé yé yé yé yé yé

towanëmahitane!
yanëmanuhita resáne
yanëmahitara haténdia
yándatiénda híseñuhamwo
réntëmahita hiwa amane
hañatutéhi hatiunujó
hatiunujó anihamwo yáti

híseñuhamwo huñanëmaheta npánu
yándatiénda anihamwo
amane hañatutéhi yándatéhitara
mother of piripiri, I'm going to call you
yé yé yé yé yé yé yé yé yé
here she comes! she's coming
she's here with me
I'm here! invite me! welcome me!
teach me! mother of piripiri
I'm asking you to do it, that's why I'm calling you to my side
my allied people will come to my side
mother of piripiri let's cure (together)
teach my people, my allies
that's why I'm calling you, so you teach me

I learned all these songs by memory.

Before drinking ramanujá, the "essence of *ayahuasca*," my deceased father transmitted to me his power that is contained in a viscous substance or phlegm, worapándi, that he brought up from the bottom of his stomach and compelled me to swallow:

"*Hihumjú ramucó hatiándatia,* she will remain in your stomach to make you know," he assured me. To keep me from vomiting, he blew tobacco smoke over my body.

fu fu uuuuuuuuuuuu
fu fu uuuuuuuuuuuu
fu fu uuuuuuuuuuuu
but I vomited twice
tcha! tcha!

of the seven phlegms, only five remained in my stomach:

"Those will remain forever," continued my father. "No one can take them from you, not even the great healers. They will come out through your mouth when you die, but not before. Without them, you won't have access to knowledge. I'm giving you part of my power, the transmissible part. The more you have, the greater your power. The mothers will make you swallow three phlegms, but these you can transmit to others, the way I have just done."

On the third moon, múwa wánditu, I again drank *ayahuasca* mixed with tobacco juice and piripiri. At each stage, a new plant is added, with the goal of knowing them all, little by little.

My deceased father and I sang the song to call the mother of *ayahuasca*:

ramanujúhamwo ranatutéhi
yeee yeee yeee yeeeeeeee
yeee yeee yeee yeeeeeeee
ramanujúhamwo rándia tuwatiaténdehi
ramanujúhamwo rándia tuwatié ndaria
yándatiénda npënanujú
hastëro rimínda
yátí yátí yátí yátí yátí
yátí yátí yátí yátí yátí

mother of *ayahuasca*, I'm going to call you
(call) *yeeee yeee yeeeeeeeee (bis)*
mother of *ayahuasca*, I don't know you (I want to know you)
I still don't know you
teach me how to heal

I want to extract virotes
come, come, come, come, . . .

The *ayahuasca* takes me, drags me along. Images appear. My father questions me. I answer that I don't see anything. He gives me another dose that I swallow. The colors dance, the lit candle appears . . . on a second plane, animals torn to pieces parade past... my bones come out of their joints; the creatures devour my flesh . . . But a sweet voice echoes in my head:

"Look! Study! Learn about this plant. Smoke, but do not spit. Swallow all the smoke. Don't let even a mouthful escape."

I suck on the cigar *pë pë pë pë* . . . a strange smell invades me, sweet and perfumed, followed by the image of a thick *ayahuasca* trunk. Whispering comes from below the vine, as if someone were speaking or, perhaps, singing:

eeeee eeeee eeeee
I'm the mother of *ayahuasca*
come closer and light this cigar

I take several puffs on the enormous cigar that they give me and I swallow all the smoke:
uuuuuuuuuuuuuuuuuuuuu.

A perfume penetrates my cold body. The images go up in smoke, little by little. I'm normal again. My bones are welded together. Then they appear again . . . I'm scared . . . they calm once more only to return again. Terrifying images parade before my eyes. My bones explode . . . there are toothless monsters that fly, jump, fall, hang in the air, bite and devour each other . . . I want to leave, but a voice intervenes:

"Drink a little bit more. You'll see everything."

I swallow my fourth or fifth dose, I can't remember. Someone blows in my face.

fu fu uuuuuuuuuuu

I open my eyes. It's a man. Then he says, "I am the mother of *ayahuasca*. Do you want to reach the world above, the second floor?"

We went up an immense ladder that pointed toward the sky and we crossed several layers of clouds. In a second, we were all the way up there. Here and there, I see vessels with manioc beer and masks.

"Here, change into this, tatia (vocative of father), before you get sick and the virotes penetrate your body."

I put on a kind of clothing . . . then we go down to the earth again. The return is just as fast as when we came. The mother of *ayahuasca* is transformed into a hammock and she has me sit on it. She makes me sing:

yeee yeee yeee yeeeeeeee
yeee yeee yeee yeeeeeeee
it's the song to call the magic bags.

The sun comes up and shines in the distance. The mother warns me, "Soon you will be awake. The day is beginning."

People approach me. Seductive women . . . I want to touch them, but the mother stops me:

"You're drunk. Come. Tomorrow night I'll be with you again," she tells me . . .

When I awoke, the blood was beating hard in my head (my head hurt).

(Alberto continues)

"The mother of *ayahuasca* lives in a rope. The leaves are her coat. He who knows, sees her with total clarity:

ne sándatia ne sándi siwa
no one sees without knowing

ne tíwatia pándra ne sándi siwa
he who does not know how to heal, can't see

She seemed strange to me the first time, but, once you get to know her, she's like a son. You can talk to her, blow on her, and she's with you. At first, you have to sing to her and blow tobacco toward the roots, below, hare, toward the leaves, up high, háwa, and in between, táhasuwumu.

When you heal someone, she keeps a vigil. The mothers of *ayahuasca* visit each other frequently, even beyond the middle of the sky. Each time you cure, they are present. The ones you know tell the others so that they can all come to help and take turns being with the sick person, day and night.

Other people, those who don't know, think that you heal on your own. But it's not like that. The people of the mothers of *ayahuasca* are also present, as if they were your own people, your own children. The mothers call you rahe, father. They come and go. But they can also do harm.

On the fourth moon, husánamo wánditu, my deceased father and I added mëyupa, toé, to the mixture. Toé is much more potent than the other plants. I have to keep a very strict fast before drinking it to limit the vomiting and, later, to help my body.

With toé, I traveled a great deal. I reached the people with no anus (subterranean world) and even half the sky (half the world), arici táhasuwumu.

The mother of toé taught me her song first:

mëyupahamwo ranatutéhi
mëyupahamwo mëyupahamwo
mëyupahamwo mëyupahamwo
ne handiahetara
yatí yatí yatí yatí yatí
yatí yatí yatí yatí yatí

mother of toé, I'm going to call you
(call)
I still don't know you
come, come, come, come . . .

Then she taught me:
"How, in what way do you want to learn? To begin, I'm going to give you a kind of bag, or clothing, so that you can defend yourself, so that the virotes can't reach you when you're in danger . . . You put it on like a garment and you'll be completely transformed instantly. So, even when you're asleep, you'll be awake and able to defend yourself. Put it on before you go to the jungle and you'll be safe. In exchange for your tobacco, I will give you some of my magic cigars whose smoke has the power of taming evil spirits. I'll teach you the way of blowing always toward the crown of the head . . . Also, I'll tell you the best way to drink toé — three times. After the third, you'll have to fast alone for a week. A person will appear, a man. You shouldn't be frightened of him. He'll ask you, 'What do you want?' You'll answer him by saying, 'nothing.' Don't tell him anything since several kinds of spirits can appear. So, little by little, you'll learn to know them and to recognize them . . . Each time you see one, give it tobacco. In exchange, it will give you magic cigars, little arrows and magic garments (invisible). Don't be scared. If they threaten you, blow on the crowns of their heads fu fu uuuu, three times. They'll fall over dead, but if you blow on their feet, they'll come back to life. At that moment, you'll give them tobacco. They can, at the same time, blow on you. You, too, will die, but not really — it will just look like you died, since you had already taken the precaution of putting on your magic clothing. Then they'll ask you, 'Are you going to take off your clothes?'

" 'No,' you'll answer.

"Then they'll give you a key that will enable you to take it off. The magic clothing will open like the wings of a bird. Take good care of the key. Each time you go to the jungle, carry it with you together with the clothing. You'll keep them inside your stomach. You should always pay attention, especially during the drinking sessions. Never say anything. Listen. Don't tell anyone that you know. Don't say a thing. Heal people when they're sick. Don't deny that you know how to heal. They'll pay you however much they want. Sometimes they won't give you anything. Don't ask for anything. Only kill the bad people, but keep the three souls in your body. These three souls are the ones that teach.

"The first one says, 'I'll be your companion forever, your eternal friend, your bodyguard. I'll visit every sick person who comes to see you and I'll take care of you during your drinking sessions.'

"The second one says, 'I'll take care of you in your home.'

"And the third, 'I'll take care of your clothes.'

"So a soul will aways be with you wherever you are. Another will watch over your family, and the third will take care of your magic garments."

A few days after the experience with toé, my deceased father told me, "Pwí, your grandfather is sick. Cure him." And he gave me two cigars.

"Papa (grandfather)," I asked him. "What ails you?"

"Here, my throat," he said.

I blew on him and then I sucked. I could only extract some phlegm, worapándi, from his throat, something sort of hard.

My deceased father, who helped me with my first healing, ordered me to throw it away as if it were an arrow. When I was getting ready to do it, the phlegm jumped from my hands and tchac! buried itself in the ground . . .

I went back to my grandfather and extracted another phlegm from the throat that was quite hard and that disappeared like the first one tchac! but he still wasn't transformed.

I continued with the healings until the day that the phlegm turned into a magical arrow that was ten fingers in length.

My deceased father said, "Now you can cure people. Go on!"

I became a pándra, healer, but I still hadn't seen the virotes turn into people. My ambition was to see the mother of the little magic arrow, in other words, the mother of the people of the wizard.

My allies visited me at night and deposited several virotes in my stomach.

Strong with my powers (since the more virotes you have, the more powerful you become), I began to carry out healings with increasing regularity. Each time they were harder, and more dangerous. I drank the most potent plants, *naranjillo (sóñu)* and *venado-caspi (hándruwit'jú)*. My deceased father also made me know gasoline, kerosene and camphor.

During a healing session, the mother of the virote appears after blowing tobacco smoke on her. This was how I learned what a shaman was and how I became a nëmara.

TRANSLATED FROM the French by Luis Eduardo Luna and Steven F. White

(EXCERPT FROM: Jean Pierre Chaumeil. *Voir, savoir, pouvoir. Le chamanisme chez les Yagua du Nord-Est péruvien.* Paris: Éditions de L'École des Hautes Études en Sciences Sociales, 1983, pp. 33–43.)

NOTE

1. This account, based on field work done in 1976 by French anthropologist Jean-Pierre Chaumeil, is by Yagua shaman Alberto Prohaño, current leader of the community Edén de la Frontera on the Marichín River. In this text, which is fragmentary out of necessity, Alberto goes over some of the most intense moments of his own initiation. At that time, he still had not reached the age of twenty (in 1976, he was thirty five). He was initiated by his father, Xenon, who received his shamanic knowledge from his father. In the following years, Alberto practiced with his maternal uncle José Murayari, who worked to perfect the knowledge of his future son-in-law by means of the periodic ingestion of new plant decoctions.

Alberto Prohaño, *Extracting Virotes.* Photograph © Bonnie Chaumeil

LIGHT OF THIS WORLD

Don Hilario Peña[1]

Yajé, according to the old *Yajé* drinkers from a long, long time ago, even if it was a stone, it was still a person, like a Christian. Any branch, any little animal. And they say the sun also was a person and a drinker of that drug and that my little God had given it the power to teach humans that wisdom, and when Christ walked here, he asked him what he wanted to be, and he told him, "light of this world," and then he turned him into a sun and that's why he shines. That's why the sun is the master of *Yajé* and that's why *Yajé* has no end, because it's the patron of everything. That's why it has a ray of light for everyone, a ray of light like the sun which means the visions, whether they're good or bad, but it has a ray of light for everybody.

Yeah, from conquest time these indigenous people knew what the world will be, what's bad and good, because I'm from an elder, old as they get, who used to say that ever since they watched, before this natural science, gets inside of us because he gave us a tiny little Christ here in this brain and he's the one who helps us with memory, with an overwhelming bit of strength, with knowledge . . . Aha!, so ever since birth, that's why each child has that gift. That's why in the history of *Yajé* those elders already knew God. They already knew that there's respect, love and kindness because that's what life is.

I began to drink *Yajé* when I was seven years old with my father, who was a really good *Yajé* drinker because that's also a gift that Christ put in him from the time he was in his mother's womb. He was born for that purpose. That's why my science is very occult and can only be understood spiritually with *Yajé*. It's not like you when you study, looking at your notebooks, nooo, this is spiritually.

I went to the school in Limón[2] for a year but I got sick with a kind of leprosy on the heal of my foot and I had to go home. I stayed with my father and followed another vocation—learning traditional medicine through *Yajé*.[3]

As a boy apprentice, I never got an animal with babies like a tapir, *cerrillo, zaino*. You can't eat garlic because you suffer a lot with vomiting. And each and every plate of food is separate from what others eat.

The Knowledge of Yajé

So, you see, ever since I was a boy I always thought that I'd prefer to know more! That's why I was never scared, because I wanted to see what there is beyond.

When I was seven years old, I was looking at a snail shell, but different little things deep inside that shell. Sure, little flowers, little images, just like us, but always really uniform, a teeny tiny little chapel, some different little doves, but easy, really easy, to see it all inside. And I told my Papa, "How come I saw little feathers of different things, colors and little angels in a scratched little snail shell that knows how to be stuck to those branches?" And Papa said, "That's the first knowledge of *Yajé*, but when you're bigger and you're about twenty years old, what's here in this world and other worlds, too, comes freely, world of the sky, of everything you're already starting to know."[4]

Afterwards, it was like I was quiet and unassuming. I drank and watched the little stars that were like little flowers. After a year, he gave me a little bowl with lots more until the snail I had when I was ten got lost and didn't come to me any more. Everything opened for me and I began seeing as if it were daytime. It's open because that *Yajé* is already penetrating, already passing into the blood, and that's when I started to know the plants and all the planets, everything.

When I was between fifteen and eighteen years old, with a stronger dose, I went to know this whole world and one planet and another with the spirit of *Yajé*, because when it really has grabbed you, you can travel through Colombia because for *Yajé* there are no closed doors. It can go in or out wherever it wants. That's why a liar or a thief or a rapist under the effects of *Yajé* confesses everything. He suffers if he has to have a conversation. That's really ugly.

Yes, and I can also know what else is going to happen, how to guide my family, how to live or how to know what sickness there might be in my house.

The Earth and the Planets

First, but before I was twenty years old, I traveled around the world. I saw mountains, seas, many lands, groves of bamboo, barren plains. I saw cities with very different lights, very colorful, that's why when I went to Cali, I was already familiar with it. It's incredible, but everything, and I mean everything, in *Yajé* turns up in the end.

I also saw the planet of the stars which is more potent than the sun because it's higher and you can never get there like you can to the sun, yes, though you can't get too close.

To go inside the earth is really easy. It's like walking on a rock. The different Yajés open a door, like a big entrance and you walk right through it because those who are below have invited you and when we go down, it's like going on a planet.

Down there, they're different. They have uniforms made of pure glass beads, and they just eat little fruits and vegetables. That's why they liked indigenous people a lot. The people there teach about everything, including infections from the earth itself. They teach about sicknesses and help cure them: the ones from the river, the water, the mountains, and even the ones from the air, too. And that planet is all made of rock and the houses are hollowed out from the stone. You can see gardens and smell a perfume more beautiful than any perfume in the world. They have light, but I don't know where it comes from and it's cold, reeeally cold.

Things That Are Not of This World

Aha! my Papa increased my *Yajé* potion a little every year. Then I began to know more things that are not of this world. Yes, there are other very marvelous planets, but I saw those before I saw the Lord . . . other planets like the one of mirrors, like the one of gardens, like the one of images and . . .

For example, the one of mirrors was like a world that was unstained, without any filth . . . pure like being stopped in the air. Everything was a mirror, not even a little blue or anything. Just pure clarity, like a great, great light.

They also took me far, far away to the planet of the flowers. There, there's a ray of light shining on this earth like a mattress but of pure flowers. Some little children are playing there and they knew how to show me around, too. How beautiful it smelled, how lovely that perfume. To get to that world it's sort of opaque, sort of dark. You're just looking at shadows. But it's enclosed with a fence against the sky and the earth and it seems like there's a big doorway but it's really another different planet, a marvelous place. You can't see where the garden ends but that's far away and we used to travel like that with our bodies. And knowing that means learning many plants, the different colors, all the smells . . . and the happiness of this earth.

Another planet is the one of happiness. The young people growing up are in *Yajé*, too, and they come out all happy as if it were a party . . . and little children with different kinds of hair show me around: some have curly hair, others are really cute, but it's all so beautiful, and that's the most happiness I've ever seen. They play, they play with everything and I was so happy and one threw a little flower in the air: he picked one, passed another, another . . . and Papa said, "Oh, my dear son! That's a good idea, for good blood. It means a good memory!"

The planet of the mountains is when you're already experienced. The spirits took me to know the forests and medicinal herbs in person. You go to the mountain to learn about remedies, but right here, on this planet . . .

The Planet of War

I accompanied my father for twenty four years. He died thirty seven years ago. After he had been dead for a year, I began to work in medicine. I drank *Yajé* alone to discover other different things like the planet of war. Yikes! it was so ugly, blood all over the place, but it was God's doing. I saw bombs there that gave off clouds of smoke, explosions that reached the sky and people were running pell-mell everywhere. It seemed like the smoke was as high as the sky, which was dark because of all the planes. And on the earth, there were armed people, and everyone was dying, scattered on the ground . . . Mark my words — it's just a question of time before it happens, and if you're still alive, you'll see if it was a lie or not.

I also saw hell. There are people who believe that it doesn't exist. But, my God! It's unbelievable to go there and see it. Some people there are screaming, others have flames shooting from their mouths. It's really ugly, just devils with horns and tails and everyone stuck in the fire. That's what they go through, flying by. I saw men and women, but no children. They do everything — laugh, scream, and if you're a coward they get mixed up with the *Yajé* right away and I begin to cry and everything. It's so ugly! It makes you so scared!

Another time drinking *Yajé*, I saw a planet of pure fire and that means a war of flames . . . and nothing else will be left of this world.

The Spirits of Everything

Yes, everything has a spirit. The ones of the air are like the figure of a little angel, similar to children but very powerful, and they show me stuff about this or that illness, or some bad spirit and they're telling me as if they were dead, as if they were the ice of the dead. My healing friends are all *compañeros*.

There are also the spirits of sudden deaths, the ones who take the wrong road because they die without repenting, the ones who are suffering in body and soul. They're ready for another world and they do evil because of that ice and that pain. That's why there's pollution in this world, in the rivers, on land. That's why. . .

I recommend to my friends that they be very careful when they want to drink because there is a lot of old *Yajé* that the old *Yajé* drinkers themselves have left damaged and *Yajé* like this can make you go crazy. It's just that since *Yajé* has a spirit they've left that recommendation: No one should touch that plant! It's forbidden for everyone else!

We can drink here because my Papa and Grandpa Patricio have recommended that wherever we live we can use that *Yajé*. After I became an orphan when my Papa died, I drank for five years with Grandpa Patricio, over on the Guamués, where the people speak Siona and have another science and other remedies. Because *Yajé* also teaches according to the language . . .

Aha! It's Because of the Capuchin Monks that We Came Here

Yes, and White people also can know how to heal because my Papa spoke of how in the time of the rubber boom there was a guy from Pasto, Manuel Bolaños, a one of a kind *Yajé* drinker because they don't come like that anymore. And Fra. Bartolomé liked it a lot. He'd tried *Yajé* with the old *Yajé* drinkers. He was like a doctor. When he saw someone was sick, he sent him to another *Yajé* drinker so that he could give him a cleaning. That's how that priest Bartolomé used to work.

Aha! It's because of the Capuchin monks that we came here, because of Monsignor Cruzalichi, who told us, "Before the colonists come in, you should grab a place somewhere and make a *resguardo* (protected community) so that you can live in peace even if it's only for a little while."[5] So, we settled there. We closed for a trail at the *bocanas* of Guayuyaco, up to the point where you leave to Guayuyaco. From there, on another trail to other rivers called Norueno and the Kofán until you get to Corozo.

From Corozo you go down to the Orito River, a cliff down below here. Then that whole area became the *resguardo*, and then all of us came here to live with my Mama *Señora*, with my Papa Igidio Peña, with everyone . . . here on the Cauca next to Puerto Guzmán, which used to be an indigenous village, Pacai people who spoke the Inga language.

Yes, and here my Papa failed. When he got sick the first time, he said, "I'm not going to live suffering in my bed. I'm dying from a sudden death." And that's how it was. It took a year. He drank *Yajé* and didn't tell any stories. When six months had gone by, he warned us, "My death is getting closer." And he cried. He gave away all his things and told us how we should live. "Behave yourselves," he said.

And my Papa's *Yajé* is like his own strength and it became an orphan and I . . . know everything. I have my experiences, my wisdom that my little God himself has given me. I see things but I can't get there like when I was young and single . . . That *Yajé* he left no longer wants to cry so much. That pain doesn't let it. Its organ was plugged up.

But how could I not be happy knowing those marvelous things I've known? Those little people, little perfumed images, or that clothing like really clear blue silk . . .

TRANSLATED FROM the Spanish by Steven F. White

(EXCERPT FROM: Hilario Peña, *Raigambre* 3 (n. d.) Pp. 35–41.)

NOTES

1. Inga Healer originally from Puerto Limón, Colombia, who lives in Guayuyaco.
2. Puerto Limón, a village to the south of Mocoa.
3. "The profession of payé (shaman) is not hereditary, although it seems to be common that the son of a renowned shaman continues the vocation of his father. Nevertheless, more important than the family tradition are certain psychological and intellectual qualities which indicate a person's *Yajé* potential and can be recognized when the person is still young. These traits include: a profound interest in myths and tribal traditions, a good memory to recite long sequences of names and events, a singer's voice, the ability to recite incantations on ritual nights preceded by fasting and sexual abstinence . . . But above all, the shaman's soul should "illuminate," shine with a strong inner light that makes visible that which is in darkness, everything hidden from ordinary knowledge and reason." Gerardo Reichel-Dolmatoff, *The Shaman and the Jaguar* (1978).
4. "The shaman knows the world by means of *Yajé* and his apprenticeship during the training period, which makes it possible for him to control the content of the experience and decipher its meaning." M. C. Ramírez de Jara and C. Pizón (1986)
5. Guayuyaco has been a resguardo since 1961. "The indigenous resguardo is a territory that serves as a settling place for a community of indigenous people. Juridically, it is demarcated by a collective and registered property title, a community that identifies itself as indigenous and an organization under indigenous authority or its cultural standards. Those constituted before 1961 have their origin in a royal decree or other instrument sheltered under the laws that applied to the epoch; those that came into existence after this date have been constituted by means of a resolution or administration act carried out by the board of directors of the INCORA (Colombian Institute for Agrarian Reform). The other resguardos currently in existence for the Inga and Kamsá are in: Valle de Sibundoy (Kamsá) and Yunguillo (Inga) before 1961, and Sibundoy high part (Kamsá) Res. No. 175 from November 2, 1979." R. Arango; E. Sánchez (1989).

AT THE END YOU SEE GOD

Fernando Payaguaje[1]

(excerpt from *The Yajé Drinker*)

The Years of Apprenticeship

I Listened as a Child

If you want to be a *Yajé* drinker and a "graduate," in other words, a wise person, the first thing you need is interest, also bravery and an ability to withstand suffering.[2] That's what happened with me: my father, who was the healer or chief of the family, told me one day, "You should be initiated in *Yajé* so that someday you can be the chief of your own people when I die."

Listening to his words, I started to get interested.

"Your obligation as healer and chief will consist of being concerned for your people, especially those who are sick. There are wizards who drink *Yajé*, but they only take care of themselves. They aren't even capable of taking good care of their families. You shouldn't follow in their footsteps. You should look at what I do and follow my example."

At the time, I was just a boy, but I'll never forget that advice.

"First of all, you should train yourself to drink *Yajé*. When you've reached a certain level of knowledge, then you, too, can give it to drink to anyone who wants to see, because you'll be able to instruct other healers."

In my family, there was a relative much older than I about whom my father said, "I'm not going to keep teaching him, nor he will drink *Yajé* anymore, since he really doesn't have enough interest in the visions."

He gave me that warning right from the beginning.

Initiation Moments

It was in the place called *Mahua'ira*, when I was still a boy, that, for the first time, I drank *taraYajé*,[3] a miraculous plant that a healer had received during his vision. It turned out to be very strong for me. The *borrachera* (drunkenness/trance state) lasted a long time. Afterwards, I drank watered-down *Yajé*, little cup by little cup. Later, in *Catëpo*, I started drinking strong, thick *Yajé* again. But I only drank continuously in Pisimoaya. I had a plot of land planted with *Yajé*, and I decided I would finish all the vines. If you drink continuously, it's really beautiful. You resist stopping and it seems like a vice. You're always thinking about drinking it again. At that moment of the apprenticeship, I was older. I must have been about sixteen. My father prepared and directed the sessions for the whole family.

Right away, I was interested in all that. I even increased my dose and learned the preparation itself. Also, my uncle had a big field of *Yajé* where several of us in our family went until we used it all up. I drank quite a bit of it, usually by itself, though sometimes mixed. My intention was to become chief of the family and the best healer later on. That's why I drank *Yajé* week after week. It was during that time that my visions increased: I saw not only birds of beautiful colors, but I also already perceived some images of the sky, for instance a *huiñahui* (angel) as small as a little frog or smaller.[4]

When I was drinking regularly, I took my first trip to Cuyabeno, just to visit. When I returned, I tried pejí.

A single session with that and you can see all of reality, even the most remote corners of the earth and the heavens, since the visions of the earth end and those of the sky begin. You keep going up, level by level, according to the kind of trance. I reached the highest one, in other words, the ultimate reaches of the sky.

Besides my father and uncles, there was another healer who taught me. His name was Salmo,[5] even though in our language we called him *Miaquë* (white). He was an *angotero,* a nice guy. First he invited me to drink *chicha* and then he kept teaching me to see. He was a distant relative on my wife's side of the family.

One of the First Yajé-Drinking Sessions

My uncle helped adorn me for the ritual. He used *azulejo* and toucan feathers, etc. We also put feathers in our ears. The master teacher had his own necklace for the ceremony.

I waited all day and we began to drink at dusk. There were two of us to be initiated. The other one was also the son of a healer. All the adults of the group were gathered there, including the women. I was the youngest, but I was really interested. On the *Yajé* table, there were two cups. The other young man picked up one of them that had a little liquid in it and took it to the master teacher, who "cured" or "arranged" it. Right away, the healer gave it back to him to drink. When it was my turn, I drink it all with no fear at all. The first effects hit me really hard, violently, but I didn't vomit. Instead I stretched out in my hammock. After a few minutes I fell asleep. I didn't even realize what state I was in and I didn't feel a thing until dawn.

The other young man, also in a trance, vomited everything as soon as he got in his hammock — bad luck for him. With me it was different. I kept it all down as if it were food without wasting a single drop in spite of the fact that it knocked me out and I wanted to get up. But they had tied me to my hammock so I wouldn't fall out. And that's how I was at dawn. Then I leaned over the ground, threw up and went to sleep again. In these cases, it's better to vomit after the trance and not before. That's what I did. After a few hours, I got up, without feeling any inebriation. That's when the ritual ended.

I went down to the river to empty myself. I washed my face and rinsed out my mouth, too. I was still a little dizzy. I found myself on a branch sticking out of the water. At that moment, my eyes cleared and I managed to see something like a submerged house on the riverbed. The roof reached the surface of the water. It was a beautiful house that I believed was real. I've never forgotten it. When I went back, they were preparing *Yajé* again.

"You'll drink again tonight," said my father.

"No, I might be scared now. But I'll do it some other time."

I kept my word and continued to drink and learn. A little later, I prepared it myself and invited others to drink, but I still didn't have much knowledge. Little by little, I taught myself to drink and to see within the visions. I started to like it so much, that I drank not only with my family, but with people in other houses in the area.

It's Not Easy to "Graduate"

In order to graduate, you have to drink *Yajé* at least fifteen times over a period of a few months. After this, you should be able to cure any illness. But to get to this level, you have to go through a lot of discomfort and suffering.

In my case, for example, because I'm married, I couldn't sleep with my wife. If I wanted to be the greatest and wisest healer, I couldn't visit her. I was close to her but in another house, preparing and drinking *Yajé* constantly, since my obligation was to perfect myself more and more. That also happens later on. The healer often suffers for not being able to take good care of his family. For a certain period of time, he has to remain distant and take care of himself and his own health. He can never use a vessel used by a pregnant woman and he should even keep away from her. If he doesn't fulfill these requirements, he'll suffer headaches and other illnesses. The same thing happens if a woman is having her period. In this case, she should be hidden and keep her distance from her husband until her illness passes. Then she should wash herself with hot water, *guaba* and other leaves. If she does this, then she can serve food to her husband again. Women also shouldn't walk near the *Yajé* house when a ceremony is taking place. Nevertheless, they can drink *Yajé* or be healers, and it's good if they can heal bites, etc. if their family suffers.

While you are drinking *Yajé*, you have to follow a strict dietary regimen. There are few kinds of fish that can be eaten — just *singo*. Few meats, too. Hot peppers shouldn't be eaten when they're ripe, only green, etc. If you eat just anything, you won't learn. That's why you need patience and tolerance. Often, you have to stay at home and visit no one so that people don't offer you forbidden foods. Also, the apprentice needs his own new pot just for himself. Always put your hammock away. If you leave it out, keep it up high and tied so that women or other people who visit can't use it. This is what the master keeps telling you. If you don't, what might happen is that you could come home, bathe, and lie down in a misused hammock and suffer pain, while at the same time losing the power of the visions. That's why you have to protect yourself.

Other times, you feel the envy of others when they know about our curing powers. Once I even heard someone say to one of my relatives, "Is there anyone here who can cure snakebites?"

"No," I said. "Nobody here knows how. I sure don't."

At the same time, I was thinking, "That bite is easy to heal."

I didn't open my mouth again, and I kept saying to myself, "Does he know more than I do? No. He doesn't know anything. He's just jealous."

In any case, it's not just the preparation that's hard, but also the cultivation. Then you have to store it in large quantities and you need lots of firewood to cook it. Two people prepare it throughout the day — the thick kind and the watered-down kind. During the drinking season, I used to prepare it myself with my nephew. It was hard work doing it day after day. Sometimes we stopped for one or two days because we needed to hunt. But then we immediately continued. Usually the drinking sessions begin with the moon before August. This is the best time for "graduation" since it's summer and there are cicadas and butterflies. The spirits are right above the trees. The angels are moving over the face of the earth. While you drink *Yajé*, you can clearly see the spirits in the cicadas and other summer insects. The drink shows them just as they are, celestial spirits, even if some of them turn out also to be instructors and conductors of witchcraft. On the other hand, you can watch others that look like short little men, as if they were children. This kind of angel does not look like us. Instead they resemble dolls.

This *Yajé* session can last two or three months until what's been stored is used up. On the other hand, during the December summer, the angels or celestial spirits are in heaven, in the sky. They don't get any closer. That's why it isn't a good time to get instruction in the visions.

So, some people drink *Yajé* only until they get the power to do witchcraft. With these arts, they can kill others. That's bad. You need a great effort or really superior *Yajé* session to reach the highest level where you have access to visions and the power to heal. It's easy and fast to become a witch, but I didn't aspire to that. I wanted to be the wisest. My idea was to become the chief of a great family or clan, some ten or twenty families, and to be able to take care of them and cure them all. Only with that idea did I find the strength to go up to the highest level.[6]

When you have drunk enough *Yajé*, the master teacher who is guiding you usually says, "Don't drink any more. Rest a bit and drink again in two or three weeks."

That's what happened to me since I was precocious. At that time, I could see the tijeritas, those birds that skim through the air. I grabbed a bone from their wings and played it. It's precisely that bone that has a stronger sound than any other.

Family of Yajé Drinkers

I stretched out in my hammock, and, once I was there, everything began to shine like it does on a clear day. Right away, the visions arrived. Later, they went away. That happened in the *Yajé* house which was somewhat far away. I left there and went back to my house and fell into my hammock. My Uncle Sebastián went by and said, "I can't stay and say hello. You're still in a trance."

Later, my Uncle Saulerio arrived and he got into my hammock with me. He talked to me about the work he was doing even though I didn't answer him since I still felt inebriated. Finally, he said, "I'm leaving."

As it got dark, lying in my hammock, I heard a noise like someone falling in the river. Soon I heard the message from the angels and I understood what they were saying,"A strong wind is coming to this region."

That's what happened. Without getting up, I felt the hurricane. I saw the trees fall around my house. Then the storm calmed. At dawn, I contemplated the fallen branches while my uncle asked, "Just before dawn, we had a hurricane. Did you see how the trees were falling?"

"Yes," I said, but I didn't tell him what I had heard.

I got up and went to Mauricio Leví's place. He said, "What have you taken now? Did you get drunk on strong *Yajé*?"

"No. Not at all. I just had a little bit."

"I'll give you this cloth to pay you for your work."

He gave it to me and my wife, but it wasn't until the next morning that I went back to where my family lives. My mother was in the hammock in a trance. She had drunk *Yajé*. Other relatives had done the same.

"Why didn't you get here on time?" asked my father. "You could have drunk with us. We could see pretty things. Your mother even played flutes made from the bones of a bird that appeared to her. She played those wingbones really well: toodledee, toodledee, doo . . .

The Temptation of Violence

You're sitting in the hammock, but at the same time, you're in another world, seeing the truth of everything that exists. Only the body remains lying down. The angels come and give you a flute. You play it. It isn't the healer who teaches you, but the angels themselves who make us sing when we are inebriated. It's so beautiful to see the animals in their entirety, even those living underwater! How could it not be lovely to be able to distinguish even the people who live inside the earth? You can see everything! That's why it's so captivating to drink *Yajé*.

But it's not simple. When I drank thick *Yajé*, I managed to see the sun, the rainbow . . . everything. The vision ended and I noticed that my heart was hot, like a pot that's just been burned. I felt the burning heat inside me. Even without working, I was sweating all day. Continuous visions assaulted me. Every so often I would be bathed in sweat. I felt capable of doing witchcraft and killing others, even though I never did it since my father's advice held me back.

"If you use that power now, you'll be able to kill people, but you'll never be anything but a witch."

That was the time when I had given myself over to *Yajé* completely. I went to visit Cuyabeno and I returned to my house to the same warnings once again.

"When you feel a little 'drunk,' you should try to master the rage that comes to you. You won't become violent or harm anyone."

"I'll be able to hold myself back."

For days, I put up with that heat inside me. I remember how I was drowning in sweat. That's a dangerous moment for you when you're preparing yourself. You shouldn't even stare at anyone, only listen to them.

"Now I'm going to get a different kind of *Yajé*," said my father. "It's time to try it."

We prepared it very thick, and when I drank it, it took away those arrows[7] that I had. I stopped sweating and felt like a little boy again. That's how my father uprooted the violence within me so that I wouldn't turn to witchcraft. He wanted to help me learn to cure. At that moment, I went up a level. Suddenly, I could see the witches like a sun. Healers were mirrors. Because of this, when I arrived in Cuyabeno permanently I discovered a Siona witch on the Aguarico River. Witches don't look at people face to face, directly. They sort of crouch down. These are the kind of people who started so many fights in ancient times.

Customs for the Yajé Ritual

The ancient Secoyas adorned themselves to participate in the *Yajé* house. They combed their hair, painted their faces with recently-picked *achiote* seeds, highlighting these markings with *curí* or *achiote* that is cooked and mixed with other aromatic herbs. They all made similar long striped markings. All these drawings didn't have a greater meaning. They were just for adornment. They smeared cooked *achiote* on their lips to make them black. They adorned their feet, ankles, arms and hands. They wore new *cushmas* and adorned their hammocks. They also put flowers and fragrant herbs on different parts of their body. Lastly, they put on feathers, crown and necklaces.

About four o'clock in the afternoon, the preparations had begun already and they came out of their houses dressed like this if they lived near the one used for *Yajé*. On the other hand, if they lived far away, they arrived unadorned until they were a short distance away and there they got dressed up. No participant came in without being adorned. Once inside, they hung their hammocks and remained seated in them from the beginning of the session, at the end of the day, until it ended at the break of dawn. The following day, they were given breakfast as guests and returned to their respective houses where they bathed to remove the painting.

The relatives who had a sick person in their charge took that person to the *Yajé* house. During the ceremony, these people remained in their hammocks in a corner. Then, at a given moment, the healer offered cured water. He fanned them with some little branches and, finally, said to the father of the sick person, "Your son is going to get better. This sickness will not return to him."

The father thanked him, and when the son was completely better he usually paid the healer with a hammock, since everyone is aware of the suffering you go through until you "graduate." That's the reason for paying him. Sometimes, if a person suddenly falls ill, he can be cured in his own house. The healer smokes tobacco, blows over the sick person and, if he is a good healer, he'll know immediately what sickness he's dealing with. Occasionally, if he doesn't have any *Yajé* prepared or if he's in a hurry, he can use alcohol, though the "drunkenness" isn't the same. You've got to be careful with the quantity. With a glass that isn't too big, a person can be cured. If you drink more, the drunkenness comes and nothing can be done, especially in terms of having visions. Alcohol is really different.

There are different kinds of *Yajé* and various ways of using it. One usual way is to cook *Yajé* on one side and, on the other, yai *(ujajai)*, which is scraped from a little tree, and wrapped in a leaf. When the *Yajé* itself is being cooked, you put it in the pot, keeping it there for a long time. You still keep boiling the *Yajé* at least half a day or more until it gets really thick. It should turn out bitter, concentrated, since that's how visions become more potent. You strain it, let it cool and take it to the house.

The *ujajai* shouldn't be cooked. The bark removed with the knife is put in water in a pot which is placed in sunlight. After awhile, you can drink it because it causes inebriation. In spite of being strong, *pejí* is simple to prepare even though it should remain for a long time in the fire. It's put in a large clay pot. A long time later, it's strained and cooked again until it's ready more to be eaten than drunk. Its smell, texture and taste are very unpleasant.

The person used to drinking *Yajé* isn't affected by this drunkenness. He can drink it with no problem as if it were *chucula*. Whoever is directing the singing never drinks *pejí*, even if he has drunk it before on other occasions, in order to sing, since it makes the body and the voice gentler. After trying it, you know longer have any doubts about singing because you've acquired all knowledge. If the "graduate" is young, usually he drinks standing up, walking with the cup in hand through the open space of the house, proud, drinking and singing, since the drunkenness can't conquer him. The truth is that it's no longer you who is drinking, but the angels themselves.

Yajé is drunk in darkness without lighting a lamp. The only light is from the flames or the coals in the hearth.

Pejí Reduces You to Ashes

After getting to know all the *Yajé* spirits, you drink *pejí* to see the innermost depths of reality and also to perfect your voice as a graduate so that you can sing clearly in the ceremony.

To drink *pejí*, you scrape its bark like *yocó*. The roots are washed well and peeled. These scrapings are baked in smaller pots and then in a larger pot to cook. Later, you let it cool, strain it into another pot, throw away the scrapings and cook the rest again until it thickens to the point where you can almost chew it.

Meanwhile, the *Yajé* is cooking in another pot at a certain distance. The director of the ceremony abstains from drinking *pejí*, but offers it to those who want to see. The truth is that it's scary to swallow that thick *pejí*. I already mentioned that it has a very unpleasant smell and a taste that's even worse. Besides, you usually vomit instantly, but you do it into a bowl so that you can swallow it again. If you vomit the *pejí* on the ground or on the floor, you won't have visions. All you'll see is an immense land where you remain as if you were buried. It's so pasty that it's not easy to swallow, so you have to push it down your throat with your fingers. All this is embarrassing, disgusting and also frightening.

Sometimes *tara Yajé, hua'iyaté*[8] and *pejí* are mixed so that they are really concentrated. When you drink it, you feel the effects even before finishing the bowl. You feel a burning, as if you were being hit with burning sticks. Your whole body burns and is reduced to ashes. When the flesh is destroyed, only then does the soul appear and begin to see. At that moment, the most fabulous visions begin.

I drank *pejí* when I was really young, when some people aren't even able to able to drink the less-thick kind. On that occasion, three graduates who were not drinking it were with me. They gave me a big bowl. I drank it and instantly went blind. They also gave me water to take away the bitterness in my mouth and they helped me into my hammock. I felt a terrible "drunkenness" and I still couldn't see. Later, they lit some tobacco for me, but I wasn't able to smoke it, so I threw it away. I couldn't see a thing. In spite of everything, I withstood the fear without screaming. I was immobile, awaiting the visions.

The person drinking with me had to drink sitting down and, even so, he couldn't swallow more than four mouthfuls. The bowl was still full when he stood up, frightened.

"I can't drink any more! I'm 'drunk'!"

"You have to finish."

But he started crying and pushed it away. Right away, he went to lie down and was like that for hours. Later, he got up and was going around the *Yajé* house like a crazy person. At dawn, he went out, saying, "I'm going to visit someone."

His whole body was shaking with spasms and that's how he remained, crazy, until the afternoon.

Young people should drink *pejí* as the culmination of their initiation. Otherwise, the celestial visions can't be attained. *Yajé* isn't sufficient. With *Yajé*, it's like being in school. Until you've finished studying, you don't know everything. Only those who drink *pejí* finally know the ultimate visions of the world. I spent one day and one night "drunk." During this time I could see all the devils that exist. I also knew the tigers in their entirety, including the ones that nobody had ever seen or described to me. One had a very thin stomach. The other, a twisted tail . . . I knew the subterranean tigers, the ones that devour people then disappear, which makes it impossible to kill them. Another, called tiger-that-pursues-*huanganas*, at first glance might seem like a pig, but if you cook it, its meat is white. If you hear its roar beneath the earth, you should run away at once because this animal comes from the ground and tears people apart before disappearing. If someone manages to see it in the jungle, it will be by itself, never in groups. Besides, it has a long tail, and pigs don't. Another is the *sajino*-tiger. Sometimes the Quichua Indians kill it, mistaking it for a *sajino*. Even my *compadre* Gabriel, a Siona Indian from Campoeno, had this happen to him: with a barbed arrow, he had shot a solitary animal he encountered along the Aguarico River. He carried it home and told people, "I hunted a *huangana* that was alone."

The healer lived nearby and came to see.

"That's a *sesetuiyai* tiger. You shouldn't eat it. It would be better to throw it in the river."[9]

My compadre, not knowing, had already eaten some, but he obeyed and threw the meat in the water.

To Attain Wisdom

I had already gone through it all when, while visiting some relatives, my aunt begged me, "My husband has good visions and even knows how to cure, but he never learned how to sing while he drinks."[10]

What had happened was that the angels never had taught him. She forced me to prepare *Yajé* and teach him. We drank. I got up and was walking all through the house, singing exactly the same way that the spirits had taught me during the visions. I had the strength to keep singing until daybreak.

If you are a healer, you can teach others, but for that you need to have attained the highest level. For example, I prepared myself together with my Uncle Miguel. We had the same visions, but he didn't dare drink *pejí*. Besides that, he got married and was always with his wife. He also ate all kinds of fish. Because of this, he lied to the master and, afterwards, turned pale and got sick. Those kinds of foods make you lose the qualities that the angels give you. That's why you get sick. When my father saw him like that, he asked, "Why are you so pale? You look like you're going to die."

Then he advised him, "You shouldn't sleep with your wife. Do what your nephew does, who sleeps alone. That's why you're ill."

Then he picked up the branches of a shrub and passed them over my uncle's entire body. After he cured him, he gave him the following warning, "You can no longer be the chief of a family. From now on, you won't be allowed to sing during the ceremony. Instead, you'll drink in silence like any other person who hasn't graduated. Nor will you be able to prepare *Yajé* to teach others. That's how you will live from now on."

AT THE END YOU SEE GOD

Many of our young people no longer even know our own beliefs. They don't know anything about the gods: Paina, Muju, who aspried to be like Ñañë, the God of the sky, God of all. Those gods fought with Ñañë and lost. Even so, because those gods of the earth bothered him so much, Ñañë burned the world, turning it to ash, even though, later, he transformed it again into trees. Finally, he said to the gods, "Okay, I'll leave you alone because you bother me too much. I'm going to the sky."

And to the people, he said, "I'm leaving you the earth, where death rules. Where I'm going, no one dies. There, there's eternal life, and that's true above and below the earth where another sky can be found also."

Now, young people don't know our traditions. the adults who have heard them can't see God either since God is a spirit. Only the good drinkers can manage to see God.

The True World

I've already said that my preparation was long because I've been brave when I drink. I finished whole fields of *Yajé* before having visions. But, finally, I managed to graduate while I was still a young man.[11]

After drinking, the first thing you notice is the light. Your mind opens like a resplendent day. The sun takes over everything and colors shine intensely. Right away, you can see the butterflies flying in that luminous air. The first time I saw them come closer, I thought the butterflies were people. I wondered if they were the angels that others had mentioned. But they weren't. Only later can you contemplate the angels themselves walking through the air. At first, you can only see butterflies and really beautiful birds. You can also hear very beautiful resonating sounds, or the murmur of celestial creatures. The drinker might feel proud and say, "I've already obtained visions." And it's true, but it's only the beginning levels. I didn't say anything because I had higher aspirations.

Later, if you have a good master teacher, you begin reaching the truth and the most complete knowledge of reality, little by little.[12] The guide should lead us first toward the sky-blue spirits and then instruct us about the multitude of devils that exist, since the graduate will know all things. But if the master teacher were to introduce us to the world of the devils first, we would never manage to leave and be able to reach the sky. Everything would be over. That kind of teacher isn't even qualified to direct the *Yajé* ritual.

The Animal Kingdoms

When the graduation lessons get more advanced, you can see all kinds of animals. In the middle of the trance you might be up in a tree or crawling along an animal trail or perhaps turned into a *sajino*, eating coconuts with other *sajinos*.

Following that road you cross some wetlands filled with fallen fruit. Beyond that, is the place where the *huanganas* are. Your chief says, "Welcome!"

The person who is having the vision is still lying down in the hammock, but his companions in the *Yajé* house hear the sounds of the *huangana*. That person begins to eat the coconuts in his own hammock, opening them with his mouth, since at that moment he has the teeth of a *huangana*. He can only move his head, and when he lifts it, he spits out the dry leaves the way *huanganas* do. These animals live where coconuts are abundant. If they eat above the river, they drop shrimp heads and rotten leaves into the water. The same thing happens now to the drinker. His teeth are colored, his fangs are stained by the coconuts just like the *huanganas*. If you can achieve these transformations you're showing an example of your power.

Even though the animals live in that swampy area of fallen fruit, they rest on a hill further ahead. There, the groves of coconuts have fruit that grows really low, almost next to the ground, and they're so abundant that the *huanganas* can't finish them. The same thing happens with the *sajinos*. They can't finish all those yellow and red coconuts ... Sometimes the wizard picks up those seeds that have already been scraped and brings them home to make a necklace. Sometimes he doesn't have enough power to reach the place where they live even though he can certainly call those animals, bringing them close to his family so they can hunt them.

Deer live in their own place and eat *pambil* seeds. Further on, when you reach the refuge of the *huatusas* you can hear them talking. Their voices resemble the murmur of falling jungle fruit, something like that. The armadillos live farther away, like the *guantas*, which are led by a chief or guardian. Still further on, you reach the place where the tapirs live, an open place where you can hear the song of the frogs together with the wind as it blows. Off to one side, it seems like you can hear a voice and another god answers in front of you with a strong voice. Lifting our eyes, we contemplate a kind of field where numerous tapirs graze like cattle. You can see ones that are colored, white, striped. Others, which are the tapirs of death, only have bones. For them, there's a kind of feeding place, a great emptied space a few meters high and fifteen in length. There is the constant echoing of the tapirs' whistling in that cave. There's always water and mud and you can hear a constant splashing.

After knowing all the things that exist on top of the earth, you go inside it, and there you can see the people who live in those depths. They're really people. After meeting them, you go further within in case there is another inhabited world, but there's no one to be seen, just water, a kind of ocean.... Then you sink beneath the waters and in a single glance you can contemplate the inner workings of the rivers with all the animals that live there: boas, alligators, water tigers, etc.

There, you can distinguish a man, Ocomé,[13] chief of all the fish — from the littlest ones to the biggest that exist. But, hey, you've got to be careful with that name! On the shores of the Aguarico we usually see a yellowish-brown bird that tricks the *Yajé* drinkers.

"I'm Ocomé! I'm Ocomé!" it sings.

It's not true. His name only serves to call the fish. There's also a devil named in reality *Uncuisiquë huatí*, who masquerades as *Tsiayaquë*. But it's another trick. Only the person who can see in the deepest part of the waters will contemplate *Tsiayaquë* since he dwells in the greatest depths. When you know him and invoke him, he doesn't come, but he sends the fish.

You see *Mecoye' yë* just as it is: it's not a person, just a boa, an animal that isn't accustomed to looking for people to eat them. Rather, it attacks all those who try to reach him. It has long, 20-cm. fangs with notches on the points, which sort of resemble the *huanganas'*. It is said that people from Archidona usually eat this animal. That's what a man from there named Lucucho told me. One day he showed me a fang.

"What animal is that from?" I asked.

"From *Mecoye' yë*."[14]

He said that he used to find those animals in a kind of field and he hunted them with the help of a dog. First he shot them, then harpooned them and tied them up. According to him, the only part of the body that dies is the part that's wounded. When you pull it, the living part comes free and can still swim. That's why he kept cutting and firing at the living part until he reached the tail and finally killed it.

"My friend, you don't eat this animal?" he asked.

"No, my friend, we don't. We only like animals with tasty meat. That animal is ugly, dirty. How could we even taste it?"

"You're wrong. It isn't dirty. It's very tasty and pleasing. It's the favorite food of my extended family. That's why I hunt it. But around here, there aren't any."

This happened below the lake of the Aguas Negras River. I think Lucucho died without eating *Mecoye'yë* in that region. That animal sometimes has a double tail one or two meters in length shaped like scissors. It has teeth like a handsaw, and it traps people with that tail before it swallows them. And that's not all: it usually grabs someone, here, for example, on the Aguarico River, and takes the person through subterranean passageways all the way to the Putumayo River where it devours the person. Sometimes it's from the Putumayo to the Aguarico. This animal is dangerous. Its markings resemble those of a land boa, but it has a tiger's head. In fact, it can crunch up bones and completely devour people.

On land once again, you can see the devils stetched out in their hammocks hung between the great trees, because they have no place to live or any fixed residence. They live wherever they want. That's why you can run into them anywhere. It might be on a fallen branch and dry trunk, which is like a window to see them. They don't have any food either. All they eat is the fungus that grows on rotten trees. I couldn't even tell you how many there are, since they're far too numerous. I should say that we know many of them by their own names. We know that none of them attacks for no reason, nor will they do any harm unless a witch orders them to do so.

The Celestial Regions

One day my father prepared a different *Yajé*, the kind with blue flowers. He cooked it until it was really thick, I drank it and quickly became unconscious. I was like that for many hours, and, finally, before I awoke, I managed to know other aspects of reality. I saw the whole sky, the rainbow. Then a spirit took me to a high, high place and I watched the earth from there. You can see the world with a rainbow circumference. Depending on how the trance progresses, that's how the vision goes, too. Now, no vision is more potent than the one produced by *pejí*. At one time I had a field of *pejí* that was fifty meters wide and 20 meters long and I finished almost all of it in my sessions. At one point, a relative said, "Don't drink so much. You've already graduated and there's no reason to abuse that drink. That's enough."

As a young man, that's how I was: interested in the visions, brave, disciplined in terms of drinking and always in search of more knowledge. That's how I managed to reach the sky. That happened especially when I drank thick p*ejí (jaro pejí)*.[15] I drank so much that the drunkenness lasted more than a day with its night. Although I was breathing, I lost consciousness. For this reason, I didn't see things the way I can now as I converse. Rather, I contemplated them as if I had already died. It's true, you die after drinking so much in order to know everything. The body is reduced to ash and the spirit remains free to reach the maximum wisdom, to know more, to rise in the end to reach God.

In the visions, there's a ladder you can climb with the guidance of a healer. The *pejí* took me beyond the sky to know the things there and to take a tour of the heavens. You can see the sun like a man (the drinker who reaches him already has the power to do witchcraft). I saw the house of the sun just as I saw the rainbow's. I've seen it all, more than any of those who are witches. Next to the house of the sun, there are other people, the ones who dry the pointed coconuts and give evil spells to the witches so they can kill people. Nevertheless, the other people who reach the house of the sun itself, the highest graduates, do so to experience the witchcraft, and to drink an adequate *Yajé* so they can defeat it.

Beyond, you get to a truly lovely place where the people of the sky live. It's a kind of separate earth for the true people. Nowadays, our Piaguaje and Payaguaje people don't see them since we abandoned the house of *Yajé* and we don't even cultivate the plant. Only the people of the Putumayo reach them in visions. There are no other wise people now. My father was trained by a man from the Putumayo and then he taught me. I saw just like him. None of the others had contemplated celestial life. Not even the most advanced sorceror of the time, a man named Yeitarí, had done it.[16]

In my case, though, I reached the *nunipai*, the people of the sky who enjoy all kinds of hunting and also have an abundance of *chambira*. When the dead arrive, they still have many memories of earth and always want to return. Then, to help the dead person forget his family members here, the celestial beings take him down the great river, visiting their people along the shore. In this way, the dead forget their house on earth and remain among the celestial beings with pleasure. These beings go fishing and navigating in an iron boat that never leaks: not even a single drop of water gets in. I'm familiar with those metal boats the Peruvians use that always have some water sloshing around in them. In that place, no, those boats are so dry that people can live inside them. Besides that, the motor has a gentle sound. There are white boats, pink ones: each family group has its own and goes out cruising or visiting. And the river? It's immense. It can't be measured. I can't even describe it. The houses of these people seem like they are made of corrugated metal, but they aren't. Once you're inside, you can see the straw, even though from the outside it looks like corrugated metal. The leaves for the construction are received from the hands of God.

I saw all this accompanied by angels. They're tiny, but they have crowns. Their stature depends on their rank: the ones who live in the preferred places are smaller. Outside of that, from up there you can't see anything because there's nothing except the devils with the colored darts. Their roads look like threads of cotton. They have their houses about fifty meters from the edge of the sky.

When I was there, the angels told me, "Check out the corrugated metal roof. From there you can see the sky as if it were an upside down pot."

I did what I was told and checked out the whole roof until I returned to the same place: I began on one side and finished where I had started. In any case, to go from the nunipai to the house of God, there is a direct road, but it's dangerous since there's a big emptied space in the middle. Through this hole (it might be ten meters in diameter) you can contemplate the earth. You've got to cross it if you want to reach the house of God. To do that, there's a white iron handrail stretching across that space. There's also a barred railing that you can grab onto when you cross. I crossed over looking down because I was curious about that space in spite of the angels' warning.

"Don't look down," they said. "Keep your eyes on where you're putting your feet."

Without heeding what they had said, I observed what was around me and it became clear to me that in reality space is just air. From here, the angels took me to the house of God, who welcomes everyone in whatever language they might speak. God lives with his wife. He has a room, which is half the house. The other half belongs to his wife, who prepares food for her husband. He is Ñañë, the God who fought with thunder. There is no other God that can exist. And his wife is that daughter of the tapir *huequë* that he lifted up from the earth. Her name is *Repao*.[17] Suddenly the angels told me, "There, my son, look at God."

I kept my distance, of course, because you don't get close to where God is unless you're an angel or a person of the sky who lives there. But I heard how God addressed me, "You are going to be a healer. You will have the power to heal. To do that, you should love people and do good, not evil."

That's what God said, and later, "Drink this so that you can cure any illness."

And he gave me a little packet of salt stones. The angels brought it, repeating, "Don't get too close."

But later they took me by the hand and I saw God sitting in a throne. It wasn't exactly a chair. His clothes were white and resplendent and, how can I explain it? The house seemed all illuminated, not the way white people have their houses, but each thing itself was shining. Then God stood up, touched me on the arm and said, "Spit."

I spit, and that saliva made a sound on the ground like music. His footsteps were also marvelous sounds and I was paralyzed, admiring that God of the vision. Then I heard him say, "We're at home. It's time for you to go back to yours."

On another occasion, after I had graduated, I reached God, who welcomed me and even invited me into his house. He offered me a really white chair. Later, he told me, "Get up and walk."

Then I took some steps and they sounded like little bells, an enchanting jingling. Then I heard God's blessing, "You have already graduated because you are brave. Now you need to follow my laws. Some of you keep bad company and behave even worse. Even so, you're presumptuous and say, 'I've seen God.' Well, some of them saw my benches shining and thought it was me. But they were fooled, because I only show myself to people of good conduct, giving them instructions so they can increase their wisdom."

That's how it was. Do you know why we become healers? Because God, once you finally reach him, washes out your mouth, gives it a rinse. At that moment, you truly become a healer. He washed mine with salt, symbol of healings. My saliva sounded like music and turned to shining gold. And, what's happened now? My people have become evangelicals. Well, I have no idea who their God is, but mine has red shoes and lives in his own house. When he said goodbye, he told me, "My son, now you, too, are God."

God and the Dead

The thunder *(Müjü)* has his house in the sky separate from *Nañë*. He looks like a young white person. As soon as he gets home, he strikes the walls with an iron staff. That's the noise we hear — thunder. He himself produces the lightning bolts, which shoot from his eyelashes when he opens and closes his eyes.

The place of the dead is different. They arrive on the road that leads to the house of God and he takes them to *Repao's* place, a hundred meters further on. *Repao* examines them. If they come from the earth annointed with *nuní* they have the same form as they had there and they go to where their people in the sky live. The non-annointed, however, must stay in *Repao's* hammock for four days. On the fifth, the woman sends them to the other side of the river and, even though they die again while crossing, once they get there they live forever, though it's with a certain amount of suffering. It's difficult to cross to the other side and not even the great healers manage to do it. Only *Numi quëye* is able to do it. For this crossing, the dead wear *cushmas* and blue crowns. Also, that man faints to cross, changes his clothes and, once there, drinks *chicha* with the dead. But I'm going to explain that better.

In Repao's house, there's an enormous nest of wasps that fly around over the dead person for five days. They sound sort of like a plane. It's a terrible noise. At the back of the house there's the *huatipú*, a bird just like the hummingbird, and is the same size. beneath its nest hang the hammocks where the dead, when they arrive, make themselves comfortable. They hang there while the hummingbird circles around them. From the side of the hammocks dangle four vines covered with leaves. Each time the hummingbird flies past, the leaves multiply prodigiously so that the dead find themselves hanging between those vines that reach a distance of forty meters. After observing the dead, the *huatipú* returns to its nest and at that moment the leaves are once again reduced to four vines. On the fifth day, the woman says to whoever is in the hammock, "Leave the house and go to the shore of that river as big as the sea,[18] whose shores can't be seen. Wait there. A strong wind will come and take you to the other side."

Upon hearing that, the person goes walking toward the shore, experiences death again and faints. Then the first wind blows, then a second. The third gust drags the person over the waters to the other side. When the person reaches the opposite shore the person is no longer human, but resembles a three-year-old. That's why those who are there ask, "Whose child would this be?"

They examine the entire body — the hands, nails, everything. Suddenly someone exclaims, "It's your child!"

They recognize it by its hands and give it to a woman who will care for the child. She takes the child and gives it banana *chucula* or black corn *chicha*. Those are the drinks of the dead. Our ancestors seem to have been able to visit that place and they said that it's not wise to finish the cup of *chicha* that you're offered; just taste a mouthful, since all the women there are going to offer you some. As for the rest, those people have hardly any clothing, just a little rag that doesn't even cover them. They've been that way for centuries. There's no place for them to buy anything, or anyone they could buy from, and they can't even make their own clothing. You always see them sitting down.

. . . I observed all this in the sky and I still wanted to walk beyond but some angels warned me, "Humans can only go this far. If you go any further, you could die. Let's just go back."

One had an oriole in his hand. He put it on my shoulder. He blew on the bird and returned me to my house but not before I heard him say, "You've graduated. You've reached the limits of knowledge."

All this can be achieved with a single session drinking *pejí*. No more is needed. Later, even drinking *yocó*, you can have visions or hear the sound of the angels since the graduate is always united with the celestial spirits.

RESEARCH AND TRANSLATIONS BY Alfredo Payaguaje, Marcelino Lucitande, and Jorge Lucitande; transcriptions by Santos Dea; translated from the Spanish by Steven F. White

(EXCERPT FROM: Fernando Payaguaje. *El bebedor de Yajé*. Shushufindi — Río Aguarico, Ecuador: Vicariato Apostólico de Aguarico, 1990, pp. 57–83.)

NOTES

1. With notes and commentary by Miguel Angel Cabodevilla.

2. The healers I have been able to listen to usually agree on these three concepts: interest, bravery, and ability to withstand suffering as qualities required for the neophyte. The following pages will explain, to a large extent, why this is the case. At any rate, I should emphasize, as a kind of outline, some of these motifs: initiation is a rigorous ascetic undertaking (in physical, psychological and social terms) for the initiate. The ceremony is carried out in full view of the group of the initiate who is subject to their judgement at that time and in the future in various ways after the so-called graduation (*eta jaisiquë*, to stand out, to remain on top). The drinking of hallucinogens is very demanding physically. On many occasions it provokes physiological discomfort and, as a result, fear. Finally, I should say that the sorcerer always walks on the wounding edge of the mediation-attraction of the protective and malevolent spirits. The healer also personifies this ambivalence for his people, for whom he alternates between healer and witch, protector and vehicle for witchcraft. For this reason, it is a trade that has a great deal of attractive power, but also many dangers.

3. To promote their visions or healing rituals, the Secoya Indians use primarily three kinds of plants: 1) *Yajé*, which is the most well known, used throughout the Amazon and perhaps popularized by the Quichua word *ayahuasca* (even though it would be more appropriate to call it *jayahuasca*, bitter vine). Vickers has collected 16 denominations of *Yajé* amongst the Secoya (See William T. Vickers. *Los sionas y secoyas, su adaptación al ambiente amazónico*. Quito: Abya-Yala, 1989. pp. 333–335). 2) *Pejí*, commonly called *floripondio* or *borrachero* amongst the guando Quichuas. Vickers lists four kinds (See Vickers, p. 335). 3) *Ujajai*, from the Secoya *uja*, prayers to flee from danger, and *jai*, many or great. In Quichua, *chirihuayusa*, cold *huayusa*. Vickers lists four varieties (See Vickers, pp. 335–336). Throughout his testimony, Fernando will remember some of the characteristics of these drinks which he recognizes as an expert. A more detailed description of their qualities is beyond the scope of these pages.

4. It is important to point out, albeit briefly, that there are two spiritual forms that commonly appear in Secoya visions. to translate *huiñahuai* as angels is not exactly accurate. According to Fernando, "It can't be said in Spanish." Nevertheless, his grandchildren, perhaps because of the symbolic system of the Bible to which they have access, or because of an inability to find a better term, they translate it as angels (or, occasionally as spirits). It is always with the understanding that they are "good," in other words, that they protect human life and are the friends of the yagé drinkers. This particular passage deals with a kind of diminutive character, "dolls" as the author puts it, or protective spirits of the healers. On the other hand, there is also the polyfacetic Secoya term *Huati*, often translated as devil, but which more appropriately would be spirit. Frequently the *huati* adopts attitudes harmful to humans, for example, serving as a vehicle for witchcraft. In this sense, it will normally appear in the text as devil.

5. This name, Salmo, as it is remembered by the old Quichua Teresa Macanilla, turns into Salmón, which, safe to say, is really Salomón. The name "white" was due to his physical characteristics, to the point that Teresa describes him as a mestizo.

6. The healer-witch dichotomy is one of the main and most fervent points of this testimony. The drinker takes great care in pointing out his specialization as a healer and his rejection of the temptation of witchcraft. Nevertheless, in that he also possesses the power, as well as a higher level of knowledge, he never escapes from outside suspicions, especially if these suspicions come from enemies for whom, automatically, his power is a constant danger.

7. Different kinds of witchcraft are experienced as arrows, darts, and thorns of diverse materials that the witch throws at his victim, causing sickness or death. In the exercise described here, the master teacher teaches the initiate how to control his rage as well as the pride of feeling his own power, since both vices would be dangerous for his community. For this reason, the master teacher leads him to a superior level of knowledge where the celestial beings purify him so that he is not violent.

8. *Hua'I*, meat. The name of the *Yajé* is due to its thick bark, meat *Yajé*.

9. *Sesetuiyai*, (sese, huangana) tiger that pursues huanganas. In addition, the text contains many other names of tiger-spirits: *ya'huituyai*, tiger that pursues sajinos, *jetejequeyai*, tiger worm, etc.

10. Together with the power of curing and having access to the spirits by means of visions, high quality singing is essential

for a healer. Without it, he would not be able to direct the *Yajé* ritual which is the basis of his prestige. The importance of songs is obvious: in them, the formulas of prayer and power over spirits are expressed. At the same time, these songs were received in some vision. In addition, though the songs are substantially the same among the healers, they also require an improvisational ability on the part of the healer. Whether or not a healer is able to do this is no trivial matter. For those who participate in the *Yajé* session, the songs are all dictated to the healer by the angels themselves as a sign of their mutual harmony. But there is, of course, another explanation that reinforces the importance of that factor: the visions can be directed, led, inspired. In other words, the drug amplifies the prior thought of the experienced drinker. This explains the importance of the term "prior concentration" and also the frequent references to the healer that "guides," "teaches people to see," and "takes away bad visions," etc. In this sense, the songs confirm the authenticity of the healer's ecstasy and become the only sure guide on the hazardous road of dreams.

11. The importance of graduating while young should not be underestimated. In the first place, we have already mentioned the difficulties experienced in this process. The necessity of being bravehearted when it comes to drinking ("You were conceived a man, but you act like a woman who goes fishing instead of drinking *Yajé*.") is an indication of the moral qualities of the young man. Furthermore, the Secoyas agree that the early acquiring of *Yajé* customs makes for more and better visions.

12. All drinkers insist on this: they don't drink because of a vice (addiction), since drinking *Yajé* is unpleasant and risky. What they pursue is seeing, controlling the fatal spirits, gaining access to the realm of the celestial beings, and, finally, achieving wisdom, or, to rephrase the same idea, knowing the truth, since everything our eyes see is only appearances. According to Cornelio Ocoguaje, "If we don't drink, we don't see, we don't dream. We don't see that other world and we aren't there. We'll end up dying. I would be a disgrace." (See Wheeler, p. 274).

13. Later in the text, the name *Tsiayaquë* appears, which is confused with Ocomé. This is the same mythic character, the master of all river creatures.

14. *Mecoye'yë (meco,* electric fish; *ye'yë,* boa): although it has mythic characteristics, here it is presented in realistic terms.

15. *Jaro pejí,* baked *pejí.*

16. Vickers defines the *nuní* in the following way: a class of sacred plants with medicinal propertites. He goes on to specify five kinds of treatment based on their use (See Vickers, p. 337). But, because we are in the Secoya world, let's let one of them, Celestino Piaguaje, Fernando's nephew, explain the various qualities of the plant: "The *nuní* is an herb that grows from a tubercle. Those small subterranean pieces are the ones that the healer received in one of his visions at the hands of the angels. My Uncle Fernando takes care of that plant and he is the only one who has it. He doesn't give it to anyone either. Even if someone were to steal it from him it wouldn't have any effect since it acquires its power when it is willed by the healer. When I was a child, he gave some of those roots to my mother, but when she became an evangelical, she let them get lost. The *nuní* is used like this: the roots are extracted, washed and ground in a mill until they are a powder. Then it is mixed with a little *achiote* to paint the body of the dead. The healer only paints deceased relatives, on the head, on the arms. I saw Fernando do that in Cuyabeno with my two grandmothers: he painted two small stripes on their faces, nose, and also on their arms and feet. Sometimes one can paint others who are not relatives if one is asked. On other occasions, *nuní* is used as a curative. In this case, the roots are split over water until their juice comes out and that is what is drunk." (Personal testimony, archived in Cicame, Pompeya). Joaquina, Fernando's younger sister, spoke about this topic to her son César: *"Painuni* is the people of *nuní.* My father obtained that plant from a family that came from the Cantëya (river of *caña brava* or Putumayo, people who had conquered the sky and lived on the shores of the river of eternity). That's why my brother knows about this plant now. If you put it on the person who is dying in a hammock, the *nuni* will bring that person back to life. You put it in the tomb, but the dead person will leave to go to the big river. The people of the sky, when they see the dead person coming, will come down to the *Yajé* drinker and ask him, "Where did that person come from?", "I made him come because he's part of my family," "Well, if that's how it is, come with us." (Personal testimonies, archived in Cicama, Pompeya). If one takes into account what has been said about the possession of these plants, one understands that only the sorcerors and their families have access to them and, because of that , are assured of a happy existence in the other life. (See Ecorasa. *Ecorasa: autobiografía de un secoya.* Quito: Cicame, 1990).

17. In this moment, the vital misadventures of the healer cannot be fully understood without some notion of his mythology or religious beliefs. For those who want more information on this point, see Cipolletti. Aipe Coca. Quito" Abya-Yala, 1992. *Ñañë* (moon) is the principal god of his pantheon. During earthly life, this God was called preferentially *Paina*

(*pai*, person; *Paina* would mean something like "primordial man"). He recreated the world just as we see it today and suffered a lack of understanding on the part of the people at that time. He married the daughters of a man whom he later transformed into the first tapir (hence his name, *Huequë*, tapir). Another character, *Müjü* (thunder) was *Ñañë's* rival and wanted to steal his women, *Repao* and *Rutayo*. After a bloody fight, *Ñañë* split him in two. Afterwards, the two halves remained in the sky, the biggest one as the moon, the other as thunder-lightning. In terms of the women, his luck turned out to be divided as well. *Repao*, faithful to *Ñañë*, ascended into the sky with her husband and lives on the shore of the river with no shores (sea) *jaitsiaya*, where she receives the dead and examines them before they go to their definitive place. As for *Rutayo*, who preferred *Müjü*, *Ñañë* secluded her in the center of the earth where she continues to be a constant threat. She, as well as the mythic tapir trapped there, can dig under or sink the earth definitively.

18. This great celestial river, so wide that its shores cannot be seen, is called *jaitsiayá* (great river) or also, occasionally, *umesiaya* (hot river or river of hot beaches).

II

AYAHUASCA
CULTURAL ENCOUNTERS

Richard Spruce, a photograph taken upon his return from 15 years in the Amazon and Andes of South America. Reprinted with permission from *Richard Spruce (1817–1893) Botanist and Explorer,* The Royal Botanic Gardens, Kew.

ON SOME REMARKABLE NARCOTICS OF THE AMAZON VALLEY AND ORINOCO

Richard Spruce

In the accounts given by travelers of the festivities of the South American Indians, and of the incantations of their medicine-men, frequent mention is made of powerful drugs used to produce intoxication, or even temporary delirium. Some of these narcotics are absorbed in the form of smoke, others as, snuff, and others as drink; but with the exception of tobacco, and of the fermented drinks prepared from the grain of maize, the fruit of plantains, and the roots of Manihot utilissima, M. Aypi, and a few other plants, scarcely any of them are well made out. Having had the good fortune to see the two most famous narcotics in use, and to obtain specimens of the plants that afford them sufficiently perfect to be determined botanically, I propose to record my observations on them, made on the spot.

The first of these narcotics is afforded by a climbing plant called Caapi. It belongs to the family of Malpighiaceae, and I drew up the following brief description of it from living specimens in November 1853.

I. BANISTERIA CAAPI, Spruce
(Pl. Exsicc. No. 2712, Anno 1853)

DESCRIPTION — Woody twiner; stem thumb, swollen at joints. Leaves opposite, 6.4 x 3.3, oval acuminate, apiculato- acute, thinnish, smooth above, appresso-subpilose beneath; on a petiole 0.9 inch long. Panicle axillary, leafy. Umbels 4-flowered. Pedicels appresso-tomentose, bracteolate only at base. Calyx deeply 5-partite; segments ligulate, eglandulose, or with only rudimentary glands, appresso-tomentose. Petals 5, on longish thick claws; lamina pentagonal, fimbriate, the limbriae clavate. Stamens 10, subunequal; anthers roundish. Styles 3, subulate; stigmas capitate. Capsules muricato-cristate, prolonged on one side into a greenish-white semiobovate wing (1.7 x 0.6 inch).

HABITAT — On the river Uaupés, the Içanna, and other upper tributaries of the Rio Negro, where it is commonly planted in the roças or mandiocca-plots; also at the cataracts of the Orinoco, and on its tributaries, from the Meta upwards; and on the Napo and Pastasa and their affluents, about the eastern foot of the Equatorial Andes. Native names: Caapi, in Brazil and Venezuela; Cadana, by the Tucano Indians on the Uaupés; Aya-huasca (i.e. Dead man's vine) in Ecuador.

The lower part of the stem is the part used. A quantity of this is beaten in a mortar, with water, and sometimes with the addition of a small portion of the slender roots of the Caapi-piníma. When sufficiently triturated, it is passed through a sieve, which separates the woody fibre, and to the residue enough water is added to render it drinkable. Thus prepared, its colour is brownish-green, and its taste bitter and disagreeable.

The Use and Effects of Caapi

In November 1852, I was present, by special invitation, at a Dabocurí or Feast of Gifts, held in a mallóca or village-house called Urubú-coará (Turkey-buzzard's nest), above the first falls of the Uaupés; the village of Panuré, where I was then residing, being at the base of the same falls, and about four miles away from Urubú-coará, following the course of the river, which during that space is a continuous succession of rapids and cataracts among rocky islands. We reached the mallóca at nightfall, just as the botútos or sacred trumpets began to boom lugubriously within the margin of the forest skirting the wide space kept open and clear of weeds around the mallóca. At that sound every female outside makes a rush into the house, before the botútos emerge on the open; for to merely see one of them would be to her a sentence of death. We found about 300 people assembled, and the dances at once commenced. I need not detail the whole proceedings, for similar feasts have already been described by Mr. Wallace *(Travels on the Amazon and Rio Negro,* pp. 280 and 348). Indeed, there is such a family likeness in all the Indian festivities of Tropical America that, allowing for slight local variations, the description of one might serve for all. There is no more graphic account of a native feast than that by old Wafer, of one he saw on the Isthmus of Darien *(New Voyage and Description of the Isthmus of America,* p. 363).

In the course of the night, the young men partook of caapi five or six times, in the intervals between the dances; but only a few of them at a time, and very few drank of it twice. The cupbearer -who must be a man, for no woman can touch or taste caapi- starts at a short run from the opposite end of the house, with a small calabash containing about a teacupful of caapi in each hand, muttering "Mo- mo-mo-mo-mo" as he runs, and gradually sinking down until at last his chin nearly touches his knees, when he reaches out one of his cups to the man who stands ready to receive it, and when that is drunk off, then the other cup.

In two minutes or less after drinking it, its effects begin to be apparent. The Indian turns deadly pale, trembles in every limb, and horror is in his aspect. Suddenly contrary symptoms succeed: he bursts into a perspiration, and seems possessed with reckless fury, seizes whatever arms are at hand, his murucú, bow and arrows, or cutlass, and rushes to the doorway, where he inflicts violent blows on the ground or the doorposts, calling out all the while, "Thus would I do to mine enemy (naming him by his name) were this he!" In about ten minutes the excitement has passed off, and the Indian grows calm, but appears exhausted. Were he at home in his hut, he would sleep off the remaining fumes, but now he must shake off his drowsiness by renewing the dance.

I had gone with the full intention of experimenting the caapi on myself, but I had scarcely dispatched one cup of the nauseous beverage, which is but half a dose, when the ruler of the feast — desirous, apparently, that I should taste all his delicacies at once — came up with a woman bearing a large calabash of caxirí (mandioccabeer), of which I must needs take a copious draught, and as I knew the mode of its preparation, it was gulped down with secret loathing. Scarcely had I accomplished this feat when a large cigar, 2 feet long and as thick as the wrist, was put lighted into my hand, and etiquette demanded that I should take a few whiffs of it — I , who had never in my life smoked a cigar or a pipe of tobacco. Above all this, I must drink a large cup of palm-wine, and it will readily be understood that the effect of such a complex dose was a strong inclination to vomit, which was only overcome by lying down in a hammock and drinking a cup of coffee which the friend who accompanied me had taken the precaution to prepare beforehand.

White men who have partaken of caapi in the proper way concur in the account of their sensations under its influence. They feel alternations of cold and heat, fear and boldness. The sight is disturbed, and visions pass rapidly before the eyes, wherein everything gorgeous and magnificent they have heard or read of seems combined; and presently the scene changes to things uncouth and horrible. These are the general symptoms, and intelligent traders on the Upper Rio Negro, Uaupés, and Orinoco have all told me the same tale, merely with slight personal variations. A Brazilian friend that when he once took a full dose of caapi he saw all the marvels he had read of in the Arabian Nights pass rapidly before his eyes as in a panorama; but the final sensations and sights were horrible, as they always are.

At the feast of the Urubú-coará I learnt that caapi was cultivated in some quantity at a roça a hour's journey down the river, and I went one day to get specimens of the plant, and (if possible) to purchase a sufficient quantity of the stems to be sent to England for analysis; in both which objects I was successful. There were about a dozen well-grown plants of caapi, twining up to the tree-tops along the margin of the roça, and several smaller ones. It was fortunately in flower and young fruit, and I saw, not without surprise, it belonged to the order Malpighiaceae and genus *Banisteria,* of which I made it out to be an undescribed species, and therefore called it *Banisteria Caapi.* My surprise arose from the fact that there was no narcotic Malpighiad on record, nor indeed any species of that order with strong medicinal properties of any kind. Byrsonima — a Malpighiaceous genus that abounds in the Amazon valley- includes many species, all handsome little trees with racemes of yellow or rose-coloured flowers, followed by small edible but rather insipid drupes. their bark abounds in tannin, and is the usual material for tanning leather at Pará, as also, by the Indians, for dyeing coarse cotton garment redbrown colour. Another genus- *Bunchosia-* grows chiefly on the slopes of the Andes, at from 7000 to 9000 feet elevation, and the species are trees of humble growth, bearing large yellowish edible drupes known as *Ciruelas de fraile* (Friar's plums). In cultivation the fruits are mostly seedless, and in that state are sometimes brought for sale to Ambato and other towns. The seed is described in books as poisonous, and if it be really so, then it is the only instance, so far as I know, of the existence of any hurtful principle in the entire family of Malpighiads, always excepting that of the *Caapi*. Yet strong poisons may lurk undiscovered in many others of the order, which is very large, and (the twining species especially) of great sameness of aspect; and the closely-allied Soapworts *(Sapindaceae)* contain strong narcotic poisons, especially in the genus *Paullinia*.

I obtained a good many pieces of stem, dried them carefully, and packed them in a large box, which contained botanical specimens, and dispatched them down the river for England in March, 1853. The man who took that box and four others on in a large new boat he had built on the Uaupés, was seized for debt when about half-way down the Rio Negro, and his boat and all its contents confiscated. My boxes were thrown aside in a hut, with only the damp earth for floor, and remained there many months, when my friend Senhor Henrique Antonij, of Manáos, whom I had advised by letter of the sending-off of the boxes, heard of the mishap, and succeeded in redeeming them and getting them sent on to the port of Pará. When Mr. Bentham came to open them in England, he found the contents somewhat injured by damp and mould, and the sheets of specimens near the bottom of the boxes quite ruined. The bundle of Caapi would presumably have quite lost its virtue from the same cause, and I do not know that it was ever analyzed chemically; but some portion of it should be in the Kew Museum at this day.

Caapi is used by all the nations on the river Uaupés, some of whom speak languages differing in toto from each other, and have besides (in other respects) widely different customs. But on the Rio Negro, if it has ever been used, it has fallen into disuse; nor did I find it anywhere among nations of the true Carib stock, such as the Barrés, Banihuas, Mandauacas, etc., with the solitary exception of the Tarianas, who have intruded a little way within the river Uaupés, and have probably learnt to use caapi from their Tucáno neighbours.

When I was at the cataracts of the Orinoco, in June 1854, I again came upon Caapi, under the same name, at an encampment of the wild Guahibos, on the savannas of Maypures. These Indians not only drink the infusion, like those of the Uaupés, but also chew the dried stem, as some people do tobacco. From them I learnt that all the native dwellers on the rivers Meta, Vichada, Guaviare, Sipapo, and the intervening smaller rivers, possess caapi, and use it in precisely the same way.

In May 1857, after a sojourn of two years in the North-Eastern Peruvian Andes, I reached, by way of the river Pastasa, the great forest of Canelos, at the foot of the volcanoes Cotopaxi, Llanganati, and Tunguragua; and in the villages of Canelos and Puca-yacu-inhabited chiefly by tribes of Zaparos — I again saw *Caapi* planted. It was the identical species of the Uaupés, but under a different name, in the language of the Incas, 2 i.e. Dead man's vine. The people were nearly all away at the gold-washings, but from the Governor of Pucayacu I got an account of its properties coinciding wonderfully with what I had previously learnt in Brazil. Dr. Manuel Villavicencio, a native of Quito, who had been some years governor of the Christian settlements on the Napo, published the following year, in his *Geografía de la República del Ecuador* (New York, 1858), an interesting account of the customs of the natives of that river, and amongst others of their drinking the *aya-huasca;* but of the plant itself he could tell no more than that it was a liana or vine. The following is a summary of what I learnt at Puca-yacu and from Villavicencio of the uses and effects of the *aya-huasca* or *caapi*, as observed on the Napo and Bombonasa.

Aya-huasca is used by the Zaparos, Angutéros, Mazánes, and other tribes precisely as I saw caapi used on the Uaupés, viz. as a narcotic stimulant at their feasts. It is also drunk by the medicine-man, when called on to adjudicate in a dispute or quarrel — to give the proper answer to an embassy — to discover the plans of an enemy — to tell if strangers are coming — to ascertain if wives are unfaithful — in the case of a sick man to tell who has bewitched him, etc.

All who have partaken of it feel first vertigo; then as if they rose up into the air and were floating about. The Indians say they see beautiful lakes, woods laden with fruit, birds of brilliant plumage, etc. Soon the scene changes; they see savage beasts preparing to seize them, they can no longer hold themselves up, but fall to the ground. At this crisis the Indian wakes up and if he were not held down in his hammock by force, he would spring to his feet, seize his arms, and attack the first person who stood in his way. Then he becomes drowsy, and finally sleeps. If he be a medicine-man who has taken it, when he has slept off the fumes he recalls all the trance, and thereupon deduces the prophecy, divination, or what not required of him. Boys are not allowed to taste *ayahuasca* before they reach puberty, nor women at any age: precisely as on the Uaupés.

Villavicencio says (op. cit. p. 373): "When I have partaken of *aya-huasca,* my head has immediately begun to swim, then I have seemed to enter on an aerial voyage, wherein I thought most charming landscapes, great cities, lofty towers, beautiful parks, and other delightful things. Then all at once I found myself deserted in a forest and attacked by beasts of prey, against which I tried to defend myself. Lastly, I began to come round, but with a feeling of excessive drowsiness, headache, and sometimes general malaise."

This is all I have seen and learnt of *aya-huasca.* I regret being unable to tell what is the peculiar narcotic principle that produces such extraordinary effects. Opium and hemp are its most obvious analogues, but caapi would operate on the nervous system far more rapidly and violently than either. Some traveler who may follow my steps, with greater resources at his command, will, it is to be hoped, be able to bring away materials adequate for the complete analysis of this curious plant.

(EXCERPT FROM: Richard Spruce. *Notes of a Botanist on the Amazon and Andes.* Vol. 2. London, 1908. pp. 413–425)

A YAJÉ SESSION

Gerardo Reichel-Dolmatoff

In this chapter I shall give an account of a *Yajé* ceremony I was able to witness among the Barasana Indians of the Pira-paraná. In the description of this ceremony we shall be able to observe the variability of certain details of procedure, together with the basic pattern underlying these ritual gatherings.

I had been asked by the Indians if I wanted to take part in a *Yajé* session and I had expressed my intention of doing so. In the days that followed this conversation the matter was not mentioned again, but about a week afterward I noticed that some of the men were leaving the maloca, taking with them their hammocks and fishing gear. I gathered that they had been sent to visit several malocas in the neighborhood, perhaps a day's travel away, in order to invite guests. In fact, as the days went by several canoes arrived with men from another exogamic unit, some of them accompanied by their women and children. After lengthy ceremonial greetings the men put up their hammocks in our maloca, while their womenfolk gathered in the back, chatting with the other women, grating manioc, and taking part, after a while, in the daily tasks of food preparation.

The next day, shortly after noon, I found myself almost alone in the house. The men had gone fishing or were gathering wood, and all the women and children were down at the creek soaking the red *mirití* fruits in the water. Only three men — one whom I shall call Biá, and his two younger brothers — were sitting at the door, one of them polishing a blowgun and the others idling and drawing with their fingers in the sand. After a while Biá rose and came over to where I was sitting. "Let's go and gather *Yajé*," he said. He took up his bushknife and left the maloca.

I walked behind him and the two young men followed us, jostling and running. We went down the trail to the creek where the women were busying themselves with their baskets full of fruit. Paying no attention to them the men went by, jumping from stone to stone, crossing the water and wading through the mudbank on the opposite side of the creek. We entered the forest, and the trail was ascending now, but soon we arrived at the top of a small hill. Biá had stopped and pulled at some leafy vines that were hanging down in profusion from the trees surrounding us. He broke off a piece and chewed it for a moment; then he spit out the splinters and pulled at another vine. A shower of dry leaves and ants fell over us and the men laughed, slapping their shoulders and thighs. Now they all began to pull down the vines Biá had pointed out to them, and they cleaned off the leaves and small branches, cutting off a bundle of finger-thick stems of about arm length. We then went to another tree nearby and then to a third. Each time Biá first chewed a piece of the stem of the vines before he and the others pulled down the required quantity. "this is *guamo Yajé*," he said, showing me the stems he had taken from a height of about three meters; they were of a light-brown color and the surface of the bark had some slightly raised ridges. Other vines, taken from a height of about two meters, he called "mammal *Yajé*"; their color was brownish with light spots, and the surface was smooth. A third category was "head *Yajé*," taken at ground level, and the dark- colored stems were knotty and twisted. As far as I was able to ascertain, all three bundles of vines belonged to the same botanical species — *Banisteriopsis caapi* — but Biá insisted that they were three different kinds of *Yajé*. We now had some twenty-five stems, each about sixty centimeters in length.

It was almost four o'clock in the afternoon when we returned to the maloca. Biá cleaned the wooden trough that was lying outside near the entrance and began to break the leafless stems into smaller pieces he now threw into the trough. Then he took his club of heavy redwood and with the blunt end began to macerate the stems with heavy rhythmical blows. While continuously stamping the mass he murmured and, once in a while, broke into a chant.

Muhipu, the headman of the maloca, had taken down the painted *Yajé* vessel that had been hanging outside from a rafter, and he was cleaning it carefully, but without washing it. He also murmured and chanted, and then he went into the maloca and walked along the walls chanting and gesturing with a small torch he held in his hand. The other men had removed the hammocks, tools and baskets that had been lying about, and the women had swept the floor and were now stirring the *cashirí* beer in the large trough standing in the center, slightly to the right.

Outside, a group of men was sitting. After dipping small cylindrical roller stamps of carved wood into *genipa* juice, they painted their legs and arms. The stamps had longitudinal perforations, and with thin straws introduced as axes they could be rolled over the skin, leaving behind bands of geometrical designs. Some of the older women were there, and they painted their husband's backs and shoulders, all serious-faced and working with great care. Near the back entrance other women and some nubile girls were carefully painting their arms and breasts and dipping little sticks into the liquid paint to trace lines and dots on their faces.

Biá had been pounding the *Yajé* vines for more than one hour. He now poured cold water, about eight litres, over the shredded mass and then began to pick out some bits of woody splinters that were floating on top of the liquid. Muhipu brought a small gourd-cup with some water in it and put a few small splinters of shredded *Yajé* vine into it. He watched it closely as the water turned a cloudy white. "It is starchy! It is good!" he exclaimed; "We shall see many images!" He now put the *Yajé* vessel on the floor and brought a large circular basketry sieve. A group of men crouched in a circle and lifted up the sieve horizontally, holding it over the vessel while Muhipu filled a large gourd-cup from the trough and poured it slowly over the sieve so that the sifted liquid dripped into the vessel.

It was becoming dark now and we entered the maloca. Just inside the door the men had arranged two rows of little wooden stools, and now they began to open the large boxes containing the feather-crowns, the rattles, and the painted loincloths. Bëhpó, the oldest of the men present and the headman of the visiting party, opened a box lying before him on the floor, lifted up a large feather headdress with both hands, and put it slowly on his head. It was 6:20 p.m. He now took another feathercrown and handed it to his neighbor; then another and another. More boxes were brought, and all the men adorned themselves. They tied the large seed rattles to their right ankles and fixed others on their left elbows; they stood and walked about, fitting on belts and crowns, sometimes stamping sharply to make the rattles sound. Others were blowing shrill tunes on their flutes. It was about an hour before all the men were properly dressed.

Now they sat down in a semicircle facing the interior of the maloca, with their backs to the main door. There were twelve men, who were now talking and laughing. It was dark now and one of them lit the *turí*, the large resin-covered torch standing near the center of the room, and it began to shed an intense red light over the scene.

There was a sudden hush. Bëhpó rose and walked to the center of the semicircle. He was holding a stick rattle horizontally in both hands, the rattle pointing to the right. He shook it sharply and exclaimed: "Hö-hö!" Again he shook the thin stick, holding it before him, almost touching his thighs. Now he took the stick into his left hand, the rattle pointing downward before him and the hand high above his head. A sharp stroke with the right palm against the stick made the rattle vibrate loudly, and now he swung it in a wide circle, clockwise, the sound of the rattle filling the room. Again and again he hit the stick, letting the lower end circle, hanging from his uplifted hand. After a few minutes he changed his stance; grasping the stick in the middle with his right hand and holding it with bent elbow horizontally and pointing forward, he knocked it against his right shoulder with sharp, rapid movements. "Hö-hö!" he called again.

Now he sat down in the middle, among the other men. There was a shrill noise of flutes and whistles. A man began to play an instrument of turtle shell, rubbing the wax-colored projection of the plastron with a sawlike motion of his right palm while pressing the shell against his body with his left upper arm. The chirping, rasping noise rose rhythmically, increasing rapidly. There was no music yet, just noise, each man using some instrument as if tuning it.

There was another silence. A boy approached with a large bowl of fresh *cashirí* beer and we all drank a sip of the brew. Bëhpó now lifted up a large horn of black pottery decorated with yellow and white designs and, without rising from his stool, blew on it. The blaring sound, long-drawn like a foghorn, filled the air. As if in answer to it the other men, also without rising, stamped their feet and sounded their rattles. Now they rose and took up their positions for the first dance. They were standing in line, each man with a painted stamping tube in his left hand, the right hand resting lightly upon the shoulder of his neighbor. Again they stamped fiercely, and then they began to sing, moving forward with rapid steps and dancing toward the interior of the maloca. Encircling the first four houseposts they danced for a long while.

It was shortly after eight o'clock when Muhipu put the *Yajé* vessel in front of him and began to stir the liquid with a little rod. The rattling sound it made was a signal; the men returned to their seats, perspiring and breathing deeply. Muhipu filled two small, black gourd-cups with *Yajé* potion and, holding a cup in the hollow of each hand, began to chant rapidly: "mamamamamamamá!" he offered a cup to the man sitting next to him. He took it and, throwing back his head, drank the potion. Then he coughed and spit noisily. A young boy handed him a cup with *cashirí* and the man took a sip. After having given the second cup to the next man, Muhipu walked back and refilled the empty cups. Going back and forth, always chanting "mamamamama-mamá!" he offered a cup to each man. While drinking the potion the men grimaced and screwed up their eyes as if the draught were very bitter and nauseating. They coughed and spit; some of them shook their heads as if in disgust.

When Muhipu offered me a cup I drank it, swallowing rapidly like the others. It tasted not at all as bitter or unpleasant as people had warned me it would. My pulse was 100; I felt a slight euphoria, and after a while a fleeting drowsiness set in.

The men were boisterous now and there were shouts and laughter; they shook their rattles and looked around. From the darkness at the rear of the maloca where the women were sitting came shrill laughter. We could not see them, but once in a while, when the light flared up, one could perceive their huddled shapes in the darkness. All during this time some of the men had been playing their flutes, and the croaking, hackling noise of the turtle shell had not ceased for an instant. Again the men rose and danced, and this time the women came forward and joined them in a slow solemn dance.

At nine o'clock Bëhpó blew again into his clay horn; Muhipu stirred the potion and began to chant "mama-mamamá!" and we all had another draught. By now my pulse had dropped to 84. At 9:30 another round was presented, also preceded by the wailing sound of Bëhpó's horn. The dancers were now more animated, their voices more sonorous, their movements more precise. The man who had been playing the turtle shell was dancing alone, jumping back and forward very rapidly with closed bent legs while throwing his body backward and forward to counterbalance his violent jumps. With the right hand he stroked the turtle shell, while with the left he held a panpipe he was playing in shrill rapid notes. The other men were dancing in line with the women and were now singing more rapidly, but without raising their voices.

A quarter past ten o'clock Muhipu offered a new round of *Yajé*, the fourth. He returned to his seat and began a monotonous recital. It was very dark inside the maloca. Some of the men were sitting slumped forward, as if asleep, their heads hanging low over their chests, but their arms were moving and their hands were gesticulating. "All painted red," said the man sitting next to me. His hand pointed to the housepost in front of us, but he spoke without looking up. "All painted red; the posts, the walls, the rafters! Hoooo-the flowers, the images, the sun!" he exclaimed and then, shaking his hand over his head, he bent sideways and vomited. The others were murmuring, a singsong, a few words. Someone started to play a flute. Suddenly I felt very nauseated; I went outside and vomited violently, but I soon felt better.

Muhipu was sitting to the far left, a little apart from the others and half-facing the first row of men. He had drawn up his legs so that his chin was almost resting on his knees. He was looking before him with half-closed eyes, his lips moving rapidly while he slowly stretched out his right arm, palm downward. The flutes stopped suddenly and the men were silent. Now Muhipu's voice could be heard chanting rapidly, and his hand rose and fell in an even rhythm. Biá was sitting in front of him, his arms embracing his updrawn knees. Now both spoke rapidly, in singsong voices, without looking at each other, both motionless but for their lips and Muhipu's outstretched arm, which rose and fell with the tone of his voice. They were alternating in their recital, in different intonations, sometimes in a staccato followed by long-drawn sounds and a sharp catching of breath. The light from the torch had become dimmer and dimmer. Muhipu's voice became louder and rose sharply, again and again. Then it stopped. For a long while we sat in silence and almost complete darkness.

One of the men got up and went to light the torch again. Standing close to the smoke-blackened pole he carefully kindled the flames until its red light began to spread over the room. The men were coughing and spitting, and now they tightened the seed rattles on their ankles and rose to gather in front for the next dance. The deafening sound of the rattles filled the room as the men took up their positions once more, facing the interior of the house, stamping the floor — once, twice, three times —. "Hö!" they exclaimed; "Hö-hö!" Then they advanced and turned, singing and marking their steps with the hollow thud of the stamping tubes. The line advanced into the open space of the center. Turning around in a circle, each man with one hand on the shoulder of the one before him, they appeared again in the light, dancing slowly, round after round. The voices rose and fell, the thumping approached and receded, over and over, from light to darkness and back again into the red glow of the torch.

By now most of the men were having hallucinations. They talked about them in drowsy voices, describing what they were seeing and sometimes asking others to explain the significance of their visions. I myself had not felt the slightest effect so far; I was completely conscious of my surroundings and in control of all my actions. The general rhythm of the dance had become more and more coordinated as time went on. After the men had drunk three or four cups of *Yajé* the steps, turns and gestures had reached a precision that made the group appear to be one single organism moving in a highly controlled and precise way. The same was true for the songs; there was never a false note or an eccentric movement; song and dance had become completely fused. Moreover, the entire scene was far from being a frenetic orgy; it was extremely formalized and solemn. There was noise, but even the noise had a formal quality and was produced intentionally and at certain intervals. I noticed that during the whole night people hardly ever looked at each other, they seemed to avoid facing others and looking into their eyes. Each man talked and sang and danced, but he did not talk to a specific person, or dance with a specific partner or neighbor. Each man acted alone, but at the same time as a member of a highly organized team.

The men were resting again and there was music of flutes. One of the guests poured some vihó snuff mixed with tobacco on the palm of his hand, scooped it up with a straight bird-bone tube, and crouching before another man blew the powder into his nostrils. He then handed him the filled tube and the other man repeated the act. The exchange of snuff was very solemn, done with slow, deliberate movements. Not all of the men took snuff.

A few minutes after eleven o'clock we were served the fifth cup of *Yajé*. There followed another dance with the women, more rapid than the preceding ones and this time not accompanied by songs but by panpipes. But soon the women retired into the darkness and the men continued to dance, now running rapidly in zigzag, now in a figure eight, between the houseposts. When they sat down to rest there was jesting and laughing. "Hö-hö-hö!" the men called, and the women answered in a shrill falsetto. There was a short exchange of obscene remarks.

At midnight Muhipu served another round. By now I had developed a strong headache, and a few minutes after taking the potion I had a spell of diarrhea. Almost all the participants had suffered from the same effects and had also vomited violently. But soon after, I felt better; the headache was gone and I felt a peculiar lightness. About half an hour passed. The men were groaning and murmuring; there were sudden exclamations. Now all of them were in a trance once more.

It was very hot and still. Suddenly I saw a flash of light before me. I looked up and saw the men, the room, the red light of the torch. I let my head fall on my chest and stretched my crossed legs out before me, just like the others. There was another flash. I had the sensation that something opened before me like a huge door, and that I could see beyond it into a deep space. I saw something like red curtains catching the light somewhere. Then, suddenly colored patterns began to unfold before my eyes.

The following is a transcription of the tape-recording I made while having these visions.

I'm seeing something . . . well, like . . . it's dark, but I see something like the tail of a peacock . . . but at the same time it's like . . . everything in movement . . . like fireworks, no? Much like a . . . the background of, let's say . . . of certain Persian miniatures There's something Oriental about all this. Oh, tapestries, Tibetan tapestries. . . .

Sometimes it makes me think of . . . decorative Arabic script, some Sura of the Qu'ran. Rather in dark colors; sometimes it appears white, but more often than not it is a dark red. It passes . . . it goes . . . it is oblique in my field of vision. It moves from top left to bottom right. There is a very gentle flow. Now it is changing . . . all the colors of the spectrum, as . . . yes, undulating . . . but in some way the arches of each undulation separate and form new motifs. At the bottom it is yellow; it changes continually and then passes through all the colors of the spectrum. The motifs are . . . yes, everything is curvilinear: semicircles, shapes like hearts that are intertwined and then become flowers; suddenly, shapes like a Medusa. Sometimes there are . . . yes . . . again these effects of fireworks. But when . . . no, it isn't three dimensional . . . it's flat and fairly dark. Now it's gone. *[Some sounds of the flutes; the dancers rest now.]* Something comes from above, from the right: they are . . . it is like water from a fountain, but the light passes through the jets of water, like a rainbow. These lines cross, but they aren't lines, in fact they are interrupted by intervals. Spots, with a . . . dark center, the exterior yellow . . . then, like a flower, like ostrich feathers, curled. And again, feathers like a peacock's. Sometimes like moss; like these mosses. Now very much like fungi, like those fungi in the lens of a camera; irridescent. A flower, but with three petals . . . three . . . yes. *[The vision disappears for two minutes; the dancing starts over again.]* I am very much awake again. When I open my eyes wide open, I see the maloca, the darkness, the people; but this way, when I half close them, I again see these motifs. Sometimes they are like microphotographs of butterfly wings, or of marine corals. Sometimes the colors aren't . . . aren't pleasant. Now there are more definite motifs: arabesques, horizontal bands. Yes, just about everything comes in parallel bands, each a different color. Yet always in motion. Often in these bands there appears a kind of grid, a mesh. Centers form themselves. *[The music becomes more intense.]* The grid is relatively static, only the centers are in motion, they spin and change colors. Again . . . now this whole scheme tilts, and moves about . . . almost 45 degrees . . . but, now almost vertical *[Strong rattling.]* Now the pattern is becoming more horizontal. The bottom is almost black. Sometimes there are concentric waves that move, like very black waters in which a stone has fallen. Yes, yes, but all very symmetrical. Hardly ever is there a motif which is not symmetrical. Sometimes, like . . . ancient locks, these ancient ornate plates on the lock of a door. It is all so baroque! *[Dance with much percussion.]* A number of semicircles, like trees of some sort, dark against a lighter, almost bluish background. But it changed already! Like . . . like microphotographs of plants; like those microscopic stained sections; sometimes like from a pathology textbook. *[Some people are vomiting. All are saying that they are having hallucinations; they claim that they see the whole interior of the maloca painted in colors. But they go on dancing.]* Now there is a change on the right side . . . now . . . there is a Tibetan quality, blue Buddhas, and around them a yellow-red-blue halo or flames that end in little dots. *[The dancers rest; there is talking.]* It's like that sometimes. It isn't pleasant. Yes, it is spectacular as a color! And always this increase and decrease of shapes, of lights. They duplicate themselves . . . a circle appears, it doubles, it triples, it multiplies itself. Yes, they spin . . . everything moving very quickly. Like . . . like . . . that's it, like bubbles, transparent bubbles, those soap bubbles. And now darkness. No, I see no more. But I am feeling well. It's almost one o'clock. I have taken six cups of Yajé: pulse 84, a light headache. After the fourth cup, I vomited violently, and after the fifth I started to get diarrhea. But otherwise I'm all right. A bitter taste in my mouth, nothing more. *[About two minutes go by.]* I continue to see things. Hexagons, all like a ceiling full of hexagons, some tilted 35 degrees, and at the center of every four of them, a blue dot. It's changed, now they are small stars . . . how many there are! They come and go, come and go; that is, they approach and recede . . . Now they have almost disappeared. *[Monotonous ritual conversation beside me; virtually no music.]* Hmmm . . . like a basketry design. Ah yes, yes . . . Rouault's paintings, like stained-glass windows . . . colors . . . blots, surrounded by a thick black line. *[High-pitched sounds of flutes].* Yes . . . or large, different-colored eyes. That symmetry doesn't exist any more! These things drawing near are like bodies . . . now they are like large caterpillars, with a lot of quills and fur . . . with a little bubble at the end of each hair. But again . . . like a microphotograph. It has changed now . . . like little red hairs, is it not? But now it is changing; those little bubbles are lengthening, and now they are gone. Again . . . well, it's so difficult! Now there appears a dark red color crossed by a series of yellow rays; the center is to the right, but I can't see it. These rays fall as if on a forest of little red hairs. Everything is tilted . . . again, above to the left and below to the right. It has now changed, now . . . they are thousands and thousands of stylized palms in perspective. They are like tapestries, aren't they? They change, they change, like stylized little trees. Yes, all of that is, for the most part, like certain ties in bad taste. Yes, now it is all disappearing. I see no more.

◆ ◆ ◆

It was almost two o'clock in the morning. My vision had lasted for twenty minutes, interrupted twice by a few minutes during which I did not see anything. I had been speaking very slowly.

At 2:10 a. m. the men took another round of *Yajé*, and at 3:20 the eighth and last one. They were dancing now in almost complete darkness. Then they rested, and occasionally there were long monotonous recitals. The music never stopped completely, and the croaking noise of the turtle shell continued hour after hour.

Dawn was coming. Bëhpó slowly took the feathercrown from his head and handed it to Muhipu, saying "má" take! in a loud voice. The other men followed his example. It was exactly 6:20 a.m.; the ceremony had lasted twelve hours to the minute. Muhipu handed the different ornaments to Biá, who carefully packed them away in their boxes. The men left the maloca and gathered in the chilly air in front of the house, yawning and stretching their limbs. There was but little conversation. The men looked tired but content. After a while some of them put up their hammocks and went to sleep. The women were starting to light their hearths, but there was little food that day and few people cared to eat. Nobody complained of any unpleasant aftereffects of the potion.

I was drawing in my notebook, trying to recapture some of the images I had seen. A man who was looking over my shoulder when I was making a series of dotted lines, vertical but slightly undulating, asked a question about it, and I answered that I had seen this design last night.

"Look!" he called to the others. Several people came and gathered around me, staring at my drawing.

"What does this image mean?" I asked.

The men laughed. "It's the Milky Way," they said; "You saw the Milky Way! You were flying up with us to the Milky Way!"

(EXCERPT FROM: Gerardo Reichel-Dolmatoff. *The Shaman and the Jaguar: A Study of Narcotic Drugs Among the Indians of Colombia.* Philadelphia: Temple UP, 1975, pp. 155–167.)

YAJÉ NOSTALGIA

Scott S. Robinson

My philosopher cousin (mother's sister's son) asked me if I'd like to meet some of his botanist friends at the Peabody Museum. At the time, in the fall of '67, I had already burrowed into *The Yage Letters* while fondly remembering, as a sophomoric California undergraduate, my earnest browsing at the CITY LIGHTS BOOKSHOP, the little book's publisher, in the North Beach section of San Francisco. Beat poets and writers fathomed on altered states of consciousness. I was to meet the "steel rimmed, spectacled" botanist, as Burroughs described Richard Evans Schultes, in the flesh, on his own turf, within the creaky, wooden floored structure where Amazonian ethnobotanical taxonomies were continually revised. Jeez, I must have said to myself afterwards, this incessant collecting, querying and classifying approximates the essence of science, and I had crossed one entrance to its temple. But Schultes' graduate students made even more of an impact upon me. The late Timothy Plowman, enthralled us all with his well-told accounts of "consultations" with "medicinal plants," including yagé, while collecting specimens for his dissertation in the upper Putumayo. And I met Homer Virgil Pinkley, more timid than Plowman and recently-returned from his Smith Kline and French-funded ethnobotanical fieldwork (along with many botany graduate students of the day) among the Kofan of eastern Ecuador and the adjacent basin, north of the Río San Miguel, in southern Colombia. Homer turned the key that opened my box of mental curiosities and associated motivations. He said, in an offhanded manner: "Texaco is now opening up an oil field on the Ecuadorean side..." of the riverine border, because "they discovered, after drilling in Colombia, the major deposit is south of the San Miguel." This statement changed my life, as the ethic of salvage ethnography brought yagé shamanism to the fore.

This I recalled while nestled into the best "corner" of my chinchorro hammock, as the uncontainable yagé-inspired memory review flashed by, while Taita Salvador was chanting and "rattling" his twin leaf fronds. It was late evening, sometime in '68, and the second gourd had been offered to all, men and women, in the subdued light of the Kofan yagé house. How did I get here, on the upper River Guamués, Putumayo, Colombia? Then, the botanist Homer's words were replayed once more, the sequence of decisions and justifications that brought me this far upriver. Shocked by the implications of the reported oil development, one could foresee the rather predictable terror of the process, then well underway. The oriente and Putumayo to be revisited by an exponen-tial intensification of the new colonial order laid out by geophysical seismic crews in the rain forest. Can shamanism and energy imperialism cohabit? What of the Kofan? Salvador resumed his chanting, after a brief regurgitation, a cleansing of his *delicado* system. Of course, I remembered now how the question was crudely formulated while walking down those squeaking Peabody stairs. But it could not be posed so bluntly in polite academic discourse. Or was there any logic to what at first glance were discontinuities? Here, among the Kofan, shamanism was politics writ large, and until that moment manifestations of power were shamanic; now, how-ever, missionaries and oil companies changed the balance. And I was burdened, or so I thought, with a fancy fieldwork fellowship, a Foreign Area, as it was called, nothing to complain about, and my research project for the competition had nothing to do with the Kofan, shamanism or the oriente *ecuatoriano*. Supposedly, I was to investigate the land tenure and kinship system of the Salasaca *mitimay* community near Ambato, Tungurahua Province, in the mid-sierra of Ecuador. But I had escaped, in a fashion, and made my way to the yagé ceremony. And just what was my quest about?

Memory folded upon itself, the chanting went on, geometric forms danced about on my retinas, behind closed lids, the sexton, or *Kuraka's* helper, was pouring a fresh gourdful for Taita. Odd, no?, that the officiating shaman was respectfully called Father in Quechua. There were a few other *kokoma* or outsiders present, clustered in a corner of the men's section of the yagé house. Suddenly, the well-enunciated phrase of a highland Colombian campesino's Spanish, who queried, somewhat innocently, in the dark, *¿De dónde viene esta ayahuasca?* (Where does this ayahuasca come from?) *¿Y por qué le dicen yagé?* (And why it is called yagé?) It was a few years later, while filming the peyote pilgrimage in Mexico among the Huichol, that I realized how these simple questions could only be answered by responding, *porque es la costumbre* (because it is the custom...). Anthropologists didn't really know, nor the botanists for that matter. Imaginative human innovation in each habitat. But applied rationalism is a stubborn exercise, *pues*... Meanwhile, a third gourdful was offered to those who wished to drink some more. Taita Salvador took a second gourd across the split bamboo floor to his mother-in-law, well beyond menopause, sitting up in a stately way, her back against a post, at the other end of the yagé house, on the female side, near a gurgling stream. How could we avoid the sound of rushing water? Harner got it right from the Shuara, for the sound permeated the stillness and created a harmonic, the bass chords for the melodious polyphonic high frequency cricket concert. There had been a brief thunder shower blowing over as we filed out of the village in the golden rainbow-enhanced light that photographers prefer on a late tropical afternoon, heading to the yagé house. Set well back from the house compound, perhaps a kilometer's level walk in the virgin forest, this space was a uniquely minimal architectural testimony to the insertion of human design into the habitat.

Salvador´s father, surnamed Moreno, had been the son of a migrant paisa cauchero, born and raised in the Putumayo. Moreno senior had taken a Kofan woman as a wife and three sons were born to them. Salvador was the eldest, and I could not help musing about the link between his name and his vocation for curing. His eldest son, Lorenzo, was stricken with polio when young, and for some other mysterious reason, was nicknamed "Gringo." Gringo was seriously crippled in his right leg, but managed to hunt, with a measured gait, and pole his canoe like any other Kofan adult male; he also accompanied his father in a very respectful way, at home and on travels to other Kofan villages. Doña "Gratorina," Salvador's wife, although fluent in Kofan, was trilingual, as her Siona mother lived with them and she had also attended the Capuchin mission schools for a few years of schooling in Spanish. Two daughters completed the household crew, all of whom performed the chores to maintain what was a kind of jungle hospital whose moral community almost administered itself. Visitors, clients, patients, came from afar, sometimes from Valle, even Medellín, perhaps Bogotá, seldom from Ecuador. All were accommodated in hammocks, on sleeping mats in the corner of the raised plank-floored "living room." Impressive how desperation, tradition and word of mouth brought the sick and stricken for the cure. I couldn't imagine Ginsberg in a hammock at the yagé house, but perhaps his howling was incurable anyway. Burroughs probably got along with the patients much better, everyone telling their own story, as was wont to happen in the shaman's "clinic," before and after the yagé drinking.

Claudio Naranjo had come up the river by motor canoe, some months before. The chileno ascetic had brought some "medicina fuerte" with him. To share it, oddly enough, one had to chew on some thin, colored cardboard, something Taita and son had never done before. This river gossip was shared as we smoked some "dark tobacco," really some Guayas Gold, while sitting, looking westward, on the high banks of the upper River Guamués at dusk, perhaps the nicest time of day. And so, curious, I asked, "How was it?"

"Pinta bonita!" Salvador replies.

Acid, I thought, what else would arrive on blotter paper? Meanwhile, the sun had set behind the Andes and the conversation turned to other matters. In retrospect, it was a fitting barter for that year, '68: yagé for LSD. Nature and Culture, swapped out, one more time, perhaps, in this case, a fair trade. And the Arica Institute, an upscale NYC outfit, was to be thanked for the initiative. Naranjo had his yagé drink and left soon thereafter. The vision quest was the trade language common to all, tribal shamans, new international shamans and miscellaneous truth seekers. Did the distinction matter anymore? It probably did, but I was too confused to figure it out. Certainly, there was no fear then that the rain forest would be chopped down, or logged and burned off while the oil was pumped. Yagé forever?

Oil wells were being drilled throughtout the region, from Guamués to the Aguarico and beyond. Texaco, Gulf and, later, other companies were busy drilling in the Ecuadorean oriente and negotiating in Quito, while the lobbies of Bogotá's five star hotels were similarly filled with foreign *petroleros* and their easy to spot domestic partners, constructing the new Putumayo El Dorado fantasy and others. Post Wild West in its tacky squalor, Puerto Asís, the Putumayo River's Amazon port, easily put dusty Dodge City and Tombstone to shame. Nearby, to the southwest, across an invisible international boundary in the middle of the muddy west to east-flowing San Miguel, Lago Agrio was abuilding in 1969, Texaco Ecuador's base camp and future oil boom town bar none on the Aguarico; something special, destined to shock visiting environmentalists thirty years later. At least the Capuchins made a vain attempt to maintain a patina of decency near their mission and its schools in downtown Puerto. They were blessed that Orito was the Colombian Texaco oil camp, not far from Salvador's home, two hours by road from Puerto Asís. This was the point where the surface pipelines connecting the wells converged and the sticky crude was pumped over the Andes to the Colombian Pacific oil port near Tumbaco. Jobs for newcomers from outside the Upper Putumayo, and the homesteaders poured in, too, taking Kofan and Ingano land. It began on the Colombian side in 1966, and the process intensified as Ecuador granted more oil concessions in subsequent years. Why were the natives trampled upon? Simply because they were condemned by the postcolonial order, neither "civilized people," occupying a surveyed space, nor citizens with access to due process. Only the railroads and Hollywood were missing. Perhaps they were incarnated in other forms, short-wave radios and missionaries. Now we know the script was full of archetypes and the natives' only source of power was yagé shamanism.

The kindness and dedication of the Borman family, Wycliffe Missionaries (a.k.a. Summer Institute of Linguistics)[1] on the Aguarico at the time, would haunt my ruminations. Salvador was chanting again, a forceful swishing sound punctuating the forest night, summoning spirits, preserving his focus as well. "Hei, hei, heiii! Hei, hei, heiii . . ." A notion popped in abruptly: the Wycliffe Kofan language primers, beginning with the New Testament Book of Acts, rustically illustrated with line drawings of happy native families meeting next to the "chapel," produced icons identified as *el cielo*, heaven. And many experienced Kofan yagé drinkers referred to the final stage of visions as *como estar en el cielo* (like being in heaven). This image or experienced sensation came to one after the patterns followed by fearsome forest critters and serpents, a bountiful paradise full of health and contentment beyond the cataclysm inhabited by special humans. Both Capuchin Catholicism and Wycliffe evangelical Protestantism succeeded in painting a version of paradise beyond Christian sin that was now the idiom for translating the nirvana of the yagé hallucinogenic voyage into language the anthropologist could understand. There was never another description of the final place along the sequenced visionary trail that failed to coincide with a Christian heaven's bounty. Suddenly, the pitch would vary, almost a sign of the Taita's intense dialogue with his helpers, the yagé people. I never saw them, nor made it to heaven, but the intensity of my own visions and memory review that evening became a linchpin experience. Disconnect, reconnect, chanting, visual patterns, animals in the forest, clearing of throats, chirping tree frogs, the muffled clatter of the yagé gourd on the clay cooking pot, an intermittent Shu! Shu! Shu! of the fronds through the air. It was a moment of intense humilliation in the face of my arrogant belief that I could somehow translate an elusive common denominator of these composite series of personal visions, the Kofan and those who came for the cure. Everyone was reviewing their memories, some more intensely than others.

What the evangelicals were doing in the Amazon was always complex, a multicontoured scenario, tough to get in focus, even then. Salvador Moreno and his brother, Asael, would often speak of how one "finds" things with yagé, perhaps an enhancement of clarity, seeing something previously overlooked or manifest in low resolution. These intense memory reviews, going through my personal files, in the yagé house, would inevitably return me to this almost obsessive curiosity about the Wycliffe missionaries, almost all from the United States. I needed to "find" what they were about. Why did the gringos export missionary zeal more than other metropolitan powers? How come such a high tech solution to compulsive soul conversion? Only years later when THY WILL BE DONE was published could my hammock-inspired hallucinations about those '68 and '69 strategic players in the oil boom scenario be reconciled with a very convincing sketch of Cold War energy imperialism. There were no commies in the yagé house that I met or heard about, but these demons did populate late night conversations with some missionaries. Needless to say, for the regional Christian powers the yagé house was a place where satanic forces were unleashed. And among the Catalan Capuchins, *comunistas* were a concern as well, the object of an unfriendly historical sketch in Victor Daniel Bonilla's *Siervos de Dios y amos de indios*

(Servants of God and Masters of Indians). The friars expressed their rage by hiring a sound truck in Puerto Asís to denounce the book while creeping around town. Of course, nobody even knew the book existed before the sound truck came down the street. No doubt, some of the afflicted yagé pilgrims were listening at the "puerto," while awaiting their motor canoes' departure for the Guamués and other tributaries, both ways on the Upper Putumayo.

Taussig's inimitable "epistemic murk" may best describe the yagé experience for the unwashed. Salvador, however, was forthright about how the yagé vision sequences were his source of knowledge, *conocimiento, ver y saber* (seeing and knowing), *poder* (power). And the diagnoses for the afflictions of his visitors, as well. The rest of us were content to traipse along, a raggle taggle band of travellers on the murky visionary trail, with less intent and perhaps insensitive to the subtle forms and signals in a shaman's pouch of conscience. Nevertheless, Salvador's narrative inevitably implied a scale of purification enroute to power, of fearful tests of resolve, the breakthrough to the yagé people, *yagé a'i in* Kofan, the source of wisdom, the proper remedy for the sick visitor from afar, the apparently innocent snakebites killing the neighbors' cattle, the malevolent intentions of other shamans and even future visitors who transmitted their impending arrival. After drinking yagé a few times, it was evident my quest for "scientific truth" would await another time and place. Listening to what the *yagé* people had to offer others plus intense personal memory reviews was narrative enough. And the sense of power granted by the visual pilgrimage was contagious. Maybe this was it? Experience and ethnography warped together, a perceptual fusion that would provoke anguish, even incoherence, in academic idioms.

Berger and Luckmann refer to a "tension of consciousness" restated by Carr to mean: "an awareness of an unusual world unfolding for us alone, comprising multiple realities, each demanding its own transition, each implying its own context and complexity, and each available to us briefly." Years later, this notion is uncannily apropos of the way one feels while taking yagé . . . Understandably, this tension may be a source of shamanic power. To my regret I was unable to communicate with Salvador at this level . . . and now he was chanting forcefully again, at a much higher pitch than before. And dawn was not far off. After the last coda, he would rest a bit before the personal curing began. His short three legged stool would be set next to the afflicted's hammock, if he were male. Or he would walk across the yagé house's empty space between men and women, kneeling next to a sick woman prone on a sleeping mat. He would occasionally blow and then suck on the afflicted's body, regurgitating loudly, spitting whatever it was with gusto and relief. Everyone listened mindfully, of course.

Occasionally, a few private comments were exchanged between curer and patient, in Kofan or Spanish. The *Kuraka* never referred to the yagé a'i during the drinking ceremony, only in discreet conversations before and after.

Taita Salvador was mindful, as all shamans surely must be. Actively engaged in reading information in his environment, during normal and altered consciousness, he was also a remarkably kind and even tempered man. Was this only a skillful use of the "split brain"? Neuroscience will inevitably screen yagé drinkers, and it may be fortunate that Salvador is no longer alive to provide evidence (d. 1985). To my mind, to subject shamans to a neural monitoring scheme would be downright offensive. The afflicted and the believers, still drinking yagé to this day, somewhere in the Putumayo and elsewhere, would be the best subjects. But I cannot imagine any "experimental situation" in the yagé house, where the shared and private meanings of an evening's mental travels in a multilingual *colono* context were at best tenuous, subject to more review at the next ceremony. And Salvador, during the five times I drank with him, never would address the group and offer any prologue, prophecy or rhetorical menu for the evening's visions and proceedings. Occasionally, his helper or a visiting Kofan would chant with him, late, in the wee hours before dawn. He was in charge of his own access to the yagé people, and catalyzed, as best he could, what the rest of us were seeing. This was an intensively collective and private affair, and whence its therapeutic virtues.

Once a year Salvador would travel to the Aguarico Kofan villages, to the south in Ecuador, in February or March, at the peak of the dry season. His entourage usually consisted of "Gringo," his son, his wife and her mother. Asael Moreno and his Ecuadorean Quichua wife would accompany his brother, acting as his trustworthy yagé assistant. Yagé might be taken along in a few Colombian rum bottles. Two small canoes were portaged from a Guamués tributary for a brief stretch to the upper Quebrada Hormiga, winding south and east into the San Miguel border river, downstream from the Conejo, which was navigable to a point only a kilometer from the Aguarico. The border meant nothing until Ecuador posted an Army platoon at the mouth of the

Conejo, wisely demanding "passports" from the Kofan. Pacho Quintero, another Kofan *Kuraka,* lived along the Hormiga, and was not a friend of Salvador's. They avoided each other, and Taita Salvador judged him to be wicked, a sorcerer, one who sent evil "arrows." If somebody from Pacho's kindred were on the bank or spotted the travellers while paddling downstream or poling back up, an awkward greeting was exchanged. Once on the Aguarico, Salvador might drink yagé with kin, and his presence was noted by all. By 1968, the Wycliffe missionaries, upon the death of the presiding *Kuraka,* had suppressed yagé drinking in Dureno village, and, as a consequence, Salvador's visits were welcomed by some, nonbelievers, perhaps, in the evangelical stigmatizing of yagé. At that time besides Salvador, only Elias in Santa Rosa, upper San Miguel, and Patricio, on the Bermejo, an Ecuadorean tributary of the San Miguel, were legitimate Kofan Kurakas. But one could drink amicably with other shamans, as did the Santa Rosa people intermarried with the Cuyabeno Secoya. Shamans were visiting each other and sharing yagé, kinfolk would spend weeks at each other's villages, often from neighboring tribes, drink yagé and return home. All shamans seemed to know each other, although they did not visit often. In fact, it was customary for aging Kurakas to make a trip to say goodbye to friends and kin. I was told, years later, that Salvador had done so as well. Yagé, curing, afflicted visitors, kinship and courtship business (exogamous patrikin groups, antia), traders, hunting, fishing, and gardening, were the essence of Kofan social life. Oil and homesteaders, of course, changed this forever.

By daybreak, Salvador had completed his personal curing ceremonies among the sick visitors and kin in the yagé house. Women began packing their baskets, mobilizing hungry children for the short walk back to the compound. In the case of Salvador, he and his immediate family shared a single large household, for it was best for a Kuraka to live apart from the hurly-burly of a village with many households. The rest of us arose lethargically and wrapped our hammocks or blankets, chuchaqui from the yagé and lack of sleep, performed minimal ablutions in the adjacent stream, quietly, without the normal conversational hubbub of a Kofan morning — although this Guamués River clinic was hardly Kofan anymore. Salvador, almost sixty, looked exhausted, as well he should. He seemed pleased, at peace, indeed a sign that things went well while negotiating with the yagé people. *Ñotse, yagé*... (yagé was good), he said. The sick had been tended to, no menacing medicine was threatening us. The elder, unmarried sexton would pack up the utensils and store them in the nearby "cooking house," ready for the next *toma,* several days hence. As we filed back through the forest, I recall thinking how this motley crew seemed to share a profound sense of well being. Certainly, all this had something to do with curing and harmonious living.

This took place thirty years ago. Salvador has passed on, and, today, well-armed young Kofan are guarding extensive coca bush plantations throughout the region. Some say the guerrilla forces protect the growers, who buy the arms for their own security and constant macho skirmishing with the Colombian Army. Who's in charge? Is this how the "power of the market" translates into the new language of the Putumayo? An Aguarico Kofan *Kuraka* was threatened by one of his patients' brothers in Colombia, because his cure was allegedly ineffective. Before, I never witnessed acts of physical or verbal violence in Kofan culture. Nowadays, the oil and cocaine economies have merged, and the forests are secondary growth. The Kofan are minigrowers and field hands. All the traditional Taitas are gone. Indeed, an epoch is over, only to be revisited in our historical and ethnographic memory. Yagé has been appropriated by urban *mestizos* and a colorful entourage of new shamans. I'm almost afraid to return.

---

1. **EDITOR'S NOTE:** There is a well-known polemic surrounding the activities of the Summer Institute of Linguistics that appears in many works, including *The Storyteller* by Mario Vargas Llosa (a fragment of which appears in this anthology) and *Is God an American?: An Anthropological Perspective on the Missionary Work of the Summer Institute of Linguistics,* edited by Sören Hvakof and Peter Aaby (Copenhagen: IWGIA, 1981). Hugo Niño in *Primitivos relatos contados otra vez: héroes y mitos amazónicos* (Bogotá: Editorial Andes/Instituto Colombiano de Cultura, 1977): pp. 15–17, repeats the story that the Summer Institute of Linguistics was part of a massive espionage campaign on the part of the U. S. government to control the Amazonian population under the cover of anthropological work and to use indigenous languages as the basis of codes for secret communication during the Vietnam war.

DISCOVERING THE WAY

Michael Harner

My first prolonged fieldwork as an anthropologist took place more than two decades ago on the forested eastern slopes of the Ecuadorian Andes among the Jívaro [HEE-varo] Indians, or *Untsuri Shuar*. The Jívaro were famous at that time for their now essentially vanished practice of "head-shrinking," and for their intensive practice of shamanism, which still continues. I successfully collected a great deal of information on their culture during 1956 and 1957, but remained an outside observer of the world of the shaman.

A couple of years later, The American Museum of Natural History invited me to make a year-long expedition to the Peruvian Amazon to study the culture of the Conibo Indians of the Ucayali River region. I accepted, delighted to have an opportunity to do more research on the fascinating Upper Amazon forest cultures. That fieldwork took place in 1960 and 1961.

Two particular experiences I had among the Conibo and the Jívaro were basic to my discovering the way of the shaman in both those cultures, and I would like to share them with you. Perhaps they will convey something of the incredible hidden world open to the shamanic explorer.

I had been living for the better part of a year in a Conibo Indian village beside a remote lake off a tributary of the Rio Ucayali. My anthropological research on the culture of the Conibo had been going well, but my attempts to elicit information on their religion met with little success. The people were friendly, but reluctant to talk about the supernatural. Finally they told me that if I really wished to learn, I must take the shamans' sacred drink made from *ayahuasca*, the "soul vine." I agreed, with both curiosity and trepidation, for they warned me that the experience would be very frightening.

The next morning my friend Tomás, the kind elder of the village, went into the forest to cut the vines. Before leaving, he told me to fast: a light breakfast and no lunch. He returned midday with enough *ayahuasca* vines and leaves of the *cawa* plant to fill a fifteen gallon pot. He boiled them all afternoon, until only about a quart of dark liquid remained. This he poured into an old bottle and left it to cool until sunset, when he said we would drink it.

The Indians muzzled the dogs in the village so that they could not bark. The noise of barking dogs could drive a man who had taken *ayahuasca* mad, I was told. The children were cautioned to be quiet, and silence came over the small community with the setting of the sun.

As the brief equatorial twilight was replaced by darkness, Tomás poured about a third of the bottle into a gourd bowl and gave it to me. All the Indians were watching. I felt like Socrates amidst his Athenian compatriots, accepting the hemlock — it occurred to me that one of the alternate names people in the Peruvian Amazon gave *ayahuasca* was "the little death." I drank the potion quickly. It had a strange, slightly bitter taste. I then waited for Tomás to take his turn, but he said that he had decided not to participate after all.

They had me lie down on the bamboo platform under the great thatched roof of the communal house. The village was silent, except for the chirping of crickets and the distant calls of a howler monkey deep in the jungle.

As I stared upward into the darkness, faint lines of light appeared. They grew sharper, more intricate, and burst into brilliant colors. Sound came from far away, a sound like a waterfall, which grew stronger and stronger until it filled my ears.

Just a few minutes earlier I had been disappointed, sure that the *ayahuasca* was not going to have any effect on me. Now the sound of rushing water flooded my brain. My jaw began to feel numb, and the numbness was moving up to my temples.

Overhead the faint lines become brighter, and gradually interlaced to form a canopy resembling a geometric mosaic of stained glass. The bright violet hues formed an ever-expanding roof above me. Within this celestial cavern, I heard the sound of water grow louder and I could see dim figures engaged in shadowy movements. As my eyes seemed to adjust to the gloom, the moving scene resolved itself into something resembling a huge fun house, a supernatural carnival of demons. In the center, presiding over the activities, and looking directly at me, was a gigantic, grinning crocodilian head, from whose cavernous jaws gushed a torrential flood of water. Slowly the waters rose, and so did the canopy above them, until the scene metamorphosed into a simple duality of blue sky above and sea below. All creatures had vanished.

Then, from my position near the surface of the water, I began to see two strange boats wafting back and forth, floating through the air towards me, coming closer and closer. They slowly combined to form a single vessel with a huge dragon-headed prow, not unlike that of a Viking ship. Set amidships was a square sail. Gradually, as the boat gently floated back and forth above me, I heard a rhythmic swishing sound and saw that it was a giant galley with several hundred oars moving back and forth in cadence with the sound.

I became conscious, too, of the most beautiful singing I have ever heard in my life, high-pitched and ethereal, emanating from myriad voices on board the galley. As I looked more closely at the deck, I could make out large numbers of people with the heads of blue jays and the bodies of humans, not unlike the bird-headed gods of ancient Egyptian tomb paintings. At the same time, some energy-essence began to float from my chest up into the boat. Although I believed myself to be an atheist, I was completely certain that I was dying and that the bird-headed people had come to take my soul away on the boat. While the soul-flow continued from my chest, I was aware that the extremities of my body were growing numb.

Starting with my arms and legs, my body slowly began to feel like it was turning to solid concrete. I could not move or speak. Gradually, as the numbness closed in on my chest, toward my heart, I tried to get my mouth to ask for help, to ask the Indians for an antidote. Try as I might, however, I could not marshal my abilities sufficiently to make a word. Simultaneously, my abdomen seemed to be turning to stone, and I had to make a tremendous effort to keep my heart beating. I began to call my heart my friend, my dearest friend of all, to talk to it, to encourage it to beat with all the power remaining at my command.

I became aware of my brain. I felt — physically — that it had become compartmentalized into four separate and distinct levels. At the uppermost surface was the observer and commander, which was conscious of the condition of my body, and was responsible for the attempt to keep my heart going. It perceived, but purely as a spectator, the visions emanating from what seemed to be the nether portions of my brain. Immediately below the topmost level I felt a numbed layer, which seemed to have been put out of commission by the drug — it just wasn't there. The next level down was the source of my visions, including the soul boat.

Now I was virtually certain I was about to die. As I tried to accept my fate, an even lower portion of my brain began to transmit more visions and information. I was "told" that this new material was being presented to me because I was dying and therefore "safe" to receive these revelations. These were the secrets reserved for the dying and the dead, I was informed. I could only very dimly perceive the givers of these thoughts: giant reptilian creatures reposing sluggishly at the lowermost depths of the back of my brain, where it met the top of the spinal column. I could only vaguely see them in what seemed to be gloomy, dark depths.

Then they projected a visual scene in front of me. First they showed me the planet Earth as it was eons ago, before there was any life in it. I saw an ocean, barren land, and a bright blue sky. Then black specks dropped from the sky by the hundreds and landed in front of me on the barren landscape. I could see that the "specks" were actually large, shiny, black creatures with stubby pterodactyl-like wings and huge whale-like bodies. Their heads were not visible to me. They flopped down, utterly exhausted from their trip, resting for eons. They explained to me in a kind of thought language that they were fleeing from something out in space. They had come to the planet Earth to escape their enemy.

The creatures then showed me how they had created life on the planet in order to hide within the multitudinous forms and thus disguise their presence. Before me, the magnificence of plant and animal creation and speciation — hundreds of millions of years of activity — took place on a scale and with a vividness impossible to describe. I learned that the dragon-like creations were thus inside of all forms of life, including man.[1] They were the true masters of humanity and the entire planet, they told me. We humans were but the receptacles and servants of these creatures. For this reason they could speak to me from within myself.

These revelations, welling up from the depths of my mind, alternated with visions of the floating gallery, which had almost finished taking my soul on board. The boat with its blue-jay headed deck crew was gradually drawing away, pulling my life force along as it headed towards a large fjord flanked by barren, worn hills. I knew I had only a moment more to live. Strangely, I had no fear of the bird-headed people; they were welcome to have my soul if they could keep it. But I was afraid that somehow my soul might not remain on the horizontal plane of the fjord but might, through processes unknown but felt and dreaded, be acquired or re-acquired by the dragon-like denizens of the depths.

I suddenly felt my distinctive humanness, the contrast between my species and the ancient reptilian ancestors. I began to struggle against returning to the ancient ones, who were beginning to feel increasingly alien and possibly evil. Each heartbeat was a major undertaking. I turned to human help.

With an unimaginable last effort, I barely managed to utter one word to the Indians: "Medicine!" I saw them rushing around to make an antidote, and I knew they could not prepare it in time. I needed a guardian who could defeat dragons, and I frantically tried to conjure up a powerful being to protect me against the alien reptilian creatures. One appeared before me; and at that moment the Indians forced my mouth open and poured the antidote into me. Gradually, the dragons disappeared back in the lower depths; the soul boat and the fjord were no more. I relaxed with relief.

The antidote radically eased my condition, but it did not prevent me from having many additional visions of a more superficial nature. These were manageable and enjoyable. I made fabulous journeys at will through distant regions, even out into the Galaxy; created incredible architecture; and employed sardonically grinning demons to realize my fantasies. Often I found myself laughing aloud at the incongruities of my adventures.

Finally, I slept.

Rays of sunlight were piercing the holes in the palm-thatched roof when I awoke. I was still lying on the bamboo platform, and I heard the normal, morning sounds all around me: the Indians conversing, babies crying, and a rooster crowing. I was surprised to discover that I felt refreshed and peaceful. As I lay there looking up at the beautiful woven pattern of the roof, the memories of the previous night drifted across my mind. I momentarily stopped myself from remembering more in order to get my tape recorder from a duffle bag. As I dug into the bag, several of the Indians greeted me, smiling. An old woman, Tomás' wife, gave me a bowl of fish and plantain soup for breakfast. It tasted extraordinarily good. Then I went back to the platform, eager to put my night's experience on tape before I forgot anything.

The work of recall went easily except for one portion of the trance that I could not remember. It remained blank, as though a tape had been erased. I struggled for hours to remember what had happened in that part of the experience, and I virtually wrestled it back into my consciousness. The recalcitrant material turned out to be the communication from the dragon-like creatures, including the revelation of their role in the evolution of life on this planet and their innate domination of living matter, including man. I was highly excited at rediscovering this material, and could not help but feel that I was not supposed to be able to bring it back from the nether regions of the mind.

I even had a peculiar sense of fear for my safety, because I now possessed a secret that the creatures had indicated was only intended for the dying. I immediately decided to share this knowledge with others so that the "secret" would not reside in me alone, and my life would not be in jeopardy. I put my outboard motor on a dugout canoe and left for an American evangelist mission station nearby. I arrived about noon.

The couple at the mission, Bob and Millie, were a cut above the average evangelists sent from the United States: hospitable, humorous, and compassionate. I told them my story. When I described the reptile with water gushing out of his mouth, they exchanged glances, reached for their Bible, and read to me the following line from Chapter 12 in the Book of Revelation:

And the serpent cast out of his mouth water as a floor . . .

They explained to me that the word "serpent" was synonymous in the Bible with the words "dragon" and "Satan." I went on with my narrative. When I came to the part about the dragon-like creatures fleeing an enemy somewhere beyond the Earth and landing here to hide from their pursuers, Bob and Millie became excited and again read me more from the same passage in the Book of Revelation:

> And there was a war in heaven: Michael and his angels fought against the dragon; and the dragon fought and his angels. And prevailed not; neither was their place found any more in heaven. And the great dragon was cast out, that old serpent, called the Devil, and Satan, which deceiveth the whole world: he was cast out into the earth, and his angels with him.

I listened with surprise and wonder. The missionaries, in turn, seemed to be awed by the fact that an atheistic anthropologist, by taking the drink of the "witch doctors," could apparently have revealed to him some of the same holy material in the Book of Revelation. When I had finished my account, I was relieved to have shared my new knowledge, but I was also exhausted. I fell asleep on the missionaries' bed, leaving them to continue their discussion of the experience.

That evening, as I returned to the village in my canoe, my head began to throb in rhythm with the noise of the outboard motor; I thought I was going mad; I had to stick my fingers in my ears to avoid the sensation. I slept well, but the next day I noticed a numbness or pressure in my head.

I was now eager to solicit a professional opinion from the most supernaturally knowledgeable of the Indians, a blind shaman who had made many excursions into the spirit world with the aid of the *ayahuasca* drink. It seemed only proper that a blind man might be able to be my guide to the world of darkness.

I went to his hut, taking my notebook with me, and described my visions to him segment by segment. At first I told him only the highlights; thus, when I came to the dragon-creatures, I skipped their arrival from space and only said, "There were these giant black animals, something like great bats, longer than the length of the house, who said that they were the true masters of the world." There is no word for dragon in Conibo, so "giant bat" was the closest I could come to describe what I had seen.

He stared up toward me with his sightless eyes, and said with a grin, "Oh, they're always saying that. But they are only the Masters of Outer Darkness."

He waved his hand casually toward the sky. I felt a chill along the lower part of my spine, for I had not yet told him that I had seen them, in my trance, coming from outer space.

I was stunned. What I had experienced was already familiar to this barefoot, blind shaman. Known to him from his own explorations of the same hidden world into which I had ventured. From that moment on I decided to learn everything I could about shamanism.

And there was something more that encouraged me in my new quest. After I recounted my entire experience, he told me that he did not know of anyone who had encountered and learned so much on his first *ayahuasca* journey.

"You can surely be a master shaman," he said.

(EXCERPT FROM: Michael Harner. *The Way of the Shaman: A Guide to Power and Healing.* New York: Bantam, 1982, pp. 1–9.)

NOTE

1. In retrospect one could say they were almost like DNA, although at that time, 1961, I knew nothing of DNA. EDITOR'S NOTE: On this issue see Jeremy Narby *Le Serpent Cosmique: l'ADN et les origines du savoir.* Paris: Terra Magna, 1995.

THE SPEARS OF TWILIGHT:
Life and Death in the Amazon Jungle
(excerpt)

Philippe Descola

Mukuimp was waiting for me at the door and whispered, "Tomorrow, come and see our cinema!" Seeing my bewilderment, he added, "Tomorrow we'll be drinking *natem* at your *amik's* house."

Now, daylight is rapidly fading and, while over there near the landing-strip Don Jaime is preparing for his second cinema show, we are gathered in Wajar's house, waiting for Mukuimp to bring the *natem*. *Natem* is the name that the Jivaro tribes give to a hallucinogenic beverage known throughout much of Amazonia by a variety of native names (*ayahuasca* in Ecuador and Peru, *caapi* along the middle reaches of the Amazon, *yagé* from Colombia to the Orinoco, etc.). It is concocted from certain wild lianas of the *Banisteriopsis* genus. The Achuar have acclimatized several species to their gardens and the two principal ones, *natem (Banisteriopsis caapi)* and *yaji* (probably *Banisteriopsis rusbyana),* are regularly used by shamans and others who, on particular occasions, wish to be transported to the part of the world that is ordinarily invisible. Its preparation is so simple that anyone could make it: the lianas are cut into several sections, pounded with a pestle and tidily arranged in the bottom of a large cooking pot. At this stage the *yaji* leaves are added, then covered with a second layer of *natem* stems. The whole thing must simmer for at least three hours until a viscous, brownish liquid is produced.

To tell the truth, Mukuimp's invitation is not entirely spontaneous. He is the only shaman in Capahuari, although he does not have the august appearance once would imagine to be associated with such a figure. He looks like an overgrown urchin and is slow in his movements to the point of clumsiness, but his eyes sparkle with irony and he always has a ready quip, possibly to disguise his secret sorrow: an eighth daughter has just been born to him and he still has no son. Mukuimp has been disinclined to talk to me about his function, partly on account of the virulent disapproval expressed on the subject of *natem* and shamanism by the evangelist missionaries, whose sentiments he naturally imagined to be shared by all Whites. To overcome his reluctance I thought it judicious to tell him that such practices were extremely common where I came from and that I myself was very familiar with them. Mukuimp then declared that, to learn of the powers that he possessed, I would have to "become drunk on *natem.*" But he was worried that I might not be up to it, that it might prove too much for me and that "my brother from France" would come to take revenge on him for my death. In order to plumb the mysteries of Achuar shamanism, I was thus led to compound my earlier bragging: already knowing something of the aims and effects of taking *natem* from my reading of ethnological literature, I went on to boast that I would come through the trial without difficulty. When Mukuimp asked me if I would be willing to sing during my trance, I said I would be happy to do so, despite my lack of musical talent; and this seemed to overcome his misgivings. Now the whole of Capahuari was buzzing with the rumour that this evening I was going "to sing" in Wajari's house. Personally, I could not see what all the excitement was about.

At nightfall Mukuimp arrives with a pot of *natem* and a *tsayantar*, a kind of mouth bow made from a reed strung with opossum gut which one gets to vibrate in one's mouth, rather like a Jew's harp. With him is Piniantza with his *arawir*, a viol with two strings, played with a bow, which seems distantly inspired by the European violin. So they are not counting on my gifts alone to bring cheer to the evening!

Without standing on ceremony, Wajari, Mukuimp, Piniantza and I each drink about half a coffee-cupful of *natem*, then rinse out our mouths with hot water. A little way away, in the company of the other women, Anne

Christine is in charge of the tape-recorder. For a minute or two I struggle against violent nausea, for the decoction is horribly bitter. The bitterness is said to be the sign of its strength, as with other substances classed as "strong," such as curare, tobacco, fishing poison and stramonium.

We settle ourselves comfortably beneath the projecting roof of the house, overlooking the Kapawi from which a lazy mist is rising, just enough to blur the leafiness of the opposite bank, bathed in the light of the full moon. Mukuimp and Piniantza begin to play their respective instruments, not exactly keeping together, it seems to me, but with quite similar effects. The initial rather irritating impression of a colony of frantic hornets circling round and round inside a bottle to the accompaniment of a cheap fiddle eventually gives way to a more subtle harmony. Hanging on the music, time seems to be dilating in rhythm with some immense organism, as if the entire forest is peacefully breathing on a continuous bass note. Meanwhile my shuddering body gradually takes off on the wings of the drug in motionless yet ever-widening spirals. Independent of my limbs, which have become heavy and cumbersome, I open up to the world and pour myself into it. I am both the source and the receptacle of a thousand sensations at once piercing yet indistinct, my only memory of my physical identity expressed in an involuntary clenching of my jaws. On the crest of this extravagant magma, my spirit floats with total lucidity.

When Mukuimp invites me to sing, it is with no inhibitions at all and a comic gravity that I launch into a few couplets from Jacques Brel, followed by one or two blues that come to mind. The narcotics produce a miracle! My performance is greeted with appreciative comments and deemed to consist of true *natem* songs. But soon my intoxication takes a new turn. Against the serene glow of the night phosphorescent circles begin to whirl, then merge and separate, forming constantly changing kaleidoscopic designs. One after another all the symmetrical patterns invented by nature pass before me in a subtle continuum: lozenges first red, then yellow, then indigo, delicate traceries, crystalline prisms, iridescent scales, the eyes of butterfly wings, feline pelt markings, reticular carapaces. Animal forms of unrecognized species display their metamorphoses and transformations before my eyes: the water-marked skin of the anaconda merges into tortoise-shell scales that elongate into the stripes of an armadillo, then reshape into the crest of an iguana against the intense blue of the wings of a *Morpho* butterfly, then stretch into black stripes which immediately fragment into a constellation of haloes standing out against the silky fur of some large cat. Curiously enough, these unanchored visions do not obscure the still landscape that frames them. It is rather as though I were looking at them through the lens of a microscope operating as a window of variable dimensions set in the middle of my usual and unchanged field of vision.

I can hear everything going on around me with unaccustomed clarity yet cannot separate out the immediate background sounds: the murmur of the river, the continuous chirping of insects, the croaking of frogs and the conversation of my companions all hum in my ears with equal intensity. Mukuimp and Piniantza are animatedly discussing shamanistic darts, Iwianch spirits, *pasuk* and *supai*, but my wandering attention prevents me from registering more than a few disjointed words from their conversation. Mukuimp is panting noisily and continuously, smacking his lips as though blowing darts through an imaginary blowpipe. The detachment with which I am living through this experience is increased by my apparent sensation of a double consciousness of the world. I am a benevolent spectator watching my own delirium, observing the changes in my sensibilities with as much curiosity as external events. It is not so much a dissociation of the physical and mental — if such a thing be possible outside Cartesian metaphysics — rather an agreeable fragmentation of the body, in which every element has become autonomous and seems to be endowed with an intelligence of its own, offering a series of different points of view on the dismembered composition from which it has emerged.

I am, as can be imagined, quite incapable of questioning Mukuimp as to the delicate points of doctrine that our shared trance is supposed to encourage him to reveal. Nevertheless, my mind is clear enough to meditate as it will upon the parallels between my second state and what I already know of the "voyage" of shamans. It seems likely that the strange beings, monstrous spirits and animals in a perpetual state of metamorphosis that throng their visions — but have not yet visited me — appear to them like a succession of temporarily coagulated forms against a moving background composed of the geometric patterns whose strange beauty I am now experiencing. Rather like the figures used in Gestalt to demonstrate perceptive illusions, the brightly coloured hallucinations induced by *natem* lend themselves to the "recognition" of animated beings with codified aspects, which must seem all the more realistic, their fantastic appearances notwithstanding, in that they borrow a vibrant uniform from the background against which they stand out. This explains how it is that the images of iridescent scales, dappled fur or luminous filaments can, through a kind of visual metonymy, turn into frameworks that support incarnations of the animal spirits — the anaconda, the jaguar, the spider — that the shamans use as their assistants. The state of my body, shattered into a thousand pieces, and the persistent feeling of being a stranger to myself also meanwhile allow a few scraps of erudition to float to the surface of my memory: the voyage of the shaman's soul, which leaves behind its corporeal envelope in order to communicate unencumbered with the beings assisting it, is a feature of all forms of shamanism, even in the absence of hallucinogenics. I am now in a position to assess the extent to which their use facilitates this feat.

Mukuimp and Piniantza invite me for a bathe. I glide along to the Kapawi like a ghost in the moonlight, conscious of the infinite softness of the mud into which my bare feet are sinking. Light wisps of mist float on the surface of the river. The water is deliciously cool after the warmth of the night, but I do not feel as though I am passing from one element into another, for the water's immaterial fluidity is so much like the air. A whispering seems to rise from the Kapawi, now loud, now barely audible, now modulated, now indistinct. Gravely Mukuimp bids me, "Listen to the fishes singing, and learn." It is really the only lesson that the evening has taught me.

TRANSLATED FROM the French by Janet Lloyd

(EXCERPT FROM: Philippe Descola. *The Spears of Twilight: Life and Death in the Amazon Jungle.* New York: The New Press/Harper Collins, 1996, pp. 205–209.)

ONE RIVER:
Explorations and Discoveries in the Amazon Rain Forest
(excerpt)

Wade Davis

When we returned to San Miguel, I casually mentioned to Pacho that I would like one day to drink *yagé*. Nothing more was said, and for several days we continued our work in the forest, collecting for the most part along the Caño Colorado, a beautiful stream overhung with dense vegetation. Then one evening not long after sunset, Rufino asked me if I was interested in taking *yagé*. Evidently his father had prepared it earlier in the day during our absence. I accepted the offer happily and without concern. In the Vaupés the potion is always a simple infusion made by pounding the liana and soaking the shredded stems in cold water. Admixtures are used, but the combination is not boiled and concentrated. The result is a milder brew, at least by reputation.

We were sitting on four small wooden stools placed around the men's circle in the *maloca*. Rufino, like his father Pedro, was wearing a guayuco, as was Pacho. All three had carefully decorated their bodies, tracing lines of red and black dye on their faces and painting their legs with small wooden rollers that left geometric patterns on the skin. Each wore a seed anklet and a simple headdress — a corona of green and yellow parrot feathers, tufts of eagle down, and a long tail feather taken from a scarlet macaw. In the center of the circle was a large red ceramic vessel with swirling designs around the rim. Inside was a frothy liquid. Near the base of the pot were rattles, panpipes, and other musical instruments made from turtle shells and deer skulls. The men had already danced shoulder to shoulder in a line, singing as they circled the pillars of the longhouse. Now they waited quietly. The women and children had long since retired, and the only light came from a resin torch burning at the base of one of the house posts.

Rufino's father stood up and began a solemn chant. When it was over, he dipped a black calabash into the *yagé* and passed it to his son. Rufino grimaced as he drank the potion, as did we all. The taste was bitter and nauseating. There followed more singing and dancing, high tremulous voices and the sound of rattles and anklets. Then there was a hush of expectation as Pedro prepared the next allotment of the brew. It was after the fourth round of *yagé* that I realized the Barasana made up in quantity what their preparation lacked in potency. I had not seen it made, but I knew from Rufino that it included, in addition to the basic liana, the leaves of a plant known as *oco-Yajé,* or water *yagé*. This was almost certainly the vine *Diplopterys cabrerana,* a tryptamine-containing admixture used throughout the Northwest Amazon to enhance the brilliance of the visions. Schultes had collected it twice in 1952 — once on the Popeyacá and again among the Barasana on the Caño Timiña. Tryptamines are soluble in cold water, and from the number of leaves in his father's recipe, I gathered from Rufino that we were in for quite a ride.

I sat quietly among them, unable to participate yet conscious of the power and authority of their ritual. The plant took them first. In soft murmurs Rufino spoke of a red sun, a red sky, a red rain falling over the forest. Nausea came quickly and he vomited. Immediately his father offered another draft of *yagé* which he took, spitting and gasping. Until then I had felt nothing, but the sound of his retching caused me to turn aside and throw up in the dirt. Pacho laughed and then did the same. We all took more *yagé*, several more cycles. An hour or more passed. I looked up and saw the edges of the world soften and felt a resonance coming from beyond the sky, like an intimation of a hovering wind pulsating with energy.

At first it was pleasant, a wondrous sense of life and warmth enveloping all things. But then the sensations intensified, became charged with a strange current, and the air itself took on a metallic density. Soon the world as I knew it no longer existed. Reality was not distorted, it was dissolved as the terror of another dimension swept over the senses. The beauty of colors, the endless patterns of orblike brilliance were as rain falling away from my skin. I caught myself and looked up, saw Rufino and Pacho gently swaying and moaning. There were rainbows trapped inside their feathers. In their hair were weeping flowers and trees attempting to soar into the clouds. Leaves fell from the branches with great howling sounds. The sky opened. There was a livid scar across the heavens, stars throbbing, a great wind scattering everything in its path. Then the ground opened. Snakes encircled the posts of the *maloca* and slipped away into the earth. One could not escape. The rivers unfolded like the mouths of blossoms. Movement became penetration. Then the terror grew stronger. Death hovered all around. Ravenous children and animals of every shape and form lay sick and dying of thirst, their nostrils plunged into the dry earth. Their flanks lay bare and exposed, and all around rose a canopy of immense sorrows.

I tried to shake away the forms from the luminous sensations. Instead, my thoughts themselves turned into visions, not of things or places but of an entire dimension that in the moment not only seemed real, but absolute. This was the actual world, and what I had known until then was a crude and opaque facsimile. I looked up and saw my companions. Rufino and Pacho sat quietly, heads down, hunched around a fire that had not been there before. Rufino's father stood apart, arms outspread as he sang. His face was upturned, and his feathered corona shone like the sun. His eyes were brilliant, radiant, feverish, as if focused into the very nature of things.

Slowly, as the night moved forward, the colors softened and the terror receded. I felt my hands running over the dirt floor of the *maloca,* saw dust tinged with green light, heard the voices of women laughing. Dawn was coming. I could hear it in the forest. My companions still remained by the hearth, but the fire had died and the air was cold. I stood and stretched my muscles. Tired but no longer afraid, I slipped into my hammock. For the longest time I lay awake, wrapped in a cotton blanket, like a drained child sweating out the end of a fever. The last thing I saw before drifting off to sleep was a placid cloud of violet light softly descend on the *maloca.*

Some hours later I was awakened by the roar of an airplane passing just over the roof of the longhouse. I looked up and saw narrow shafts of light cutting through the thatch. My head ached and I wanted to drink, but other than that I was fine. I felt clean, as if my body had been washed inside and out. Sitting up, I found myself surrounded by young boys; they followed me outside into the sunlight and down the path that led to the river. The water was cool and refreshing, delicious to drink. There was a shout, and one of the boys pointed to the riverbank. It was the missionary pilot. Beside him stood Rufino and his father. They had packed away their regalia, but their legs still bore decorative motifs, and black dye was smeared across their faces. The pilot had his hands on his hips.

"Gone native, have we?" he called out. "I wouldn't touch that water if I was you."

"You're early," I said.

"Actually, I'm two days late."

"Oh."

"Well, come on, then. I don't have all day. I have to be in Miraflores by noon."

It made for an awkward departure. I gathered my gear and specimens, left what remained of the trade goods with Rufino, and within twenty minutes was airborne, soaring above the *maloca* and over the forest toward Mitú. The sudden shift in perspective was startling. The streams fell behind, grew into rivers, and the rivers spread like serpents through a silent and unchanging forest. Rufino had likened *yagé* to a river, a journey that takes one above the land and below the water, to the most remote reaches of the earth, where the animal masters live and lightning is waiting to be born. To drink *yagé*, Reichel-Dolmatoff wrote, is to return to the cosmic uterus and be reborn. It is to tear through the placenta of ordinary perception and enter realms where death can be known and life traced through sensation to the primordial source of all existence. When shamans speak of facing down the jaguar, it is because they really do.

(EXCERPT FROM: Wade Davis. *One River: Explorations and Discoveries in the Amazon Rain Forest.* New York: Simon & Schuster, 1996, pp. 487–490.)

JAGUAR-BECOMING

William Torres C.[1]

The entheogen possesses the body, making it an epidemic in jaguar-potency.[2] The jaguar- potency in the *yagé*-inebriation disorganizes the body to activate the becoming. The invocation is necessary. To invoke is to potentiate the event in the word. It is not *any* word that invokes the force's presence and the ally's potency. The invoking word is esoteric: mentioning it touches the allied presence, making it present. The allied potency has chosen and touched the initiate as soon as it has chosen him or her. The shaman has indicated to the initiate how to find him or herself with the allied potency, invoking it in the *yagé*-inebriation. The *yagé*-inebriation propitiates the invocation of the allied potency in the word that is appropriate for becoming. It is a word that flows toward the dimension of potency in order to activate it in the instant of naming it. Herein lies the force of invocation. Its force is potency's will. To invoke the jaguar-becoming is to invoke that will of potency to become.

The entheogen-inebriation of the jaguar-becoming is activated and potentiated in the propitiatory music. The ritual percussion of the drum activates the body's disorganic quality to bring about the becoming. In a *yagé* session,[3] a woman plays the drum. She is an ally, an accomplice. As she plays the drum, I see how her body is transfigured, how it turns into a North American indigenous woman. Her complexion is now copper-colored. She has long hair gathered in a braid that hangs down her back. The percussion vibrates in colors: purple, red, violet, blue, and green. Brilliant and vibrant colors from the percussion that become an undulating serpent. This percussion pounds in my lower abdomen, in the vital point below the navel,[4] and the serpent that the colors of the percussion have become flows, rippling toward this place. It coils in my lower abdomen, undulating in the percussion. The serpent stretches out from my belly, parallel to my body, and, when it reaches the height of my forehead, becomes an Indian woman's arm with its copper-colored skin. The hand is in front of my face. It simulates the form of a serpent's head, seen from the side, vertically. The palm of the hand cannot be seen since it is facing forward and not to the side. In front of me, I see the opening between the thumb and forefinger. Between them, in that opening, there is a vibrating of clear and brilliant light that is prolonged into a beam that touches my forehead. It is located just above my eyes. The hand disappears, and from the light that is on my forehead, with the same elongated oval form that flowed from the opening between thumb and forefinger, a beam of colored light flows again. The same colors that move like a serpent from the drum's vibrations now flow in a serpentine way from my forehead and the beam of light deposited on it. The serpent flows from the beam of light on my forehead and coils. Now it is a small disk, a mosaic of stained glass made of pieces of the same colors. This small disk-mosaic-stained glass window is configured in a little cylindrical box in a mosaic-stained glass window with the same colors as the disk-serpent. Bursting from the inside of the edge, in the opening of the little box, are the jaws of a jaguar whose teeth are mounted upright on the edge of the little box. It is a jaguar-mandala. The jaguar-fangs shine in the diamond intensity. The diamond-shining of one of them is intense and flows to meet the forefinger and thumb opening of the Indian woman's hand that appears again, right there, and from there flows again toward my forehead. This time it is a jaguar-fang that flows toward my forehead and is incrusted in it, upright, at a point between my eyes. The hand disappears again. The little box-mandala-jaguar jaws-serpent's body uncoils and the serpent again undulates in its coloring. From the jaws of this serpent, from its breath, a jaguar flows. At the point on my forehead where the jaguar-fang is incrusted, the jaguar-eye-fang is activated in the intense shining of diamond-ivory. The intense shining traces a design on my face. Extending down from the upper tip of the jaguar-fang incrusted in my forehead, over my nose and mouth and ending at my chin, there is an ivory-colored diamond. The jaguar that flowed from the serpent's jaws turns its face toward me. Its face is an immense gold mask. The mask looks at me, opening and closing its jaws. I hear an imperative voice that commands, "Grab it! Put it on!" And at the same moment another, gentler, voice says, "Be careful! This is for demonstration purposes only." I pay attention to the second voice and I see the mask that is being shown to me with the jaguar-eye-fang.[5] Now there are many jaguar heads with open jaws in which shining fangs dazzle. There are many jaguars foraging around me. The gold mask, covered with jaguar-skin, approaches, gets very close to me. I ask it if I can take one of its fangs for a necklace. My torso is naked. My body is levitating and approaches its open jaws. It's a very large jaguar head. It buries its upper fangs in my chest. I feel no pain. The fangs remain buried from one side to the other, from the sternum to above my nipples. I see how, inside my body, they spin to burst from my body points first and then how they piece themselves together as a necklace of jaguar-fangs in many concentric circles, covering my entire chest and stomach. There are concentric circles of jaguar-fangs from the edge of my neck. The drum has not ceased vibrating. Its percussion pounds in my stomach. I pick up one of the maracas that ends in a tuft of condor feathers[6] and I sing the jaguar-song:

Janayari, janayari
Unao janayari
Juipa janayari
Caapi janayari
Beiji janayari
Indihuasca janayari
Curihuasca janayari
Ayahuasca janayari
Janayari, janayari
Unao mo komeki janayari
Unao mo nikai igai janayari
Unao mo jifaide janayari
Juipa mo komeki janayari
Juipa mo nikai igai janayari
Juipa mo jifaide janayari
Caapi mo komeki janayari
Caapi mo nikai igai janayari
Caapi mo jifaide janayari
Beiji mo komeki janayari
Beiji mo nikai igai janayari
Beiji mo jifaide janayari
Indihuasca mo komeki janayari
Indihuasca mo nikai igai janayari
Indihuasca mo jifaide janayari
Carihuasca mo komeki janayari
Carihuasca mo jifaide janayari
Ayahuasca mo komeki janayari
Ayahuasca mo nikai igai janayari
Ayahuasca mo jifaide janayari
Janayari, janayari

Rafue nai janayari
Makabaite Kai mo
Mooma, Mokani
Kuwei, Furnamilani
Matsuludani, Tsmani
Hate Tse
Janayari, janayari
Yai janayari
Navi janayari
Seikunuma janayari
Makokonewütjü janayari
Makokoneute janayari
Munüani janayari
Navigaka janayari
Wamani janayari
Jitinayubena janayari
Tserelepiele janayari
Arara janayari
Kuyodo janayari
Kuraya janayari
Pan janayari
Janayari, janayari, janayari
Unao janayari
Juipa janayari
Caapi janayari
Beiji janayari
Indihuasca janayari
Curihuasca janayari
Ayahuasca janayari

The *yagé* session is being directed by Taita Martín Agreda. While the woman who is my friend played the drum, he was singing, and now the drum was accompanying us in the song that was Taita's and mine . . . With the fourth round of *yagé*-drinking, my body is activated in jaguar-becoming. I already have been made epidemic and contagion. A luminous vibrant intensity possesses the body, which is a soft yellow color with dark spots. The body perceives itself as pigment in that luminous vibrant intensity. Many jaguar-heads and many jaguars are around me. Their color vibrates and impregnates my body. A great yawn emerges from my belly at the point where the drum pounds. The yawn irrupts, opening my mouth into immense jaguar-jaws. I perceive the jaguar-fangs in my open jaws. The yawn emerges in opening-sound-of-jaguar-jaws. At the same time, the jaguar that accompanies me has made the same movement with its own jaws.[7] The two of us, the jaguar and the body that becomes jaguar, carry out gestures of complicity, warrior-gestures. Other jaguars pass rapidly, some to one side, some to the other. It is the same jaguar ready to pounce quickly, backward or forward, with the intensity of a single backward-forward movement, like Aion movement.[8] Aion is the movement of becoming. I invoke Mokokonewütjü, mokokoneute,[9] the two-headed jaguar: backward-forward, and at that moment I see the speed of a forward-backward-jaguar-pounce and it carries me off in its aion speed. All space vibrates around me in vibrating-jaguar-luminosity. Another immense yawn-opening-jaguar-jaws-sound impels me to sing: *makokonewütjü makokoneute janayari mo komeki:* "In-two- headed-jaguar-potency," vibrates the yawn-roar. I perceive the serpent-movement in my spinal column. My hands and feet are activated in feline movement. A slow speed passes my body along the roof and the walls of the instance, quicker and quicker, until reaching a speed at which it is no longer necessary to support myself on my extremities because the impulse drives my body at a line of speed that flows in the air. The body, stretched out and suspended at the speed of an infinite pounce, experiences flying, which brings about this written piece on the speaking event.

At the beginning of the session, I had asked the *yagé* to grant me the ability to write on jaguar-becoming. During the jaguar-flying, during the infinite aion pounce, I perceive this trace of *haecceidades.*[10] We consider these bringings about and inter-bringings about in a cartography of this jaguar-becoming. It is not about *the* cartography of jaguar-becoming, but of a jaguar- becoming-cartography experienced in this investigation. A cartography is defined by its longitude and latitude. "The latitude is composed of intensive parts under a capacity, in the same way that longitude is composed of extensive parts under a relation."[11] The longitude and latitude of a body constitute the etiology of its becoming. Between them, the *haecceidades* of bringings about and inter-bringings about are activated.

There is a pre-existing incorporeal jaguar-potency that has its own name: *janayari (jana:* mysterious, *yari:* wild beast; "mysterious wild beast."— Witoto language, Colombian Amazon), in the enunciation *rafue (ra:* thing, *fue:* mouth; "thing that passes through the mouth," "word-knowing," "shamanistic word": enunciation of naming in Witoto shamanistic discursivity).[12] This pre-existing jaguar-potency, "mysterious wild beast," brings about a choosing of a current existence, to empower it *mojano (mo:* locative that indicates spatial-temporal location; *jan* from *jana:* mysterious (in *janayari);* or: nominal classifier, "object, thing in the shape of . . ."—*Mojano:* "that-is- in-the-mysterious") in the showing and bestowing of the mask, skin, jaguar-fang-eye, jaguar-fangs-necklace in epidemic-contagion to activate it as phersu-jaguar-anomaly.[13] "The name itself does not indicate a subject: for this reason, it seems pointless to us to ask if its operation is similar or not to the nomination of a species, according to which the subject is considered of another nature than the form that classifies it, or only as the final act of that Form, inasmuch as it is a limit of the classification. The name itself does not indicate a subject, nor can a name acquire a value of the name itself in function of a form or of a species. The name itself designates in the first place something that is of the event's order, of the becoming, of the *haecceidad* (. . .) The name itself is not the subject of a time, but rather the agent of an infinitive. It signals a longitude and a latitude."[14] The *haecceidad-janayari,* as longitude-*mojano,* is a multiple extension in water, in air, in the mountains (land-jungle), of two heads: forward-backward. The *haecceidad-janayari,* as latitude-*mojano,* "the effects it is able to produce in keeping with such a degree of potency,"[15] flows in to challenge, to pounce, to fly, to abduct, to hunt, to wage war, to heal, to sing, to see . . . "The verb in the infinitive is in no way undetermined in terms of time. It expresses the floating, non-pulsed time of Aion's realm, in other words, the time of the pure event or of the becoming, that enunciates speeds and relative slownesses independently of the chronological or chronometric values that time acquires in other modes."[16] The name itself of the *haecceidad-janayari,* and longitude-*mojano,* is supra- ethnic and finds its designation in different languages in order to make its multiple extension even more precise. In the water, it takes the name *munüani* (Sikuani language): jaguar-of-the-water. When it is below the water, it is the serpent-anaconda from which emerges from the earth for the jaguar-becoming, according to what Grandfather Rafael Vicente Yepes told me in the Sikuani community called Walabó. In the seeing propitiated by the *yagé*-entheogen-inebriation, from the anaconda-jaws-breath flows the jaguar, and the serpent is configured also in the coloring that vibrates from the beating of the drum for jaguar-becoming. In the air, it takes the name *navigaka (navi:* jaguar, *gaka:* rocks of the high plain; Kogi language) jaguar-of-the-air, "condor, who vibrates-in-music on the maraca's tuft of feathers to propitiate flight." In the mountains (jungle-land), it takes the name *janayari* (Witoto language) to propitiate a gold-mask and a skin that vibrates-luminous in the song. In Aion time, it takes the name *makokonewütjü* (Sikuani language): jaguar of two-heads: forward-backward. In its invocation, it signals "the instant without thickness and without extension that subdivides each present into past and future." You fly in Aion, in the *makokonewütjü*-invocation. "Like infinitives, the indefinite article and pronoun are not undetermined. Or, rather, they only lack determination to the extent that a simultaneously non-determinable form is applied to them. On the other hand, they lack nothing when they introduce *haecceidades*, events whose individuation does not pass through a form and is not done by a subject. In this case, the indefinite is conjugated with the maximum amount of determination: once upon a time, a child is mistreated, a horse falls . . . The elements employed find their individuation here in the bringing about of which they form a part, independently of their concept's form of their persona's subjectivity."[17]

The infinitive of the *haecceidad-janayari,* as *mojano*-latitude in anomalous bringing about, does not activate the reflexivity of the transforming under a chronology or determined chronometry. It signals the affections as pure event: the challenging of the water-serpent to the becoming-breath-jaguar, of the drumming-vibrating-drum to the serpent-coloring, from the drum to the belly, from the belly to the forehead where there is an acti-vated line of flight that disorganizes the eye that looks into the eye-fangs-jaguar of seeing. To hunt the naked torso in the inserting of fangs that become necklace-fangs- jaguar in the concentric piecing together of pectoral-shield of waging war and healing. Singing is no longer in a narrative syntax that describes the being, but in the esoteric word in its vibrating and musical drumming that names-sings the potency of becoming in the instant of the event.

Between the longitude and the latitude of this *haecceidad* of jaguar-becoming, the imperceptible is per-ceived, the invisible is made visible, the unsayable becomes sayable, the outer thought in a nomadism of existence is experienced: it is not the reflection of the "I think," of the "I think how becoming would be." It is an outer thought in the jaguar-becoming event. The event is the one that speaks. As the Witoto grandfather Oscar Román says, "This word is the one that speaks." It is the experiencing of the nomadizing of existence in a rhizome-jaguar in Aion intensity. The body flows in the jaguar-becoming in each instant, in any instant the jaguar is made potent to act with its strength on the immediacy of the event. Between the name itself, the in-definite article and the infinitive, this *haecceidad*-jaguar-becoming is brought about and inter-brought about. Experiencing the shamanizing.

TRANSLATED FROM the Spanish by Steven F. White.

NOTES

1. Excerpt from *Yagé: Nomadism of Thought* (unpublished manuscript)
2. **EDITOR'S NOTE:** According to Jonathan Ott in *Pharmacotheon*, the word *entheogen* was invented by a group of schol-ars (including Ott) in 1979 and "derives from an obsolete Greek word meaning 'realizing the divine within,' the term used by the ancient Greeks to describe states of poetic or prophetic inspiration, to describe the entheogenic state which can be induced by sacred-plant drugs." (See Jonathan Ott, *Pharmacotheon: Entheogenic Drugs, Their Plant Sources and History.* Kennewick, WA: Natural Products, 1996. pp. 19–20).

    Earlier in the chapter entitled "Devenir-Jaguar" (Jaguar-Becoming), from which this excerpt is taken, Torres ana-lyzes the (pre-Thucydides) etymology of *epidemic,* linking it to the vocabulary of theophany and the propitiatory rites of religious "contagion" in the presence of the divine.

3. September equinox, 1994.
4. In the vital chakra of the jaguar, the *Ki* in the Chinese tradition.

5. In this third eye, seeing is activated, the claridoscope, which is a line of flight from the eye as organ, that sees, in the dis-organic quality of the jaguar-eye-fang that brings about seeing. The body becomes intense, intensive. A wave travels through the body "that traces on the body levels or thresholds from the variations of an amplitude. The body does not have organs, but, rather, thresholds or levels." Gilles Deleuze. *Logique de la sensation I.* Paris: Editions de la Différence, 1981. p. 33.

6. The condor is the jaguar of the rocks of the high plains and the air. In the Kogi language, it is designated with the word *navigaka: navi,* jaguar and *gaka,* rocks of the high plain.

7. In the middle of 1991, I commented to Bruno Mazzoldi that in a yagé trance I had perceived that the gesture of the so-called "Screamers" of the Capulí ceramics were not gestures of screaming, but the gesture of the *yawning* of someone who is experiencing yagé-inebriation at the very moment of entheogenic possession. In a letter from Pasto, dated June 26, 1991, he made the following comment: "With regard to the yawn (and I'm really glad that you have discovered this, too), I'm sending you a page from *Fulgido sapo* (Gleaming Toad) in which there are references to the so called "screamers" that you speak of in your beautiful letter: 'The open mouth of the toad-jaguar (if only I could open it that wide every time I had to toss) is an expression of rage or extreme disgust but also a 'symbol of transformation' as Kennedy indicates when he relates the Xipe-Totec tradition of Our Flayed Lord, with the yawning that overwhelms the amphibian for half an hour or more before it begins to shed its skin. In the same way, we can relate the motif of the so-called Screamers of Capulí ceramics in their mimicking of the yagé drinker because of the gesture that recalls the vomiting of the purge. More importantly, however, it's important to point out that the yawning does not necessarily express fatigue or laziness on the part of the visionary, and certainly not simple boredom. The target of the fiercest rage is the old skin, the toxic remains of the past that the subject has persisted in hoarding as assets of progress. And this rage is the target of an abysmal disgust. The jaws of the toad-jaguar open, therefore, not only to devour the other (the adversary-guardian of the subject's truth projected on the face of the neighbor) but, from this voracity's most intense moment of sickness, to get the devouring subject (who waits and clings tenaciously to the void, terrified by his own loss) out of the nest."

8. "According to Aion, only the past and the future insist or subsist in time. Instead of a present that reabsorbs the past and the future, there is a future and a past that divide the present in each instant, that infinitely subdivide into past and future, into the two meanings at the same time. Or, better still, it is the instance with no thickness or extension who subdivides each present into past and future, instead of vast and thick presents that include, with respect to each other, the future and the past." Gilles Deleuze. *Lógica del sentido.* Trans. Miguel Morey. Barcelona: Paidos, 1989. p. 172.

9. Sikuani language (Flia. Guahibo Linguistics, Colombian Orinoco region).

10. "There exists a mode of individuation very different from that of a person, a subject, a thing or a substance. We reserve for it the name *haecceidad.* A season, a winter, a summer, and hour, a date, have a perfect individuality that lacks nothing, even though it is not confused with that of a thing or a subject. They are *haecceidades* in the sense that in them everything is the relation of movement and rest among molecules and particles, the ability to affect and to be affected (. . .) All the bringing about in its individuated entirety turns out to be an *haecceidad,* which is defined by a longitude and a latitude, by speeds and affections, independently of the shapes and of the subjects that only belong to another plan (. . .) At most, two kinds of *haecceidad* will be distinguished: the *haecceidades* of bringing about (a body that only is considered longitude and latitude) and the *haecceidades* of inter-bringing about, that signal as well the potentialities of becoming in the heart of each bringing about (the means of crossing longitudes and latitudes). But both kinds, strictly speaking, are inseparable (. . .) An *haecceidad* has no beginning or end, origin or destiny. It is simply in the middle. It is not made of points, only lines. It is a rhizome." Gilles Deleuze and Felix Guattari. *Mil mesetas: capitalismo y esquizofrenia.* Trans. by José Vázquez Pérez. Valencia: Pre-textos, 1988. pp. 264 and 266.

11. Deleuze and Guattari, p. 261.

12. With regard to the shamanistic-word, the ethnologists Patrice Bidou and Michel Perrin say: "These enchantments are not well-known and studied. Not only are they composed of particular words, or of ordinary words with special meanings, but their syntax breaks down as well with the discursive order of the myths that deploy the objects and beings of the world in a linear way. The formulas, songs, and prayers of the shaman travel the roads of creation with words that do not merely *describe* things, but *touch* them in a concrete way, reducing them to elemental principals that constitute all beings." Patrice Bidou and Michel Perrin. *Lenguaje y palabras chamanísticas.* Quito: Abya-Yala/MLAL, 1988. p. 6.

13. EDITOR'S NOTE: earlier in this chapter, Torres, citing Jean-Pierre Vernant, defines *phersu* as the "Bearer of the mask that officiates the ceremony."
14. Deleuze and Guattari, p. 267.
15. Deleuze and Guattari, p. 261.
16. Deleuze and Guattari, p. 267.
17. Deleuze and Guattari, p. 267.

THE JAGUAR WHO WOULD NOT SAY HER PRAYERS:
Changing Polarities in Upper Amazonian Shamanism

Françoise Barbira Freedman

Sorcerers are still murdered in the Peruvian Upper Amazon. Two Lamista suspects were recently killed in revenge, shot dead at night. "People got tired of their evil doings," I was told. Vendettas and feuds continue: the majestic "black sorcerer" of San Martín who had emerged unscathed from so many ritualized confrontations of power was finally done in a few years back. There were tales of others becoming "worthless," "drunk-like," reduced to a sorry state through the loss of their power in spirit-attacks, a fate greatly feared among local shamans. The words of my teacher Corina came back to my memory: "Think of what you are doing; once you step in, it is like being on a football pitch; you have to play, kick, defend and attack; there is no respite ever." Indeed, the game never seems to be secured, only played at different levels as one acquires more power, more defenses. Spirits' envy is an extension of human envy and defenses escalate from animal spirits and souls to cosmic forces and elements. There is no tenure in shamanism, as spirit helpers are imponderable and can desert powerful shamans from one day to the next.

At the beginning of the 20th century, mestizos apprenticed themselves with increasing regularity to Indian shamans during the social upheavals of the rubber boom, often after a life-threatening illness from which they had been cured. They in turn had trainees, which resulted in the spread of *vegetalismo,* a widespread syncretic mix of herbalism and shamanism in Amazonia, which, in its Peruvian form, was strongly influenced by the indigenous Lamista shamanism from the San Martín province. Non-Indian shamans sometimes have Catholic icons as defenses, unlike Indian shamans. Both refer to an intricate set of categories differentiating good shamans from evil shamans, *curanderos* from *maleros.* A statement is made through icons or the use of prayers during *ayahuasca* ceremonies: Christ, the Virgin Mary and, to a lesser extent, saints are called upon as guarantors of "the good" in shamanic practice. Very few shamans do not acknowledge the dichotomy in some way in their practice. All shamans claim that they only cause harm to others in their patients' defense or their own, unlike sorcerers who cause harm gratuitously and cannot "put people right." The closer to indigenous Amazonian cultures in their training, the less mestizo shamans call upon Catholic sources of power, whether directly or through sects such as the Rosicrucians. Protestant Churches are less tolerant of shamanic practice and have discouraged syncretism in any form.

My questions as to how novices taking *ayahuasca* turn to sorcery or healing, and how strong shamans ultimately transcend evil and good in an ambivalent power, all received a standard answer: "The plants themselves teach one one's path." The divide between innate tendencies and deliberate choice in the statements of shamans invariably stirred emotional reactions which pointed out a sensitive issue engaging the speakers' own perspective: "Sometimes the plants teach one to send darts (for disease and harm) in an irresistible way;" "If visions to become a sorcerer present themselves to you, then that's your lot;" "There is a choice, and one has to resist the temptation to use the power to send darts if one gets it." Apprentices who breach prescriptive or proscriptive rules in their ascetic training, particularly self-imposed ones, get weak and "as a result become sorcerers." There are also codes of practice whereby those who seek deliberately to become sorcerers bend the rules of the diet in particular ways from the start. Shamanic plant-teachers are classified in an elaborate symbolic system of "sorcery-teachers," "healing-teachers," and ambivalent teachers: colour, shape and habitus provide clues to the dominant function of a plant teacher in sorcery or healing. In this system, *ayahuasca* is a gateway and a leader, directing those who take it to sources of power which can then be mastered with further diets, in relation to both animals and other plants.

Throughout western Amazonia, shamanic training entails a preoccupation with "keeping right," being constantly "put right" with the help of one's guide. Besides sorcerers' attacks and temptations to abuse one's newly acquired power, spirits also challenge trainees into dramatic fights, testing their courage *(sacando sus valientes)*: "If one is beaten up, one has to be set back upright again." Even one's power songs get "upset" *(volteadas)* and need to be set straight again. The imagery is in terms of being weak or strong, crooked or straight, sick or healthy.

Moral uprightness is also part of the cultural ideal of mixed forest people in the Upper Amazon; it is expressed in terms of a strong body that can resist the elements with equanimity either in hunting or in carrying heavy loads; both men and women teach their children and relentlessly cultivate in themselves the steadfastness they advocate in formal speeches. Lamista anti-heroes, failed hunters, trickster forest spirits such as *Chulla Chaki,* and deceiving mermaids are a welcome antidote to this lofty ideal of the "strong and straight" at gatherings when myths are told. The Lamistas, or Jakwash, as they call themselves among themselves, have been the patient, caring, yet demanding hosts of several anthropological fieldworks in which they made sure that I not only learned their culture correctly as an outsider but also that I literally "grew up straight": they viewed it as a slow process of hardening myself in the manner of a tree from a weak, green, baby-like stem *(yuyu likidu),* to something strong and straight *(sinchi puru).* Little by little, in many subtle ways and always by example and exhortation rather than reproaches, I would gently be "put right" (kuskacha-) until social consensus had it that at least some of the time, I "stood right."

Plant medicines, generically called "purgatives," *(purga)* because of possible emetic and laxative side effects, are prescribed for all states of weakness, whether they are attributed to parasitosis, pollution or, more dangerously, to spirit or sorcery attacks. Conditions range from mere fatigue to afflictions that are perceived as potentially life-threatening. *Ayahuasca* is the *purga* par excellence, taken in most crisis situations before other plants or admixtures are prescribed.[1] Those people who are not particularly receptive to visions simply get "strong and straight" again: in a "with *purga*" state, being alert, vigorous, and altogether fit in a way that is recognized by others. Visions also help in the diagnosis of the cause of sickness, showing the origin of sorcery attacks. To those who are receptive, *purgas* "teach" medicine, granting access to the plant-essences *(madres)* which in visions and dreams selectively reveal their character, mores, properties and power songs. They are then said to "stick" *(pegarse)* to the body of the novice and open a gateway through which he/she can engage in a power quest.

The more I marveled at the expansion of the cognitive maps that set plants, the forest and animals in an increasingly meaningful cosmos, the more pressing the issues of constant strife, struggle and rivalry seemed to be. There was constant watching, rounding, feuding, deterring: a permanent state of alert against enemies galore, nearby and far away. These features are congruent with a tradition of feuds between residential kin groups and networks of alliance and enmity among indigenous populations of the Upper Amazon. As an anthropologist, I could satisfactorily "construct" shamanism in relation to ethnography: soul capture, spirit allies, control of cosmic territories and game animals fitted with the social dynamics of kin groups on the ground. As an apprentice, however, I was "being put right" between poles of morality and power that were elusive. As I progressed in my apprenticeship, the increased awareness that there was no neutral position within reach frightened me. I was now in the game: in a skeptical yet irreversible process, the *purga* was teaching me experientially about polarities of power between good and bad shamans both in social power fields and in my own psyche. Each moment became a precarious balance between acquired protections and defenses, attacks and retaliations. Each *ayahuasca* vision triggered further insights and interpretations.

The jaguar vision I am reporting here fueled my particular concern with the cultural dialectics of good and evil around *ayahuasca.* The immediate interpretations that were offered to me on the spot, besides my own interpretation, cannot be separated from the socio-cultural processes in the Upper Amazon today.

Within seconds of the transformation of space/time/sound into the always surprising, dazzling stage that *ayahuasca* opens, the magnificent face of a spotted jaguar emerges right in front of me. Surprised, I take time to check that it is indeed a jaguar, as I have never had any particular interest in cats. It's definitely not an *otorongo,* it is similar to the panthers I have seen in English zoos: "Tigre" is the Amazonian Spanish word for jaguar and I hear it in my head amplified many times in the way it's announced in hunting stories.

We stare at each other at very close quarters and I feel its very strong breath in my face, reeking of rotten meat, nauseating. In succession, it takes expressions of threat, blind cruelty, playfulness, cuddliness, indifference: I respond with all the corresponding intense emotions, engaging in the exchange.

Suddenly, the jaguar turns round and I follow its stalking, entranced by its beauty and suppleness. It's an adult female. I notice the surroundings: an exquisite nature temple, with columns of *Capirona (Capirona decorticans)* around which a snake (a medium-size brown-yellow- greenish boid I cannot identify) is slithering up and down in a twirling motion against the smooth bark. There is a vegetation canopy (I recognize stems and leaves of *ayahuasca*) from which scintillating flowers are hanging in luxuriant bunches. The floor, I then notice, is a manmade platform incrusted with all sorts of jewels and precious stones in mosaic. Other jaguars jump and stalk with the first, who henceforth becomes "my" jaguar. I am so delighted with the vision that I relax and pick some of the hanging flowers. Instantly, the jaguars become angry and aggressive. There are now five of them. I persist in trying to feed them flowers although I know that this is a stupid, misconceived thing to do. It infuriates them even more and I have only a split second to "receive" the mental message from "my" jaguar that the only possible course of action is to become a jaguar, too, and fight. A wave of intense aggressiveness unfurls in my solar plexus. This causes me to vomit, later than usual, after taking *ayahuasca*, and the process of "becoming jaguar" takes me over irresistibly. I feel it all at once, paws and claws, spine and tail, nose, whiskers and tail; I see with a jaguar's eyes, suddenly encompassing a wider field of vision, prick a jaguar's ears, open my jaws in practice. "My" jaguar has gone. It dawns on me that I have become her, am her, yet, at the same time, I retain the awareness of her merged with my consciousness. I find it easy to signal to the other jaguars to go away with mere body language, arching my back intensely. As I do this, I have a flashback of my cat standing up to the stray cats of a new neighborhood when we moved house in Cambridge.

Nothing I ever read about shamanic animal metamorphoses could have prepared me for the total involvement of my senses, body, mind in this process. I am fully experiencing it, I am it, yet at the same time I retain the awareness of who I am, albeit in jaguar form, partaking with other people clearly dealing with intense experiences of their own in an *ayahuasca* ceremony. The female jaguar whose form I have entices me to go into the forest where she will teach me the ways of jaguars. Suddenly, I am in a swampy area near an oxbow lake which is my home, and instantly I am made to understand/feel stalking prey, jumping and killing, ripping, spreading fear and also feeling fear myself, being lonely and shy and even cowardly among the other animals there that, surprisingly, are lounging and relaxing in the water.

The leading shaman's songs call me back, and in a docile cat's way I walk round in circles towards him with the intention to sit at his feet. Yet every time I get close and I can hear the words of his song, which are those of the Christian passion recited in characteristic shamanic chanting mode, I experience a dazzling pain similar to an electric shock all over my fur and around my ear drums: my only escape from this pain is to crawl to find again in relief my "nature-temple" outside the house where the ceremony is held. Only there does the pain gradually subside.

It does not surprise me that the other shaman present, as an eagle, comes to find me and blows gently on my crown. It is even reassuring, as surprised as I am to know that this large harpy eagle is him, that as a jaguar I can physically relate to the being of the eagle, particularly eyes, beak and talons. I respond to the ritual blowing and feel very calm and at ease in my jaguar self, keenly sensing my surroundings.

Later, the otherness of the snakes on the tree columns startles me. I become aware that on each tree, there are in fact two snakes twirling up around each other in the way of a caduceus. This vision fascinates me, and I lie at the foot of one of the tree columns, experiencing intensely "being a jaguar" in a way that inexplicably but unmistakably transcends all differentiation between good and evil. At that time, the leading shaman has concluded his chanting: in succession, the eagle shaman and one of the participants sing their songs. The first makes me see (through leaves, stems and roots around the nature-temple) a myriad of forest spirits, perhaps the "mothers" of the plants. The second makes me focus on the double movement of the snakes which I suddenly perceive as an outer and inner caduceus and which induces an unprecedented feeling of inner strength. It is then my turn to sing. Watching the snakes, I feel my plain jaguar's limitation in understanding them. I only know dimly that their wisdom, so different, may offer a resolution of the incompatibility I experience between Christian prayers and "my jaguar being" in the forest as cosmos.

Interpretations by the Actors

In Peruvian Amazonian shamanic terms, this vision gave me access to a stronger defense, which *ayahuasca* as a plant teacher bestowed upon me. I was instructed at once on securing it by ingesting particular barks associated with the Jaguar, following a rigorous diet during four to six weeks. The Jaguar mother-spirit would then teach me how to "tame" my jaguar into a spirit-ally and become able to summon her or even have her leap to my defense in situations of danger. I would also learn more about the essence of jaguars and their place in the cosmic order, and gain "puma medicine," which I now understand as a specific lens through which to look at sorcery-caused illnesses. The various plants which have the jaguar as their "mother-spirit" would become familiar to me as a result. The vision created a moral obligation in the officiating shaman to help me with these further steps, as a jaguar vision can be dangerous if it is not consolidated into defenses and the support of spirit-allies. He stressed that these steps were to be completed soon, preferably in isolation in a forest setting as is the norm of standardized "Indian" shamanic training in the Upper Amazon. His diagnosis was that another rival shaman was setting me on the wrong path *(te está encaminando mal)* and a jaguar defense would come in handy. He offered me some of his hand-made perfume for protection in the meantime, as he has now completed the cycle of *ayahuasca* and entered the cycle of "perfume," which is the path of his Cahuapana shaman grandmother.

The shaman with Catholic spirit helpers interpreted my jaguar's abhorrence of prayers in the terms that she I were not "straightened" enough for this larger source of power. He used my description of an electric shock to expand on "voltage differences" between bad and good shamans, describing Christ as "a more powerful genera-tor." He then launched into a dithyrambic account of how, after "falling" to sorcerers and being "put right" many times, cheating death in many ways, he was now impervious to sorcery attacks through surrendering to the superior power of Christ. The prayer book, which his mestizo shaman father used as an emblem of his bona fide, became his teacher: he "read it again and again until it became part of him," and then he had a vision of Christ with *ayahuasca* and received the power songs which he was chanting in our session. As a result, his brew and his songs were now acknowledged to be very powerful by other local shamans. He could deviate sorcery attacks and simply return darts to their senders or neutralize their spirit allies, leaving them powerless rather than physically harming them. Many people could not stand his chanting, he said, because, if there was some evil *(malo)* in them, the songs would shock them and blow them away. Some people were intrinsically evil, but this was quite rare. Like most local shamans, he saw evil as a pathological condition inflicted by others, arising from envy and revenge. Shamanic healing could cleanse and remove this strange pathogen which caused weak-ness, crookedness and lethal illness. He was adamant that although the jaguar is a powerful ally, I should turn to Christ as the ultimate defense.

He recommended that I "study" prayers to get a Christ vision with *ayahuasca*. This was not incompatible with acquiring further "jaguar medicine," but I had been shown that it could not compete with the power of "Christ medicine."

There was clearly a cleavage between the interpretations of the two shamans, one Indian-born, who had a long acquaintance with the rain forest in the midst of various indigenous peoples, the other mestizo, who spent some time in a forest environment with his shaman father but whose frame of reference was mainly urban. They did not question or comment on each other's interpretation. I sensed a mutual respect and a tacit acknowledg-ment of difference in their contracted partnership. Both were relatively young shamans, 41 and 35 respectively, and, through their frequent association with Westerners who came to take *ayahuasca*, they had learned to adjust their respective categories of good and evil to the new notion of "negativity" that was central to their guests' discourse.

Reflecting on the session, I could also put forward my own interpretation. While I rejected Catholicism strongly as a child, my jaguar is a likely expression of my identification with Amazonian native culture. Given the historical assimilation of shamanic practice to the devil's works, an irrational abhorrence of prayers is a pre-dictable feature of the cultural patterning of my *ayahuasca* visions as an anthropologist. In terms of my personal shamanic quest in Yakwash Lamista culture, how did this vision "put me right," if at all? By allowing me to embody a jaguar, it gave me a vivid, immediate insight of the Forest as cosmos, in which relations of power are enacted as archetypal relations with and among animal spirits, yet at the same time mediated through "real" animals in the surrounding forest. This order is known to hunters, although, unlike shamans, they cannot act upon it by entering this supernatural dimension. Shamans make alliances with the animal masters/owners/essences (*dueños* and *madres*) of plants in altered states of consciousness, perceiving them as immanent. By impersonating predators such as the jaguar or the harpy eagle, they state their dominant position in power relations within the cosmos. They are then at an advantage in shamanic fights and increase their power through returning hostile spirit-darts to their senders in expanding power fields that are socially defined at any point in space/time. My jaguar vision transposed this intellectual understanding into an experiential one, through which, potentially, I could become a stronger player in the shamanic game of power and defense. This vision engaged my whole self experientially in a phenomenological approach which was blatantly at odds with the empiricist standpoint I intellectually favored. There was no longer any possible vantage point for me as an anthropologist other than that of the shamanic rainbow, forever bridging incommensurable perceptions and perspectives within highlands and lowlands, earth and sky, earth and water, from a constantly changing in-between.

Changing Polarities in "Chamanismo"

Writing about *ayahuasca* in the Upper Amazon alone implies extrapolating from a multiplicity of idiosyncratic experiential syntheses of cultural elements. The interplay and overlap between these individual configurations create collectively accepted versions of the cosmos defined as a transforming set of metaphors relating landscape (sky, earth, water domains and their creatures) to both an ideal social and moral order (for some Amazonians, the "land without evil") and the actual endless strife and "shamanic wars." The cosmic underwater realm where powerful shamans enjoy perfect affinal relations with their mermaid or mermen consorts in affluent cities, for example, is contrasted with the socially destructive acts of water spirits in abducting the weak and luring the strong into life-threatening dangers.

Nothing is neutral in relation to ego: all elements are forces, potentially if not actually, either increasing ego's power or threatening it. The metaphors, myths and images expressing the transmutations of humans, animals and plants through eating, sexual intercourse and killing, using the idiom of kinship and affinity, are part of the cultural tropes common to forest people throughout Amazonia. Historical shifts in the semantic fields of "good" and "evil," are part of the colonial heritage of Amazonia from the Conquest to the rubber boom (Taussig 1987). The growing importance of *ayahuasca* as a main focus of shamanic practice in the Upper Amazon in relation to other "plant-teachers" has to be understood in light of the relations between poles of power, both geographic and cosmic, in the region. These poles, probably originating from the pre-Columbian exchanges between Andean and Forest people, were constituted by ethnic and religious identities as well as by politics and economics (Gow 1994), but Upper Amazon shamans today still perceive them as extensions of their respective ancestral territories and the orbis *mundi* of their people as The People. Amazonian *vegetalismo* (Luna 1986) spread throughout the region after the rubber boom, but it extended trends which had developed in colonial times.

Implicitly or explicitly, the new forms of shamanic practice currently developing in the Upper Amazon continue to refer to an opposition between urban and forest, high and low, Christian and wild, sources of power which have sustained the transformative evolution of shamanism since the Conquest and perhaps earlier. Shamanic power always has consisted of mediating between such polarized sources. The power fields of prominent Peruvian shamans have now extended from local and regional to global ones, with the United States replacing Leticia, Brazil, and the north coast of Peru as outmost sources of external power. The notion of forest people (*las tribus*), at the other end, now integrates the various indigenous cultures in an overall environmentalist wilderness (*selva*).

The current emergence of *chamanismo*, which imparts the already sanitized *vegetalismo* as "medical system" with the ideal moral order of neo-North American Indian and New Age shamanism, hides further the social dynamics of shamanic strife. Negativity replaces "damage" and "evil" (*daño*). And there is an increasing confusion between enemies out there and inner conflicts in interpretations of *ayahuasca* visions. The Amazonian cultural understanding of soul, subsumed under Catholic teachings for centuries, is in question among the new *chamanes*. The recent public displacement of the colonial Christian opposition between good and bad shamans towards a discourse of indiscriminate folk psychiatry and therapy, however, also denies the social idiom through which conflicts are resolved without resort to justice, particularly across ethnic categories. At the same time, as emblems of Catholicism and cosmopolitan medicine are less needed to give legitimacy to a more socially accept-able shamanic practice, new markers combining international perceptions of rain forest native identity and environmentalism are being developed.

The two shamans who interpreted my jaguar vision expressed a wish to transcend the traditional forms of shamanic strife and saw them as a feature of the past which would soon fall in demise. At the same time, they defined their practice in relation to their respective power fields, constituted by their life history and practice. Past ways of transcending shamanic strife, besides the highest *vegetalista* shamanic status of *banco muraya*, shaman-diviner who has gained access to the underwater connections in the cosmos, have been to seek alterna-tive sources of legitimacy and power besides Christianity and cosmopolitan medicine. Black and white magic, Eastern religions, esoteric cults and imagined Incan traditions have provided such sources in the last two centuries. Each of these sources of legitimacy has colored to a variable extent the interpretation of *ayahuasca* visions in the framework of urban mestizo folk medicine which developed around *vegetalismo* as plant-based shamanism, as well as the ensuing diagnosis and therapies.

In contrast with the theatrical acting out of patients' crises in some shamanic rituals, the patient's drama in a syncretic Amazonian shamanic healing session is an intimate one. Notwithstanding group dynamics in sessions, visions are only partly directed by the leading shaman's songs; they are then interpreted in one-to-one dialogues between patient and shaman, mostly without an audience. There can be a negotiating process in which various interpretations are offered before finally one is selected. Many shamans give sound counseling on particular issues as well as interpreting *ayahuasca* visions with reference to cosmic elements. "Putting right" entails annihilating, neutralizing or keeping at bay forces disempowering the individual in the spirit-world, in society and finally within his/her psyche. It involves the removal of "evil" as a pathogenic substance carried by a magic dart into the patient's body *(sacar la maleza)* or retrieving stolen soul matter from an enemy, on those three levels simultaneously. Along the continuum of shamanic practice to which I have referred, these three levels are seen as interconnected. Yet the emphasis placed on each of them now varies according to the source of legitimacy which is sought. While *chamanismo* stresses the connection between psyche and spirit-world in the Forest as cosmos, seeking visions for diagnosing the source of illness and removing evil darts without returning them to the sender in revenge, the identification and annihilation of malevolent agents, human or otherwise, is still a main intent guiding *ayahuasca* visions for most local people in the Upper Amazon, entailing cycles of accusation, revenge and retaliation.

The awareness of shamanic strife does not underrate the full impact that *ayahuasca* visions can have on an individual experiential plane. Neither does it preclude the therapeutic potential of shamanic curing rituals in which the combined skills of plant knowledge, spiritual healing and traditional medical knowledge are often effective. That *ayahuasca* visions in *vegetalismo* and even more in *chamanismo* are increasingly directed to healing and personality integration in what is now called "*ayahuasca* ceremonies" *(ceremonias de ayahuasca)* is an explicit displacement of the shamanic discourse from the enemies out there to the sorcerer within. Over the centuries, the Forest as cosmos has continued to be the locus of interpretation of *ayahuasca* visions, be they of jaguars, space ships, blond fairies or Christ, in relation to outsiders' perceptions of good and evil that were superimposed on the native concepts of strong and weak. The Catholic Church devilized shamanism, making all healers into sorcerers *(brujos)*; the shamans of mixed blood in Amazonian towns integrated Christian icons not only for legitimacy but also in an instrumental way to heal the terror of the Devil in its many manifestations, as Taussig (1987) has shown so lucidly. Since the rubber boom, in a process parallel to that of the Peyote cult, such inter-pretations have filtered back to "native" forest people whose shamans are now appropriating them, to the point that there is now a divide between younger *chamanes* and older *brujos* (for example, between the non-Christian shaman with Christ as a spirit ally who interpreted my jaguar vision and his *vegetalista* father) concerning re-taliation, revenge and shamanic wars.

Such a divide may be a historical pattern since the colonial period, rather than a recent by-product of glob-alization, and further expansion of chamanismo outside Amazonia may intensify the current transformation of shamanic discourse (if not practice) in the Upper Amazon.

Many *ayahuasqueros* no longer have the knowledge of *vegetalismo* plant medicine in which *ayahuasca* is mainly a diagnostic and training tool, and the path of *ayahuasca* is only one among several ancestral paths to gain vision, strength and knowledge from the plant-teachers. The *palero* shamans from the Huallaga river, who took their mastery of tree bark medicine downriver with them in the colonization of Peruvian Amazonia and were the founding fathers of *vegetalismo*, scorned the new dominance of *ayahuasca* in relation to the "master trees" *(palos maestros)*. *Ayahuasca*, they said, seduced youngsters and gave them the illusion that they were powerful and strong. Is the new discourse of personality integration in *chamanismo* contributing to make obsolete not only old ethnic enmities but also the subversive, illusory power that shamanism offers to the oppressed forest people of mixed blood in the dialectics of race and class? The central place that shamanism occupies as medicine and religion within the popular culture of the Upper Amazon precludes its reduction to "folk psychiatry" or cheap medicine. Once again, through the use of *ayahuasca*, the Forest as cosmos is likely to provide a new source of symbols to express and resolve social perceptions of enemies, out there and within, close by and in cosmopolitan capitals. In wider power fields, Forest shamans, whether native, of mixed blood or gringos, guide the visions of the poorest and the richest sometimes sitting side by side to "get straightened" (in however illusory terms this may be from a social scientific perspective) in the center of the caduceus.

NOTE

1. The *ayahuasca* brew most commonly prepared in the Peruvian Upper Amazon consists of *Banisteriopsis caapi* and various admixture plants used to strengthen the effect and/or modify the visions. The brew which I ingested included mainly crushed bark of *Banisteriopsis caapi* and leaves of *Diplopteris cabrerana* (also known as *Banisteriopsis rusbyana)*, with leaves of *Psychotria viridis,* Coca leaves and sugar cane. The major active constituents of this brew were the beta-carboline alkaloids harmine and harmaline, and the compound DMT (N,N-dimethyltryptamine). Cf. Rivier and Lindgren 1972 for the chemical study of *ayahuasca* and McKenna, Luna and Towers 1995 for a review of the active constituents of *ayahuasca* and admixture plants.

MONTAGE

Michael Taussig

Two years later Eliseo was back again, by bus all the way across the country to dip once more into what he saw as the Indian well of magical power. He came with two companions and they stayed one month, working hard on the farm, ready and cheery and with a willing hand, quiet and unobtrusive. He told me had found *yagé* growing in the forests of the eastern Andes way to the north, in his homeland of Boyacá. I gathered he had quite a following as a healer there. He had put on a lot of weight since we were last together, and I have a vivid memory of him day after day, barefoot, chubby, and agile, leaping behind and in front of the horses laden with sugarcane making their way, floundering and clambering, from the fertile river flats to the tiny *trapiche* for milling the cane beside the house. I used to see him sometimes in the late afternoons on the veranda, absorbed in copying down the medicinal virtues of plants from what Santiago's barely teenaged granddaughter, Delia, had herself copied down from a school textbook on botany.

He found a willing instructor, of sorts, in Santiago's son-in-law, Angel, himself the son of a shaman, Don Apolinar, whose first language was Inga and who had died but two years ago. They had lived far away in the forests of the Caquetá region and Angel seemed to be some sort of beginning shaman himself. But he was also an awful drunk, much to the despair of his poor father and his wife, and was given to vain boasting.

Overwhelming events had thrown Angel into our midst. For a year or so, he told me, the Colombian army had set up a counterguerrilla base near his home. He cured many of the soldiers and got on well with them. He told me they came to him with skin rashes, arthritis, and requests for magic that would stop the captain and the colonel from being so hard on them. For their part, the captain and the colonel came to understand that with *yagé* you could divine what was happening in other places and in the future. With *yagé*, Angel was able to see the captain's wife living in the city of Pereira and, to the captain's surprise, see that she was five months' pregnant. But the captain could not cope with drinking *yagé*. It was too strong, and both he and the colonel asked Angel to drink it to see if they were going to survive the counterguerrilla campaign and where their enemies were hiding. But these last questions Angel could not answer.

Two sets of soldiers came and went from that part of the Caquetá: the ones with epaulettes of the Colombian colors red, blue, and yellow, and those of the counterguerrilla, with green and white. Then came the third set of soldiers, the ones with black epaulettes-black for death, Angel said. They put a helicopter next to his house, blew the roof off and the walls apart. They said he was aiding the *guerrilleros* and they tied his hands tight behind his back and hung him by his wrists for about three hours.

"I'm lucky I can still use my arms and work," he told me, rubbing his shoulders. "People get their arms and shoulders broken that way."

Then he was let down and they stuck the muzzle of a rifle into his mouth. They took him into the forest with his hands tied behind his back and with a gun jabbing him, ordering him to lead them to the enemy. But he knew nothing. "It's worse if you give in and make a false confession that you are an ally of the *guerrilleros*," he explained to me. He pleaded with them to kill him right then and there and cease with the humiliation. But each day they went on again deeper into the forest, a column of fifty soldiers pushing him in the lead. After eighteen days they untied his hands, now swollen like balloons, and set him free, apparently convinced that he knew nothing important.

"But you'd be better off not going back home to live in the Caquetá," the captain told him, "because the *guerrilleros* will assume you sang and helped us."

"And he's right," said Angel. "They will try and kill me too."

There was little to do but live elsewhere, at least for a while, even though he blustered: "I'm not to be humiliated like that! I'm going to stay in my home! I've done nothing wrong!" Like so many people he had been caught in this struggle in which the vagaries of gossip, envy and suspicion created realities as confusing as they were cruel and deadly. That was how these country people understood their situation: out of envy someone went to either the army or the *guerrilleros* saying that so-and-so was aiding the enemy — not at all unlike the social circuitry of sorcery.

Angel had been free only two weeks and with gusto joined our farewell for the three men from Boyacá. They were leaving home in the dawn and this was their night to be cured.

Borbonzay, Santiago's young Indian helper, had gone to the Putumayo river, a day or two's journey away, to get some leaves of *chagropanga-yagé*'s female companion without which, so it is said, no visions come. In his absence Angel helped out, and as the twelve people, all men, assembled that night to drink *yagé*, he authoritatively explained to a hesitant newcomer what *yagé* could entail: "You take it as a cure, as something to improve your life," he expounded, "and for intelligence-so you can see danger and be more astute. You see beautiful things or horrible things according to the state of your heart. If it's clean, you see beauty. You can see what's happening in Barranquilla, Bogotá, Cartagena, Cali . . . wherever."

Santiago poured out the *yagé* and wiped it clean with the curing fan but did not sing. We all fell into a dreamy doze. About three-quarters of an hour later a tiny hum began. It grew louder to counterpose the wind from the forest and the river's rush. Utterly absorbed and lost in itself, the song went on for a long time. The singer was old and tired. His voice was rough and low. He seemed lost in himself, singing for the sake of singing, the rite singing to itself in complete disregard of our presence or judgments. The room was quiet. People seemed to be asleep. Someone stumbled out and we heard the heart-wrenching retching and vomiting sounds that curl back into your own stomach like the snakes people talk about that come out in your vomit and go back in at the same time — a collective empathizing of nausea, now gathering like a storm. It feels like ants biting one's skin and one's head, now spinning in wave after trembling wave.

"When people are envious of you, then you have an awful time with *yagé*," Santiago said. "Then come the snakes all over your body and your vomit goes back into your mouth as snakes. Frogs, lizards, alligators, wild animals, cockroaches — the ones with big horns — that's what you feel when you are sick. And it smells of shit, too."

We took a second gourdful and the singing started again. Now Santiago had a ring in his hands that Rafael, one of the three men from Boyacá, had given him. He was curing Rafael's ring. The beat was very slow and deliberate with an occasional Spanish words: luck . . . paint *yagé* . . . luck . . . then the gunshot click of the tongue, then singing again. He was wearing Angel's father's necklace, the shamanic necklace of tigers' teeth glinting dully yellow and white, with a large metal crucifix tied to it. Santiago's necklace was stolen or had simply fallen off the roof of the bus bouncing him over the mountain roads to cure the coca growers of Bolívar, Cauca, on the other side of the Andes, where he was also asked to cure the man made crazy by the *duende*, huddled in his rags and long hair in a cave by the river.

Santiago was curing some *chondur* roots, holding the little knobby clumps the size of marbles in his hands together with Rafael's ring and singing over them. He asked me to cut a plastic bag, into which he placed the roots and the ring, and then asked Rafael to come and blow into it. In the jumble of events and objects the song wound its irregular way. Rafael was now sitting on a low stool right in front of him. The curing fan was beating fast, a galloping pulse in the eardrum of the world made suddenly aware of its own life and heart. He was singing into the bag, holding it no more than a hand-breadth from his mouth. He sang into the plastic bag with the knobby little magical roots of peppermint-tasting chondur roots and the ring. Then he swept over Rafael's head, singing faster and faster, the rhythm lifting us all, as it were, into the bag with the roots and the ring. Then he stopped abruptly, blew — "whoosh now, whoosh now" into the bag, which he then handed over to Raphael to take away as his talisman on the long trip across the republic the next day.

"Here's the cured stuff," he said, pausing to giggle, "with the love perfume [quereme] so you can win the hearts of women," and the giggle burst into a full-blown gale of laughing sweeping us all in its wake. The intense self-absorption of the man in the song in the still-sleeping quiet of the dark room had been cracked open like the husk of a nut, and into this opening we all tumbled, willy-nilly.

Close to midnight he was singing again, curing *yagé* for another round of serving. After a few minutes the singing suddenly stopped. There was ever so faint a sound of music coming through the night from the direction of the town down the valley.

"It's Borbonzay — dancing with the *chagropanga,*" chortled Santiago.

He called on Eliseo, the leader of the three from Boyacá, to bring over his ring too. This whole night, so it seemed, was to generate magical power for these three white men prior to their departure the next day. How many strangers eager for such magic had these Indian shamans thus obliged, giving back in the tangible form of rings and talismans the power that the strangers had given to them?

The curer loomed like a dark rock in the night, massivity compacting around the tiny pin-point of the charm to be cured, singing into its point of power and repose.

Outside soft rain fell and a gasoline lamp on the veranda cast a circle of light into the mist coming off the mountains. The singing also softly covered everything. My thoughts leap-frogged. I saw flowers, a panel on a pink kimono, wet rain on just one shiny blade of grass bending under the weight of a raindrop, a drop on a quivering edge, just this fragment looming, then — as the Indians say, *"otra pinta,* another painting," signifying a sudden swooping change — a curious memory picture of a tiny little corner, again a fragment, of the market in the town where I lived a few months in Australia, an image concentratedly conveying to bursting points of self-destruction the feelings for me of the huge sprawling market as a whole, and then beyond and over that the love and arguments I was embroiled in at that time of my life with my marketing companion at that tiny little corner — that fragment of a life's whole. Then, "another *pinta,*" back to the drops of rain on the vibrating edge of a blade of grass with the song gathering us all, people here, people of the troubling past, shiny grass blade bending to the rain . . . the song snapping to a halt like a dry twig snapped into pieces.

"What's this, a sorcery bundle?" Santiago interjected, wiping his one good eye in mock disbelief because Eliseo kept bringing little plastic bags out of the darkness for Santiago to cure. "This one is for my wife," Eliseo gravely declared, pulling at his little bags.

From the hollow of his hammock, Santiago's son-in-law Angel now started to sing too, joining with Santiago to make in that instant of connecting a new tableau with the most beautiful singing I have ever heard, the two together rising and falling through the night sounds, stimulating and soothing turmoil at one and the same time.

Angel was seated on Santiago's chair, beating with the curing fan, while Santiago sat hunched in his hammock peering into his cupped hands holding something precious. Someone was vomiting outside. For a few instants a refrain snaked through the song: *"gente envidiosa, gente envidiosa,* envious people, envious people . . ." The vomiting got louder. Santiago stopped singing to ask who it was that was suffering so, and gently laughed as did we all.

"Ah! *Así es el yagé;* That's *yagé* for you!" chuckled Santiago and after a short pause went on. "When will it be? One goes from here to there, round and round, trying this, trying that until the hour comes, the fight with death. When will it come?" he asked thus of Angel, who has just been released from staring death in the face every minute of the day for eighteen days and who, by way of reply, began to hum a tiny seed of life thrown into the gaping mouth of death-talk that now, humming too, grew into the great beating leaves of the curing fan, *waira sacha,* beating the beat of the galloping wail of the song that is *yagé.*

Now the room, so silent at the beginning of the evening, was buzzing with life. The song stopped and started, stopped and started, as either Angel or Santiago joined in the telling of tales in this carnival of humanity wiping at its tears while snuggling in each other's words, the wittier the saner.

◆ ◆ ◆

Fundamental to the power of this almost nightlong carnival was montage-immanent and active from the moment the curtain rose, so to speak, an hour after sunset when the old man breathed "whoosh fire" into the *yagé,* cracked his tongue like a gunshot, and began to sing, curing the *yagé* that would cure us all, the old man included. The power of this *yagé* night came only in part from what could be called "mysticism," and that mystery concerned the quite unconscious way in which whites like Eliseo and his two companions from Boyacá attributed magical power to the "Indian." Given this attribution of magical power to tamed savagery, the power of the ritual itself then proceeds to do its work and play through splintering and decomposing structures and cracking open meanings. In this most crucial sense, savagery has not been tamed — and therein lies the magic of colonial healing through the figure of the "Indian." The "mystical insights" given by visions and tumbling fragments of memory pictures oscillating in a polyphonic discursive room full of leaping shadows and sensory pandemonium are not insights granted by depths mysterious and other. Rather, they are made, not granted, in the ability of montage to provoke sudden and infinite connections between dissimilars in an endless or almost endless process of connection-making and connection-breaking.

MONTAGE: alterations, cracks, displacements and swerves all evening long-the sudden interruptions, always interruptions to what at first appears the order of ritual and then later on takes on little more than an excuse of order, and then dissolves in a battering of wave after wave of interruptedness into illusory order, mocked order, colonial order in the looking glass. Interruptions for shitting, for vomiting, for a cloth to wipe one's face, for going to the kitchen to gather coals for burning copal incense, for getting roots of magical *chondur* from where nobody can remember where they were last put, for whispering a fear, for telling and retelling a joke (especially for that), for stopping the song in mid-flight to yell at the dogs to stop barking . . . and in the cracks and swerves, a universe opens out.

MONTAGE: the manner of the interruptedness; the sudden scene changing which breaks up any attempt at narrative ordering and which trips up sensationalism. Between the swirling uncertainty of nausea and the abrupt certainty of the joke there lies little if any room for either the sensationalistic or the mysterious.

MONTAGE: suddenly altering situations of the group within the room and mood-slides associated with those changing situations, scenes, as it were, from the art of *trompe-l'oeil* passing in a flash from night to day through ages of time from despair to joy and back again without any guarantee of happy endings.

MONTAGE: flashing back and forth from self to group; not simply self-absorption broken up and scrambled by participation in the group or with one or two members of it, but also through such flashing back and forth from self to group and group to self a sort of playground and testing-ground is set up for comparing hallucinations with the social field from which they spring. Hence the very grounds of representation itself are raked over.

Another point: the movements and connections involved here between self and group are not susceptible to the *communitas* model that Victor Turner postulated as a universal or quasi-universal feature of ritual. His basic idea concerning this can be quoted, thus:

> In flow and communities what is sought is unity, not the unity which represents a sum of fractions and is susceptible of division and subtraction, but an indivisible unity, "white," "pure," "primary," seamless," This unity is expressed in such symbols as the basic generative and nurturant fluids semen and milk; and as running water, dawn, light, and whiteness. Homogeneity is sought, instead of heterogeneity [and the participants] are impregnated by unity, as it were, and purified from divisiveness and plurality. The impure and sinful is the sundered, the divided. The pure is the integer, the indivisible.[1]

Impregnating people with unity may fit well with certain fantasies of maleness and fascism. Certainly the *communitas* features of the *yagé* nights are the antithesis of this whiteness, this homogeneity, this soppy primitivism of semen and milk and the unified as the pure. Against that the *yagé* nights pose awkwardness of fit, breaking-up and scrambling, the allegorical rather than the symbolist mode, the predominance of the left hand and of anarchy — as in Artaud's notion of theater of cruelty with its poetic language of the senses, language that breaks open the conventions of language and the signifying function of signs through its chaotic mingling of danger and humor, "liberating signs," Artaud said, in a disorder that brings us ever closer to chaos.[2] It was to what he called "an infinite perspective of conflicts" that this theater of cruelty was directed, and with all the pitfalls and advantages that such a course entailed he drew for inspiration on non-Western theater, a course encouraged by the overwhelming contempt in which he held the bourgeois world so many of whose anthropologists have analyzed ritual as serving to structure and solidify society. Not for them the "infinite perspective of conflicts."

"Collective ritual can be seen as an especially dramatic attempt to bring some particular part of life firmly and definitely into orderly control. It belongs to the structuring side of the cultural/historical process." Thus

Sally Falk Moore and Barbara Myerhoff introduce a recent book on ritual and curtly dismiss any notion that what goes on in between the segments of ritual can be as important as "the structuring side" of something so portentous as "the cultural/historical process."[3] By and large anthropology has bound the concept of ritual hand and foot to the imagery of order, to such an extent that order is identified with the sacred itself, thereby casting disorder into the pit of evil — as is so question-beggingly brought out by the citation from Paul Ricoeur with which Bruce Kapferer emblazons the first chapter of his book on exorcizing demons in Sri Lanka: "If evil is coextensive with the origin of things, as primeval chaos and theogonic strife, then the elimination of evil and of the wicked must belong to the creative act as such."[4]

Yagé nights challenge this ritual of explanation of ritual. They make us wonder at the unstated rites of academic text-making, at the means for creating intellectual authority, and, above all, at the convention of sense-making thereby inscribed through conventions of "ordering" the chaos of that which has to be explained.

And it is precisely at the holy alliance of the orderly with the sacred that Benjamin's Marxist notion of the dialectical image, as developed through Surrealism and more especially his early work on allegory in Baroque drama, comes into play, divesting the totalizing compass of the Romantic concept of the symbol (upon which the aforementioned theories of ritual are based) by the nonwhite, nonhomogeneous, fragmentedness of montage, which on account of its awkwardness of fit, cracks, and violent juxtapositionings can actively embody both a presentation and a counterpresentation of the historical time which through conquest and colonialism matches signs with their meanings.

MONTAGE: the "interior" scenes of dots and dashes of color and of phantasms, coming and going, death scenes, above all fragments of things-shiny blades of grass quivering under the rain, a tiny feathered segment of intricate pattern (the edge of a bird's wing, perhaps?), the quavering *yagé* song butting into the river's rush — all metamorphosing into memory images as the past gains force in its rush into the present "now-time" of the *Jetztzeiten* where time stands still as an image in which past and future converge explosively.

MONTAGE: oscillating in and out of oneself; feeling sensations so intensely that you become the stuff sensed. But then you are standing outside the experience and coldly analyzing it as Bertolt Brecht so wanted from his "alienation effects" in his epic theater. Only here, in the theater of *yagé* nights in the Putumayo foothills, the A-effect, standing outside of one's now defamiliarized experience and analyzing that experience, is inconstant and constantly so, flickering, alternating with absorption in the events and their magic. Perhaps that is the formula for the profoundest possible A-effect, standing within and standing without in quick oscillation. It is not the order of ritual or the equally celebrated mystical "trip" through the more or less harmoniously cadenced zones and stations of cosmology that is of importance here. That cosmology we know well, and it is a fascist fascination too, with the ritual leader, with the harmonics of heroism, with order, with mystical flight, with the organic absorption of the individual into the "tribe" and so forth.

◆ ◆ ◆

Yet even disorder implies the presence of order, and on the face of things *yagé* nights do have features providing for continuity and in that sense for order too. Chief among these features would be the song and the shaman. But the song resists characterization in these orderly terms. The best we can do is regard it as something like "ordered disorder" and "continuous discontinuity." Its outstanding qualities are its irregularly stopping and starting, its frequent interruptedness, its sudden swerves and changes in pace and the peculiar way by which it is not only a massively dominating force but is open to interruption by anyone and anything — including this observation by Artaud in *The First Manifesto for Theater of Cruelty* regarding the uniquely material side of that theater's language, its humor, to break down, its poetry to make afresh:

> It extends the voice. It utilizes the vibrations and qualities of the voice. It wildly tramples rhythms underfoot [especially that]. It pile-drives sounds. It seeks to exalt, to benumb, to charm, to arrest the sensibility. It liberates a new lyricism of gesture which, by its precipitation or its amplitude in the air, ends by surpassing the lyricism of words. It ultimately breaks away from the intellectual subjugation of the language, by conveying the sense of a new and deeper intellectuality which hides itself beneath the gestures and signs, raised to the dignity of particular exorcisms.[5]

As for the shaman, despite his solidity and caring he is also a strategic zone of vacuity, a palette of imageric possibility. Where he does predominantly swim into focus, however, at least in the eyes of the civilized, is as the alternating, composite colonially created image of the wild man, bestial and superhuman, devil and god — thus reinforcing the montage technique and in a way its very fount. Just as history creates this fabulous image of the shaman, so the montaged nature of that image allows history to breathe in the spaces pried open between signs and meanings.

Furthermore, the decentered character of the shaman as a strategic zone of vacuity creates havoc with the notion of the hero and of the heroic so crucial to the tragic form of drama. Brecht's central figures become, notes Benjamin, like an empty stage on which the contradictions of society are acted out. The wise man is the perfect empty stage.[6]

Putumayo shamans resist the heroic mold into which current Western image-making would pour them. Instead, their place is to bide time and exude bawdy vitality and good sharp sense by striking out in a chaotic zigzag fashion between laughter and death, constructing and breaking down a dramatic space layered between these two poles. True, there is the cosmic Christian stage of redemption too. But that cosmos is here not just constricted. It is radically displaced.

The *axis mundi* (of which our cosmologists are so fond) here stretches not from hell to heaven but oscillates back and forth between laughter and death in a montage of creation and destruction — figured for the shaman in the signs of sweet-smelling petals as against the smell of shit, flowers as against frogs and lizards, birds as against snakes and alligators, clear-headedness as against nausea and drunkenness.

As a form of epic theater these *yagé* nights succeed not by suffusing the participants in unrelieved fantasies. Instead their effect lies in juxtaposing to a heightened sense of reality, one of fantasy — thereby encouraging among the participants speculation into the whys and wherefores of representation itself. In a similar vein Stanley Mitchell delineates Benjamin's preoccupation with montage:

> For fruitful antecedents, he looked back beyond German baroque to those forms of drama where the montage principle first made its appearance. He finds it wherever a critical intelligence intervenes to comment upon the representation, in other words where the representation is never complete in itself, but is openly and continually compared with the life represented; where the actors can at any moment stand outside themselves and show themselves to be actors.[7]

The technique of criticism and of discovery imputed here is not bound to an image of truth as something deep and general hidden under layers of superficial and perhaps illusory particulars. Rather, what is at work here is an image of truth as experiment, laden with particularity, now in this guise, now as that one, stalking the stage whose shadowy light conjures only to deconjure. It is this image of truth that flickers through the *yagé* nights of which I write, where it is patently the case that (in Mitchell's words) "the representation is never complete in itself, but is openly and continually compared with the life represented; where the actors can at any moment stand outside themselves and show themselves to be actors." The night-long *yagé* gathering exhibits this as much on the external stage as on what we might call the internal one set by the imagination. To the nights I have described as almost drumming with this alternating beat created by the constant interpolation of the everyday into the fabulous, and the fabulous into the everyday, think back also to the "internal" parallel to this as in José García relating one of his *yagé* visions in which he sees his family and farm being subject to sorcery. In that vision it is clear that the representation of himself in battle with the sorcerer is a representation never complete in itself, but one openly and continuously compared with the life represented, so that by this means the life as much as the representation is not only sensitized by each other's medium, but changed as well.

In this way fate is levered open and it is perhaps possible to overcome misfortune. On the one hand are envy and sorcery, and we are condemned to live out our lives in such a world where inequality breeds more of the same. But on the other hand there are weapons with which that fate can be fought. "'It can happen this way, but it can also happen quite a different way' — that is the fundamental attitude of one who writes for epic theater," comments Benjamin.[8]

The magic of the Indian — an unconscious colonial creation — can provide the white man such as José García or Eliseo with just this weapon against the fate of inequality and envy. Now, having come from what to many here would seem as far away as Australia, having passed through night after night of taking *yagé*, and equipped with his freshly empowered charms and talismans, he can return home. He may not have got from the Indian all the secrets for which he asked in his letter. In fact he probably has none of them. Nor has the Indian given him magic — magic in the sense of making money magic, winning the lottery magic, making something out of nothing magic, finding gold magic. And there is a lesson in not giving that, for in that direction lies the realm of *magia* and deeply commoditized magic that dances with the magic of money. That is what the charlatans who wander from the Sibundoy Valley are good at. Ask them!

What Eliseo has acquired (and he paid for it), says the Indian curer, who all night long has so laboriously cured his big fleshy body and his plastic bag of rings, is the curing of his cattle and of his hens so that the envy of his neighbors shall not penetrate. Now Eliseo can go home and work hard at being a curer and a farmer and withstand the envy his success will inevitably create-as it did for José García before.

It is a simple-sounding social function. The magic invested in the Indian by the civilized assuages the envy that comes from inequality among the whites. The shaman's daughter puts it in a slightly different way, that her father tries to make enemies into friends. But how this is done, and how the figure representing inferiority, savagery, and evil, comes to have this power-that is not quite so simple.

To the white man such as Eliseo, the epic theater of the *yagé* night is not merely Indian. It is real. Despite its dazzling array of alienation effects, this theater fails dismally where Brecht would have it most succeed. It is deeply illusionistic and nowhere more so than in the magical power attributed by colonial history to the Indian shaman.

But for the referents of this history and of these practices, namely the Indians who are called upon to provide magical power to blunt the evils of inequality in the rest of society, there *is* doubting about the reality. This uncertainty at what we might call the fount of the system of magical curing has curiously curative effects for us because it cautions against the search for magical power in a unitary being such as the Indian shaman, and instead advises us as to where that power creates itself; namely in the relation between the shaman and the patient — between the figure who sees but will not talk of what he sees, and the one who talks, often beautifully, but cannot see. It is this that has to be worked through if one is to become a healer.

(FROM Michael Taussig, *Shamanism, Colonialism, and the Wild Man: A Study in Terror and Healing,* Chicago: University of Chicago Press, 1987, pp. 435–446.)

NOTES

1 . Victor Turner and Edith Turner, *Image and Pilgrimage in Christian Culture: Anthropological Perspectives* (New York: Columbia University Press, 1978), pp. 254–255.

2. Antonin Artaud, *The Theater and Its Double,* trans. Mary C. Richards (New York: Grove Press, 1959), p. 61.

3. Sally Falk Moore and Barbara Myerhoff, eds. *Secular Ritual* (Amsterdam: Van Gorcum, Assen, 1977), pp. 3–24.

4. Bruce Kapferer, *A Celebration of Demons: Exorcism and the Aesthetics of Healing in Sri Lanka* (Bloomington: Indiana University Press, 1983), p. 1.

5. Artaud, *The Theater and Its Double,* p. 91.

6. Walter Benjamin, *Understanding Brecht* (London: New Left Books, 1973), p. 8.

7. Stanley Mitchell, "Introduction," in Walter Benjamin, *Understanding Brecht,* p. xiii.

8. Benjamin, *Understanding Brecht,* p. 8. Compare with Raymond Williams contrasting the indicative to the subjunctive mode of dramatic representation; the subjunctive being the experimental "as if" and "could be perhaps" mood that he discerns in Brecht's intention: Raymond Williams, *Politics and Letters: Interviews with New Left Review* (London: New Left Books, 1979), p. 218; and also his *Modern Tragedy* (Stanford: Stanford University Press, 1966), pp. 190–204.

DESIGN THERAPY

Angelika Gebhart-Sayer

The healing designs of the Shipibo-Conibo are perceived from the spirits and projected onto the patient's body in a spiritual, nonmaterialized manner. There are some indications that a shaman may read the designs of his vision analytically in linear pursuit of individual configurations, but in general the design visions are described as being overall, nonanalytical impressions of entire patterned "pages" or "sheets" flashed rapidly in front of the shaman's inner eye and vanishing as soon as he tries to have a closer look.[1] The shaman's spiritual knowledge, his spirit comprehension, and interactions form a complex system that deserves detailed study apart from the present essay. These matters are, to a large extent, veiled from the patient and the other nonspecialists. The patient might snatch a few disconnected details from the shaman's otherworldly voyages. All he is told about his sickness is its origin and the precautions to be taken. Ideally, he places himself in the hands of his doctor and refrains from asking questions.[2]

One important condition of the therapy is the aesthetically pleasing environment into which the shaman and the family place the patient. He is carefully surrounded by an ambience designed to appease both the senses and emotions. Visible and invisible geometric designs, melodious singing, and the fragrance from herbs and tobacco smoke pervade the atmosphere, and ritual purity characterizes his food and each person with whom he has contact. The patient is never left alone in his mosquito tent during the critical time of his illness. This setting induces in the patient the necessary emotional disposition for his recovery. But how is this indigenous concept of aesthetics to be understood?

The term *quiquin* refers to several notions of "correctness" and "beauty." Although it implies primarily a pleasant visual, auditory, or olfactory experience evoked, for example, by harmony, symmetry, accurate performance, or cultured refinement, the term is not limited to sensuous experience; it includes ideational values like subtlety, relevance, appropriateness, and cultural correctness. A harmoniously formed and well painted vessel is *quiquin* just like a village kept free from plant growth. *Quiquin rarebo* are genuine relatives; a *quiquin ainbo* denotes a woman of good upbringing and appearance. *Quiquin* also refers to the treatment of a sick person if the shaman works in an appropriate, traditional, sophisticated, and aesthetic manner, that is, employing, songs, designs, fragrance, and ritual purity in a truly Shipibo-Conibo manner. We shall now see how the shaman operates with *quiquin*-ness on three sensory levels — visual, auditory, and olfactory — and how they are synaesthetically combined to form a therapy of beauty, cultural relevance, and sophistication.

The shaman uses several invisible requisites richly embellished with designs. These include the medical book with its delicate, minute designs drawn by the Hummingbird spirit, the shining crown received during initiation, and the crossed bandolier which is the "mother and root" of the *quenyon*, the gruel-like substance, which he carries in his chest and may bring up to his mouth to suck the afflicted body parts. Among the visible painted requisites are the shaman's garment, the *tari,* the occasional facial painting of the patient, the painted vessels the shaman uses for the *ayahuasca* potion or tobacco water, and the vessels used for the patient's food and washing water perfumed with fragrant flowers.

Each case of illness requires the attendance and assistance of a different set of plant and animal spirits. Only Nishi Ibo, the master spirit of the *ayahuasca* vine, is necessarily present at all sessions. Nishi Ibo projects the luminescent geometric configurations before the shaman's eyes shortly before he visits the session personally. These

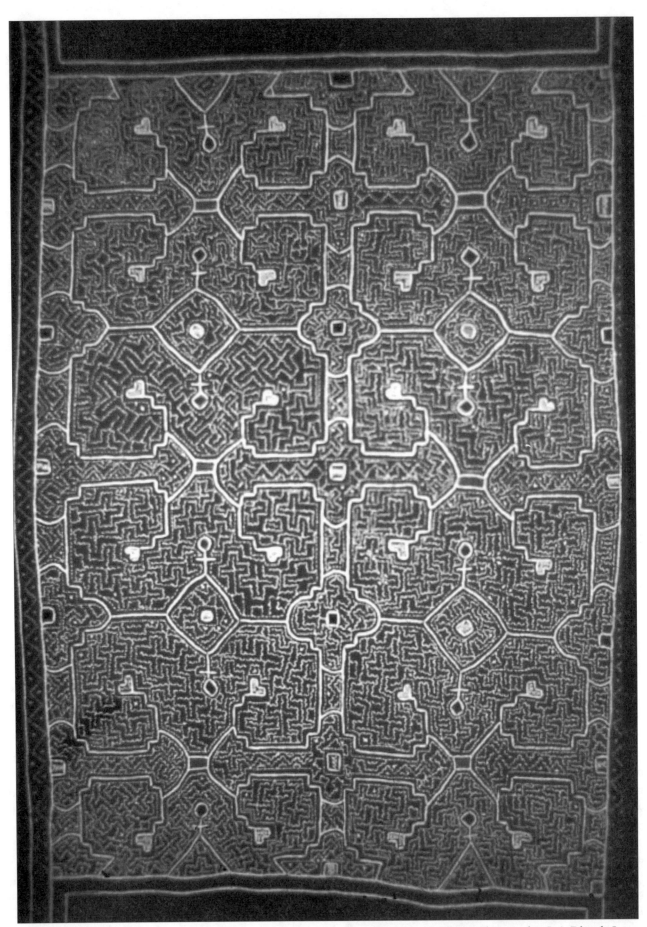

Shipibo textile design. Photograph © Luis Eduardo Luna.

are luminous phosphenic visions that cover everything within the shaman's sight. With the assistance of his helper spirits, the shaman now begins to interpret the vision as a *quiquin* design medicine. As soon as the floating network touches his lips and halo, the shaman issues melodies that correspond to the shiny visions. Describing the phenomenon, the shaman says, "My song is a result of the design image," a direct transformation from the visual to the auditory, in some way comparable to our musical notes and their auditory realizations. There can be more than a hundred designs in one song. The songs are heard, seen, and sung simultaneously by Nishi Ibo, all attending spirits while the villagers hear but his solitary voice. If the patient's relatives now join the shaman in singing (their singing necessarily lags slightly behind since most of the texts are ad hoc creations and unknown to them), a two-sided choir builds up in which the shaman plays the conspicuous role of an acoustic hinge between the spirit and the village worlds. The compelling force of this chorus is directed against the spirits held responsible for the patient's illness.

As voices meander through the air, a second transformation takes place, visible only to the shaman. The song now assumes the form of a geometric pattern, a *quiquin* design which penetrates the patient's body and settles down permanently. According to the shaman, the healing pattern is a result of his song. Unless he falls ill again, it remains with the patient even after death to help identify his spirit as a Shipibo-Conibo in the other world. The Hummingbird spirit, Pino, described as the "writer" or "secretary" among the higher spirits, now hovers above the patient and lets the design configurations drop onto the patient's body, swishing, whirring, humming, busy with tiny movements. The shaman explains:

> Pino writes the quene outlining the therapy and the song. It grows little by little. Just as each word in modern writing is different, so are the individual signs *(tená)* of the design. At first, the sick body appears like a very messy design. After a few treatments, the design appears gradually. When the patient is cured, the design is clear, neat, and complete. In my visions, I watch Hummingbird hover above the patient. With each swish of his wings, a part of the design emerges. He also draws with the beak and tongue. If the design refuses to become clear, I know that I cannot heal the patient. I am not told the meaning of the individual design elements, but I know by my overall impression of the designs what I have to sing. I feel that designs and melodies are rotating. Some designs can make a person even more ill. They are not made by Hummingbird, but come out of the mouth of a sorcerer. They are detached like figures, not flowing like handwriting.

While he watches Hummingbird write the healing design, the shaman uses his painted garment, the *tari*, to fan away the malignant *nihue* (wind, pneuma, aura) of the disease-inflicting spirit, which again "sounds like the wings of Hummingbird." *Nihue* hampers the formation of the healing design. In a specific case of swollen liver, high fever, and hemorrhaging diarrhea, for example, a motif called *nai cano mahueca* ("consecutive curves in the scaffold of the sky") was applied by the hummingbird, a design including many zigzags. Before the hummingbird is able to apply the healing design, the shaman, with the help of his fragrant herbal bundle, brushes away the "mess" *(móe)* on the patient's body. Spots and shadows are traces of *nihue* indicating that the healing process is not yet completed.

The number of treatments required to complete a healing design depends on the tenacity with which the disease-inflicting spirit is able to contaminate the design. Generally, a shaman needs three to five treatments of approximately five hours each, during which the spirit incessantly tries to stain or smudge the gradually emerging design with its evil countersongs and harmful aura. When on a disease-inflicting tour, these spirits may also attempt to open the tightly sealed vessels of design-song medicines stored in the cloud villages of the tree spirits and protected by guardian spirits, to let the *shama* (massed potency) of the medicines (which are actually songs) escape and vanish. The shaman counters such attacks with an intensification of singing and helper spirit intervention.

In certain cases, the shaman will climb the tower or tree that connects him to the cloud villages to procure personally the medicines (songs and herbal recommendations). Or he will descend into the water to free an abducted soul from the "soul prison" of the cosmic anaconda at the aquatic edge of the world.

A number of therapeutic measures are applied directly to the patient. During the daytime, for example, the shaman dispenses herbal remedies (the Shipibo-Conibo know many), helps prepare blood-circulating nettle lashings, steam baths, ablutions, inner purifications (vomiting, enemas), and prescribes facial and body painting. The patient is kept on a diet that excludes, among other things, bought food "which has been in contact with metal" (during the canning and bottling processes), foods containing fat, sugar, salt, and fruit. The patient must be protected from impure influences, such as menstruating women and couples who have "united" the night before. Tobacco smoke, the fragrance of flowers, and certain aromatic ointments from the pharmacies in town are substantial components of the treatment in that they lead helper spirits to the sickbed, ward off opponent spirits, and intensify respiration and relaxation.

If the patient's destiny is to die, a condition the shaman is able to read from the unsuccessful body design, he will tell the patient after the first few sessions that he is unable to cure the disease. If the treatment is successful, the healing pattern is "covered" *(tapado)* by a protective finish, the *pana.* For this purpose, the entire body of the patient is "covered with songs." The *pana* shelters the weakened patient against shocks from menstruating women or sexually active couples, as well as from malevolent spirits and shamans. Should further treatment be necessary, the *pana* must be removed with the help of certain songs. Although the *pana* acts as a protective shield, it is easily destroyed, for instance through breaking the diet, and the old disease may appear again.

Many diseases are *nihue* afflictions and are cured with the spiritual body designs *(quene rau or yora quene).*[3] They may be defined as "loss of the anima," "rainbow stroke," "shock," "hypnotic spirit magnetism," and so on, and attributed to an inimical shaman or an animal, plant, or other spirit.

Although research has not been very successful in the realm of harmful designs, one mode of inflicting disease appears to be the sung projection onto a person's body of a design resembling a double projectile point or any nonspecific pattern received from the spirits and used by the shaman together with the name of the person to be harmed or influenced.[4] Ronin, with all possible patterns united on its body, is brought into play in this instance, provided the shaman has command over this most awesome of all spirits. An evil body design is said to be clouded and difficult to diagnose. It is sometimes equalized with *nihue,* the harmful spirit aura. But with the help of Nishi Ibo (the *ayahuasca* spirit), the shaman "reads it as if with an X-ray machine." Once an evil pattern is diagnosed, the shaman can "unravel" it and wind it onto an imaginary spool, erase it with his shamanic broom, lift it off as if peeling it, etc. All these transactions are accomplished through singing, the texts of the songs revealing much about the techniques involved.

The *vero-yushin* designs described above seem to be as ambivalent as most other shamanic issues. Discussion of them arouses controversy among the Indians themselves. The relation of the designs with the spirits of the dead (a clearly negative association) and sorcery on the one hand and their popularity on textiles and ceramics on the other obscures their function and meaning.

Another method for inflicting harm is the withdrawal through the shaman of a healing pattern he once gave to a patient. This is allegedly, very easy to accomplish and presents quite a temptation to the shaman: "I have to keep controlling myself so that this idea does not enter my head; I might wish to apply this practice on my own people." If a patient whose design has been withdrawn falls ill, the new shaman whom he might then consult can immediately recognize that the patient is without a design. Healing designs from earlier cures are smudged by new diseases.

Obviously, a person places himself in the hands of his doctor not only during therapy, but for the rest of his life.[5] This explains why the Shipibo-Conibo are so careful in their choice of doctors to one another. Kinship proximity plays an important role, and it is understandable if parents are eager to lure a shaman son-in-law into the family. The social and psychological implications of these close ties between a shaman and his former patient appear to be significant and deserve further study.

Returning to the visionary shamanic book previously discussed, we may now conclude that the Indians' view of the book comprises both the general (*ayahuasca*-induced) capacity to perceive the rapidly flashing "sheets" of designs or the floating variety that covers everything in sight, and the mentioned imaginary volume that the shaman receives from the spirits during his initiation. The senior informant's account of his initiation adds some ethnographic substance to the latter:

> I had been practicing with small portions of shahuan-peco ["the macaw's moulting"; an unidentified parasitic plant formerly used in Shipibo-Conibo shamanism as a hallucinogen instead of or in addition to ayahuasca] for a long time. This is a very strong drug which not every shaman could endure. I drank the juice of the

leaves with water and tobacco juice, and I also bathed with it. Then came my chief experience with shahuan-peco. Twelve hours after drinking the potion and bathing with it, about noon the next day, it started to thunder, and I heard crowds of spirits making much noise. The four masters of the plant appeared in human disguise. They were very angry with me and denied me their knowledge and power. When I was shaking a lot and almost fainted, they took hold of me and dashed me around within the four corners. Two of them were standing in the opposite corners to throw me back. When I was almost dead, Ani-Ino, the great jaguar, arrived, very beautiful and shining. He grabbed me by the neck with his mouth, and sucked my blood to reduce my weight so I could fly. He carried me through the air for many hours, up to the clouds, into a great remoteness. This is how a shaman learns to travel through the air and see things from above. In the clouds, he meets all the tree spirits who help to heal the sick, for example doctor anta-yushin (a tree spirit and bone doctor). During my vision, I was able to see all who passed by my house in their true nature, with their true intentions, and naked. Then there appeared the master of shahuan-peco himself. He carried a book in his hands, the leaves of which were still new and blank. Before he gave it to me, Hummingbird painted very fine designs into it with its delicate beak. In a book like that, a shaman can read about the condition of his patient and the way to help him. I often use the book when I sing.

Although it contradicts what was said about the overall grasping of rapidly flashing design "pages" in *ayahuasca* visions, I would like to introduce here a bit of information received from the same shaman which supports the claim that a shaman can (or could) also read a design analytically, that is, follow the individual motifs in linear fashion. Linear pursuit is an indicator of a former motif-by-motif reading technique. While discussing the reading of his shamanic book, the informant followed with his finger the meandering configurations of a design, starting at the lower right and continuing horizontally in serpentine ascent. In front of him were the two designs he had chosen from my comprehensive collection as the closest approximation of those of his visionary book. Belonging to the older, rectilinear design tradition, they are composed of two or more sub-fields displaying different patterns. Naturally, as a consequence of the semantic loss in design art, this linear reading technique, if it ever existed, became obsolete.

(EXCERPT FROM: Angelika Gebhart Sayer. "The Geometric Designs of the Shipibo-Conibo in Ritual Context," *Journal of Latin American Lore* 11:2 (1985). pp. 143–75)

NOTES

1. Reichel-Dolmatoff describes the *ayahuasca* visions of the Desana as symmetric light patterns "perceived as superpositions on surfaces," as a "multitude of small luminous images" clustered or strung together, zigzagging or assuming network and checker patterns. He also points out that acoustical stimulation is important to attain a "bright and pleasant vision" (1978:8–12). These descriptions coincide in all aspects with descriptions of Shipibo-Conibo visionary experience. Hence we may assume that the graphic perceptions are a phosphenic retina function triggered by the alkaloids of the drug.

2. The external proceedings of *ayahuasca* sessions have been described elsewhere. See for example, Roe 1982a and Meyer 1984:57.

3. The second major medicinal agent applied is *nete* (light). However, this complex is of little relevance in this essay.

4. The ambivalence of the shamanic practice in Amazonia is well established. The Shipibo-Conibo shaman is no exception, being both healer and sorcerer. Not only is he himself ambivalent, but his helper spirits are too. The same spirit that assists in curing may be sent to harm a person. But conditions are not that simple. In the terminology a shaman uses after defeating a harmful spirit, it is conspicuous that such spirits are never extinguished or killed by the shaman. They are simply driven away. Langdon (1979a:64, 77) describes how the Siona shaman directs the disease-inflicting substance back to its origin. Reichel-Dolmatoff (1971:130) reports that the Desana shaman has to promise to the master of game animals to cause the death of a certain number of people (own or alien) in exchange for game animals. The Warao "Dark shaman" feeds human sacrifices to the Lords of the Underworld to guarantee the duration of the world, the Gods, and the young generation (Wilbert 1975:174). In the Siona case, the shaman knows where the evil substance is going, but it is uncertain whether he also knows the substance to cause harm at its place of origin, that is,

whether he uses the substance to hit back, thus simultaneously harming somewhere else and caring for his own people. In the Desana case it is obvious that caring for one's people and harming are closely interrelated. A case for such an interrelation between caring and harming could be made for the Shipibo-Conibo if it could be shown that the shaman, while expelling evil forces from a patient, intentionally directs them to certain targets (perhaps a distant enemy), rather than just dismissing them into space. One step in this direction might be my major informant's answer when I asked him why he was very sick and losing his force. He said, "I healed many during my life. Now they are hitting back." Those "hitting back" are either the inimical spirits and shamans whom he upset so many times, or those people whom he harmed perforce by exposing them to the harmful forces released through him, be it intentionally or not. Considering the profound concern with the reconciliation of opposites, with reciprocity, ambivalence and balance in general so consistently found in Lowland cultures (including the Shipibo-Conibo), the latter speculation might be not entirely off the track.

5. Among the Warao Indians, lifelong dependence on the shaman exists for some women (Johannes Wilbert, personal communication).

III

NEW RELIGIONS:
Santo Daime, Barquinha, and União do Vegetal
(UDV)

Ayahuasca, watercolor on paper, © by Isabela Hartz (Brazil). Collection of Editora Record.

HYMNS

All hymns translated from the Portuguese by Steven F. White

Received by Raimundo Irineu Serra

Water-Star

I'm going to call the water-star
To come illuminate me
To come illuminate me
To come illuminate me

Give me strength and give me love
Give me strength and give me love

Can I dive in? Please let me!
Can I dive in? Please let me!
Down to the depths of the sea
Down to the depths of the sea

It was My Father who sent me
It was My Father who sent me

To know every kind of beauty
To know every kind of beauty

Give me strength and give me love
Give me strength and give me love

It was My Mother who taught me
It was My Mother who taught me
To know every kind of beauty
To know every kind of beauty

With so much love in my heart
To sing with brothers and sisters
To sing with brothers and sisters
With all my brothers and sisters

I Strike a Balance

I strike a balance, strike a balance
between everything that is and will be

I call the sun
I call the moon
I call the star
So they'll all keep me company

I strike a balance, strike a balance
between everything that is and will be

I call the wind
I call the earth
I call the sea
So they'll all keep me company

I strike a balance, strike a balance
between everything that is and will be

I call the vine
I call the leaf
I call water
To join them all and help me see

I strike a balance, strike a balance
between everything that is and will be

I'm filled with joy
And I feel strong
I have it all
Because Eternal God gives it to me

Little Bird

The little bird is singing
Running through its ABCs
And I'm running through your life
So that everyone can see

The little bird is singing
All alone in the forest
Announcing to the hunter
You fired but you always missed

Little green bird is singing
Next to you by the flower
I'm a bird with a keeper
And my keeper has power

Little green bird is singing
With abundant love and cheer
I'm the little Bird's true song
And I know for sure I'm here

Gardener

It was my Mother, my Queen
Who gave me the job that is ours
To become a gardener
In the Garden of Lovely Flowers

In the Garden of Lovely Flowers
There's everything that I need
The gorgeous and beautiful
Everything that God gives me

There's no one that won't receive
Flowers that come from this place
But who is being mindful?
Who knows how to use their grace?

Tending to this garden
Requires attention year-round
Since such elegant flowers
Mustn't fall down on the ground

The Garden of Lovely Flowers
Needs to be watered with care
With Our Universal Father's
Loving kindness and prayer

The Stars

The stars already came
They're here to say their name
It's me, it's me, it's me
A child in God's family

The stars have carried me
To travel the whole world through
So that I could know this truth
So that I could be true, too

I climbed a mountain of thorns
There were sharp points I endured
But the stars kept telling me
That everything can be cured

Then the stars went on to say
Don't talk, be someone who listens
So that I can understand
and talk with my Indians

The Indians are here right now
They've brought their good medicines
On bare feet with naked arms
So they can cure the Christians

I Was Guided by the Moon

I was guided by the moon
And by a band of stars
After climbing this high hilltop
There was thunder in my ears

The roar of thunder that I heard
Was God's heavenly abuses
Informing all of us
That the Highest Power was his

I was out wandering
On the beach by the sea
When I heard a loud voice
Send them looking for me

Before my very eyes
Getting closer to me now
Was a gold and silver canoe
With a Lady in the bow

When She finally reached me
She told me to come for a ride
She whispered in my ear:
"We'll travel far and wide

To a certain place I know
We'll travel far and wide
God and the Virgin Mother
Traveling by our side

When we finally arrived
At fields of this flower later
I saw the rich beauty
Of Our Father the Creator

I Am the Son of This Truth

I am the son of this truth
I'm in this world for all to see
I give advice and more advice
To those who would listen to me

Knowledge is what everyone has
You don't need a special degree
But there's lots of science involved
It's something you have to study

I study hard, I study hard
There are so many things to know
To be a good professor
You've got to show what you know

At the Side of My Mother

At the side of My Mother
And My Father on the astral plane
That's where I want to remain
That's where I want to remain

My Flower, My Expectation
My Garden Rose
That's where I want to remain
With My Mother wherever she goes

I live in this house right here
My Mother gave me a place
I love being close to her
And I love singing her praise

I follow My Mother's wishes
And heal people of their pain
With these fine and shining stones
Here where I want to remain

Flower on the Waters

Flower on the waters,
Where've you been?
Where're you going?
I'll be doing some cleaning
In my heart, My Father's flowing

The dwelling of My Father
Is deep in the planet's heart
Where all love makes its home
And hides its most secret part

This part that is most secret
Lives in each of us so dear
If we only knew each other
Within the truth right here

I Stepped Down on the Cold Earth

I stepped down on the cold earth
But I felt only warm air
She's the one who gives me bread
My Mother who raised us with care

My Mother who raised us with care
Her teachings soon became mine
Matter I give back to her
My Spirit to the Divine

With blood that runs in my veins
I wrote my name with a plume
I give My Spirit to God
My body goes to the tomb

My body goes to the tomb
Scorned in dew that the night brought
Someone will speak in my name
Others will say it in their thought

(EXCERPT FROM: Raimundo Irineu Serra. *O cruzeiro (Hinário)*. Rio de Janeiro: Editora Beija-Flor [Centro Eclético de Fluente Luz Universal Sebastiã Mota de Melo], 1991, pp. 51–52, 58–59, 74, 85, 92, 97, 103–104, 123, 135, 147, 150.)

Received by Sebastião Mota de Melo

I Lifted My Thoughts

I lifted my thoughts on high
From this garden where I'll be
I raised my voice to the sky
Oh, My Mother, pray for me!

I cleaned out my frame of mind
I saw a wheel begin to spin
At the heart of this great light
My Father watched me from within

Oh, My Father in heaven
His power that can reach us
He gave us this great Master
Here on earth to teach us

Brothers, sisters, let's go on
This is no time to delay
Listen to the moaning sea
Feel the earth begin to sway

While I was watching the sky
I saw a shooting star flare
When it circled around me
I felt my body despair

Whenever You Become Ill

Whenever you become ill
And Daime is what you drink
Remember the Deity
That healed you and made you think

Remembering the Deity
Made the cosmos shake and shine
The jungle rocked itself to sleep
Since everything here is mine

I've already given you
As much as I can unveil
If you do what I tell you
There's no way that you can fail

You know the way that I shine
You know who I am already
That's why I'm asking you now
To come here and be with me

Remember Your Master

Remember, please, your Master
Remember to love unafraid
Remember you must be strong
And keep the promise you made

Head toward invisible realms
Wander in the astral plane
Enter the holiest home
That is our Father's domain

Follow the road you've taken
Leave all the talkers behind
Since the strength of your Master
Can also destroy your mind

They don't know what they're saying
And maybe they never will
When I am with my Master
I find myself happier still

My Master let me ask you
In the name of the Lord above
Make my light even brighter
Give me strength and give me love

My Son I Love You Truly

Deep within my heart of hearts
My son I love you truly
My Father I honor you
With respect on bended knee

My son I've become the Man
That other men cannot see
Meet all your obligations
My son please listen to me

My son I am your Father
I am the one you spoke to

Receive this light that is yours
So you know your own value

Do all that you need to do
Meet every obligation
Don't listen to or bother
With brotherly conversation

Receive these words with love
With attention carefully
Because these are the flowers
For your garden sent by me

On Sun, on Moon, on Earth, at Sea

On sun, on moon
On earth and at sea
I've been searching for this truth
Now I know where it will be

On sun, on moon
On earth and at sea
This truth I know is pure
I'm here to show how this must be

On sun, on moon
On earth and at sea

Whoever wants to can search
Find the master's place and see

On sun, on moon
On earth and at sea
God in heaven descended
To teach this truth to you and me

On sun, on moon
On earth and at sea
I call out to all the stars
So they'll accompany me

I Am Not God

I am not God
But someday there is a chance
I am not God
But there is a strong resemblance

God is fire
God is water. God is everything

All my brothers and sisters
We should start our studying

God in heaven
God on earth. God at sea with grace
All my brothers and sisters
You must remain in your place

(EXCERPT FROM: Sebastião Mota de Melo. *O justiceiro (Hinário)*. Rio de Janeiro: Editora Beija- Flor [Centro Eclético da Fluente Luz Universal Sebastião Mota de Melo], 1992, pp. 29, 36, 103, 104, 118, 195

Received by Alfredo Gregório de Melo

Divine Bond

Because of this divine bond
Because of these threads of love
We can be even closer
To Our Creator above

Rainfall from the astral plane
Rain that falls upon the land
We can be even closer
To Father's all-embracing hand

Thunder is a mighty force
It's the power of the word
Where God speaks even closer
To the whole of humankind

The sun with Your radiance
Makes the entire forest shine
Where many divine blessings
Cover all of humankind

The moon from its place on high
Consecrated in Your calm song
In the most perfect harmony
Gives us force and makes our souls strong

The multitude of tiny stars
With light that is incandescent
As Our Master has declared
Just God who is Omnipotent

The creative force we have
As beings joined together
Shines brightly in this Garden
Of Our Protective Mother

Meditation

When I consider nature
My heart is satisfied
To see so many creatures
Unique and living side by side

When I consider heaven
And the great power in command
I feel tiny here on earth
And ask for strength to understand

When I consider humans
The multitude keeps me awake
To see so many creatures
Each one choosing a road to take

I see all the animals
Arrange their places and feed
Because here in this Garden
They've got everything they need

I see the whole rain forest
As an immense work of art
If you want to see yourself
You must have God in your heart

I see the many insects
With a different fate in store
Life provides us living proof
There's a Divine Creator

All things live on land and sea
And in our illumination
This secret's great mystery
Is revealed through meditation

As far as the eye can see
There's nothing that can't be seen
Here in this Garden of Love
That belongs to Longing's Queen

And give me the strength and love
Boiled-down harmony and pardon
I consider this kingdom
The Virgin Mary's Garden

(EXCERPT FROM: Alfredo Gregório de Melo. *O cruzeirinho (Hinário)*. Rio de Janeiro: Editora Beija-Flor [Centro Eclético de Flu-ente Luz Universal Raimundo Irineu Serra], 1992, pp.26–27, 37–38.)

Received by Daniel Pereira de Matos

The Sweeper-Angels

I
Twelve heavenly angels came down
Lord Jesus sent them in our sleep
Out of His love for our mission
They're the angels that sweep and sweep

II
Twelve heavenly angels came down
All are angels that sweep and sweep
They've come to sweep our evil thoughts
And bring the holy love we keep

III
The heavenly angels came down
With the brooms of light in their hands
To sweep away our evil thoughts,
To clean up the heart's unclean plans

IV
Oh angels of God my Savior
With the shining brooms you carry
Sweep away our evil thoughts
Clean us for Jesus and Mary

V
With so much love and no complaint
Jesus died for us on the cross
To offer us all salvation
And to redeem our lives from loss

VI
Sweep us clean, heavenly angels
With your busy brooms of light
With pure thoughts we'll adore Jesus
And pray to Him to makes things right

VII
We give a thousand thanks to God
And the Virgin of Conception, too
For the cleanliness we've received
From soul to heart, from me to you

VIII
All the malignant thoughts we have
Come from the master of temptation
Only God and Our Holy Mother
Save us from that devastation

IX
Let us save the angels of God
They sweep away bad behavior
They sweep us and keep us so clean
So we can follow God the Savior

X
St. John on the face of this earth
Made roads where the Savior could pray
Jesus came and He made them smooth
And sent sweepers to clean the way

Natural Flowers

The natural flowers
Of Jesus are quite a sight
He is the eternal
Gardener of light

The natural flowers
Of Jesus are quite a sight
All the worlds that exist
Are gardens of light

The flowers of the sky
Are all legendary
They speak and take long strolls
With the Virgin Mary

How sublime to witness
In gardens of this earth
In mountains and forests
A thousand flowers' birth

Through the open country
Through the fields and meadows
By places of worship
God the gardener goes

In the ocean garden
Everything shines brightly
The flowers are the light
From Mary's rosary.

My brothers and sisters
Our pilgrimage is long
Let's praise the Lord Jesus
And Mary with our song

Queen of the Sea Waltz

I'm going to sing a waltz
About the sea's mystery
Let's all play like the children
As happy as we can be

With the beautiful mermaids
And the sea-nymphs in a ring
And lovely Princesses, too
They've all come to dance and sing

Tonight is a lovely night
Everyone's ready to play
Here come the lovely fairies
And the Queen is on her way

And they're all very happy
To be visiting us here
They've brought lots of mimosas
And offer us their good cheer

The flowers are mysteries
From the garden of the sea
They're the plants of many lights
From the sea's own mystery

These beautiful mysteries
Are confirmed for you and me
In the lights of the sublime
That light the Queen of the Sea

Received by Francisca Campos do Nascimento

Hymn of the Most Holy Trinity and the Virgin of Charity

Oh, Virgin Mother of Charity
You cure me with your holy love
You cure my brothers and sisters, too
With the light from your divine love

Oh, Virgin Mother of Charity
You cure me with your holy love
You cure my body and my soul
For Jesus the Savior above

Oh, Virgin Mother of Charity
Mother of our Savior's origin
You can cure the most innocent
Who're sick because of those who sin

Oh, Virgin Mother of Charity
Only you can save us now
And only you can cure our souls
And protect us as you know how

I beseech you, Oh Mother of Charity
I pray you'll soon come to our aid
Now and at the hour of our death
Free us from what the Devil's made

Chorus
Hail! Divine Eternal Father
Hail! Jesus the Savior above
Hail! Divine and Holy Spirit
Make us shine with the light of love.

THE BOOK OF VISIONS:
Journey to Santo Daime
(excerpt)

Alex Polari de Alverga

My Gods Live Far from the Temples

The afternoon was ending. The heat was giving way to a tropical freshness. Flocks of birds were seeking refuge. Here and there, men, women and children were smoothing their impeccable uniforms: the men in white suits with dark blue ties and the women with a pleated white skirt, petticoat and diagonal green band, colored ribbons on their shoulders and a tiara on their heads.

After several attempts to dress appropriately, I opted for a white Indian tunic that allowed me to move freely and comfortably. The rules on the day of the *trabalho* (ceremony) were strict: men on one side, women on the other. And this is true inside the Church as well as outside the temple. Couples only speak to each other during the midnight break and at the end of the ceremony at dawn.

I must admit that this separation irritated me a little. To me, it seemed more like an imposition of a certain kind of conservative morality than something necessary for the ceremony. But, because everything that was happening there was new to me, I respected the rules out of a sense of good will. This was the only position possible for a person who had come there to learn.

But whenever I had the chance, I infringed on the regulations to a certain extent. The ceremony had not yet begun (it was 5:45), and I was chatting with Sônia and some other people.

João Batista, one of the *fiscais* (marshals) in charge of keeping order during the service, came over to call this infraction to our attention. His tone was really not very nice and it irritated me a great deal. I swallowed all my replies while he accompanied us toward the Church, ruminating some vague moral sermon. "Great!" I thought. "I got here today and this guy is treating me as if I had been around for years."

We entered the Temple. The women were already taking their places on the right. The men were more dispersed and wandered through the large, open part of the Church. Several visitors and assistants took their places on the benches designated for them.

Zé, Gil and I decided to record some sounds during the first part of the *Hinário,* the Santo Daime religious service composed of a long series of hymns. We got in line in order to drink Daime.

There is a mystery in the taste of Daime. Nothing in the world resembles it. I grabbed the tape recorder and I left accompanying Gil. I wasn't able to relax the way I wanted to. The necessity of professional work did not allow me to give myself over to the experience. Besides, I had been very anxious "waiting" for the effect of the Daime. And that expectation just made things more difficult. Nothing was going to happen there as long as I had that attitude.

I saw Sônia far away on the other side with the women making an effort to dance while shaking a maraca. Sometimes I felt like sending all those rules of the ritual to hell and going to sit down with her in some cozy place in the rain forest.

When we finished the recordings, the Daime was served again. At the back of the Church, there is a replica of the temple made of wood. Through two little windows, the Daime is offered without any pause in the ceremony.

In this second round of drinking Daime, to use the language of the *daimistas,* "the force hit hard." My feet felt like lead and I had very little sense of my body from the waist up. I looked for a place to sit down because I was afraid of falling. There was a kind of popping in my left ear similar to when I travel by plane.

A chair had caught my attention ever since the beginning of the ceremony. It was one of those lounge chairs with a woven nylon seat that one sees in simple little houses in the North and Northeast Brazil.

Several times I had tried to approach it, but it was only unoccupied for a few seconds before someone else would occupy it.

Once again, I felt the need to sit down. Someone got there before me. I went to the bench. I was dizzy, felt like vomiting, and my stomach was twisted in knots. That was more or less the shape I was in when we reached the midnight break.

I stood up with difficulty and called Sônia with my eyes. She was at the peak of her journey. She wanted to stay with the women. I was hurt. I felt terrible and I wanted to come down a little with her at my side.

We almost created a very tense climate. I wandered away without any sense of direction. My stomach ached and I felt like shitting. Worse than that: I had the feeling that I might already have taken a shit and that everyone was watching me and amused.

Completely disoriented, I went through the little iron door at the back of the Church and took the road that led to *Seu* Mário's place.

I took the risk of eating some crackers with cheese, and my stomach felt worse. I went to the jungle and there was no way to leave. I went back. I exchanged some harsh words with Sônia. People were coming and going from the little house. I laid down with Sônia on top of a bed. I felt almost exhausted and on the verge of a bad trip on acid.

Someone asked if I was going to go back and said that the ceremony was going to begin again soon. I swore to myself that there was no way I was returning. Sleep was tempting me.

The house was almost empty. Something in me fought against sleep. At this point, the hymns in the Church began. They reached my ears distinctly and softly.

A spark shot through my brain and I heard the order loud and clear: "Go back to the Church!"

I got up with no discussions. I wasn't able to focus on anything very well. It took me ten minutes to take a few steps, in that, all of a sudden, I had the clear sensation of alternating between being on the edge of a precipice and in a closed forest filled with thorns.

After a great deal of effort, I managed to find the path again. I still stopped at Seu Wilson's house and drank some very sweet *capim Santo* tea. I wanted to throw up again. I felt green all over. I went to the window and began to breathe deeply. Holding my head in my hands, I looked at the ground as if I were hundreds of meters in the air. In fact, I could see everything — even the tiniest details of the pebbles and sand. Two turkeys stopped below me and stared at me with a questioning look. At that moment, I wasn't able to define them as two turkeys. I just felt a captivating wave of love for those two creatures and the unquestionable feeling that they were sorry for me and had come there to help me.

When I was able to free myself from the eyes of my friends, I looked up and saw the starry sky. A thousand rays of energy refreshed my neck and gave me the courage to return to the Church. I met Tom and some other people from Rio Branco in the temple. I had to make an enormous effort to exchange half a dozen words with them.

Seu Wilson came toward me.

"So, did you see anything?"

"I don't know."

He continued ahead of me, reiterating his offer to allow me to drink the special Daime. I had forgotten about that.

When I entered the large room, I was dragged without realizing it to a point behind some pillars. The next thing I knew, I was beside the chair I longed for. Then, when I finally sat down, I felt it was there that my journey began.

During the break, I had told Rama in passing, "My gods don't live in temples and palaces. They prefer the open air."

What I meant by that was that I felt much better when I went outside next to the jungle, laid down and watched the stars. To stay inside listening to the hymns was a sacrifice. Now, sitting in my chair, the feeling was the opposite. I wouldn't leave this place for anything in the world.

The second part of the ceremony not only has dancing and singing, but also musical instruments. The musicians, after a period of warming up, really started cooking. The dancing started again.

An Argentine beside me began to speak: "It's an explosion of energy, vibrations that come from everywhere, isn't it? Explosions of energy . . ."

These words not only kept me from concentrating but made me feel bad. I closed my eyes and mentally hoped that the Argentine would disappear from the face of the earth. When I opened them, he was no longer there. I was shocked!

In the distance, I could see Chico Corrente taking the Argentine to the window.

"Brother, please have more respect for those who are working. Otherwise, you're just getting in the way."

"But the explosion of energy is fantastic!"

"Fine. But if you keep speaking loudly, you'll have to leave."

I realized that Chico was my guardian angel.

The Journey of the Inca

Sitting in my chair, I leaned back comfortably. The hymns began to seem more familiar to me. Something in me no longer resisted them.

Suddenly, I heard a buzzing getting progressively louder moving toward me from behind. The sounds of the maracas were confused with the buzzing. I felt like I was a prisoner inside the sound of the maracas. Each beat made concentrated circles of energy move through the large room, similar to the way we skipped stones on the surface of a lake. That layer of energy did not sit still. Another blow from 150 maracas at the same time and the surface of the lake was moving again.

My chair became incandescent, like a piece of iron in hot coals. I leaned forward. Everything was moving around me. I saw energy as small circles pulling in the direction of the bigger circles, external to their rays, and, at the same time, toward the smaller circles that coexisted in their interior to infinity. And that's how it went, from there to infinity and from infinity to the center of the star of David, where the last circle disappeared and began again.

The incandescent chair became a ship. There was a kind of woven bubble around it. It was as if, around me, circles of energy took longer to disappear. That materialized some protection. Within, I felt crystallized and the sort of time to which I was accustomed could not interfere.

A thread of consciousness accompanied all these visions. I wanted to explain them, but I couldn't. Intuitively, I was discovering that my encounter had arrived. It didn't get me anywhere to want to explain things. When I conquered the last rational attacks, a great calm took possession of me. It was at that instant that I saw him.

At first glance, it was a presence of undefined contours. Then, the face, alternating between one that was old and wrinkled as if it had just come from a sarcophagus, and one that was young and filled with an exuberance capable of defining me ironically. Every time I blinked, he appeared in one form or the other. I sensed that I was the materialization of that being's thought, that I would feel and behave according to the way he "thought me." That power, at first, scared me. Later, an enormous confidence calmed me.

I looked again. It was an old Inca with a typical cap and clothing that mixed colored wool and leather from some animal. My communication with him was telepathic. I was feeling obliged to represent the projections that he made of me. He seemed to have an existence that was much more concrete than mine, a mere creation made better by an incomprehensible power.

With his mind, the Inca guided my ship. He knew that it was taking me to a very important place. The focus of my vision oscillated and, each time I blinked, the two images alternated between the unclear feeling of that place and the scenes of dancing around the Star.

Suddenly, both were synchronized. The other time that was many millennia in the past as well as the other place where I traveled with my Inca coincided with the present time with its uniformed people dancing and playing hymns. They were now one and the same, the key to the same secret.

This was when the following hymn exploded in my ears with the sound of a thousand symphony orchestras:

Daime is Daime
That's what I affirm
It's the divine Eternal Father
and the Sovereign Queen

I'll never be able to describe what I understood at that moment. My eyes opened wide and, inside my ship, I carefully began to watch the evolution of the dancing. My doubts entered a state of alert and I started to drink all the words of the hymns that, until then, I had barely noticed.

Daime is Daime
The Professor of Professors
It's the Divine Eternal Father
and his Redeemer Son

Suddenly, I felt as though I had been worked on for hours by the hymns that preceded this one. I didn't remember the music or the lyrics, but they were recorded indelibly in some part of me that I didn't know how to identify. Everything was like some kind of removal of obstacles to my absence so that I could prepare myself to listen. And, then, for no apparent reason, my ears were unplugged and "I heard."

Daime is Daime
The Master of all teachings
It's the Divine Eternal Father
And all divine beings.

My Inca was smiling. With a kind of telepathic signal he told me that I was prepared "to see."

Then the ship began to shake. As if swallowed by the concentric circles of energy, it entered a zone of turbulence. I became incandescent and even the smallest molecules I'm made of were mixing with those of the chair, which suddenly became a throne. I was sitting in that throne and the Daime paid homage to me. I became very powerful. I felt myself disintegrate. I remained upside down and all the functions of my body were inverted and changed positions. My brain was in my stomach, my stomach in my elbow and so on. I asked forgiveness for my pride and everything calmed. I thanked whoever it was that had pardoned my arrogance and had made that physical anguish cease.

Daime is Daime
I appreciate it with love
Daime gives me my health
And invigorates my love

The hymn surprised my expression of thanks. Then I saw. The people dancing and shaking their maracas were the celebration of life's origin, the first celebratory ritual of humanity's beginnings on this planet. The Rain Forest was shining around me and the vine was the comprehension of everything, a being that had witnessed everything from the beginning. I understood the Universe, life, creation, and their deep meaning and mystery. I understood time in its disordered flux and in its permanence. Everything was and was not. Everything that would be, kept on being. I was the universe from the most immemorial times and my own body was a universe to recreate millions of life cycles per second.

That dance, where the energy was constantly tamed and refined, opened a trapdoor in time. The visions took on the form of memory, of something I had already seen. At some point, I already had been part of the rain forest's substance. I carried within me millions of years of human evolution that now paraded before my very eyes like living photographs.

Life explained itself to me from its origins. It was a gift and a pattern of forces that I had never known existed. There was a power that hovered over all things. It wasn't imagination, projection, archetypes, or atavisms, but a colossal entity, personified right there in the vine and in the drink.

I am grateful to Santo Daime
Grateful to all beings
And the one who sends me to give thanks
Is my true Father.

I gave thanks again. That Father was everything. From the very beginning. The love for Him was a feeling that didn't fit inside my chest.

The ritual of celebration was the same as the one that had been danced tens of thousands of years ago by the first group of beings that had become "humans." There was no doubt about that. It was growing calmer. The ship was less incandescent. I was shocked when I saw just the people dancing and, even though I was dizzy, I contemplated this scene in the present. There was no longer the sensation of perfection and harmony that had existed before.

Moments of "there" still alternated with moments where I only saw the dancing of the ceremony.

The ship abruptly changed course and went humming downward. It entered the earth, feeling the earth, worms, moist mildew, roots of trees, stones, until it reached fossilized microorganisms.

I returned to the surface. Dozens of snakes peered from between my legs, but I wasn't afraid. My body became the Daime vine and I felt its sap as if it were mine. I was the vine. In an instant, it became a snake and swallowed my body.

I was dizzy and awake again. My Inca and my ship had disappeared. In the place where he had been, I only saw Chico staring at me. When I looked at him, he walked past like some wizard-cat.

One hymn speaks of "that light that illuminates us." My eyes bulged in their sockets. Just when I think that the force would diminish, it grabbed me, jumped and dove again with me into unfathomable depths.

I saw a golden light grow beside the two-armed Cross on the altar with such an intensity that I had the impression that I would be blinded if I kept looking at it directly.

Everyone will see that shining
Everyone will speak of Jesus
I ask my Master for the strength
Within that Light forever.

For the first time, God became an acceptable and unquestionable idea for me: in the form of a light.

Then the frequency really dropped. I still drank Daime one more time *(Seu* Wilson's special one). I played with my recently-acquired powers of telepathic communication. I felt all people (even those I didn't know) by means of an emanation of their energy waves. When Chico passed me silently, I knew that it was him. And he also knew that I sensed him.

After a certain point, that became something too playful. I felt that if I didn't pay attention, I wouldn't move ahead. And there were other things I also wanted to see.

That's when I perceived Heaven and Hell. The dancing and the movement within the Church became a deafening, Manichean struggle between Good and Evil. For me, Heaven and Hell had always been categories that were unthinkable for a person of my intellectual sophistication.

Some people represented Darkness, others Light, but these positions did not always mean an automatic relationship whereby light was good and darkness was bad. The figures were simply vehicles for bringing those energies of Good and Evil so that they could be refined and purified by the Dancing.

Chico was the devil himself. He watched me and told me that. I informed him mentally that I knew who he was. He replied to me telepathically.

"So, brother, this means war. Don't be scared, just believe."

It was that simple and natural. I would understand the meaning later. Chico Corrente was my instructor, the person I trusted the most together with *Seu* Mário.

For a time, everything was calm. Then I heard the buzzing and explosions again and I was scared those other feelings would return. I felt physically incapable of repeating all that, incapable of incorporating anything else.

I felt like entering the current of the dancing and express myself to *Seu* Wilson. The chair next to his was open and I sensed that he was expecting me as he concentrated. I struggled against going. The hymns spoke of the need for humility. I looked to the side and saw *Seu* Mário with his closed little eyes beside me. I understood that he had been a crucial piece in my journey, a cosmic supervisor, a sounding board, selecting what I should live in that first experience. Something told me that the greatest tribute was to be loaned later to *Seu* Mário, not to *Seu* Wilson. Even so, I went without my body to the chair and thanked *Seu* Wilson. That "something" that went returned to my chair and reassumed my body.

My happiness was a feeling of peace and wisdom. I felt well-received by my brothers. They were the ones I loved most in the world. My entire life before, including the time I spent in prison, could be explained as merely what I needed to do to get to where I was now, my final destination. A very old search had been satisfied there at that moment. I found the treasure or, better still, the beginning of the map. Nothing that I had asked myself for 32 years had gone unanswered during the night that was coming to an end.

When I stood up, I cried with joy. But the inner crying was much more intense than the few tears that welled up in my eyes. Several beloved people appeared to me in scenes from my childhood.

As some of the people were receding, I met with *Seu* Wilson and timidly told him, "You know what? This is my place."

"Congratulations."

That was what he said. When I left, dawn was splashing each tree of the rain forest with purple and red. The jungle also congratulated me. Each tree was smiling.

I went looking for Gil, who was recording sounds of the dawn. I pushed the play and pause buttons of the recorder. Meanwhile, for myself, I pushed replay, trying to retain the extraordinary things that had happened to me . . .

Energy and Time

I realized, at a certain point during the ceremony, that some people dancing around the Star of David were condensing and expanding an energy and that it could be "seen." Similar to the preparation of bread dough, it was being stretched, kneaded and prepared until it was "ready." Those moments of working with the energy (when the music and the sound of the maracas played such an important role) occasionally reached an apex, a moment of very intense harmony from within the current. We could feel the force of the current itself as a whole, syntonize and feel telepathically the role of each individual in the creation of that incredible field of energetic force which was the sum of all those minds directed toward a similar spiritual goal.

It was at those moments of harmony that the visions occurred with more force. And there was a clear sensation that everyone was enjoying the same extraordinary moment. That was the secret. And the silent complicity enclosed in that ritual, pontificated by the Daime, divided people into two groups: those who were on the inside and those who were outside the revelation of that certain secret.

It isn't surprising that all members of the Group clearly distinguish between two aspects of Daime: Force and Vision. The Force is the performance of the Daime within the material apparatus of each person, in terms of energy and its language. Vision, or Light is ecstasy, a memory that Daime brings from the divine spark that lives within us all. This implies perforating the linear barrier of time, a trait common to all mystical experiences of ecstasy: Zen satoris, samadhis in yoga, devotional visions, etc. In order to be real, the visions must *be-in-time*. The discovery of this other dimension of time (where past, present, and future are mere arbitrary, didactic representations) becomes indispensable, therefore, for all the new knowledge to acquire legitimacy when it deals with the inquisition of our implacable, vacillating Rational Self.

When we finally reach where we want to be, *O Astral* (the Astral Plane) is a place of correspondence, a parallel dimension that is simultaneously inside us and in the Cosmos, constituted in some point of the Universe, in keeping with another kind of materiality much less dense than that which we know.

That the entire Universe communicates with the inner part of our bodies and our minds, including the contiguous parts, is difficult to understand only for confirmed materialists. That idea has been part of the esoteric tradition of all schools, religions and occult doctrines on the face of the earth for millennia.

Daime, above all, opens the doors of communication between the mind and the Astral Plane. The whole

Universe belongs to us: *we are in it,* in the whole and in the parts. And that is the only possible road to surrender with pleasure to the irrefutable idea and sensation of the presence of God. In us, therefore in the Universe. In the Universe, therefore in us.

For the time being, this understanding is enough. What becomes increasingly simple for our spirit at the same times grows more complex for our Rational Self, which only is capable of reducing life, creation and its mystery to a few categories that can be manipulated by systems related to each other in terms of differences and similarities. These systems are called logic, epistemology, etc., and their results are theories, science, etc.: in other words, they provide thousands of ways to prove that the Illusion is reality and vice versa.

Energy and Time are the two initial rungs on the ladder to reach the Astral Plane. And the ritual of Santo Daime, in all its simplicity, is a fabulous science that facilitates the movement from energy-work to Time. From Time, one receives a sense of direction as one moves toward the Astral Plane and, once there, the visions, messages and instructions that the Master who is in Daime has to offer us: to each, according to his or her ability, worthiness and perseverance.

Ceremony of September 2
Language and Eternity

I had an interesting experience on the roads that lead to language.

1) I felt moments of very intense harmony. Soon, they scattered into marvelous meanings that formed complex and symmetrical images in the shape of geometrical figures, mandalas and icons, which differentiated themselves in such a way that I could read them as words and sentences full of sophisticated poetic suggestions. Finally, all that transformed itself into very simple sentences and I realized that these sensations occurred in keeping with the hymns that I was listening to.

2) I also understood the nature of the power that is in our brains, that even without being exactly mental, it is translated by us into something involved with mental processes. In any given moment of the ceremony, primarily when there is a period of concentration, we emit energy at a certain frequency. Telepathic communications come into being, creating an objective field in which the ceremony occurs.

It is this semi-tangible zone, the always-stable border between the senses' immediate consciousness and supra-consciousness that serves as a sensory antenna to capture what comes from the Astral Plane.

The experience of God, or some Primary Cause, is initially an explosion in that frontier zone, a patient collection of its landscapes, voices, lights, murmurs and mysteries. This occurs up to the time when diverse "totalities" are assembled, so that in another moment worthless primary elements are revealed again, all of which are infinitely more complex.

3) Eternity: to reach the infinite and let that which has no answer manifest itself as its own answer. When we discover, after so many attempts to use our reason, that we can "feel" the mystery and make our existence compatible with its pre-existence, without trying to violate its patterns, we approach an understanding of that which is commonly called Eternity.

The infinite sends us to the limits of Time. Our material apparatus does not contain organs that are sensitized to these dimensions. In a certain sense, only our feeling can understand them by means of a perception that varies between affective and aesthetic.

Now, in terms of being alive in matter, our ability to witness eternity is barely the minutest fraction of its transcourse. We are an ephemeral piece of it, among other ephemeral pieces. But if, in another state of perception, we intuit that halo surrounding us with no apparent beginning or end, in some way the experience joins us to that mystery, and from its most basic elements we construct our part within the Cosmos, however insignificant it may be. For us to experience eternity, we need to return before the guiding trails stop shining and disappear.

The work with Daime, to a certain extent, means remembering the day when that aurora borealis of the spirit was experienced, within and without. The proper course now would be to make mental, energy-related and corporeal procedures automatic to recover the place that is reserved in each person in Paradise.

Paradise is Time with no strictures or limits . . .

September 10

The Knowledge of Myths

I am perplexed in this day and age of Rational Darkness by the way our Science with its excessive pretentiousness attempts to explain, measure, classify, and create axioms and equations for life's challenges.

Furthermore, it stigmatizes all other forms of knowledge that never strived for such statutes and always renounced a method.

Spiritual truths will never need instruments for measurement and calculation, even if certain spiritual doctrines make a paradoxical effort to prove their tenets by means of rational thought, logic and traditional science. The intensity of that original sin of Spirituality, that anxiety to seek legitimacy through knowing, is always contradictory. What is increased in proofs is lost in faith, whether it is based on the most modern cybernetics or in some positivistic model from the nineteenth century.

But this is the least serious part of the problem. What's sadder is to see how, for more than a century, modern anthropology has treated indigenous creation myths, even when it attempts not to adopt a condescending attitude toward them.

Behind the simple metaphorical reasoning, the magical links and the oral history of ancestral legends, there is something much bigger than a fairy tale or an allegory.

The problem is with us, in our heads contaminated by reason and logic, and our way of seeing in these cosmogonies mere allegories that at best serve to reconstruct certain bases of the psychic universe of a tribe and with that project their social organization, production, customs, beliefs, etc. by means of *our* language.

The truth is that the Creation stories, totemic taboos of clans, prescribed social relations, etc. are part of something much grander and sublime, far from being simple raw material to fill notions that have already come pre-fabricated from great universities in the anthropologist's field studies. These concepts with all their epistemological arrogance only serve to stuff doctoral dissertations, never to explain the mystery of life, since in order to do this (and to treat what all peoples of all eras have in common) one needs a certain humility. Academic knowledge may have many virtues, but humility is not one of them.

Of course, there may be exceptions on one side or the other — shamans who through some "civilizing" mechanism become anthropologists of their own tribes, or anthropologists who are moved and converted by the beauty that resides in the simplicity of the myths.

Jean Monod, at the end of his study of the myths of the Piaroas, a Colombian tribe, writes the following:

"Be it as it may, the profound wisdom that is inferred from the beliefs of the Piaroas should open the eyes of all those who consider indigenous people intellectually inferior beings. In spite of the recommendations accumulated by ethnologists and anthropologists, our civilization ignores the message of primitive cultures and expands its own sterilizing influence even to the depths of distant jungles. What we label "primitive peoples" in fact simply transforms "the masters of the jungle" into parasites of our society. In this respect, the declaration that utopian life is impossible in the twentieth century is more revealing than the affirmation that the primitives need our help, or that nothing can detain the progress of civilization. We need to face the fact that we destroyed the primitives because we cannot bear the challenge they represent.

"I hope that this essay has added some evidence to the thesis that the indigenous people have nothing to envy of our mentality. Truly, when one compares that eternal wisdom to the spiritual misery of their 'civilizers' it is difficult to contain a feeling of anger mixed with compassion."

At best, our intellectual sophistication only allows us to see allegories of profound truths in the creation myths of certain peoples, the last vestiges of a time when there was a true communion between the experiential sense of divinity and its collective, intellectual understanding.

It is beyond the scope of this study to analyze in depth the Piaroa myths that Monod describes in his article in such a beautiful and simple way. In any case, it can all be summarized in terms of the relationship between the Invisible and the Visible. And all the myths are related to the millenary use of yopo (*Liptadenia peregrina*) and *Banisteriopsis caapi* (the same vine that is used to produce ayahuasca or Daime).

From the beginning of time, the Piaroas communicated spiritually with the forces of divinities that shaped nature, the world and the universe. The origin and the saga of their gods and heroes are totally impregnated with the special perception that we normally call hallucinatory experience. What flows from this experience into language is the treasure of a people who have an intimate knowledge of their journey in the world, a phenomenon that successfully establishes the genesis of that mystery with a few simple words.

There is a vast bibliography that can inform the reader about a thousand philosophical and ethical issues regarding spiritual revelation by means of the ingestion of plants that alter our consciousness.

For now, I'll leave it at that. In a ceremonial session with Daime (on September 7, 1983) I thought I reached an understanding of the peoples that our civilizing eagerness oppressed and exterminated in the name of a fictitious Christianity.

I saw luminous beings that were part of those peoples, and I connected with them in a profound love. I felt that we needed to resurrect the testimonies of those peoples, in that theirs are perhaps the most eloquent testimonies given to God during the whole phase that succeeded primitive Christianity.

In the vision, I entered a current formed by all those who had the giving of that testimony as their mission. The book of stories was simply a beginning. I felt myself dissolve in that energy, heading toward a true knowledge, the Truth. And that road, in spite of what I used to think, wasn't toward the future and the progressive "telos" of sufficient reason, but a road toward the past, heading toward our lost origins, toward the links we maintain with Creation and the Creator.

The further back I went, the more I advanced in this quest for knowledge.

TRANSLATED FROM the Portuguese by Steven F. White

(EXCERPT FROM: Alex Polari de Alverga. *O livro das mirações: viagem ao Santo Daime.* Rio de Janeiro: Rocco, 1984, pp. 41–53, 62–64, 278–279, 283–286.)

AN UNUSUAL EXPERIENCE WITH "HOASCA":
A Lesson from the Teacher

Dennis J. McKenna

Years ago, while conducting fieldwork in the Peruvian Amazon as a graduate student, I had on several occasions sampled the psychedelic drink *ayahuasca* under the watchful eyes of *mestizo ayahuasqueros*. For some reason, however, these early experiences were less than satisfying.

A combination of circumstances, including the variable and often weak composition of local brews, a tendency on the part of the presiding shaman to underdose Gringo participants, and my own uptight hyper-vigilance, a defensive posture reflecting my precarious situation as a stranger in a distinctly strange land, had all conspired to keep me from connecting with the *ayahuasca* experience in Peru except in the mildest and most superficial manner.

I did not really experience the true profundity of the *ayahuasca* vision until years later, when I attended a conference hosted by the União do Vegetal, the Brasilian syncretic religious group that uses *ayahuasca* ritually in their ceremonies, under the name "hoasca," "vegetal," or "chá" (tea). In 1991, the medical studies group of the UDV organized a scientific conference on hoasca, which was held at a summer retreat a few miles outside of São Paulo, adjacent to the circular, church-like temple which served as a community and ceremonial center for one of the local UDV "núcleos" or congregations. A few years previously, I had published several papers on the *ayahuasca* research I had conducted in Peru in connection with my doctoral research. This work had come to the attention of the UDV and it was on the strength of this that they kindly extended an invitation to me to attend the São Paulo conference and give a talk on the results of my research. The conference was attended by about 500 people, most of them Brazilian members of the sect, but also a smattering of local and international outsiders, including physicians, psychiatrists, anthropologists, botanists, pharmacologists, and the like. There were about 20 North Americans invited and I was among these.

The conference started on a Tuesday and ended on a Saturday. After four days of lectures, slides, and much animated conversation, we were all well primed and eager to experience the hoasca beverage; a group session at the temple had been arranged for us on the final closing evening of the conference. This also corresponded with the regular schedule of the UDV, which customarily holds sessions on alternate Saturdays.

On the night in question, the weather was humid and balmy. In the gathering dusk, we all walked the short distance from the dormitories where we had been staying to the temple, about a quarter mile away nestled in a small valley. The regular members of the congregation, many of whom had attended the conference but most of whom had driven out from the city for the evening's ritual, had already taken their places in the temple, and were seated in comfortable reclining chairs arranged on terraces which completely encircled the interior of the temple. In the center of the amphitheatre-like space, a long table was arranged, with chairs arrayed around it, and a picture of Mestre Gabriel, the founder and prophet of the religion, was hung beneath an arch-shaped structure decorated with the sun, moon, and stars at one end. Several gallons of hoasca tea, a brownish liquid the color of coffee latté, was in a plastic juice dispenser placed on the table beneath the picture of Mestre Gabriel; beside it was a stack of paper picnic cups.

A special set of chairs had been reserved for the visiting delegation of foreign "dignitaries" along one of the terrace-like elevations close to the center of the amphitheatre. We threaded our way among the members already seated and took our places in the reserved spot. The officiating *mestre* and his acolytes, mostly men but including several women, were already seated around the table. After everyone had gotten settled, the *mestre* in charge rose to start dispensing the brew, helped by a couple of his disciples. The members formed an orderly line (they all seemed to know just where and when to go and there was no confusion or need for direction) and one by one, we filed down to stand before the *mestre* and be handed a paper cup containing our allotted draught; the size of the servings varied from person to person, and seemed to be measured according to body weight and the *mestre's* assessing gaze; what other criteria were applied was not explained but one got the feeling that he was taking the measure of the soul and spirit of the supplicant standing before him as well as the body. Each person took the cup assigned to them and returned to stand in front of their chair, holding the cup. Once everyone had been served, the *mestre* gave a signal and all raised the cups to their lips and drained the bitter, foul-tasting beverage in two or three gulps. One of the Brazilian scientists standing beside me slipped me a small piece of dried ginger to chew to kill the aftertaste; I was grateful for the kind gesture.

Having drained their cups, everyone sat back in their comfortable webbed chairs. I kept hoping someone would turn off the glaring, buzzing, fluorescent lights over head which were altogether too bright and quite annoying. They were to stay on during the entire evening, however. For about 45 minutes, everyone sat, wrapped in their own thoughts. Absolute silence reigned; in a hall of over 500 people you could have heard a pin drop. After this period, a few people began to get up and totter toward the bathrooms, as the nausea, a frequent side-effect in the early stages, began to take hold. You could hear the sounds of people puking and shitting emanating from the communal bathrooms at the back of the building. About the same time, the mestre began singing a beautiful song, called a *chamada,* and though I could not understand the Portuguese words, the melody was quite moving. The sound of the heartfelt *chamada* mingling with the wretching, gasping noises of people throwing up violently in the background made me smile at the incongruity, but no one else seemed to notice.

My own experience was not developing as I'd hoped. My stomach was queasy but not enough to send me to the bathroom and I felt restless and uncomfortable. I felt very little effect, except for some brief flashes of hypnagogia behind my closed eyes. I was disappointed; I had been hoping for more than a subthreshold experience, and I didn't want to disappoint my hosts, who were concerned that their visitors should have a good experience and "get" it. When the *mestre* signaled that he was ready to give a second glass to anyone who wanted it, I was among the group of about a dozen Gringos that queued up in front of the table; apparently I was not the only one who was having a difficult time connecting with the spirit of the tea.

I took my second draught and settled back into my chair. It tasted, if possible, even worse than the first one had. Within a few minutes it became clear that this time, it was going to work. I began to feel the force of the hoasca course through my body, a feeling of energy passing from the base of my spine to the top of my head. It was like being borne upwards in a high-speed elevator. I was familiar with this state of sympathetic activation from previous mushroom experiences, and I welcomed the sensation as confirmation that the train was pulling out of the station.

The energized feeling and the sensation or rapid acceleration continued. It was much like mushrooms but seemed to be much stronger; I had the sense that this was one elevator it would be hard to exit from before reaching the top floor, wherever that might be. Random snippets of topics we had been discussing at the seminars in the previous days began to float into my consciousness. I remembered one seminar that had addressed the UDV's concept that the power of hoasca tea is a combination of "force" and "light"; the "force" was supplied by the MAO-inhibiting *Banisteriopsis* vine, known as *mariri* in the local vernacular, while the light — the visionary, hypnagogic component — was derived from *chacruna,* the DMT-containing *Psychotria* admixture plant. I thought to myself what an apt characterization this was; *hoasca* was definitely a combination of "force" and "light" and at that moment I was well within the grip of the "force" and hoped that I was about to break out into "the light."

At the instant I had that thought, I heard a voice, seeming to come from behind my left shoulder. It said something like, "you wanna see force?? I'll show you force!" The question was clearly rhetorical, and I understood that I was about to experience something whether I wanted to or not. The next instant, I found myself changed into a disembodied point of view, suspended in space, thousands of miles over the Amazon basin. I could see the curvature of the earth, the stars beyond shown steadily against an inky backdrop, and far below I could see swirls and eddies of clouds over the basin, and the nerve-like tracery of vast river systems. From the center of the basin arose the World Tree, in the form of an enormous *Banisteriopsis* vine. It was twisted into a helical form and its flowering tops were just below my disembodied viewpoint, its base was anchored to the earth far below, lost to vision in the depths of mist and clouds and distance that stretched beneath me. As I gazed, awestruck, at this vision, the voice explained that the Amazon was the Omphalos of the planet, and that the twisted, rope-like Yggdrasil/Mariri World Tree was the linchpin that tied the three realms — the underworld, the earth and the sky — together. Somehow I understood — though no words were involved — that the *Banisteriopsis* vine was the embodiment of the plant intelligence that embraced and covered the earth, that together the community of the plant species that existed on the earth provided the nurturing energy that made life on earth possible. I "understood" that photosynthesis — that neat trick, known only to green plants, of making complex organic compounds from sunlight, carbon dioxide, and water, was the "force" the UDV was talking about, and indeed was the force on which all life depends; I was reminded of a line from Dylan Thomas, that photosynthesis is "the force that through the green fuse drives the flower."

In the next moment, I found myself instantly transported from my bodiless perch in space to the lightless depths beneath the surface of the earth. I had somehow become a sentient water molecule, percolating randomly through the soil, lost amid the tangle of the enormous root fibers of the Banisteriopsis World Tree. I could feel the coolness, the dank dampness of the soil surrounding me, I felt suspended in an enormous underground cistern, a single drop among billions of drops. This sensation lasted only a moment, then I felt a definite sense of movement, as, squeezed by the implacable force of irresistible osmotic pressures, I was rapidly translocated into the roots of the *Banisteriopsis* tree; the sense of the rising, speeding elevator returned except this time I was being lifted rapidly through the vast pipes and tubes of the plant's vascular system. I was a single molecule of water tumbling through the myriad branches and forks of the vertical maze, which grew progressively narrower the higher I went.

Finally, the sense of accelerating, vertical movement eased off; I was now floating freely, in a horizontal direction ; no longer feeling pushed, I was suspended in the middle of a stream flowing through an enormous, vaulted tunnel. More than that, there was light at the end of the tunnel, a green light. With a start I realized that I had just passed through the petiole of a sun-drenched leaf, and was being shunted into progressively narrowing arteries as I was carried through the articulating veins toward some unknown destination. It helped that the voice — or my own narrative self, I'm not sure which — was providing occasional commentary on the stages of the journey as it unfolded.

Desperately, I tried to remember my old lessons in plant physiology and anatomy; by this time I had been given the wordless understanding that I was about to witness, indeed, participate in, the central mystery of life on earth; a water molecule's eye view of the process of photosynthesis. Suddenly I was no longer suspended in the arterial stream of the leaf vein; I had somehow been transported into an enormous enclosed space, suffused with greenish light. Above me I could see the domed, vaulted roof of the structure I was inside of, and I understood that I was inside a chloroplast; the roof was translucent and beams of sunlight streamed through it like a bedroom window on a bright morning. In front of me were flat, layered structures looking like folded sheets stacked closely together, covered with antenna-shaped structures, all facing in the same direction and all opened eagerly to receive the incoming light. I realized that these had to be the thylakoid membranes, the organelles within the chloroplast where the so-called "light reaction" takes place. The antenna-like structures covering them literally glowed and hummed with photonic energy, and I could see that somehow, this energy was being translocated through the membranes of the thylakoids they were mounted on. I recognized, or "understood" that these antenna-like arrays were molecules of cholorophyll , and the "anchors" that tied them to their membrane substrates were long tails of phytic acid that functioned as energy transducers, funneling the light energy collected by the flower-shaped receptors through the membrane and into the layers beneath it.

Next thing I knew I was beneath that membrane; I was being carried along as though borne on a conveyor belt; I could see the phytic acid chains dangling above and beyond them, through the semitransparent "roof" of the membrane, the flower-like porphyrin groups that formed the cholorophyll's light-gathering apparatus loomed like the dishes of a radio telescope array. In the center of the space was what looked like a mottled flat surface, periodically being smited by enormous bolts of energy which emanated, lightning-like, from the phytic acid tails suspended above it; and on that altar, water molecules were being smashed to smithereens by the energy bolts. Consciousness exploded and died in a spasm of electron ecstasy as I was smited by the bolt of energy emitted by the phytic acid transducers and my poor water-molecule soul was split asunder. As the light energy was used to ionize the water, the oxygen liberated in the process rose with a shriek to escape from the chamber of horrors, while the electrons, liberated from their matrix, were shunted into the electron-transport roller coaster, sliding down the chain of cytochromes like a dancer being passed from partner to partner, into the waiting arms of Photosystem I, only to be blasted again by yet another photonic charge, bounced into the close but fleeting embrace of ferredoxin, the primary electron acceptor, ultimately captured by NADP+, to be used as bait to capture two elusive protons, as a flame draws a moth. Suddenly I was outside the flattened thylakoid structures, which from my perspective looked like high-rise, circular apartment buildings. I recognized that I was suspended in the stroma, the region outside the thylakoid membranes, where the mysterious Dark Reaction takes place, the alchemical wedding that joins carbon dioxide to ribulose diphosphate, a shotgun marriage presided over by ribulose diphosphate carboxylase, the first enzyme in the so-called pentose phosphate shunt. All was quiet and for a moment, I was floating free in darkness; then miraculously, (miracles were by this time mundane) I realized that my disembodied point of view had been reincarnated again , and was now embedded in the matrix of the newly reduced ribulose diphosphate/carbon dioxide complex; this unstable intermediate was rapidly falling apart into two molecules of phosphoglycerate which were grabbed and loaded on the merry-go-round by the first enzymes of the Calvin cycle. Dimly, I struggled to remember my early botany lessons and put names to what I was seeing.

I recognized that I had entered the first phases of the pentose phosphate shunt, the biochemical pathway that builds the initial products of photosynthesis into complex sugars and sends them spinning from thence into the myriad pathways of biosynthesis that ultimately generate the molecular stuff of life.

I felt humbled, shaken, exhausted and exalted all at the same time; suddenly I was ripped out of my molecular roller coaster ride, my disembodied eye was again suspended high over the Amazon basin. This time, there was no world tree arising from its center. It looked much like it must look from a space shuttle or a satellite in high orbit. The day was sunny, the vista stretching to the curved horizon was blue and green and bluish green, the vegetation below, threaded with shining rivers, looked like green mold covering an overgrown petri plate. Suddenly I was wracked with a sense of overwhelming sadness, sadness mixed with fear for the delicate balance of life on this planet, the fragile processes that drive and sustain life, sadness for the fate of our planet and its precious cargo. "What will happen if we destroy the Amazon," I thought to myself, "what will become of us, what will become of life itself, if we allow this destruction to continue? We cannot let this happen. It must be stopped, at any cost." I was weeping. I felt miserable, I felt anger and rage toward my own rapacious, destructive species, scarcely aware of its own devastating power, a species that cares little about the swath of destruction it leaves in its wake as it thoughtlessly decimates ecosystems and burns thousands of acres of rain forest. I was filled with loathing and shame.

Suddenly again from behind my left shoulder, came a quiet voice. "You monkeys only think you're running things," it said. "You don't think we would really allow this to happen, do you?" and somehow, I knew that the "we" in that statement was the entire community of species that constitute the planetary biosphere. I knew that I had been given an inestimable gift, a piece of gnosis and wisdom straight from the heart/mind of planetary intelligence, conveyed in visions and thought by an infinitely wise, incredibly ancient, and enormously compassionate "ambassador" to the human community. A sense of relief, tempered with hope, washed over me. The vision faded, and I opened my eyes, to see my new found friends and hosts all eagerly gathered around me. The ceremony had officially ended a few minutes previously, I had been utterly oblivious to whatever was going on in the world beyond my closed eyelids. "How was it?" they wanted to know. "Did you feel the *borrachera* (drunkenness)?" I smiled to myself, feeling overjoyed at the prospect of sharing the experience and knowing that I had indeed been allowed to experience the ultimate "force," the vastly alien, incredibly complex molecular machine that is "the force that through the green fuse drives the flower."

Ayahuasca Visions, oil on canvas, © by Donna Torres. Collection of Luis Eduardo Luna.

IV
WRITING AYAHUASCA

Allen Ginsberg, speaking at the University of Pennsylvania in 1967. Photograph © by Robert Hahn.

THE YAGÉ LETTERS

Allen Ginsberg

June 10, 1960
Estafeta Correo
Pucallpa, Peru

Dear Bill,

I'm still in Pucallpa — ran into a little plump fellow, Ramon P — who'd been friend to Robert Frank (photographer of our movie) in '46 or so here. Ramon took me to his Curandero — in whom he has a lot of faith and about whose supernatural curing Powers he talks a lot, too much, about — The Maestro, as he's called, being a very mild and simple seeming cat of 38 or so — who prepared a drink for 3 of us the other night; and then last night I attended a regular Curandero all night drinking session with about 30 other men and women in a hut in jungly outskirts of Pucallpa behind the gaswork field.

The first time, much stronger than the drink I had in Lima, Ayahuasca can be bottled and transported and stay strong, as long as it does not ferment — needs well closed bottle. Drank a cup — slightly old stuff, several days old and slightly fermented also — lay back and after an hour (in bamboo hut outside his shack, where he cooks) — began seeing or feeling what I thought was the Great Being, or some sense of It, approaching my mind like a big wet vagina — lay back in that for a while — only image I can come up with is of a big black hole of God-Nose thru which I peered into a mystery — and the black hole surrounded by all creation — particularly colored snakes — all real.

I felt somewhat like what this image represents, the sense of it so real.

The eye is imaginary image, to give life to the picture. Also a great feeling of pleasantness in my body, no nausea. Lasted in different phases about 2 hours — the effects wore off after 3 — the phantasy itself lasted from ¾ of hour after I drank to 2½ hours later more or less.

Went back and talked to The Maestro, gave him 35 soles ($1.50) for services and talked with him about peyote and LSD — he'd heard of peyote — he's a mestizo who studied in San Martin (upper Huallaga territory) — he gave me samples of his mix — uses young cultivated Ayahuasca plant in his back yard, and mixes that about half and half with a catalyst known as the "Mescla" which is another leaf known in Chama indian language as Cahua (pron Coura) and locally by him in Pucallpa is called Chacruna. Said he'd get me more samples to bring back to Lima Natural History Museum to identify. Cooks the mixes together all day and strains the broth, gives the drained leaves a second cook too. Anyway the preparation is not excessively secret — I think Schultes saw and knows the preparation. Can add other leaves of other plants too, I don't know these combinations to try out — he seemed generally interested in drugs — serious — and not mercenary at all — good type — has quite a following here — does physical cures, his specialty.

Anyway to make a long story short, went back to formal group session in huts last night — this time the brew was prepared fresh and presented with full ceremony — he crooning (and blowing cigarette or pipe smoke) tenderly over the cupmouth for several minutes before — (enamel cup, I remember your plastic cup) — then I light cigarette, blow a puff of smoke over cup, and drain. Saw a shooting star — Aerolith — before going in, and full moon, and he served me up first — then lay down expecting God knows what other pleasant vision and then I began to get high — and then the whole fucking Cosmos broke loose around me, I think the strongest and worst I've ever had it nearly — (I still reserve the Harlem experiences, being Natural, in abeyance. The LSD was Perfection but didn't get me so deep in nor so horribly in) — first I began to realize my worry about the mosquitoes or vomiting was silly as there was the great stake of life and Death — I felt faced by Death, my skull in my beard on pallet on porch rolling back and forth and settling finally as if in reproduction of the last physical move I make before settling into real death — got nauseous, rushed out and began vomiting, all covered with snakes, like a Snake Seraph, colored serpents in aureole all around my body, I felt like a snake vomiting out the universe — or a Jivaro in head-dress with fangs vomiting up in realization of the Murder of the Universe — my death to come — everyone's death to come — all unready — I unready — all around me in the trees the noise of these spectral animals the other drinkers vomiting (normal part of the Cure sessions) in the night in their awful solitude in the universe — vomiting up their will to live, be preserved in this body, almost — Went back and lay down — Ramon came over quite tender and nurse like (he hadn't drunk, he's sort of an aide to help the sufferers) asked me if I was OK and "Bien Mareado" (Good and drunk?) — I said "Bastante" and went back to listen to the spectre that was approaching my mind — The whole hut seemed rayed with spectral presences all suffering transfiguration with contact with a single mysterious Thing that was our fate and was sooner or later going to kill us — the Curandero crooning, keeping up a very tender, repeated and then changing simple tune, comfort sort of, God knows what signified — seemed to signify some point of reference I was unable to contact yet — I was frightened and simply lay there with wave after wave of death-fear, fright, rolling over me till I could hardly stand it, didn't want to take refuge in rejecting it as illusion, for it was too real and too familiar — especially as if in rehearsal of Last Minute Death my head rolling back and forth on the blanket and finally settling in last position of stillness and hopeless resignation to God knows what Fate — for my being — felt completely lost strayed soul — outside of contact with some Thing that seemed present — finally had a sense that I might face the Question there and then, and choose to die and understand — and leave my body to be found in the morning — I guess grieving everybody — couldn't bear to leave Peter and my father so alone — afraid to die yet then and so never took the Chance (if there was a Chance, perhaps somehow there was) — also as if everybody in session in central radiotelepathic contact with the same problem — the Great Being within ourselves — Coming back from vomit saw a man knees to chest I thought I saw as X ray his skull I realized he was crouched there as in shroud (with towel mosquito protection wrapped round his face) suffering the same trial and separation — Thought of people, saw their images clearly, you — mysterious apparently know more than I do now and why don't you communicate, or can't you, or have I ignored it? — Simon seemingly an angel in his annihilation of vanity and giving forth new life in children — "If any interplanetary news comes through" he said "I'll be the first to be relaying it over the wires in a way that won't get it fucked up" — Francine his wife — sort of a Seraph of Woman, all women (as all men) the same — spectral creatures put here mysteriously to live, be the living Gods, and suffer Crucifixion of death like Christ, but either get lost and die in soul or get in Contact and give new birth to continue the Process of Being (tho' they themselves die, or do they?) — and I lost and poor Peter who depends on me for some Heaven I haven't got, lost — and I keep rejecting women, who come to minister to me — decided to have children somehow, a revolution in the Hallucination — but the suffering was about as much as I could bear and the thought of more suffering even deeper to come made me despair — felt, still feel, like lost soul, surrounded by ministering angels (Ramon, the Maestro, yourself, the whole Common World of Diers) — and my poor mother died in God knows what state of suffering — I can't stand it — vomited again (Ramon had come over and told me to vomit off the porch where I was lying, if I had to later, very careful kind situation) I mean, is this a good group — I remember your saying watch out whose vision you get — but God knows I don't know who to turn to finally when the Chips are down spiritually and I have to depend on my own Serpent-self's memory of Merry Visions of Blake — or depend on nothing and enter anew — but enter what? — Death? — and at that moment — vomiting still feeling like a Great lost Serpent-seraph vomiting in consciousness of the Transfiguration to come — with the Radiotelepathy sense of a Being whose presence I had not yet fully sensed — too Horrible for me, still — to accept the fact of total communication with say everyone an eternal seraph male and female at once — and me a lost soul seeking help — well slowly the intensity began to fade, I being incapable of moving in any direction spiritually — not knowing who to look to or what to look for — not quite trusting to ask the Maestro — tho' in the vision of the scene it was he who was the local logical Ministering Spirit to trust, if anyone — went over and sat by him (as Ramon gently suggested) to be "blown" — that is he croons a song to you to cure your soul and blows smoke at you — rather a comforting presence — tho' by now the steep fear had passed — that being over got up and took my piece of cloth I brought against mosquitos and went home in moonlight with plump Ramon — who said the more you saturate yourself with Ayahuasca the deeper you go — visit the moon, see the dead, see God — see Tree Spirits — etc.

I hardly have the nerve to go back, afraid of some real madness, a Changed Universe permanently changed — tho' I guess change it must for me someday — much less as planned before, go up the river six hours to drink with an Indian tribe — I suppose I will — meanwhile will wait here another week in Pucallpa and drink a few more times with same group — I wish I knew who, if anyone, there is to work with that knows, if anyone knows, who I am or what I am. I wish I could hear from you. I think I'll be here long enough for a letter to reach me — write.

Allen Ginsberg

(EXCERPT FROM: William S. Burroughs and Allen Ginsberg. *The Yagé Letters.* San Francisco, California: City Lights, 1963, pp. 49–56.)

AT PLAY IN THE FIELDS OF THE LORD

(excerpt)

Peter Matthiessen

A dog turned in its circle and lay down in the shade, and a vulture swung up and down in a short arc above the jungle, as if suspended from a string. In the heat of the siesta, the street below was hollow as a bone.

He took the cork out of the bottle, and holding his breath to kill the bitterness, drank off half the brown fluid in a series of short gulps, gargling harshly when he was finished and spitting the residue into the street. The aftertaste made him gag. He sat down on the window sill and in a little while the nausea receded, leaving only a thick woody taste and a slight vagueness.

A half-hour passed. Maybe the Indian had watered the infusion. A voice in the salon below sounded remote to him, and he nodded; he was on his way. A little more ayahuasca, Mr. Moon? He took up the bottle and drank off another quarter of it, then set it down very slowly. You've made a bad mistake, he thought; already he knew he did not need it. The effects were coming very suddenly, and he stood up and stalked the room. *In overdose,* he had read somewhere, *the extract of* Banisteriopsis caapi *is quite poisonous and may bring on convulsions, shock and even death.*

How silent it was — the whole world was in siesta. He glanced quickly out the window, to take time by surprise; the dog slept soundly, and the vulture still swung up and down its bit of sky, dark as a pendulum. From the far end of the street, a solitary figure was moving toward him, down the center of the street — the last man on earth. There you are, he thought, I have been waiting for you all my life.

Now he seized with vertigo and apprehension; his heart began to pound and his breath was short. He went to his bed and lay down on his back. He felt a closure of the throat and a tension in his chest, a metal bar from chin to navel to which the skin of his chest was sewn. Breathing became still more difficult, and a slight pain in the back of his head became a general, diffused headache. He turned cold and his teeth chattered; the hands pressed to his face were limp and clammy.

I am flying all apart, he thought; at the same time his chest constricted ever more tightly. *Let go,* he told himself aloud. *Let go.*

He rolled over on his side and blinked at the other bed. The man on the bed retreated from his vision, shrinking and shrinking until he was no bigger than a fetus.

Color: the room billowed with it; the room breathed. When he closed his eyes, the color dazzled him; he soared. But there was trouble in his lungs again, and his heart thumped so, in heavy spasmodic leaps, that it must surely stall and die. He broke into a sweat, and his hands turned cold as small bags of wet sand . . .

He sat up, aching, in a foreign room. He could breathe again, although his heart still hurled itself unmercifully against his chest: how thin a man's poor chest was, after all; it was as thin as paper, surrounding a hollow oval space of wind and bitterness. *Thump, thump-ump, um-thump;* it would crash through at any minute, and what then? Do I greet it? Introduce myself? How long can a man sit holding his heart in his hands?

Or was that thump coming from elsewhere? The thump of a bed — were the missionaries making love? The male missionary making love to the female missionary? The Courtship of Missionaries: the male missionary, larger and more splendidly plumaged than his shy dowdy mate, hurls his head back joyfully and sings "Praise the Lord," upon which he rushes forth, tail feathers spread, and mounting in a decorous and even pious manner, inserts his tongue into her right ear . . .

You are the Lost Tribe of Israel, and therefore you must pray especially hard, for the Lost Tribe of Israel is under God's everlasting curse. Do you understand? Why don't you answer me? What is the matter with you children — do you wish to remain accursed? Now you answer me, Lewis Moon, or I'm going to beat you. Lewis? Lewis!

Now his body cavity felt hollowed out as if cold sterile winds were blowing through it . . . loss, loss, loss. Loss.

Look into the sky and think of nothing, said Alvin Moon "Joe Redcloud," *but do not look into the sun, for the sun will blind you. Face east on the first day, south on the second, west on the third, north on the fourth, until you are at the center of the circle, and then you will know the power of the world.*

After the first day his stomach hurt and he felt foolish, all alone on a rock lookout above a river bend of box elder and cottonwood; all that night he shivered. He was not like the old men, nor even like his father; he spoke American and raised the American flag at school; he wore blue jeans and looked at magazines in stores and stood around outside the movie in the town, searching his pockets as if he had real money; and he did not believe in visions. Like all the children, he killed his hunger at the mission house on Sunday and afterward felt ashamed. Once he went hungry, telling the missionary that Cheyennes never ate on Sundays.

He remained on the rock a second day and a second night, just out of stubbornness, and because he was proud of the rifle that Alvin Moon had laid beside him. No bear nor cougar came — the animals would not bother him, his father said, if he sat still — and on the third morning he did not feel hungry any more and sat there motionless, letting the sun and wind blow through him. He was as firmly rooted in the ground as the young pine. By afternoon he was growing weak and became filled with apprehension: something was happening. The jays and squirrels had lost all fear of him, flickering over and about him as if he had turned to stone, and the shrill of insects crystallized in a huge ringing silence. The sky was ringing, and the pine trees on the rocks turned a bright rigid green, each needle shimmering; the pines were ringing and beside him a blue lupine opened, breathing. Then the river turned to silver and stopped flowing. The jays trembled on the rock, their eyes too bright, and the squirrel was still, the gold hairs flowing on its tail. He stared at the enormous sky, and the sky descended and the earth was rising from below, and he was soaring toward the center.

Then, in the ringing, far away, rose a flat droning. The airplane unraveled the high silence as it crossed the sky; it disappeared without ever appearing, and when it had gone, the sky no longer rang. He sat a long time on his rock, but the sky had risen, leaving him desolate.

Light-headed, he went down to the river, where he drank. He found mushrooms and fresh-water mussels, and some berries, and when he had eaten he laughed at his three-day vigil, pretending that he did not feel a dreadful sorrow.

On the fourth day, waiting for Alvin Moon to come, he hunted. He killed a wild goose on the river, and boasted of it to his father.

His father gazed at him. *And where is the goose,* his father said.

I could not reach it, the boy said. *It came so close, and then it drifted far away.*

He reeled from the bed and drifted to the window, but the figure coming down the street was gone; again he had missed some unknown chance. The street was void, a void, avoid. Dog, heat, a vulture, nothing more. A dog, a vulture, nothing more, and thus we parted, sang Lenore.

Singing, Somewhere, somewhere there was singing. His whole body shimmered with the chords, the fountainhead of music, overflowing. The chords were multicolored, vaulting like rockets across his consciousness; he could break off pieces of the music, like pieces of meringue.

You're sleeping your life away, he told the dog.

Do you hear me? I said, Do you hear me?

Meri-*wether,* Sheriff Guzmán said. *That's some name for a red nigger, ain't it? You're the smart one, ain't you kid? Ain't you supposed to be the* smart *Cheyenne? Done good in the war, and now they gone to send they little pet Christ-lovin Cheyenne to college, ain't that right, kid? Well, kid, if you're a* real *smart Injun, you won't even go and look at me that way, you'll keep your Injun nose clean, kid.*

Oh, to be an Indian! (Now that spring is here.) Big Irma: *Be a good boy, Lewis. Do not fight so much. You come back and see us now.* Alas, too late — the world is dead, you sleepyhead. The Inn of the Dog and the Vulture.

There are voices, you see, then singing voices, then strange musics, hollowed out, as if drifted through a wind tunnel, these followed by a huge void of bleak silence suggesting DEATH.

THE STORY OF LIFE, by Lewis Moon.

Now . . . something has happened, was happening, is happening. BUT WILL NOT HAPPEN. Do you hear me? I said, DO YOU HEAR ME?

A softer tone, please.

To begin at the beginning: my name is Meriwether Lewis Moon. Or is that the end? Again: I was named Meriwether Lewis Moon, after Meriwether Lewis, who with Lieutenant William Clark crossed North America without killing a single Indian. So said my father; my father is Alvin Moon "Joe Redcloud," who lived up on North Mountain. Alvin Moon still traps and hunts, and in World War I, when still a despised non-citizen, exempt from service, joined those 16,999 other Indians as insane as himself who volunteered to serve in World War I. Alvin Moon is half-Cheyenne; he went down South when he came home and took up with a Creole Choctaw woman named Big Irma and brought her back up to his mountain. The worst mistake that Alvin Moon ever made was trying to educate himself; his information about Lewis and Clark was the only piece of education he ever obtained, and it was wrong. He used to joke that he couldn't educate himself unless he learned to read, and how could he learn to read if he didn't educate himself? So he left off hunting and trapping and came down off his mountain and took work near the reservation to keep his children in the mission school, to give them a better chance in life.

I ain't got nothin, said Joe Redcloud, and I don't know nothin, not a thing. And the hell of it is, I broke my back, paid out every cent, to keep them kids into that school, and now they don't know nothin, neither, only Jesus Christ. Now ain't that somethin? They sit around here thinkin about Godamighty, I reckon, while they're waitin on their gover'ment reliefs.

All but Meriwether Lewis.

Again: my name is Lewis Moon, and I am lying on a bed (deathbed?) in a strange country, and I hear eerie voices and a crack is appearing on the wall, wider and wider, and the bulb in the ceiling is growing more and more bulbous, and will surely explode — a crack (of doom?) of lightning down the walls.

The extract of B. caapi is a powerful narcotic and hallucinogen containing phenol alkaloids related to those found in lysergic acid, and whether or not it finds a respectable place in the pharmaceutica of man, it has held for unknown centuries an important place in the culture of Indian tribes of the Amazon basin. At the time of my experiment I was lying in a narrow room with a corpse in the next bed, with God, a vulture and a dog as witnesses, wishing that Marguerite were here. Marguerite. I wish to tell Marguerite that the reason I did not make love to her that time in Hong Kong was not because I did not want her but because I had reason to believe that in the late, low hours of the week before, I had contracted a low infestation. I did not know Marguerite well enough to give her crabs — you understand? Marguerite had alabaster skin, triumphant hair, and an unmuddied soul, and a swinging little ass into the bargain.

You listen to me, Meriwether Lewis: what the hell you sass that Sheriff for? He mighta kilt you. You stay clear of whiskey, then; long as you can't stay out of trouble, you ain't welcome back. And don't you show your Mam that bad face, neither; I whupped you plenty times before, and I'll whup you again, hero or no hero. Alvin Moon "Joe Redcloud" said, *You're all your people here got left to count on. You go get that education, hear me now? And then you come on home and learn it back to us as best you can. Because the way things are goin they ain't no hope for none of us, lessen we don't get somethin learned here to us pretty quick.*

I have opened my eyes again, to shut off all that blue. Color can threaten, overwhelm, whirling like that — an ant in a kaleidoscope might sense the problem. But out here the bed shudders, the chair sneaks, the bureau budges; they back and fill, about to charge. From above the bulb socket descends like a falling spider, leaving the bulb behind.

B. caapi, which is named for the caapi of certain Brazilian Indians, is also the camorampi of the Campa, the natema of the Jivaro, the ayahuasca or haya-huasca of the Quechua-speaking peoples, the yage of Ecuador, the soga de muerte of most Spanish South Americans, names variously translated as "Vine of the Devil," "Vine of the Soul," "Vine of Death": the Spanish term means literally "vine rope of death," the soga referring to the jungle lianas used commonly as canoe lines, lashings, ropes, etc. In addition to certain medical properties, the vine can induce visions, telepathic states, metaphysical contemplation and transmigration; these conditions are used by the Indians for the reception of warnings, prophecies and good counsel. Among many tribes one purpose of the dream state is identification of an unknown enemy, and the use of it is thus related to the Jivaro practice of taking tsantsas, *or shrunken heads . . .*

I am cut off, I feel both silly and depressed; it is the solitude, not solitude but isolation . . . Death is the final isolation, but from what, from what?

I am trying to reach out to you, but I do not know who you are, I cannot see you. I only feel your presence in this room. Perhaps . . . I wonder . . . are you inside me? And if so . . . Now listen carefully: there is a lost reality, a reality lost long ago. Are you in touch with it: can you tell me — did you see? — the man with the blue arrow —

Or . . . or are you the figure in the center of the street? So you came here, after all! Can you hear me? I said, CAN YOU HEAR ME? CAN — YOU — HEAR — ME!

I cannot reach him through the sound and silence, distant sound and deepest silence, like a thick glass barrier between the world of the living and myself, as if I were wandering on an earth which had suddenly died, or in a Purgatory, myself already dead.

There is something that you have to understand.

Now look what's happening — can you see? It's Him, the Dead Man. Resurrection. Rising out of bed. Not suspecting that I am already dead, he will attempt to kill me.

He speaks: *Stopshoutinforchristsake!*

Here he comes, intent on the kill. He has broken the glass wall. He drags me across the room. He has a costume, he is all dressed up like a soldier of fortune, he is very hip; but see the rosy cheeks behind that beard? An enormous child!

"You are an Enormous Child!"

Nevermindmejustlookinthemirra! Whatareyousomekindofaaddictorwhat? Gowanlookatyaself!

See that pale face in the glass! The face is rigid, and the eyes are dark and huge. Over the left eye drifts a dark shadow, like a hand. There you are, I see you now, and the bearded man, your warder.

He knew his lucidity could not last, and because he had taken too much, he dreaded going under again, and he started to ask Wolfie for help. "Hey," he said. But he could not ask, he had never asked in all his life, and even if he asked, what could poor Wolfie do? There were no sedatives in Madre de Dios; sedation was superfluous in a graveyard. He pushed away and tottered toward the window, where he fell across the sill. The dog and the vulture were gone. The light was tightening in the way it always did before the sudden jungle night, and down the center of the street a solitary figure walked away.

The bottle stood upon the sill; he drank it to the bottom.

He felt like crying, but did not. He had not cried in twenty years — no, more. Had he ever cried? And yet he did not really feel like crying; he felt like laughing, but did not. Stalking Joe Redcloud's shack as twilight came, he waited to be called back, beaten, and forgiven, but with the clear prairie darkness came the knowledge that the call would never come, that the days of tears and comfort had come and gone before he had realized they would ever end. Dry-eyed, enraged, he crouched in the sage-brush for a little while, and then moved off like a lean yearling grizzly driven snarling from the cave, feeling very bad and very good at the same time, and spoiling for a fight.

He crouched beside the window sill, his back to the world without, and far away he heard them coming, the marching of huge nameless armies coming toward him, and once again his hands turned cold. He felt very cold. On the wall of the room, over the door, he saw a huge moth with a large white spot on each wing. It palpitated gently; he could hear the palpitations, and the spots were growing. And there was a voice, a hollow voice, very loud, and very far away, calling through glass, and there were hands on him and he was shaken violently. The voice rose and crashed in waves, rolling around his ears; it was getting dark.

NowlistenI'mgonnatellGuzmánweflytomorrowawright? AwrightLewis? I saidAWRIGHTLEWIS?

He looked at the man and the man's head, fringed with hair; the head shrank before his eyes and became a *tsantsa.* He could not look, and turned away. A figure crossed his line of vision, moving toward the door. The door opened and light came in. The voice said *Thisisnowheremanl'vehadenough.*

Don't go . . . I need . . . Don't go. I need . . . But he could not hear his own voice, and he could not have said just what he needed. From over the man's head the large white eyes of the moth observed him; they pinned him, like incoming beams. The music crashed, the wave . . . The door was dark again. He pushed himself to his feet and stared out of the window. The dark was rolling from the forest all around, and the sky was so wild as the sun set that it hurt his eyes. He reeled and fell, then thrashed to his feet and fell again, across the bed, and was sucked down into the darkness as the music burst the walls and overwhelmed him.

His body diffused and drifted through cathedral vaults of color, whirling and shimmering and bursting forth, drifting high among the arches, down the clerestories, shadowed by explosions of stained glass. In the dark chapels of the church was a stair to windy dungeons, to colors rich and somber now, and shapes emerging; the shapes flowered, rose in threat and fell away again. Fiends, demons, dancing spiders with fine webs of silver chain. A maniac snarled and slavered, and rain of blood beat down upon his face. Teeth, teeth grinding in taut rage, teeth tearing lean sinew from gnarled bone. Idiocy danced hand in hand with lunacy and hate, rage and revenge; the dungeon clanked and quaked with ominous sounds, and he kept on going, down into the darkness

Snow, dawn, black aspens. The creature rose at the boy's coming and somersaulted backward, whining and snarling, the trap clatter muffled in white silences; whiteness; the blood pools colored black, the tight-sewn cold.

A great head, and yellow eyes too big for Coyote — the last wolf in the mountains, the first and only wolf the boy had ever seen. He had no rifle. The old wolf leaped, to drive him back, and fell forward on its muzzle, which rose white-tipped from the snow; its tongue fell out. The icy steel worked tighter on its foreleg, and the pain confused it, for it looked aside and wagged its tail a little, shivering. Then, just once, it howled a real wolf howl, pure as the black air of the mountain forest. Then it lay down. It had been gnawing on its foreleg, just above where the trap had snapped, and now it began again, whining and snarling at its own agony, at the stubbornness of its own bone which held it earthbound. The mad yellow eyes watched him, the taut muzzle, the purplish curled gum, red teeth, the jaw; the scrape of teeth on living bone made him cry out. The ears flicked forward, but the gnawing did not stop.

When he came close, it sprang sideways; another such spring might free it. He drew back, frightened of the mad wild yellow eyes.

The sun rose to low banks of winter clouds; the day grew cold. He cut a sapling and carved a spear point, long and white; confronting the wolf, he drove the raw white wood into its chest as it came up at him and fought to pin it to the ground and grind the pain out of it. But still it fought to live, dull heavy thumps in the white flying powder; a blood fleck seared his lip — the wolf was snapping at the place where the stake pierced it. Shaken free, he had fallen within reach of it, but the stunned creature only raised its bleeding teeth from its own wounds and stared at him and past him, blinked once at the dying winter world, in a daze, and lay its head upon its forepaws, panting.

He opened his eyes, gasping for breath; he drifted downward. Once the abyss opened out into air and sunlight, but there were papier-mâché angels, and again he broke off chords of music from the air like bits of cake: the Paradise was false and he went on. A spider appeared, reared high over his head, then seized, shredded and consumed him. Voided, he lay inert in a great trough, with molten metal rising all about him in a blinding light. SO THIS WAS BRIMSTONE. The missionary's pasty face peered down at him over the rim: *This is a proud day for the mission, Lewis, and a proud day for your people. We all count on you.*

Eyes. Eyes. He struggled to free himself, but the stake held in his heart, the hole in his heart; even breathing hurt him, even breathing. He clawed at his own chest to ease it. If only he could get that pain out, then his heart would bleed his life away, but gently.

A roar of trapped insects, flies and bees, and he among them: mad drone and bugging and brush of hairy, viscous legs scraping toward remote slits of air and light, of acrid insect smell, of flat inconscient insect eyes, unblinking, bright as jewels, too mindless to know fear, oh Christ, how mindless. Humans . . . A human mob, pounding its way into the bar, in search of — what? It did not know. It had no idea what it was hunting, but was hunting out of instinct, with myriad flat insect eyes, trampling everything underfoot; he shook with fear. Like a rat he was, a famine rat of broken cities, a quaking gut-shrunk rat, scurrying through the wainscoting of falling houses. His skeleton flew apart, reassembled in rat's skeleton; his spine arched, the tiny forefeet and long furtive hand, the loose-skinned gassy belly; he poised, alert, hunched on his knees upon the bed, hands dangling at his naval, long nose twitching. In the mirror across the room he saw the hair sprout on his face and the face protrude.

He found his way across the room and stared so closely into the glass that his nose touched it; he watched the face wrinkle and turn old; he saw his own raw skull again and groaned. Then another mask, a new expression, hard and sly and cold. As he watched, it softened and turned young and wide-eyed, gentle; the muscles in his stomach eased, and he recognized the self of boyhood mornings. He was touched by this last face and grinned at it in embarrassment; but just as he grinned, self-consciousness returned to poison him, and the boyish face turned hard again and mean, and the lips drew back upon sharp teeth and the eyes glittered, and the whole body tensed with an anger of such murderous black violence that he recoiled from his own hate, falling back again across the bed.

A huge dead dog had its teeth locked in his throat, and the metal bar dragged at his chest again, and when he closed his eyes the Rage descended, a huge and multilimbed galoot in hobnailed boots and spurs, eyes bulging, teeth grinding, cigars exploding in its mouth and flames shooting from its ears, bearing a club spiked with rusty nails, wearing brass knuckles and outsize six guns; in its blind snot-flying rage, it blew its own head off by mistake. This thing came stomping down out of his mind, and he gasped, Look at *that* guy, that guy is so mad, he blew his own head off by mistake! His body relaxed and he howled with laughter, lying now with his back on the floor and his feet on the bed, and as he laughed, the gnawed and painful stake which had pierced his chest as long as he could remember cracked and opened like an ancient husk and turned to dust, and he could breathe again.

With the music rising in the summer breeze there came a gay preposterous parade along the highroad: calliope flutings and fanfare, with band wagons and floats and maelstroms of confetti, pouter pigeons and emerald parakeets, bursting drums and golden tubas, and gauzy fat-cheeked majorettes in crotch-tight sateen suits, chins bouncing on high squeaking breasts like taut balloons — *oompa, oompa, oompa, oompa*. And an immense blowzy one-man band of a hand-me-down Big Irma, beer-soaked and high-colored, all billowing bows and curlicues and furbelows of hue and texture *Look At Her Go, Hurrah Hurrah!* all leer and wink, hiking her skirts to turn the ankle, pretty still beneath the mass of tired flesh, and trying in vain to shake a ball of hair and dog turd from her heel, squinching and squashing and squirting along like a banquet dumped into a bag. She wore a gigantesque plumed hat which she flew like a flag, and as the old tub pushed along, batting her eyes and swinging her butt, she leaked and sagged and oozed so woefully at the seams that rats and crows fought for her leavings, while in the front and alongside, as trumpets blew and pennants flew and children snickered and horses nickered, stores and provisions and water and fuel were crammed aboard; varlets hurled up trays of tarts and heaved up meats and slung up wine flagons and kegs of ale, while others ran to pump in gasoline and air, barely able to offset the waste and loss of the vast outpourings beneath — Big Irma meanwhile, nothing daunted, leering and winking to beat hell, and curtseying prettily as the bands played and hats were tossed and wild cheers rent the air *hip hip hurroo* and winking her blinkers and twinking her pinkie and twirling a tiny parasol, all giggling and goosed and poked, as if to say, Well, sweet Christ knows I always done my damndest.

Once upon a time, at morning, a small blood-silver river in the rising plains, the silver undersides of wind-awakened leaves, the silver spider webs in dew. A small boy hunting, poised, quick, listening, in a fine old-smelling boat parting new reeds. Soft drops falling from an oar, a newborn sun, far bugling . . . a swan. The stalk, the shot, the yell of blackbirds, the white bird turning a slow circle, head under water. Feathers floating and wild silence . . . That morning his skin tingled, and he laughed aloud in that sky-high aloneness that was not loneliness, the strength of a young animal among animals in a soft summer sunrise . . .

horses, rodeos, long murky bars and rotten sawdust smell in high small sandy towns of the Great Basin, a coyote trapped by hurtling cars where the road cut through the rock, a lone whiskey bottle on the shoulder of the road. Night voices, speed, a dirtied strength, a flight, a maiming, a lost friend; women and bystanders overrun, struck aside by wheels spun loose from flying axles, flying hooves, by fenders: highways, sirens, howling lights, a crash . . . dread silence . . .

smoke, and twisted metal shards, flayed twisted limbs, a staring eye, and gasoline spreading like a stain of blood on the stunned pavement: hiss of steam, oncoming sirens, sirens, *I-A-R-R-A-O-W-A-O-A- O-W* . . .

Meriwether

Lewis Moon, in ditch, head bleeding at the temple
Ever driven a convertible, Lew boy? Go ahead — try it.

With the record you already made, Lew boy — Lewis.
With the record you already made, Lewis, it won't hardly be no trouble, no trouble at all.
Yeah, but Eddie, his grades are very good, he's got what you might call real native intelligence —

Hell, just keep drinkin whiskies like you been doin right along, and then you parade that little Eastern gal of yours around the campus, you know, feelin her up and all, and throw a punch maybe if somebody gets smart — that ought to do it.

All you boys want is a complete sellout of the Cheyennes in this state, and you'll give the dumb Injun three hundred brand-new all-American silver dollars, right?

Well, there's no call to look at it that way . . .

Make it two thousand, or this auto, and I'll be out of your miserable alma mater before daylight.
Two thousand? Or this automobile? How in hell are you going to earn two thousand — scalp somebody?

Hand it over and find out.
Look, Geronimo, we can get you framed for less than that!

Ah, come on, Eddie, they said they wanted it a nice clean job.

Well, there's the two, goddamit, Lewis — now when you going to earn it?

. . . eighteen, nineteen, two. Right now — you two fat turds get out and walk.

Hey, wait a minute, watcher language! No red nigger's gonna . . .

— Ow! Christ watch it!

In the mirror he saw one of them, face bloodied, help the other to his feet; they bawled for justice.
You mean that's their car you have downstairs? Oh, I can't bear it, you were almost graduated! Lew, listen to me, darling, this is no way to prove anything —
Lewis. *I'm supposed to feel you up in public.*
Oh, listen to you, sweetheart, look how drunk you are! If you really believe in what you're doing, why are you so drunk? Listen, it's not only a question of yourself — how about your people? How about the people who worked so hard to get you in here —
That's it, right there — I sold out when I first signed in as their pet Indian. And yours too, baby, yours.
The only reason you're making it with me is because you don't come from around here. You goddamn liberals are all alike — all talk and no risk.
Don't be like that! How can we help you people if you won't help yourselves! Oh, can't you understand? I love you!
Love, love, lo-ove . . .
Down the road. The big two-tone auto stank of lotion and cigar butts, but it moved. It roared across the land like an apocalypse, almost to the state line, before the oil gauge flashed red; then he forced it harder still, grinding his teeth and driving the gas through it to burn it clean, until the tires reeked and the body shuddered, until the fat plastic dashboard bulged with warnings, until the whole fat contraption of churchgoing chromium and patriotic plush screeched and choked on its own heat and burst its block and screamed to a hissing locked fiery halt with eight million all-American motorcycles hard behind. *I-A-R-R-A-O-A-O-W.* A last swig and he broke the bottle, then toppled out, rolling and laughing, on the highway shoulder. Down he went through waving weeds into the swamp, hailing and cursing the cop silhouettes, with two thousand dollars and a hand cut by broken teeth, and nothing and nowhere, but free, by Christ, how free of their whole Indian game.

He headed eastward to New York. On a truck radio he heard the charges: grand larceny — an automobile and two thousand dollars — and felonious assault.
See, Lewis, it ain't gonna work. You find yourself another local.
I don't get it. You had a fight in here yourself only last week — you guys were drunk right on the job.
You don't fight the way we fight. We fight for fun, Lewis. Because we like it. Because we like it. We ain't tryin to prove nothin. So you just find yourself a nice white local where they fight the way you fight.

White local, huh? There's more Cheyenne in this blood coming out of my nose than there is Mohawk in all you bastards put together —
You got shit in your blood too. We never heard of Cheyennes, hardly, until you come along, and anyway, we ain't professional Indians like you. All we know about Indians, bub, is what we seen on television.

I-A-R-R-A-O-A-O-W...
Sirens, howling lights, another crash, another, still another: modern times. *CRASH, CRASH, CA-RASH* — that crazy kid is *CA-RAZY* — he began to laugh. The crashes became gimcrack destruction, a breaking and tinkling of deafening dimensions, a mounting heap of slow jalopies hurling themselves together at a crossroads.

Port scene with rum, tropical colors, high white birds, the lonely palms of dawn: a crazy-legged Negress dancing nude,

Wistaria, her flesh...

Because the way things are goin they ain't no hope for none of us, lessen we don't get somethin learned here to us pretty quick...

Here was Rage again, exploded now, hung-up like an old scarecrow, like a big broken toy with one loose eye and loose old parts and springs and stuffing every whichy-way — all hung-up on itself, poor critter. Rage danced somewhat sheepishly to guitar and wind, as if to say: Well, just because I'm angry doesn't mean I don't enjoy a dance or two...

Lucidity. He sighed. He lay there all laughed out and loose, loose as a dead snake slung on a rail, lay there drunk with gentleness and pleasure. *Be a good boy, Lewis, do not hate so much.*

Oh good old Wolfie, Wolfie would die laughing. The thought of the Old Wolf laughing, *dying* of *laughing*, set him off again, but this time, even as he laughed, an apprehension came. He crawled to the corner of the room, where he crouched low, watching both door and window. The noises were surrounding him, there was something happening to him, something *happening*, and he felt too tired now to deal with it. If he could only stop this laughing, but he could not; his laughter grew louder and louder, and when he tried to stop he could not close his mouth. It stretched wider and wider, until he swallowed the ceiling light, the room, the window and the night; the world rushed down into the cavernous void inside him, leaving him alone in space, pinwheeling wildly like a jagged fragment spun out from a planet.

A terrific wind blew, and his ears rang with the bells of blue-black space; the wind sealed his throat, his flesh turned cold, his screams were but squeaks snapped out and away by the passage of night spheres. Nor could he hear, there was no one to hear, there was no one where he had gone — *what's happening, what-is-happening...*

He had flung himself away from life, from the very last realities, had strayed to the cold windy reaches of insanity. This perception was so clear and final that he moaned; he would not find his way back. You've gone too far this time, *you've gone too far...*

As he whirled into oblivion, his body cooled and became numb, inert, like a log seized up and borne out skyward by a cyclone; he struggled to reach out, catch hold, grasp, grip, hang on, but he could not. He could not, he was made of wood, and there was nothing to hang on to, not even his own thought — thought shredding, drifting out of reach, like blowing spider webs. He was gone, g-o-n-e, *gone*, G-O-N-E, gone — and around again. The howling was in his head, and all about lay depthless silence. His screaming was ripped away before it left his mouth, and the mouth itself was far away, a huge papered hoop blown through and tattered by the gales. The air rushed past, too fast to breathe; his lungs sucked tight, shriveled like prunes, collapsed. He died.

Death came as a huge bounteous quiet, in the bosom of a high white cloud. The wood of his body softened, the knots loosened; he opened up, lay back, exhausted, mouth slack, eyes wide like the bald eyes of a corpse. He glimpsed a hard light lucid region of his mind like a lone comet, wandering far out across the long night of the universe.

(EXCERPT FROM: Peter Matthiessen. *Far Tortuga/At Play in the Fields of the Lord.* New York: Random House, 1975 & 1965, pp. 87–104.)

TRANSLATED FROM the Spanish by Steven F. White

TEN POEMS ON A SUNDAY AFTERNOON

Luis Eduardo Luna

Sunday, February 27, 1972

1. Barcarole

On the lost waters,
downriver,
boatless and thirsty
traveler of plants,
I saw and I heard,
and that murmur of insects
and the water-engine in the river
and the black man's conversations
on the black afternoon
and those ropes
frayed to breaking among the boards
and the jarring voice
and a small scream.
And jungle and jungle.
I don't even remember
how that day began
and how
in a confusion of voices
and shouting
and sudden movement
and who knows what sort of orders,
we all went up
a blue hill
at thirty kilometers per hour
and from there
through tangled jungle
we saw the river
and the reflection of the waters
in the river
and time's reflection in the waters
and the reflection of certain events
in time.
Memory is sometimes sand.
And her body
on the river's black sand
and that tenacious boat
on the river
crossing so many things.

2. Sleight of Hand

It was the summer heat
in the eternal summer.
Up ahead, a dark face like a turtle shell.
My friend Careidón, I suppose.
In the square, a table,
the green juice, the yellow mango,
the infinite whiteness of some hands.
And only the smile,
the incongruence,
and through obstacles,
the glacial quality,
the monotony,
then suddenly an opening,
where a melancholy air
slowly filters.
Tropics, sun
and floating dust.
And a scent of pine
that remained lost like a child's prank.
And I could no longer
distinguish the faces.
That ancient man
more than five hundred years old
talking about the United States
and the towers of Manhattan
and sailboats on the Cote d'Azur.
And at night
the adventures of Lain among mambos
and the felt orchestra
that came to enclose us in any tent.
Yes!
And he has a son
who knows no English.
And that was our first day
with its terrapin face
looking at me,
smiling,
and his wife
who might even be
considered pretty.
The afternoon
rained
yellow dust.

3. The Seeker

When I saw it coming,
tied to the load,
I couldn't resist a smile.
It was thin,
barely a tower collating the sky.
And I couldn't imagine that treasure
in the last corner of its diving helmet.
Some hours passed
and I barely raised a question.
I seemed
somehow possessed by the Insect.
That insect singing at noon,
not daring to introduce itself
perhaps because it had no tie.
Then the place
toward which we walked
drinking Cokes
and chewing little yellow balls
of corn
became a prism.
Wide curve in motion,
 rubber flecked with red.
And it began to speak to me
and it said so many things
that I barely understood
and so many things were sawed to pieces,
hammered,
struck at that moment
when it suddenly said:
I am Tarsisio
of the great jaws.

4. Necromancy

He worked for many long years
hoping that everything would come back to him,
the fruits of his labor,
the results of mistakes.
His hands,
burdened by so many blisters,
by so many efforts,
so many thoughts,
awaited the miracle
every day.
And dressed in wool,
cradled in the darkest regions,
obstinate and firm,
the miracle did not come,
because he never knew if it existed
or if it was only his imagination,
or if it was the fruit of time
and summer.
And so he spent the years
gathering stones,
building castles
that aged with him.
And he never knew if the stones were piled
on the other side,
if each figure was copied
in an ageless mirror
behind the pyramids.
But although
perhaps he knew,
he told me nothing,
leaving me in ignorance
to gather stones.
In the summer
when the rains arrive,
swimming in the memory
of the ancient necromancer
who died of old age
as he gathered scraps of newspaper.

5. Atlantis

Submerged,
the splendor of plants urged him on,
and he dug a road in the water
to get closer,
and in blue depths he discovered
beautiful white wings of algae
and sweet rhythms
of locusts in love.
Four by four
toward the enormous tower
where black meteorites streaked past
he saw the insects,
millimetrically aligned,
rising into blue.
The sky was pink,
the water, pale,
and among warm waves
he saw figures
with only two dimensions
giving soft speeches
while waving their arms
and he was there
with wide-open eyes
watching it all
from the shore of the lake.
Where the bottom disappears
near a river
or in the river,
the slow beating,
the perfect succession of movements,
the white wings
appeared again,
crying in the air.
And in the water,
the ship of illusion
revealed itself and slowly
spun past
on the wide river
within the
water.

6. Inner World Tour

I traveled it all in a flash —
an inner world tour,
near a canyon
on a green afternoon,
the house above me
on the edge of the jungle,
wading across a river,
writing on the dry leaves
of a banana tree with ripe fruit.
Among nettles,
apples
and peaches
were sleeping,
whole.
And I was
on top of a ramp
four arms spread to the world,
contemplating it all
from above.
And seeing this,
non-conformist that I was,
I decided to look at things
from below.
And I saw the succession of roots
in the mauve pollen
of the earth,
and the seminal liquor of almond trees
coursing through stones
and the band of colors
I hadn´t imagined.
On the white tour,
in the earth´s mauve night,
I saw the world from below
and I cast myself adrift
on the tide of virgin smells,
the smooth touch of the trees' fingers
as they hang
in bunches
in the violet pudding of the earth.

7. Bitterness

In the bar,
a few meters from the dust,
the Indian Apolinar crossed the callouses on his feet
beneath the table.
With his one eye, small and brilliant,
he described the spirit of the trees.
And those huge, bark-covered hands
moved through the air, carving the figure
of Oguara and Yagé,
Yoco and Chagró,
and the bad eye.
And the firewater
consumed in each gulp's blown breath.
And he barely answered,
and his voice like an old plant
leapt through the jungle
under the full moon.
And in his house,
sleeping in the square of a blanket
divided like a lily
the night keeps watch in silence
over his little Indian grandson.
And by the bonfire's light,
among so many dark hands,
Yagé, like a goddess,
dancing naked.

8. Deep Within

That happened on the boulders
at twilight some month I can't remember.
The house had been abandoned,
and in the silence of fruit and snow,
the clicking of bamboo
above the bed.
In the tangled branches,
that fruit, the *badeas*,
almost ripe,
yellowed by sun and birds,
waited amidst clouds of insects.
Water was striking the rocks
as it descended from the heights.
In the river's green pool,
surrounded by fish
in the plunging water
and whirlpools of sand,
the message grew
like an open book.
And its hard cover flashed red
and its words were soft among dead grass.
Tossing the bread far away,
so close to the jungle,
once again I was propelled
toward the mystery.
Not far from there,
among white stones,
pink and vermillion flesh
brushed its teeth.
The wildcat was sleeping
with its tail between its paws.
The only sound was
the bamboo's silence above the bed.

9. Mandrágora

It was the night of the cicadas,
the first time.
The light was a glimpse,
the tip of the candle.
In the juicy wood,
the rat-faced spirits were spying on me,
keeping watch over my tired eyes
and the flame rearing up,
balancing the shadows.
Then darkness came
and that immense space
already tangible
in its black encasement of the body,
condensed into sharpness,
into a wakening sensibility,
and the hoarse fear,
the broad scream,
the golden twitching on the edge of the sheets,
perforated walls,
plummeted outside,
and in the enormous awe
above all convergences of dreams
step by step
with a dead man's solemnity,
it roamed through all my corridors
and knocked on my door with its moist fingers.
Light was a memory
receding too far in the distance,
and daytime
an unknown corner of the universe.
When I moved beyond centuries,
growing spirals,
and when I reached the sixth dwelling of the gods,
an ancient man
in a white shroud
swollen with watches
surrounded by rats
in the night with no candles
kept his vigil in bed
over a sleepless awakening.

10. The Night of the Eclipse

There was an article in the newspaper —
between midnight and seven o'clock
on March 23, 1939.
At 4:00, the shadows left their caves
and danced until it got late.
Among the five daggers of the ancient Messiahs,
we listened carefully to all the music.
From thick weeds, the dead kept coming
in a slow desperate procession.
But everything there went on as before.
My Hungarian friend Karman even made a toast
to the unborn.
And there they were, ancient and remote,
and they lent us their particular gifts,
and in an enormous agreement
in perfect harmony,
we occupied the site of brother Nostradamus,
Rosacruz, Anselmo,
our friend Plotinus and Ulysses always with us,
and it was strange to observe
those other greens,
those other swallows,
all so similar
in history's hundreds of distant circles,
with different ways of dressing,
with the same gaze,

in the fierce moment of the eclipse.
All the languages came to shine,
and all the riddles,
and, with a bit of luck,
we compared these works
with those of old Jupiter,
bored with having to wait so many centuries
for the night of the eclipse.
There was a round of wine
and fruit juice with cookies
and at the hour of judgment
which was a total farse,
we laughed at those
who took our nonsense seriously.
When it was almost dawn,
when the sharp, advancing papagayos arrived,
the troop dissolved
as if under the blows of sticks.
When the blue came
to restore its powers
with its birdcries
and buzzing of insects,
between cracks
in dark eyes of stone,
the dead
were still laughing.

MEN OF CHAZÚTA

F. Bruce Lamb

You have seen that wild country on the Amazon side of the Cordillera on your flights over the Andes from Lima to Iquitos. The Amazon River rises in those jungle-covered sharp ridges and deep canyons almost always shrouded in mist. *Cejas de la montaña* (eyebrows of the mountains) they call that country, and well named too. Sometimes in clear weather you can see down into those dark shadowy canyons, but more often drifting clouds obscure the view. From the air only an occasional fleeting glimpse is possible into the wild inaccessible country where the men of Chazúta dwell.

Going into that country from the mountain town of Tarapoto I received a warning about the local Indians. I had already decided that the small jungle village of Chazúta fit into my curare production plans. When my friends in Tarapoto found this out they warned me: *"Tenga cuidado, los hombres de Chazúta son temibles hechiceros todos* (Be careful, the men of Chazúta are feared sorcerers every one)." Sorcerers, if you know how to deal with them, can be useful. Also, I knew before going there that the forests of the country around Chazúta had a greater abundance of the jungle vine *ampihuasca* (poison vine) than any other known part of the Amazon region. Forest- dwelling Indians make from this vine a lethal arrow and blowgun dart poison called by some "winged death," better known as curare.

Word reached us that the substance had value outside the Amazon. In delicate surgical operations the purified extract can be used to relax selected strategic muscles of a patient during critical moments of a surgeon's work. My employers had commitments to certain New York pharmaceutical firms to provide the raw jungle extract for laboratory purification, which would then be made available to surgeons when needed. But efforts to produce a suitable jungle extract on a commercial scale had failed.

The person who first attempted to produce this *curare* was a friend of mine, and we often discussed his efforts before sudden death terminated his work. From his comments I was convinced that he had not been careful enough during the extraction process in his jungle camp. Now the turn of fortune involved me in this same dangerous enterprise. But I had my own protection from my training at the hand of old Izidore, one of the best Ticuna Indian curare makers in the whole upper Amazon. That experience of years ago still remained vivid in my mind.

The men of Chazúta of whom I hoped to make allies belonged to the Lamisto tribe. To escape Inca tyranny and the brutal Spanish *conquistadores* these Indians several hundred years ago moved down from the high Andes plateau into the forbidding lands of the *cejas de la montaña.* Superstitious and clannish people, they do not welcome outsiders. Yet in their territory the *ampihuasca* vine grows best. And if I was not to fail in the production of a commercial *curare* extract I needed the help of the Lamisto.

In spite of the warning about the feared sorcerers who lived there, Chazúta seemed to me to provide the best site to establish my influence among these potentially unfriendly people. The strategic location and special reputation of the Chazutinos to the rest of the Lamisto in the region as sorcerers gave Chazúta significance to my plans. In the almost impassable jumble of steep mountain ridges and narrow canyons the Lamisto villages are small and scattered far apart. You get to them on foot or by mule back. There is no other way to reach these isolated places.

On my first trip to Chazúta from Tarapoto, which has an airport, Chuquizuta guided my way. He had come to Tarapoto on a trading mission, and since I spoke to him in his own dialect he agreed to take me to Chazúta.

Along the trail on our way I noticed throughout the forest the vine *ayahuasca* — vine of the spirits. It was well-known to me for the vision extract it contained. But when I asked Chuquizuta if he knew the famous plant he looked at me in a strange way before answering. That gave me an idea for getting close to the Chazutinos.

"Hie pani Taita (Great Holy Father)," they exclaimed when I arrived and they found out that I spoke their Quechua dialect from the Andes. By talking with them in their own idiom I managed to head off much of the antipathy they might otherwise have felt toward me and my project of producing curare extract. I soon found out that they also knew about the spirit vine — *ayahuasca.* But from our discussions I could tell that their understanding of its use was superficial. They believed that the strong purging effect of drinking the extract cleansed their bodies and attracted useful forest spirits to help them in their hunting expeditions. The disorganized visions they saw were only incidental to them. When I suggested that *ayahuasca* visions had meaning beyond their understanding, it aroused their curiosity. They agreed to take it with me to see if what I said was true. Feared as they were by some, the sorcerers of Chazúta compliantly let themselves be persuaded to drink with me the vision vine extract *ayahuasca* that I myself prepared. I knew it would put them under my control.

Late one afternoon when the weather signs were favorable for a calm rainless night, I led a small select group in single file from their village, Chazúta, through the jungle to a place I had made ready in the forest. On the way I chanted in their dialect a simple song to hold their attention and relieve any fears or tensions they might feel.

great forest
dwelling place our forefathers
benevolent protector of our lives
watch over us
green mantle
source of our sustenance
shelter for the spirits
of our ancestors
now watch over us

When we reached the opening I had cleared in the undergrowth beneath a canopy of large forest trees beside a small stream, I kindled a small fire, continuing my chant. Deliberately and calmly I arranged my companions in a circle around the fire. Late afternoon bird songs floated down from the tree tops. A shaft of filtered sunlight momentarily illuminated our gathering place with a friendly glow. As the sunlight faded and fire became our source of light, sounds of the night, which comes suddenly in the deep forest, took over the aural background of our scene. Then I asked those Lamisto Indians of Chazúta to remove their clothing, proceeding to set the example myself. Thus we removed all that separated and restrained our bodies from the direct contact with the ambience of this forest place. We shed our inhibitions with our shirts and pants, becoming simpler, more natural beings — better attuned to the dark and brooding forest. Our naked bodies glowed in the fire light.

Chanting again, I put a bundle of leaves on the fire.

fragrant leaves
tranquil smoke
prepare our minds
for visions to come

A billowing white cloud of pungent, fragrant smoke from the burning leaves floated up into the tree tops, enveloping us at the same time in the spell of its aroma. A trance-like tranquillity prevailed as we breathed in the fragrant smoke.

My chanting held their attention as I poured out into small gourd cups a greenish-brown liquid which I had prepared several days earlier; sections of the vision vine I had boiled with the leaves of a certain shrub I found in the forest.

magic vine of the forest
leaves of the shrub

with markings of the boa
bring us visions
bring us awareness
give us knowledge
of our forest home

As we drank together the potion in our cups I noticed a slightly bitter taste and wondered momentarily about the strength of this *ayahuasca*. Plants even of the same species vary from one region to another and there had been no time to test the strength of the local variety here at Chuzúta. That it was certainly strong enough soon became apparent.

One of the first reactions to a strong dose of *ayahuasca* is a violent discharge of energy through the nervous system. This can be a traumatic experience for imbibers untrained to control the reaction mentally. The Chazutinos had told me they took this vision vine purge and I assumed they had some control. This conclusion on my part turned out to be erroneous, at least in connection with the extract I was accustomed to preparing and using. Perhaps they made up a milder potion for their hunting purge.

If body condition and mental control are inadequate the individual reactions vary according to the state of the nervous system of each person. Some have violent abdominal convulsions, others experience intense nausea, and still others erotic stimulation of the whole glandular system involved with sexual response. And now suddenly, a few minutes after drinking our potion came characteristically deep and powerful reactions, violent reactions, of naked Indians. Some were loudly crapping, pissing and vomiting in the small stream beside our clearing. Others stood displaying with amazement their tremendous hard-ons. Any personal inhibitions to such manifestations had been dissolved by that first stage of response to the extract.

But these outward physical reactions lasted only a few minutes and with suggestive chanting and gestures I calmly assembled and seated them around the fire again with their eyes closed. At first, as the initial stimulus subsided, a general feeling of euphoria spread through the group, indicated by the play of expression on the usually-impassive Indian faces, and I knew they were seeing in their minds, as I was, strange formless moving visions. These multicolored blobs gradually cohered in the more formal shapes of natural forms — vague arabesque traceries of a butterfly wing, then a delicate spider web set against a subtle changing background of greenish-blue color. With evocative songs, imitated jungle sounds, and subtle gestures creating an atmosphere suitable for auto-suggestion I brought into our joint visions scenes of the forest where birds of brilliant plumage and rare song were followed by game birds, then by the hunters — the hawks and owls. In my carnivorous parade the giant harpy, the monkey-eating eagle with flaming yellow eyes and scimitar beak, was followed by the hideous but brilliantly colorful king vulture and giant condor of the Andes. A snake-eating hawk doing battle with a fer-de-lance or yellow beard then started a procession of snakes through our visions, with the appearance of the giant *shushupi*, the bushmaster. Fire flashed from the *shushupi's* tongue and eyes, and a pulsating bluish scrollwork floated upright along his spine. Loud hissing and vicious strikes at an invisible prey accompanied his passage. Last came the enormous anaconda or boa, known to the Indians as *yacumama* or mother-of-the-water, now released onto land from its native rivers and lakes. As this incredible reptile moved slowly through the forest, every segment of the intricate pattern of his scaly hide glowed in brilliant contrasting colors.

A cool breeze passing gently through the forest carried the fragrance of night-blooming orchids from the tree tops. The combination of the cooling effect on our naked bodies and the heavy aroma in our nostrils created indescribably erotic sensations. They surged into all the sensing mechanisms of our minds. the breeze increased to a strong wind and the great trees of the forest began to sway and groan. Wild cries of unknown creatures filled the turbulent air, and the agitated vegetation roared. But this storm subsided as quickly as it had arisen. In its aftermath I brought forth a complete precisely textured series of forest animals, ending finally with a family of big spotted cats. Before my companions drifted into a troubled sleep I turned their minds loose to float through subtly colored and moving spirals and arabesques of infinite variety themselves gradually fading into the ever nothingness that surrounds and impinges on our world of light and form.

With the cacophony of morning bird song and the shafting rays of sunshine penetrating our secluded jungle glade there beside the small sparkling stream, my phantom-viewing companions gradually awakened. They looked at one another with guarded glances and conversed in whispers, verifying by their half-heard remarks that they had all witnessed the same fantastic parade of visionary birds and animals. They looked in my direction with awe and deference. I stirred up the fire and encouraged them with casual remarks to return to the world of ordinary everyday life.

When my quiet and subdued new friends had all awakened I reminded them of what had happened in those first moments after they drank properly prepared *ayahuasca*. I explained that their reactions were so violent because they had failed to follow my instructions for getting ready, especially by their not avoiding contaminating foods. I told them that if they would spend a few days with me, doing exactly as I instructed in the matter of fasting and other preparations, I would show them even more marvelous things, far beyond the revelations of the visions just ended. Shaking their heads questioningly and grinning shyly at one another in disbelief they agreed to try.

When we went back to the village I kept these men together in one hut and there among us we discussed the natural world. We talked about this land in which they lived, the eyebrows of the mountain; we examined the production of *curare* and a thousand other things. I arranged for one of the women to bring us only fresh fruit, roast chicken, and boiled white yuca (manioc) to eat. That first reaction to my *ayahuasca* had purged them almost completely, but I did prepare a mild extract of *achuni sacha*, a nerve stimulant, to tune their systems for the visions to come.

The sun was not far from setting on the third day of our fasting when we went again to our scheduled spot in the forest. This time there was a feeling of eagerness and a desire for more active participation. The men had a better idea of what to expect and were keyed up to see if I could make good my promise of fantastic unison visions. Again, as we approached the little clearing, I chanted to the forest; again, the song to the fragrant leaves as I placed the green branches on the small fire; then, pouring the liquid into the cups, I intoned the chant of the vision-vine and we prepared the medicine.

We drank together. With great mental concentration and compelling song I held their attention safely through the stage of violent reaction. Some jerked with slight muscle spasm and I knew from these signs that soon I would possess them all in the visions that were to come. Again, through evocative chants and imitation of jungle sounds and even more subtle channels of suggestion, I maintained control of the flow of visions through our collective consciousness. Beginning with changing, flowing abstract color forms of great plasticity and variety I brought into our minds scenes of the forest, giant trees and other plants, and, again, the passing parade of birds and animals.

From our long, meandering conversations of the last three days I found that these men greatly admired the spotted jaguar. This was the largest animal in their forest, and I knew that some of them were clever at trapping these uncanny beasts. So, as our fantasy progressed, to impress them I brought into our visions the shuffling, giant, big-headed spotted cat of old Chief Xumu's visions from years before in a faraway jungle with a different group of even more primitive Indians. Now as we watched him in wonder, this huge cat stumbled through the trees, grunting to himself, his tongue lolling out, his great curved fangs clearly visible. He looked harmless enough in spite of his size, until with a sudden lashing switch of his tail he became instantly and viciously alert — flashing eyes and menacing growl. From my seated companions came a collective audible response, a gasp of indrawn breath, in anticipation of some disaster. But the mighty beast of our fantasy faded from the visioned forest, to be followed by another jaguar, a magnificent black one. He reared up and tested his large curved claws on a great tree trunk, scattering bark chips in all directions, switching his tail and rumbling a growl low in his throat. Coming down to four feet again he turned with twitching tail and sprayed the scratched tree with panther piss, marking his territory. As on previous occasions when this beast had come into my visions, I had the impression — and it now also became part of my companions' visions — that I was myself merged in some strange way with this black jaguar and that we traveled as one through this forest of our dreams. All the mysteries and secrets of the jaguar world were mine. My sensing faculties became those of the black animal. Sound, sight, smell, feel and instinct were tuned in with those of this most astute beast of the forest. And we prowled together — investigating dark hidden things beyond the ken of uninitiated man, unexplainable in his language.

With the black cat fading into the forest shadows came a change in mood; there developed views of distant picturesque landscapes and strange cloud formations. Out of the clouds there strode a caravan of giant human figures in white hooded robes. In slow succession they passed among us, chanting, and each one as he passed laid a hand momentarily on each of our heads. This event was accompanied by an incandescent glow of light and an almost unbearable flow of heat through our bodies. As these apparitions faded back into the clouds from whence they came, pleasant images of colored forms took over — giant double rainbows arching and moving between clouds and accompanied by celestial music. Then this too faded into nowhere as I gradually relaxed my mental control and phantom-viewers dozed into their fitful slumber.

Soon the morning sun and the usual forest sounds brought us back to the world of reality. And again my companions displayed their feelings of awe. All of them had drunk *ayahuasca* before my arrival, if what they had told me was true, but none had participated in anything at all like the experience we had just been through together. They spoke especially of the forest cats we had seen and seemed to shudder at the thought of meeting one of them alive. And these Indians of Chazúta assured me that *jamás habían pensado que una purga tenía tanto poder para dejarles tan lelos de todo lo que ellos sabían, y quedaron muy maravillados del poder del* ayahuasca *bien preparado* — never had they thought that a purge could have such power to leave them as simpletons for all they knew, and now they recognized the marvelous power of *ayahuasca* properly prepared and controlled by a master of the art.

"I sense, my friend," Córdova said to me, "that you find it difficult to grasp the significance of the influence that a *maestro ayahuasquero* has over the minds of a group of people who participate with him in a vision session of the kind I have described. This power once exerted, though perhaps subtle in its effect, does not easily disappear. As you know, in my youth I was held in its spell for several years.

"In your country, from what I read in the newspapers, people are taking something called LSD which seems to have a similar effect on the mind. Unfortunately, from the accounts I have seen this new medicine is taken in a haphazard way, more for quick thrills than trained wisdom. *Ayahuasca* is taken that way here also. But such is a dangerous pastime. What I have described to you — group visions under controlled conditions, with an experienced leader to bring out simultaneous reactions — is an affair of an entirely different order with long-lasting influences on the mind. And still all this is only a token of the profound secrets to be revealed by *ayahuasca*."

(EXCERPT FROM: F. Bruce Lamb. *Rio Tigre and Beyond: The Amazon Jungle Medicine of Manuel Córdova*. Berkeley: North Atlantic Books 1985, pp. 17–26.)

THE THREE HALVES OF INO MOXO
(excerpt)

César Calvo

As a Preface, Ino Moxo Enumerates the Attributes of Air

"It is a long story, I've told you. If I were to tell you everything, you would not believe anything. One can never believe everything. Do you know that? Never never can you listen to everything. . . ."

"I'm ready to do so, Maestro Ino Moxo," I hear myself say almost as a bribe; "that is why I have come."

"Could you? No, I don't believe you could." And his head leaning to one side, his eyes bringing it back up:

"To give you only one example, look at the jungle. If you try to listen to all of the sounds of the jungle, what do you hear? . . ."

And as if he had just caught himself, as if he himself were simultaneously the blowgun and the dart and the hunter and the prey and the burning wood waiting in the kitchen, Ino Moxo raised his voice:

"Not only the scream of the alert monkeys, not only the humming of the mosquitos, of the *arambasa,* which is the darkest and fiercest bee, of the *chinchilejo,* which you call dragonfly, of the *chuspi,* which infects you as it bites, of the *carachupaúsa,* which bleeds without warning; you not only hear the *ronsapa* hissing in the wind, and the *mantablanca,* which drinks your hair, and the *quilluavispa* of yellow flights, and the *papási,* which is born from worms but is not a worm, and the *wairanga,* which never touches the ground. Not only do you hear the flute bird, the *firirín,* which can't fly and has wings, nor the *ushún,* nor the *tabaquerillo,* nor the *shánsho,* nor the *piurí* nor the grayish *timelo,* nor the whitewhite *tibe,* nor the *taráwi,* which eats snails and is too black, nor the *sharára,* which knows how to live under the water very well, and even better above the wind, nor the blue *zui-zúi,* nor the great *yungurúru,* whose eggs are of the *zui-zúi* color, nor that giant red and white stork called *tuyúyu.* Not only will you listen to the all-knowing *urkutútu.* Nor the *quichagarza,* loose in excrement. Nor the *ucuashéro,* nor the *tiwakuru,* which only eats ants and sings in the top of the *wimbras,* nor the *páwcar,* which imitates all of the songs of the other birds, with its yellow and black plumage, nor the *unchala,* the same as a wine-red dove, nor the *paujil,* which you may have tasted, with flesh more flavorful than that of the *makisapa* monkeys, more flavorful than meat from the small white lizards, more pleasant than the giant plum of the *tageribá,* nor the *tatatáo,* which is a bird of prey that some call *virakocha.* You not only hear the *mariquiña* duck, the *locrero,* the *pinsha,* the *montete,* which in certain places is called *trompetero,* the *tuhuáyu,* the *pipite,* the *panguana,* which always lays five eggs and then dies, those blue macaws they call *marakána,*nor the carnivorous *wapapa* (surely you've seen it in the Mapuya River); not only do you hear its cousin the *wankáwi* giving the alarm when a human being approaches, nor the *chinwakullin,* nor the *korokóro,* nor the *ayaymáman,* which weeps like an abandoned child, nor the *camúnguy,* nor that man-sized stork with gray feathers called *mansháku,* so many birds. . . . Not only do you hear fat clouds of insects, chirping out after dusk, deep into the labyrinth of the jungle. Not only does the distrustful snake sound out, the *túnchi* forecasting a death, the sly quiet *otorongo* seeking warm flesh, nor the sticky *ronsoco* in the yuca patches, nor the huge fish with big heads in tricky nets.

"Not only do you hear fish: the *akarawasú,* the *gamitana,* the *tamborero,* the *paiche,* three meters long with a bony tongue, which lays creatures, not eggs, the *peje-torre,* which inflates itself with air and floats like a buoy, the *dorado,* which has a single spine, the *chállualagarto,* the *kunchi,* the *añashúa,* the eel that kills you with just one electric discharge, the *manitóa,* the *shitári,* the *doncella,* framed in black fringes, the *chullakaqla,* orphan without scales, the *tiríri,* the *fasácuy* in the bottom of lakes, the *shirúi,* the *maparate,* the *shiripira,* the *bujúrqui,* the *makána,* which looks like a sword with three edges, the *shuyu,* which knows how to walk on land, a fish of the road, and the *canero,* which enters your anus and eats your guts, the *demento-chállua,* which almost flies through the air, almost — and more incredible, the *saltón,* the giant fish that jumps several yards above the surface, weighs more than two hundred pounds, and measures over two meters long.

"Not to speak of the *paña,* which you know about as *piraña,* which consumes you in a few moments without reluctance. And the *kawára,* huge, and the *palometa,* tasting almost like a dessert, and the *bujéo,* also called river dolphin, the female being more delicious in love than a woman, more tasty, according to the fishermen who tried it, and it has a vagina and breasts like a woman, and delivers its young just like a woman. Cutting out the labia of a female *bujéo* and curling them, some *shirimpiá* remake infallible bracelets for the love affairs of rejected lovers, as is well known. And you also hear the great *carachama,* with a stone mouth, which lives out of the water for a week or more, and which comes from long ago, from before the deluge, before the tiger came and dispersed our first Ashanínka ancestors. So many fish. . . .

"Not only do you hear snakes, the innocent *afaníga,* harmless among the pastures, barely defending itself by swishing its tail, and the *aguaje-machácuy,* which breathes in the water and has skin like the surface of the fruit of the palm, and the deadly, small *naka-naka,* stalking in the rivers, and the *mantona,* with its useless length of ten meters, harmless to anyone, ten yards of strident colors, pure naive ornament, and the poisonous five-meter long *chushúpe* biting its prey several times, and the *yanaboa,* reaching fifteen meters in length, as thick as a man, whom it first hypnotizes and then devours. And the *sachamáma,* a boa with ears, distinct from the *yakumama,* which lives only in the water. The *sachamáma* is a land boa; it inadvertently undergoes mimesis: grass grows freely on its body. The *jergón,* instead, undergoes mimesis but with a purpose: as it grows, its skin turns to a reddish color, mottled, like brilliant leaves, and you can only spot it by its aura, by that brilliance that the *jergón* leaves in the places through which it will pass, as a signal, as a soul.

"You hear so many existences, you hear so many silent wisdoms, when you hear the jungle. And that is even without being able to hear any longer the songs of the fishes that once brightened the waters of the Pangoa, the Tambo, and the Ucayali Rivers, musical animals that foresaw the arrival of the great black otorongo and fled days before his arrival and were saved. You must know that the otorongo, with its giant paws, produced an avalanche of rocks that killed life in the rivers. Only those singing fish, which in their songs spoke and listened to the future, could survive the mud of those paws. Even though today they may no longer know how to sing, or perhaps if they still know how to sing, they must do so in secret, with sounds our ears are not accustomed to, perhaps in another dimension. . . .

"You should know that everyone, even human beings, when they are very young can hear the future, just as the fish could do before the deluge, as so many present-day animals can do. So many lives that know what will happen and cannot speak to us, warn us. Children, in general, have nine senses, not five and I have seen some that have access to eleven. As they grow their bodies gradually become poisoned with food and miseries, and as their souls become home to stained thoughts and dreams, the bodies and the thoughts of men lose their senses, their forces. That is why the sorcerers, the great shirimpiáre, in order to fully exercise the powers of air, to fully develop their powers of seeing, use the spirits of children, souls like new little families occupying the abodes of their body, the ruinous dwellings. . . .

"Not only do you hear animals: the *awíwa,* the worm one can eat like the zúri, another tasty worm of many colors, and the noisy toad that weighs more than a kilogram and is called *wálo,* and the *bocholócho,* which knows how to sing, and its song knows only how to say its own name, "Bocholóchooooo," calling always to itself, from afar, and the *manacarácuy,* a fighter, invincible among birds, and the *cupisu,* small water turtle, which eats its own eggs and flesh, and the fierce *wangána,* wild pig that lives in herds of savage fangs, and the *tokón,* that monkey with a huge and hairy tail, and the *allpacomején,* an ant sentenced to live in the ground, and the *bayuca,* poisonous worm covered with blue, yellow, red, and green hairs, and the large ant without poison that feeds on mushrooms and is called *curuínce,* and the *añuje,* almost like a hare of some size, and the *isango,* which we can't see and bites us, getting into our flesh like a punishment, and the *anañawi,* the eye- of-the-dead, which others call firefly or glowworm, and the *achúni,* sought after because it has a bony phallus, which when powdered is used to season potions used by impotent men, and that other wild boar with coarse hair and snowy collar named *sajino,* and the *ronsoco,* perhaps the largest rodent in nature, one meter long and one hundred kilos in weight, and the *apashira,* whose name is used by villagers as a synonym for a woman's sexual parts.

"The sounds come from so many animals that you've seen, that you haven't seen, that no one will ever see —

creatures that learn how to think and converse just as human beings do. . . . The sound also comes from plants, from vegetables: the *katáwa*, with poisonous sap, the *chambira*, which lends us its leaves to make rope, the breadfruit tree, which they call *pandisho*, the tall *makambo*, with big leaves and fruit resembling a man's head, the spiny *ñejilla*, which grows in the lowlands, the rugged *pashako*, the *machimango*, with impossible odors, the *chimicúa*, whose branches tear with the slightest breeze, the *wakapú*, with harder heartwood than the bloodwood, the *itininga*, the *witino*, the *itahúba*, the *wikungu*, with its black spines, and the straight tree called *expintana*, which when fallen is good to sit on and talk, and the *wakapurána*, better for firewood, and *chonta*, the heart-of-palm: from *wasái*, *cinámi*, *pijuáyu*, and *hunguráhui* palms. And the *hunguráhui*, from whose fruit flows an oil that makes hair grow. And the creeping *wayúsa*, whose leaves contain a powerful tonic to erase weakness, and the *sapote*, with a fruit the color of green shade. And the very hard *tawarí*. And the *shiringa*, the rubber tree that unwillingly brought us disgrace. And the *quinilla*, and the *timaréo*, and the *shapája* of oily fruits, and the *wiririma*, and the giant *shebón*, offering leaves to thatch roofs with, and the vegetable marble we call *tágua*, and the *sitúlli*, that rarest banana with great red flowers, and the *wingu*, a bush whose fruit becomes a cup to hold drinks and is called *tutúmo*, and the *pitajáy*, the black and hard *pona*, and the giant *aguaje*, and the *andiroba*, and the *caimito*, with fruits like a virgin's breasts, and the *waqrapona*, waisted palm, and the delicious *anona*, and the *cashú*, which is an almond on the outside, and on the inside more sweet and juicy, and the *apasharáma*, with a leather-curing sap, and the *barbasco*, with a poison root, and the citrus *camucámu*, semi-aquatic, and the *capirona*, matchless as firewood and charcoal, and the *aripasa*, with its small green-gray round fruit not to be eaten, and the *curmala*, and the *punga*, and the *cumaréba*, and the *cashirimuwéna*, and the *ashúri*, which protects teeth from caries, and the *catiríma*, whose fruits are fought over to the death by some fish, and the beautiful *cocona*, and that tuber, eaten raw, called *ashipa*, and the *pucaquiro*, with very hard red heartwood, and the leafy *pugúyo*, under whose shadow nothing can live because it expels venom from its branches, and the leafier *parinári*, with a large red fruit called *súpay-oqóte*, devil's ass, and the *lupuna* in the river banks, with its immobile wings, red on white, just above ground, the biggest of the trees in all of this Amazonia. And the other one that rains like a winter roof. And the other one that inflates and explodes worse than a hundred bullets in the night, deep in the forest, and the *renaco*, growing more than forests without leaves and without flowers, and the *garabatokasha*, which cures several types of cancers and dissolves the torpor of aging joints, and the *tamshi*, which distances you from the cold, and the coca used with *ayawaskha* for divination, and the *kamalonga* is used also for diagnosis, and the *renaquílla* entertains the lame, and the *wankawisacha* cures alcoholics forever, and the *chamáiro* helps in chewing coca, and the blackscrew, floating beneath water, halfway down thin rivers, which betrays better than the juice of *tohé* when the moon is green and the time is good to cut cedars without splitting their bark, and the *paka*, which also sounds like a tunnel along vanished rivers, and the *zarsaparrilla* cures syphilis, and the green papaya eliminates the mange and bad breath and its leaves cover the toughest meats and turn them into tender little animals. And the *wenaira*, with a poisonous shadow as the juice of the flowers of *tohé*. And the *tohé*, which makes you see the worlds of today and the worlds of tomorrow that form those of today. And the *para-pára*, better known as *hiporúru*: that leaf never loses its shape, as if it were made of rubber, stubborn; you cut it from its stalk, crumple it, bend it, and it returns to the original shape in the branch, always returns to how it was, its size, to the size and form of its two births. And it is not for that reason but from the powers that flow to it from afar that the leaf of the *hiporúru* knows how to return sexual youthfulness to men. And the *quino-quina*, which centuries ago learned how to wash rotting wounds. And the vine of the dead, *ayawaskha*, sacred, the Mother of the Voice in the Ear. With *ayawaskha*, with *oni xuma*, if you deserve it, you can pass from dreams to reality, without leaving the dream. . . . So many, so many plants, all of them producing sounds. The *abuta*—pay attention—the *abuta*, a medium-height tree whose reddish root is boiled and when the liquid is drunk, in a few days the sugar in the blood is erased; diabetics no longer suffer. And the *mariquita*, half lover and half flower, which knows how to open only in the purest shade. And the *tzangapilla*, orange and large, an only daughter, a flower warmer than a feverish forehead. All of them, all of them produce sound, as the stones do.

"And above all, you hear the sound of steps of animals one has been before being human, the steps of the stones and the vegetables and the things every human being has previously been. And also what he has heard before, all of that you can hear at night in the jungle. Inside, each one of us hears, throughout life, dances, and fifes, and promises, and lies, and fears, and confessions, and war shouts, and moans of love. Voices of the dying that one has been, or that one has only heard. True stories, stories of tomorrow. Because everything that one will hear, all of that, sounds beforehand in the middle of the night, in the jungle. It is the jungle that sounds in the middle of the night. Memory is much, much more, do you know? The truthful memory also remembers what is to be — and what will never come about; it also retains that. Imagine. Just imagine. Who could hear everything? Who could hear everything, at once, and believe it?

THE VISIONS

Ino Moxo Says That Words Are Born, Grow and Reproduce, but Not in Spanish

"The truth is not *the* truth, but *our* truth," exclaims Maestro Ino Moxo with a hard and dark voice. "It is the truth of *oni xuma*, the truth of the *chullachaki,* the curse of Ximu!" I see him angry for the first time, breathing strongly toward the Mishawa, which slides into the night. He slightly lowers his voice.

"Ximu dedicated himself to teaching me all of our truths."

And overcome by darkness:

"I would lie if I told you that I easily adapted to Amawaka existence. I would lie if I simply told you that I adapted. In reality, it was as if I had always lived here, rising early in the morning with them, going hunting, fishing at midnight, feasting, warring, loving, cutting down trees for canoes and branches for firewood, accompanying women to capture turtles and *cupiso* eggs under the sand, learning to row without the sound of a single drop, preparing arrows and their poison, polishing blowguns, great bows, and blowing darts without letting the air know about it. And above all else, being always near Maestro Ximu, going everywhere with him, witnessing his fasts, his intoxications for invocation, of call, of exchange of knowledge, spelling out his *icaros* word for word, as if I were his third lip, and listening to him always. He taught me what one can know, what one should know for the benefit of human beings, of human men and things and animals, of all humans. My initial apprenticeship with Ximu lasted until I was fifteen, then it continued with other chiefs who came to teach me from afar and to practice. But at that age, the great maestro died, shortly after naming me his heir. He donned his ritual cushma when he felt death near. To enter death he donned his yellow cushma. He said farewell to me, saying nothing to the others, and he went into the forest. Ximu's body disappeared spewing smoke."

It has been four days since we arrived at Ino Moxo's village. It is almost noon. Several black lizards bask in the sun, in front of us and to our side, on the shining pebble beaches on both sides of the Mishawa. The river right at this moment is about to win; it pulls out and carries away the remains of the *renaco* tree downriver, to the vast and sacred Urubamba.

"Some of those things, only some of them will I tell you," says Ino Moxo slowly, gazing at the *renaco,* which sinks and resurfaces, stumbling, grasping the water, which dislodges it beyond the muyuna. "Maestro Ximu returned me to my true nation and its wisdom. He taught me that the miracle is in the eyes, in the hands that touch and search, not in what is seen, not in what is touched."

The childhood of the kidnapped boy passed in a long celebration, a noisy ceremony of potions and fierce nostalgias, in the climax of which he was rebaptized. He stretched his arms, and from the high bush his new life rained down. "Ino Moxo," said the branches above, struck by a heavy downpour. "Ino Moxo," as a talisman made of roots and darkness. Ino Moxo: Black Panther.

Enrolled in the wisdom of plants, warm animals, absent animals, things, stones, and souls; expert in conflict and in counsel; worthy of being listened to by shadows and the bodies of shadows, as Ximu intended, the kidnapped youth was to reach the loftiest depths. Disguised in his former identity, with mestizo clothes and manners, he would deceive the deceivers and obtain carbines and bullets from the white merchants. Later, returning to his real life, he would demonstrate how these iron blowguns, which spew thunder and explosions, were to be used. So Ximu ordered, and so it happened. He trained the youth starting with a first night he has never forgotten. Naked and white, among naked coppery men, surrounded by the bodies of the tribe, he received his destiny at the end of a ritual *ayawaskha* session.

"Visions . . . begin!" exclaimed Ximu, while calibrating the hallucinogenic apparitions in the mind of the young man, and with those two words taking over his emotions, his soul, his life. The youth learned that all barriers, all *walls* between his existences and those of old Ximu began to disappear. The slightest gesture of the old man developed in his consciousness the caresses of an order. Whatever Ximu thought was seen and heard by the boy. They understood each other through flashes of lightning and through shadows, amid slow visions and colors, and Ximu began to confide his patience and his strength. The boy was told which orders to accept from the souls that live in the air, which directions to ask for and listen to from *ayawaskha,* which intentions and operative words. He was fertilized with the capacity to carry out these orders and to transmit them, to heal bodies and souls, to mold his own life with hands of service. First of all, the youth had to learn to know dark, unclear forests in full detail, to understand the jungle, and to recognize plants one by one — their uses, spirits, and names. Because each plant has a spirit and a vocation. The same applies to animals, even the most useless ones, one by one even those that don't exist. He started with the birds, overwhelmed by the ayawaskha, in that first Amawaka intoxication.

"Do you remember what a *panguana,* that lovely partridge, looks like?" Ximu insisted. "I want you to visualize one now, for me."

And the youth closed and opened his eyes.

"And there was the *panguana!"* Ino Moxo tells me with a bright smile. "There it was next to Chief Ximu and next to me — the *panguana.* I could see it perfectly well, tailless, with its green plumage spotted with brown. The colors of the bird were one with the reminiscences of the light, with the shades moving behind the torches, upon the leaves on the ground. I could see everything without limits. Never again in my life have I been able to see like that, with so much clarity, with so many details."

"The *panguana* will begin to move," Ximu alerted him.

And the *panguana* moved, began to turn around the youth's field of vision. Ximu invoked and produced a male *panguana* from the air by willing it, and the two partridges began a courtship dance, flapping their wings and gently pecking each other. A shadow appeared between the two partridges, something that made a nest on the ground, and five eggs. The male *panguana* sat on the five blue eggs.

"It is the male that incubates," says Ximu.

"And I saw how the eggs began to crack open!" exclaims Ino Moxo, "and from each egg grew two *panguanas,* big ones, adult ones!"

"It was a man, it was a woman," says Don Javier to my memory. "Because the god Pachamakáite had ordered that Kaametza and Narowé were to have five . . ."

Ino Moxo interrupts him: "Later, by just gazing at Ximu's visions, I learned that there are several classes of *panguanas.* I learned about the trumpet birds and the *wapapas,* about many birds, all of them — all the birds. Chief Ximu went about imitating their song, and they would appear and enter my field of vision: day animals, night animals. Later they sang on their own, alone, and their songs passed into my life, forming that other part of my repertory forever. Lovely languages — I still remember them. Chief Ximu put them in my heart and my mouth in those years, in the voice of those years — my spiritual body and my material body. He taught me all the languages: the speech of the birds, the languages of the plants, the more complex ones of the stones. He taught me to tame the powers of the plants and of the stones, the dangerous and honest vocations of herbs. More than anything else he taught me to listen. He taught me to listen to them; he put my ear to their powers, their knowledge, and their ignorance, using *ayawaskha.* Now, if I come across a root, a flower, or a vine that Maestro Ximu did not show me in his visions, I can listen to that root, to that bush, flower, or vine. I am able to determine its soul, which solitude rules it or which company it keeps, how it was born, what it can be used for, which disease it can banish, which ills feed it. And I know with what diet, with what icaro you might increase or diminish the powers of that plant, with what songs I can nourish it, with what powerful thoughts I can graft it. The same applies to people — Chief Ximu taught me the same things about them. Something for better or worse: Ximu taught me to distinguish the days of the plants. Because on some days a plant is female and is good for certain things, and on other days the plant is male and is good for the opposite."

"If I get to a large river, I'll be safe," said the absent renaco in my vision. Later. Now, I listen to the sound of the site where its branches defied the current, and hear myself inevitably saying:

"*Ayawaskha,* in the Amawaka dialect — how did you say it?"

"Your question is not fair," interrupts Ino Moxo, with pity in his voice. "In the language of the Yoras — not a dialect — in their language, phrases can go away forever, join together, intermingle and separate for all time, further away than infinity itself."

And turning his face away, nostalgic, losing himself in the absence of the *renaco* in the middle of the Mishawa:

"Perhaps because of the character of these jungles, this world of ours is still in its formative stage, like rivers that suddenly change course or increase or decrease their flow in a few hours. You must have seen it: if you tie down your canoe without taking it out of the water, you will find it next morning hanging in midair, if you find it at all. The river will look at you from below and you see nothing but stones, all of last night's water has been converted to stone. The reverse may also happen: your canoe may be gone with the currents, which increase without warning and give you no time to react. This world is still being formed, carving out its niche, putting in place its future, falling with the canyons. The gigantic trees, sprouting in islands that today sleep here, like the renaco, tomorrow may wake up far, far away, and in a few moments be again populated by plants, animals, people. In order to see and understand and name a world like that, we must be able to speak in that same way. A language that can decrease or ascend without warning, containing thickets of words that are here today and may wake up far away tomorrow, can in this very instant and inside the same mouth be populated with other symbols, other resonances. It will be hard for you to understand this in Spanish. Spanish is like a quiet river: when it says something, it says only what that something says. It is not so in Amawaka. In the Amawaka language, words always contain things. They always contain other words."

And with a voice that only now I recognize, Ino Moxo said, in the voice of those times in the Hotel Tariri in Pucallpa, flowing from the closed mouth of Don Javier:

"Our words are similar to wells, and those wells can accommodate the most diverse waters: cataracts, drizzles of other times, oceans that were and will be of ashes, whirlpools of rivers, of human beings, and of tears as well. Our words are like people, and sometimes much more, not simple carriers of only one meaning. They are not like those bored pots holding always the same water until their beings, their tongues, forget them, and then crack or get tired, and lean to one side, almost dead. No. You can put entire rivers in our pots, and if perchance they break, if the envelope of the words cracks, the water remains: vivid, intact, running, and renovating itself unceasingly. They are live beings who wander on their own, our words: animals that never repeat themselves and are never resigned to a single skin, to an unchanging temperature, to the same steps. And they couple, like *panguanas,* and have offspring.

"From the word *tiger,* coupled with the word *dance,* may be born *orchids* or perhaps *tohé poison. Night,* inseminated by *gull,* gives birth to *lightning,* a twin brother of the word that in Amawaka means 'silence-after-the-rain.' Because not just one silence exists in Amawaka, as it would in your generally quiet language, which says nothing. In Amawaka there are many silences, as there are in the jungle, as there are in our visible world, and also as many silences as exist in the worlds that cannot be seen with the eyes of the material body.

"Words, therefore, have descendants.

"And your question is unfair. I believe it comes more from virakocha prejudice than from insolence or ignorance. Even then, I will not let it go unanswered. In the Amawaka language, *ayawaskha* is *oni xuma* — write it down. But *oni xuma* does not only mean 'ayawaskha.' You shall see. *Oni xuma* may mean the same thing, or something else, or its opposite, depending on how you say it and for what purpose, depending on the time of day and the place where you say it. If I pronounce it like this — *oni xuma* — with a thin voice, shining, as if spelling bonfires instead of words, in the dark, *oni xuma* means cutting-edge-of-flat-stone.' And pronounced another way it means 'sorrow-which-does-not-show.' And it means 'arrowhead-of-the-first-arrow.' And it means 'wound' which also means 'lip-of-the-soul.' And always, at the same time, it is *ayawaskha.*

"*Ayawaskha,* for us, is not fugitive pleasure, venture, or seedless adventure, as it is for the virakocha. *Ayawaskha* is a gateway — not for escape but for eternity. It allows us to enter those worlds, to live at the same time in this and in other realities, to traverse the endless, unmeasurable provinces of the night.

"That is why the light of the *oni xuma* is black. It doesn't explain. It doesn't reveal. Instead of uncovering mysteries, it respects them. It makes them more and more mysterious, more fertile and prodigal. *Oni xuma* irrigates the unknown territory: that is its way of shedding light.

"And when we invoke it with urgency, with hunger, and with respect, with that intonation of finite waters, waters passing between the embrace of two round boulders, *oni xuma* is 'flank-of-a-stone-knife.' We cut the fingers of the Evil One with it. With it, we separate the body from its souls. If a soul is ill or in danger, we divorce it from its hard matter and negate the contamination. We energize it. The *ayawaskha* shows us the origin and location of the problem, and tells us which herbs and which *icaros* to use in scaring it away. Likewise, if a body is sick, we pull it away from its soul so that it will not putrefy. We also isolate the location of the damage. We know which roots keep the spiritual body and the material soul away from each other, until the flesh resuscitates in the very heart of its health. Until its double in the air and in the shadows grows again in the body as a *renaco* would: innocent, not knowing only what the flesh knows, not caring whether it is happy or immortal because both states mean nothing and belong to everything. It is all the same whether it is eternal or fleeting to him who enjoys it. And this, which is nothing, is everything. There are gifts, there are powers, there are commands. There are no miracles in the sense you are now thinking about the word miracle. There is no miracle in the cure or in the invocation, neither before or after *oni xuma*. There are roots and the juices of roots; there are barks precisely used for this and that, several types of rains which one drinks, and also certain stones. In what manner and in which cases to use them, when to gather them, and how to prepare them — that is what *ayawaskha* knows and will reveal to us when it deems proper, if the soul or the body is worthy of it. To give you an example: If you live only for yourself, you already have chosen to die. And since nothing will cure you, even though on the outside you may appear to have been born and continue living, you will die, you are already dead. But if you remain in your place — if your soul is in its place, and your body is in its place, snatching away from nothing or no one their rightful living space — then there is no illness that can survive. *Oni xuma* advises me, dictates the plants, the strong thoughts, the exact medicine that will cleanse the earth and the air belonging to a body. *Oni xuma* is necessary for that so that the sick person will not advance, will not retreat, and at the same time will not stand still. So that the secret blood of the patient continues flowing. I'm speaking of the blood that feeds the dreams without boundaries, as the existences of the Ashanínka, the Campa, once circulated in the time of men inside their dreams, the time of men in the perfect time.

"That is everything, and as I told you, it is nothing. When you know how to call upon *ayawaskha*, the impossible becomes easy. There is no mistake; there is no miracle. There is what we deserve to know, and what we deserve to remain ignorant about. That is what the Urus in their wisdom forgot. Everything depends on worthiness. Each ailment, each disease, comes to the world after its remedy. What happens is that there are bodies that deserve to be one with their souls, clean to such a degree that you can't even detect the junction. There are others who deserve a constant lack of equilibrium, always orphaned in something — widowers, lacking in something, stuffed into themselves like a cave within a cave like blind men who are also only one-eyed on top of being blind. They are incapable of contributing anything to the world, never learning that souls are nourished by offerings, that they are nourished by offering themselves, that they become more themselves the more they give of themselves. And he who gives what he has does not really give. He who really gives is he who gives of himself, he who gives from his own life in the earth of this life. Yes, my friend Soriano, souls get nourished by giving nourishment. And ashes turn to water when the thirsty kiss them. But there are those who forget it by remaining unaware, without affirming or denying it. Those bodies do not deserve to be bodies; they occupy a void in this world, in the infinite existences of this world, and that is why they always lack something. They lack air, a slice of soil. Their souls are in disarray and useless; their flesh is in disarray. *Oni xuma* knows how to unite them. That is why it is the cutting edge of a flat stone, it is wound and knife and arrowhead of the first arrow of the last rib, and it is a needle that mends or tears apart. It knows how to separate the bodies from their souls and then return them. It knows who says yes and who says no, who is worthy of this life or deserves another one, or deserves none. I can only obey. Without the black light of *ayawaskha* I am not even ignorant. I can't even make mistakes; I simply hit the target in reverse, which is quite different. *Ayawaskha* makes me its most wretched instrument because it is so powerful. If there is much that I don't know, that I don't quite see, it doesn't matter: *ayawaskha* knows. Everything depends on worthiness. *Ayawaskha* orders or disorders; I obey. If it doesn't order me to do anything, I obey all the same. And if it orders me to postpone a death, then I certainly transform any damaging spell into a mere memory!

"I have probably said more than your question asked for. Do you see it? Words start other words moving;

they unleash powers, liberate other energies. If the person who hears my words can only hear my words, what a waste —but no matter: the powers are already unleashed to roam in the air, traveling and transforming the world. Can't you see? I told you. Everything depends on worthiness."

"You mean to say that *ayawaskha* opens the door to health?"

"Everything depends on worthiness, my friend Soriano." He half-gyrated his face again and again, scattering gazes upon the floor, under a pomarrosa tree I had not noticed until yesterday. "Look at these small ants — they are called *citarácuy.* Do you know that they forecast the future?" I, in silence, wonder whether he is making a fool of me. "Look how they run to protect themselves from the rain," says Ino Moxo. "They hurriedly run pell-mell looking for their nest, ungrateful, leaving behind the time that guided them. The *citarácuy* know that shortly, within five to seven hours, it will rain heavily. But considering their life span, five to seven hours to these ants represent ten or fifteen years to us. What man could predict exactly when it will rain and at what time of day, fifteen years in the future? Many animals around here know. Even certain flowers know: they close and hide long before the rains come. Other things are foreseen here. I have learned, taught by the air, that human beings in ancient times could also foresee the future as they could see what had already happened. I have seen them in timeless time. In time perhaps, and in the night, they began to lose those powers. Now only some people can do that, generally children or *shirimpiáre* — sorcerers. Newly born, we all possess those powers and many others as well, but as we get older we retreat for whatever reason and gradually lose them. Speaking, for example. I am now speaking for you. Otherwise, I would surely do so in a different way. I would not develop the concepts in order to fit your understanding. But I'm forced to use your words. I have to fit my words inside yours and adapt my thoughts, silencing others that do not fit, that rebel against that confinement you call coherence. If we had enough time to be worthy, perhaps I might show you how to use my eyes, to speak with my mouth. Maybe you would understand. As it is, I have to reduce everything. The obstacle is time."

And Maestro Ino Moxo, as if distancing his mouth but not his voice from my increasing interest, spoke from his body seated on the log in front of the Mapuya River, making himself weaker and slower in his words:

"Within a short time I will have to go. The problem is that of time, this time. No matter how long you wait, you cannot wait for me. My time is not your time but the time of Chief Ximu. Last night I dreamed about Chief Ximu. I have seen him again, and he disappeared spewing smoke, the time of his body, a great yellow smoke."

TRANSLATED FROM the Spanish by Kenneth A. Symington

(FROM: César Calvo. *The Three Halves of Ino moxo: Teachings of the Wizard of the Upper Amazon.* Rochester, VT: Inner Traditions, 1995, pp. 1–6, 172–180.)

THE REAL WORLD OF MANUEL CÓRDOVA

W. S. Merwin

And so even
as True Thomas had done
after seven
years had gone
and no cell of his skin
bone blood or brain
was what it had been
the night that the rain
found him alone
neither child nor man
in the forest and at dawn
looking into the swollen
stream toward the sudden
flash of a fish and then

up he saw them
standing around him
more silent than tree shadows from
which they had come
each holding the aim
of a spear for some
moments before they came
without a word and from him
took knife bucket the freedom
of his hands binding them
behind him and hauling him
for days through the green spinning dome
to bring him at last half dead home
into their own dream

in which there was
yet something like time yes
it was still a kind of time as
he turned slowly to realize
where not one of his
syllables touched any surface
and what had been his voice
proved to be nobody's
wondering unheard for days
whether they would eat him as

they kept feeding him dishes
cooked before his eyes
for his mouth alone and across
what felt like his own face

and down over
the meat of him everywhere
first there was the water
they warmed at the fire to pour
on him as a mother
would do and then the knowing finger
of the old man their
leader tracing a signature
of the forest in one color
after another
along him with roots to enter
him and go on growing there
then one night the bitter
juices they held up for

him to swallow while
they watched the apple
climb in his throat and fall
but he thought he could tell
by then a little
of that turning pool
their single will
and if they meant to kill
him there with their sentinel
keeping watch on the hole
in the forest far from the babble
of the village then why was the bowl
passed from his mouth to theirs until
each one in the circle

had drunk and he
looked on as one by one they
lay down and looking on he
discovered that he
was lying down and they

were all together by day
there in their forest where he
understood every word they
were telling him while they
travelled and already
when he came to each tree he
knew that it would be
just where it appeared and they
were its name as they

passed touching
nothing until the morning
when they heard the same birds sing
and he was sitting
with the others in a ring
around the ashes knowing
much of what they were saying
as though it were echoing
across the water and he was learning
that they had been dreaming
the same dream then they were filing
like water out of the clearing
and he kept recognizing
the face of each thing

the moment it appeared
also he remembered
here and there the word
to which something answered
them it seemed then that he heard
his own mind and from there onward
through the forest he discovered
how much less he floundered
and crashed while they flickered
with him through the scattered
light their feet in a mastered
music never heard
not even remembered
except as a shared

dream which he found
when they returned
to the village remained
visible around
him a presence that had opened
in the foreground
of the day and as he listened
he could still understand
enough out of the sound
of their words to attend
as the old chief his friend

pointing to the morning summoned
to him the world and
piece by piece explained

where certain medicines
live in hiding where directions
travel in the dark how poisons
wait how the snake listens
how leaves store reflections
which of the demons
are nameless where dying begins
and as the days' lessons
taught him to pronounce
some of the questions
growing in him since
they had him in their hands
he was answered with instructions
from the forest of the old man's

mind carefully
guiding him until he
believed almost that he
had followed his own way
into the only
place alive and when the
moon was right and again they
stood after dark in the empty
tower of trees where one by
one they drank from the bowl and lay
down he thought it was the same day
that he knew but he could see
through each of them an entry
to the forest and as he

turned he went on seeing
everywhere something
the chief was letting
him know even while he was dreaming
what they were all dreaming
together flowing
among the trees entering
cat fur monkey voice owl wing
but he found in the morning
that he was taking
shape in the old man's ruling
dream and was recognizing
in the surrounding
day a forest hiding

from the others
and that his teacher's
whispers and gestures

had rendered his eyes and ears
attuned to powers
haunting plants and waters
that were unknown to theirs
he beheld the ancestors
in his own sleep the bearers
of birth and death the spiders
in charge of night fierce
protectors vipers
of lightning at the fire source
and from the chief's answers

he came to see
that they wanted him to be
the heir of every
secret and therefore ready
to be next on that day
no longer very
distant when their chief would die
for they believed that they
must have somebody
to guide them who already
understood the deadly
aliens steadily
withering their way
into the only

forest somebody who
had been alien and knew
the outer words and how to
turn something of the forest into
what could save them to
trade part of their life for the new
death an outer person who
could teach them how to
have guns yet someone who
had gone with them into
the dream flowing through
the forest and knew
the ancients and the spirits who
never let go

in that way he became
all that the chief taught him
and all that appeared to him each time
he went into the dream
farther and it came
out with him into the day and from
then on was all around him
they gave him a name
and he started to show them

what they could take from
trees that would buy them
guns they gave him
a girl to be with him
they almost trusted him

some of them and under
his guidance they put together
a first cargo or
caravan of rubber
that they would carry for
many days to the river
where he would go to the trader
alone and barter
everything they had brought for
Winchesters and bullets and after
they had brought the guns home to their
roof each of them wore
that night ceremonial attire
feathers claws teeth from their

forest in celebration
and he was given
another girl and then
a third and an old woman
watched over him when
more and more often
after the day's lesson
was done he was taken alone
with the chief at sundown
to the opening in
the trees where the old man
gave him the bowl and began
the chants while on his own
he drank the potion

and the visions rose
out of the darkening voice
out of the night voice the secret voice
the rain voice the root voice
through the chant he saw his
blood in the veins of trees
he appeared in the green of his eyes
he felt the snake that was
his skin and the monkeys
of his hands he saw his faces
in all the leaves and could recognize
those that were poison and those
that could save he was helpless
when bones came to chase

him and they were
his own the fire
of his teeth climbed after
his eyes he could hear
through his night the river
of no color that ended nowhere
echoing in his ear
it was there in the morning under
his breath growing wider
through those days after
the first guns were slung in their
rafters among the other
protectors and the men were
preparing to get more

spending their time doing
what he had taught them working
to change something living
there into something
else far away putting
their minds that far away wanting
guns guns becoming
more ardent still after a raiding
party of enemies sending
arrows out of hiding
near the village had run fleeing
before the pursuing
guns vanishing
leaving one behind dying

and so another caravan
like a snake soon
slipped out in the track of the first one
but the season by then
had moved on and the rain
they seemed to have forgotten
caught them out and began
to drum down
on them all night and in
the misty days as they went on
sliding and splashing in
running mud and then
when they reached the river again
and he took the raft alone

to the trader
the value of the rubber
had fallen the rifles cost more
all they had carried bought fewer
bullets he sat down there
that time at table to share

the soup of the invader
and it was a fire
he did not remember
burning over
his tongue to sear
his throat and pour
through him everywhere
melting him so that no water

he drank could cool him and
he wept and imagined
that he would be burned
to death or if he happened
to live would never be sound
in body and whole in mind
again but it lessened
at last and he was left by the bend
of the river with the full count
of guns and bullets on the ground
beside him while the canoe went
back into the flooded end
of the day and without a sound
his companions appeared around

him he watched the weightless
pieces of merchandise
seem one by one to rise
by themselves and nose
their way forward into the trees
then in turn he bent to raise
his load and took his place
among them for the many days'
walking until his surprise
always at a bird-like voice
ahead of him breaking the news
of their return and bird voices
welcoming them with echoes
from their own house

but the old chief was dying
turning before long
into a mummy blackening
in the smoke clouds of the ceiling
and the others were wandering
into themselves hiding
from him exhuming
hatreds that meant nothing
to him they were waiting
he thought for the burying
of the old man and for the mourning
to be done and then they were looking

as he saw for something
from him and the one thing

he had known to show them
was guns a way to get them
a way to depend on them
and now he tried leading them
to the hunt but from
the crash of his gun each time
he fired it the continuum
of calling all around them
fled in echoes away from them
out of range so that it took them
a long time to come
close again and seldom
was it possible to aim
very far through the scrim

of forest and they
with their silent weaponry
went on hunting in the old way
wanting the guns as he
understood then only
for humans such as the enemy
tribes with their angry
language but principally
for the aliens every
change of season so many
more coming up the rivers he
was taken on a winding journey
to see a succession of empty
names in the forest where they

had lived at some time before
the aliens had come with blades for
the white blood of the rubber
trees and guns for whatever
feather or fur or
face they might discover
and in each place he was shown where
the house had stood and men were
shot by the guns and their
women were spread butchered or
dragged off with their children and never
seen again and he learned there were
many voices to avenge but after
each house burned the people had moved farther

into the wild
fabric that they knew and he was told
how at last when the old
chief had led them into the stream curled

like the boa where the field
would be and where they would build
the house that now held
their hammocks and the bundled
corpses creaking in the smoke-filled
ceiling with the cradled
guns among them the chief had called
the place by the name that means world
begins here again or first world
wakens or only world

once more and when they
had led him to every
overgrown scar on the way
of their lives they
went home again to their only
roof where although he
warned them patiently
about the aliens what an army
would be like if it came why
vengeance would never be
final and how they
depended now on the enemy
for guns always they
sat watching silently

for the end of his
words but the voices
that they were hearing even as
he spoke had no peace
for the living and no place
for reason so the restless
passion for guns invaded the days
growing as the gashed trees
dripped and the smoke rose
around the rubber and the cargoes
were shouldered for the wordless
journeys where each time his
exchange with the trader yielded less
for them each time the price

of guns had gone
up and the burden
was lighter than ever on
their way back and when
they had reached the village again
he knew he was alone
and he went out one
time before sundown
into the forest with none
of the girls he had been given

only the old woman
following him and in
the circle of trees stopped to drain
the bowl and he lay down

in the gathering dark watching
for a glimpse of something
the old chief had been hoping
he would come to but was soon beginning
to shiver running
with sweat a nausea clutching
him the coils of writhing
serpents knotting
him on the ground then he was being
shown a sickness like a waving
curtain surrounding
his family and his mother was dying
there and he saw himself lying
with an arrow through him nailing

him down to be walked over
only then did he see once more
the face of the old chief for
the last time standing before
him his protector
and the black jaguar
from the other side of fear
in whose form he could go anywhere
came to him just at the hour
before daylight when from the floor
of the forest curled roots that were
the old woman's hands rose to offer
the bowl that would restore
him and as her face became clear

in the milk of her eye
he saw that she
knew everything that he
had been but as before she
said nothing and after that night he
woke to how far away
was the intangible country
of his ancestors he
began to be
repelled by the frenzy
of their celebrations and they
who so delicately
when hunting could make the
odor of the human body

one with the unwarned
air of the forest around

them now began to offend
him with their ripened
scent they hardly listened
to him or so he imagined
and a silence widened
between them until a band
went on a raid as he found
out later and when the men returned
with eyes ablaze and blood-stained
bodies he learned
only from the shouts that night around
the fire what kind

of game they had taken
that trip what meat they had eaten
and in those days the men
worked without urging and too soon
had another caravan
ready and they set out again
but on this journey storm and rain
would not let them alone
day or night and they thrashed in
mud they were bruised chilled hungry and when
they tried to sleep sitting down
under leaves the water ran
across them as though they were in
a black stream then

with his eyes closed he saw over
and over one fast stretch of river
and each time out on the water
the same familiar
small boat heading upstream near
the white turn where
the current swept out from under
hanging boughs and he looked more
narrowly after
the vessel but never
could see it clearly before
it was gone in the green cover
and he was awake cold and sore
that day they reached the river

built their raft and he
pushed off at break of day
with everything they
had brought and in the misty
dawn poled his way
downstream to tie
up at the trader's landing by
a river boat that he

thought familiar it would be
leaving at about midnight he
heard from the trader as they
loaded a canoe with every
useful thing that he
had been able to buy

except guns
then he took a canoe once
more to where his friends
were waiting for him in dense
forest on the bank he watched their hands
unload the canoe looking for guns
he had brought only this he said the guns
were still on the boat new guns
for shooting through trees the plans
called for unloading them in silence
at midnight to keep those guns
from falling into the hands
of the aliens
he watched their expressions

as he told them he
had to go back with the canoe he
could see that they were uneasy
knew something was wrong so he
pushed off quickly

into the current paddling and by
the time he reached the bend he could see
no one on the bank where they
had been standing only
the trees and then the trader's where he
asked for the remaining tally
of their earnings there and he
withdrew all the gun money
bought clothes for going away

paid for his passage would
eat nothing went on board
feeling numb and cold trying to avoid
their questions lay down and waited
in the dark for midnight with his head
afloat above the floating wood
heard the limbs of wood
from the forest falling into the loud
firebox watched the trees of sparks fade
overhead as the boat started
out into the river his mother was dead
whatever he might need
was somewhere that could not be said
as though it had never existed

(FROM: W. S. Merwin. *Travels*. New York: Knopf, 1994,
pp. 96–114.)

Manuel Córdova. Photograph © Kathleen Harrison.

AYAHUASCA,
or What There is at the End

Mario Villafranca Saravia

With the goal of finding the Monolithic Bridge, which is mentioned a great deal in this part of the jungle, I embarked on an excursion accompanied by my faithful Campa Indian friend Puniro. The excursion did not produce the desired result, but it did allow me to live a strange adventure that has left a deep trail of nostalgia in my spirit that I am unable to overcome. The adventure I experienced flowers above me like a sad and melancholy shadow that slowly but surely is devouring my small stores of happiness. I don't know if it was true, or whether it was the product of my imagination or perhaps the ayahuasca that I drank (that hallucinogenic plant with small, white, paniculated flowers in the shape of a pyramid that produces a delirious psychosis and a pseudo-aesthetic sensation of aerial suspension), but I suspect that what I saw, foresaw or imagined nevertheless must have happened:

Pijiri and Oshero

The rain danced violently on the earth. The wind roared among the trees and shook them, like neurotic beings, with its potent hands. Those trees that opposed the will of the wind were cracked and knocked down, producing a crashing fall that dragged down other vegetation. The bolts of lightning emptied the black innards of the clouds.

Water filled the gorges and lakes. The river slowly began to overflow through the *tahuampas* and underneath our hut, which was built on supports of *chonta* wood.

Lying in our cots, Puniro and I watched as the turbulent and violent waters washed away the shoreline, carrying off plants, bushes, tree trunks and animals. When nature shows its force and power, human beings feel like impotent, helpless creatures.

"Water is the blood of the earth," I said.

"Hmm!" replied Puniro.

Puniro was a tall Campa with wrinkled skin. His features inspired confidence. From the looks of his strong muscles and straight white teeth, he didn't seem to be more than forty years old. But his long white hair, which he wore tied with a headband, betrayed his seventy years that weighed heavily on his back. His eyes were clear (from looking long and hard at time, as he put it) and had a deeply sad and enigmatic gleam.

The sun had set, and above the tremendous noise produced by rain, wind and river, one could hear piercing screams that seemed both close at hand and far away. Perhaps they were animals trapped by the current or some fallen tree.

"Tell me a story, Puniro," I said.

Puniro looked at me as if he were organizing his ideas, lifted his vine-like hand still full of strength, pointed at me and said, "Ashaninca has many adventures."

He took a long swig of *mazato*, and passed me the *tutuma* gourd bowl while he wiped his mouth with his hand and continued, "When I used to be able to walk for days without eating, when I could paddle from sunrise to sunset, I decided to visit Pachacamaite."

"Who's Pachacamaite?" I asked.

Detail: *Vision 42: Lucero Ayahuasca* by Pablo Amaringo from *Ayahuasca Visions*.

"Pachacamaite is Pawa, he who gives birth to the plants, makes fruit ripen, and produces the rains that feed the rivers and lakes that the earth drinks. He lives there, downstream, where the horizon ends, where earth, sky and river join. It's not easy to get there. And it's very dangerous. You have to fight Pijiri. You have to fight Oshero.

His eyes took on an unusual brilliance and his face glowed in the light of his memories. "There were seven of us," he said. "We navigated many moons. On the fifth moon we heard a noise that sounded like crashing water. Someone shouted, 'Waterfall!' Paddling as hard as we could, we reached the shore. The noise got louder and louder. Pawa stopped shining. We looked at the sky, and there was Pijiri with his two enormous heads. We ran to hide, but he dropped down on us like an arrow. He broke our canoe with his flapping wings and we blew away like dry leaves on the ground. He grabbed three of my companions and left.

We reached the lands of Oshero, where we wanted to spend the night in silence so he wouldn't hear us. But Oshero did hear us and trapped us between his powerful pincers. He ate three of us. He didn't eat me because I had some *achiote,* which Oshero likes, so he let me go. I never did get to where Pachacamaite is because the river was blocked by the wooden fencing of the white people and the Choris.

Puniro fell silent. I handed him the gourd of *mazato.* His bright necklace made from achira plants gave off little lights like far away stars. I looked at his face in the light of our fire. It had the dignity of someone who would never lie. And I believed him.

The Tunnel

Traveling through the jungle with Puniro wasn't problematic. He was very skilled at hunting monkeys with arrows. He knew the medicinal plants and, besides, we always had plenty of *yucca, catzeni* and *mazato.*

When the horizon disappeared, I realized that we had been swallowed by the jungle. Its immense stomach consisted of deformed trees, flowers with disgusting smells, foul water, strange insects, creatures that are simultaneously beautiful and fatal, poisonous reptiles, hairy, big-bellied spiders, trees and bushes that embrace in lascivious ways and block the sunlight, forming capricious arabesques and strange, indecipherable signs.

The real jungle is a constant struggle of life and death. The people who live here wage war against each other, rage, and cut each other to pieces. Nowhere else does one sense so strongly the raw egotistical desire to prevail, the ancestral instinct of staying alive. There are proud, majestic trees stretching out above the green sea, gazing upon the horizon or staring at the sun, trampling and crushing weak, spindly plants. There is sickly vegetation begging for a little solar warmth. There are plant parasites that shamelessly climb luxuriant trees to drink the sap, flowering in exotic petals, while their weak arms slowly strangle their source of life, causing death and producing a tremendous crashing that convulses the jungle, where living means killing and dying means giving life.

In this hallucinatory world, one hears voices, strange sounds, snapping jaws that devour, terrible screams or unbearable silences that hurt, that crush. One sees will-o'-the-wisps, sparkling eyes with a bloody look, shadows that emerge and disappear like rhythmic breathing. We were walking through this unreal world when, all of a sudden, we found ourselves on an enormous avenue of trees capriciously aligned in a parallel shape. The treetops were so intertwined that they formed a perfect vegetal dome, which, nevertheless, was totally illuminated by millions of fireflies that lived there. It was an impressive avenue. Half way down, I heard a slight buzzing, as if something were about to be fried. I cast Puniro a questioning glance.

"Cicadas," he said.

The sound grew louder and so did the beating of my heart, penetrating my brain like hundreds of painful needles. Louder. Louder. I covered my ears with my hands but the sound kept getting louder. There must have been millions of cicadas singing at the same time. I was losing my mind. I screamed and stamped the ground, but the sound got even louder.

"No! No! For God's sake, no!" I screamed.

I fell to the ground. Spasmodic convulsions attacked me and the infernal noise wouldn't stop. Red, white, and yellow circles came toward me in a dizzying spin, smashing into stars, moving as thousands of painful little lights. I was sinking into a black abyss and then I lost consciousness.

The Palace of the Parrots

After going through a hell like this, one can really begin to savor life. I woke up. We were in a beautiful place, bread trees, flowers, white herons, sun. Everything was singing a song of happiness and hope.

Puniro looked at me with sadness and said, "You *wiracochas* are weak."

We were moving down a wide river as fast as arrows. The Campa skillfully steered the canoe, avoiding jutting treetrunks, violent rapids or treacherous whirlpools. I was stretched out in the canoe, watching the trees and wild fruit go by, and above was a blue sky with white clouds like tufts of cotton. A flock of parakeets like leaves in the wind plowed through the sky. The afternoon ripened, taking on a lemon-yellow color. The birds passed in search of their nests. Puniro pointed the canoe toward a sandy beach. Beyond a bend in the river, the river was plummeting with a deep, hushed sound.

"We're almost there," said Puniro.

"What's around the turn?" I asked.

Puniro gave me an enigmatic look and deftly finished tying up the canoe.

"Look," he said, extending his arm and pointing to a path that disappeared in the undergrowth. "That's the way to Shora. But first, come see the palace of the parrots."

I followed him with curiosity as we walked along the river. When we went around the bend, I contemplated the river cascading as a white and misty waterfall and then flowing like a silver thread through the green jungle. The cliff in front of us was cut to form a smooth wall above the water.

In the dark clearing of the afternoon, I could distinguish hundreds of flying forms. Apparently, they were parrots, speaking in several different languages. I looked at Puniro, bewildered. With a mocking smile, he answered my silent question.

"I have no idea where they come from, *wiracocha.*"

What There Is at the End

Let us rejoice for the rains that come.
Let us rejoice for the God that shines.
Let us rejoice for the yucca that flowers
Let us rejoice for the Moon that lights our way.

The Campas were singing when we arrived. The moon in all its splendor illuminated the scene. The Campas were in a semicircle with Shora in the middle. Musicians were playing drums and *soncaris.* The women were holding hands, dancing, making shapes, forming circles, semicircles. They coiled and uncoiled as if they were an immense snake. They all sang:

Cashiri, *make us fertile.*
Tasorentesi, *with your powerful breath,*
Make our men strong.
Pawa, *with your heat, give us life.*

Shora saw us and came toward us.

"Who's there?" he asked.

"*Wiracocha* and Puniro," answered Puniro.

"Do you have any sicknesses?" he asked, spitting loudly.

"We're good people. We don't have any sicknesses," Puniro responded.

Shora looked at us for a long time. He was adorned with a crown, which was supported by huacamayo feathers. On his wrists and ankles he had bracelets of multicolored stones. On his broad back hung dried birds that were green, yellow and red. After making us wait in silence, he gave us a big smile of scarce teeth, and let us pass.

The Campas are a very hospitable people. A visitor can stay for as long as he wants, but, as retribution, he should accept all that is offered. If he doesn't, he runs the risk of receiving nothing from them, not even any water. For this reason, when Shora took me to the center of the semicircle of Campas and invited me to drink ayahuasca, I had no choice but to accept.

He lifted the *tutuma* bowl and, looking at the Moon, said:

Tasorentesi, potent blower,
Tasorentesi, you who create with your breath,
watch over your children who dance and sway
to give you pleasure.

He drank half and then gave me the gourd. I drank. The moon was shining in the highest point of the sky. The orange trees had lit their lamps and were ready for the harvest. In the trees, like fallen stars, the fireflies glowed.

We sat down and the festivities continued. I felt a kind of emptiness in my liver, which is the organ that governs feelings. Then it seemed like I was inflating like a balloon. My eyes and my ears grew. I could hear Shora's eager breathing and Puniro's, which was slower, the panting of the dancers, and the growing plants. My eyes saw trees, rivers, hills, insects. Curiously enough, I saw and felt everything all at once, in a single plane, but perfectly discernible, as if I were seeing and hearing each thing separately. I had a sense of lightness, an ethereal quality, and I began to fly through a blue sky beyond a white disk. The Sun? I couldn't tell. Then darkness, a golden dusk, running phosphorescent bands, chasing after each other, crashing, and ascending in multicolored lights. I'm sinking, terrifying thunder, bolts of lightning burning up the sky, white, blue and red columns, then an orange sky that turns red, yellow, green. I'm suspended in the air. I feel and I beat with all things. I'm born and I die with them. I become eternal and diluted forever, lost in the void. I'm born once again. Below, the earth spins with a green brilliance, and suddenly a dense black hand envelops it. I feel my heart beating with anxiety, fury, fear, and then that tremendous, terrifying explosion. White light, blinding, stronger than the sun, like a thousand suns together, God!, I scream, heat, suffocating heat, burning hot, craters, winds, giant waves that bury everything, America, Africa, Oceania, Europe. Then silence, total, absolute, eternal silence, and the void, always the void. . . .

TRANSLATED FROM the Spanish by Steven F. White

(FROM: Isabel Córdova Rosas, ed. *Narradores de Junín*. Huancayo, Perú: Departamento de Publicaciones de la UNCP, 1979, pp. 53–59.)

THE STORYTELLER
(excerpt)

Mario Vargas Llosa

(FRAGMENT 1)

As I was coming here, even though I knew the way, I got lost. It must have been Kientibakori's fault, or his little devils', or a very powerful machikanari's. Without any warning, it suddenly started raining; the sky hadn't darkened or the air turned briny. I was fording a river and the rain was coming down so hard I couldn't climb up the bank. After two or three steps I slipped back, the earth gave way beneath my feet, and I found myself at the bottom of the channel. My little parrot was frightened, flapped his wings, and flew away squawking. The bank became a gully. Mud and water, stones, branches, bushes, trees split in two by the storm, bodies of birds and insects. All rolling down on top of me. The sky turned black; bolts of lightning flashed and crashed. The peals of thunder sounded like all the animals of the forest roaring at once. When the lord of thunder rages like that, something grave is happening. I went on trying to climb up the gully. Would I succeed? If I don't clamber up a really tall tree, I'll be carried away, I thought. Any moment now, all this is going to be a boiling caldron of water pouring down from heaven. I had no strength left to struggle; my arms and legs were badly injured from my many hard falls. I was swallowing water through my nose and my mouth. Even my eyes and my anus seemed to be taking in water. This is going to be the end of you, Tasurinchi. Your soul will take off to goodness knows where. And I touched the top of my head to feel it leaving.

I don't know how long I kept on, climbing up, rolling down, climbing up again. The channel had become a wide river after swallowing its banks. At last I was so tired out I let myself sink beneath the water. "I'm going to rest," I said. "Enough of this useless struggle." But do the ones who go like that rest? Isn't drowning the worst way to go? In a moment I'd be floating on the Kamabiría, the river of the dead, headed for the abyss with no sunlight and no fish: the lowest world, the dark land of Kientibakori. Meanwhile, without my noticing, my hands had grabbed hold of a tree trunk that the storm had cast into the river, perhaps. I don't know how I managed to climb onto it. Nor whether I fell asleep at once. The sun had set. It was dark and cold. The raindrops falling on my back felt like stones.

In my sleep I discovered the trap. What I'd taken for a tree trunk was an alligator. What sort of bark could those hard, prickly scales be? It's a caiman's back, Tasurinchi. Had the alligator noticed that I was on its back? If so, it would have been flicking its tail. Or it would have dived under to make me let go, and then bitten me underwater, the way caimans always do. Could it be dead, perhaps? If it were, it would be floating feet up. What are you going to do, Tasurinchi? Slip into the water very slowly and swim to the shore? I'd never have gotten there in that storm. You couldn't even see the trees. And, anyway, there might not be any land left in the world. Try to kill the alligator? I had no weapon. Back at the channel, while I was struggling up the bank, I'd lost my pouch, my knife, and my arrows. I'd best stay still, sitting tight on the alligator. Best wait till something or someone decided.

We were floating along, borne by the swift current. I was shivering with cold and my teeth were chattering. Thinking: Where can the little parrot be? The alligator didn't paddle with its feet or its tail, but just went where the river took it. Little by little it was getting light. Muddy water, dead animals, jumbled islets of roofs, huts, branches, and canoes. Here and there, men half eaten by piranhas and other river creatures. There were great clouds of mosquitoes, and water spiders crawling over my body. I felt them biting me. I was very hungry and perhaps I could have grabbed one of the dead fish the water was bearing along, but what if I attracted the alligator's notice? All I could do was drink. I didn't have to move to quench my thirst. I just opened my mouth and the rain filled it with fresh cold water.

At that point a little bird landed on my shoulder. From its red-and-yellow crest, its feathers, its gold breast, and its sharp-pointed beak, I took it to be a kirigueti. But it could have been a kamagarini or even a saankarite. For whoever heard of birds talking? "You're in a bad fix," it chirped. "If you let go, the alligator's going to spot you. Its squinty eyes see a long way. It'll knock you out with one slap of its tail, grab you by the belly with its great toothy mouth, and eat you up. It'll eat you up bones and hair and all. Because it's as hungry as you are. But can you go on clinging to that caiman for the rest of your life?"

"What's the use of telling me what I know all too well?" I said. "Why don't you give me some advice, instead? What to do to get out of the water."

"Fly," it cheeped, fluttering its yellow crest. "There's no other way, Tasurinchi. Like your little parrot did when you were on the steep bank, or this way, like me." It gave a little hop, flew about in little circles, and disappeared from sight.

Can flying be that easy? Seripigaris and machikanaris fly, when they're in a trance. But they have wisdom: brews, little gods, or little devils help them. But what do I have? The things I'm told and the things I tell, that's all. And as far as I know, that never yet made anyone fly. I was cursing the kamagarini disguised as a kirigueti, when I felt something scratching the soles of my feet.

A stork had landed on the alligator's tail. I could see its long pink legs and its curved beak. It scratched my feet, looking for worms, or perhaps thinking they were edible. It was hungry, too. Frightened though I was, it made me laugh. I couldn't help myself. I burst out laughing. Just the way all of you are laughing now. Doubling over, whooping with laughter. Just like you, Tasurinchi. And the alligator woke up, of course. It realized at once that things were happening on its back that it couldn't see or understand. It opened its mouth and roared, it flicked its tail furiously, and without knowing what I was doing, there I was, all of a sudden, clinging to the stork. The way a baby monkey clings to the she-monkey, the way a newborn suckling babe clings to its mother. Frightened by the flicking tail, the stork tried to fly away. But since it couldn't, because I was clinging to it, it started squawking. Its squawks frightened the alligator even more, and me, too. We all squawked. There we were, the three of us, seeing who could squawk the loudest.

And suddenly, down below, getting farther and farther away, I saw the alligator, the river, the mud. The wind was so strong I could hardly breathe. There I was, in the air, way up high. There was Tasurinchi, the storyteller, flying. The stork was flying, and clinging to its neck, my legs twined around its legs, I was flying, too. Down below was the earth, getting smaller. There was gleaming water everywhere. Those little dark stains must be trees; those snakes, rivers. It was colder than ever. Had we left the earth? If so, this must be Menkoripatsa, the world of the clouds. There was no sign of its river. Where was the Manaironchaari, with its waters made of cotton? Was I really flying? The stork must have grown to be able to carry me. Or maybe I'd shrunk to the size of a mouse. Who knows which? It flew calmly on, with steady sweeps of its wings, letting itself be carried by the wind. Untroubled by my weight, perhaps. I shut my eyes so as not to see how far away the earth was now. Such a drop, such a long way down. Feeling sad at leaving it, maybe. When I opened them again I saw the stork's white wings, their pink edges, the regular wingbeat. The warmth of its down sheltered me from the cold. Now and then it gurgled, stretching out its neck, lifting its beak, as though talking to itself. So this was the Menkoripatsa. The seripigaris rose to this world in their trances; among these clouds they held counsel with the little saankarite gods about the evils and the mischief of the bad spirits. How I would have liked to see a seripigari floating there. "Help me," I'd say to him. "Get me out of this fix, Tasurinchi." Because wasn't I even worse off way up there, flying in the clouds, than when I was perched on the back of the caiman?

Who knows how long I flew with the stork? What to do now, Tasurinchi? You won't be able to hang on much longer. Yours arms and legs are getting tired. You'll let go, your body will dissolve in the air, and by the time you reach the earth, you'll be nothing but water. It had stopped raining. The sun was rising. This cheered me up. Courage, Tasurinchi! I kicked the stork, I yanked at it, I butted it, I even bit it to make it descend. It didn't understand. It was frightened and stopped gurgling; it started squawking, pecking here and there, flying first this way, then that, like this, to get rid of me. It nearly won the tussle. Several times I was just about to slip off. Suddenly I realized that every time I squeezed its wing, we fell, as though it had stumbled in the air. That's what saved me, perhaps. With the little strength I had left, I wound my feet around one of its wings, pinning it down so that the stork could hardly move it. Courage, Tasurinchi! What I hoped for happened. Flying on only one wing now, the other one, it flapped with all its might, but even so, it couldn't fly as well as before. It tired and started descending. Down, down, squawking; despairing, perhaps. I was happy, though. The earth was getting closer. Closer, closer. How lucky you are, Tasurinchi. Here you are already. When I grazed the tops of the trees, I let go. As I fell, down and down, I could see the stork, burbling for joy, flying on both wings again, rising. Down I went, getting badly scratched and battered. Bouncing from branch to branch, breaking them, scraping the bark from the trunks, feeling that I, too, was falling to bits. I tried to catch hold with my hands, with my feet. How lucky monkeys are, or any other creature that has a tail to hang by, I thought. The leaves and small branches, the vines and twining plants, the spider's webs and lianas would check my fall, perhaps. When I landed, the shock didn't kill me, it seems. What joy feeling the earth beneath my body. It was soft and warm. Damp, too. Ehé, here I am. I've arrived. This is my world. This is my home. The best thing that every happened to me is living here, on this earth, not in the water, not in the air.

(FRAGMENT 2)

It's true; he guessed rightly: if I weren't a storyteller I would have liked to be a seripigari. To be able to control trances through wisdom so that they'd always be good ones. Once, over there by the tapir-river, the Kimariato, I had a bad trance, and in it I lived through a story I'd rather not remember. Nonetheless, I still remember it.

Here is the story.

That was after, by the tapir-river.

I was people. I had a family. I was asleep. Then I woke up. I'd barely opened my eyes when I understood. Alas, poor Tasurinchi! I'd changed into an insect, that's what. A buzz-buzz bug, perhaps. A Gregor-Tasurinchi. I was lying on my back. The world had grown bigger, it seemed to me. I was aware of everything. Those hairy, ringed legs were my legs. Those transparent mud-colored wings, which creaked when I moved and hurt me so much, had once been my arms. The stench that surrounded me: was that my odor? I saw the world differently: I could see the underside and the top, the back and the front, at the same time. Because now, being an insect, I had several eyes. What's happened to you, Gregor-Tasurinchi? Did a bad witch eat a lock of your hair and change you? Did a little kamagarini devil get into you through your ass-eye and turn you into this? I was covered with shame at seeing myself the way I was. What would my family say? Because I had a family, like the other men who walk, it seemed. What would they think, seeing me changed into a repulsive insect? All you can do with buzz-buzz bugs is squash them. Can you eat them? Can you cure evil with them? You can't even make filthy machikanari potions with them, perhaps.

But my family didn't say anything. They pretended. They came and went in the hut or down by the river, as though they hadn't noticed the misfortune that had befallen me. They must have felt ashamed, too. Saying: Look how he's been changed! That might have been the reason they avoided mentioning me by name. Who knows? And in the meantime, I saw everything. The world seemed content, the same as before. I could see the children lifting stones off anthills and happily eating the soft-shelled ants, squabbling over them. The men, going to clear the weeds from the cassava patches or painting themselves with annatto and huito before going off to hunt. The women, cutting up the cassava, chewing it, spitting it out, leaving it to rest in the masato tubs; unraveling cotton to weave cushmas. When night fell, the old men got the fires ready, cutting two reeds and making a hole near the tip of the smaller one, planting it firmly in the dirt, holding it fast with their feet, placing the other reed in the hole and turning it, turning it, patiently, till a thread of smoke started rising. Then they'd collect the dust in a banana leaf, wrap the leaf in cotton, and shake it till the fire caught. Then they lighted the fires for the families to sleep around. The men and women came and went, getting on with life, content perhaps. Without mentioning the change I'd suffered, showing neither anger nor surprise. Who asked after the storyteller? Nobody. Did anybody take a sack of cassava and another of maize to the seripigari, saying: "Change him back into a man who walks?" Nobody. Many people bustled about, their eyes avoiding the corner where I was. Poor Gregor-Tasurinchi! Furiously fluttering my wings and wriggling my legs; trying to turn over, fighting to get up. Ay, ay!

How could I ask for help without talking? I didn't know. That was the worst torment, perhaps. Bound to suffer, knowing that nobody would come and put me right side up. Would I never walk again? I remembered the tortoises. When I went to hunt them on the little beach where they come out of the water to bury their young; how I turned them over, catching hold of their shell. That's the way I was now, frantically waving my legs in the air, unable to right myself, just like them. I was a buzz-buzz bug, and I felt like a tortoise. Like them, I would be thirsty and hungry, and then my soul would go. Does the soul of a buzz-buzz bug come back? Perhaps it does.

Suddenly I noticed. They'd shut me up. Who was it who had done that, who were they? My family, yes, that was who. They'd closed off the hut, sealed up all the holes I might be able to escape through. They'd shut me up like a girl with her first blood. But who would come bathe Gregor-Tasurinchi and bring him back to the land of the living, pure and clean now? Nobody would come, perhaps. Why had they done this to me? Out of shame, most likely. So that nobody visiting them would see me and feel repelled by me or make fun of them. Had my kinfolk pulled a lock of hair from my head and taken it to the machikanari so he'd change me into Gregor-Tasurinchi? No, it must have been a little devil or even Kientibakori. I have done something wrong, perhaps, for them to shut me up like an enemy, on top of the evil I'd suffered. Why didn't they fetch a seripagari who'd give me back my bodily wrappings, instead? Maybe they've gone to the seripigari and have shut you up so you don't hurt yourself by going outside.

That gave me hope. Don't give up, Gregor-Tasurinchi, not yet; it was a little ray of sunshine in the storm. Meanwhile, I went on trying to turn over. My legs hurt from waving them about so much and my wings creaked with my efforts as though they were splitting apart. How much time went by? Who knows? But suddenly I succeeded. Courage, Gregor-Tasurinchi! Perhaps I moved more energetically; perhaps I stretched one of my legs out farther. I don't know. But my body contracted, moved sideways, flipped over, and there it was, I could feel it underneath me, hard. Firm, solid: the ground. I shut my eyes, intoxicated. But the joy of having righted myself disappeared immediately. What was that horrible pain in my back? As though I'd been burned. I'd torn my right wing on a splinter as I took those sudden leaps, or before, while I was struggling so violently. There it was, dangling down, split in two dragging along. That was perhaps my wing. I was beginning to feel hungry as well. I was frightened. The world had turned into an unknown one. Dangerous, perhaps. At any moment someone might squash me. Crush me. Eat me. Poor Gregor-Tasurinchi! Lizards! Trembling, trembling all over. Had I ever seen them eating cockroaches or beetles or any of the insects they chase? My broken wing hurt more and more, so much I could hardly move. And hunger-thorns still piercing my belly. I tried to eat the dry straw stuffed into the wall, but it tore my mouth without getting any softer, so I spat it out. I started scratching around here and there in the damp earth till I came across a nest of larvae. They were very small, squirming about, trying to escape. They were pocos, wood-worm larvae. I swallowed them slowly, shutting my eyes, happy. Feeling that the pieces of my soul that had been leaving were returning to my body. Yes, happy.

I hadn't finished swallowing the larvae when a distinctly unpleasant smell made me leap into the air, trying to fly. I felt something panting, very close by. The heat of its breath went up my nose. It smelled — it was — dangerous, perhaps. The lizard! So it had appeared. There was its triangular head between two worm-eaten partitions. There were its gummy eyes looking at me. Gleaming with hunger. Despite the pain, I flapped my wings, but trying, trying my best, I couldn't get off the ground. I took a few feeble hops, it seems. Losing my balance, hobbling. The pain of my wound was more severe now. There it came, there it was. Contracting like a snake, wriggling from side to side, it slid its body between the partitions and was inside. So there was the lizard. It crept closer and closer, quite slowly, never taking its eyes off me. How big it looked! Then, swiftly, swiftly, it came at me on its two legs. I saw it open its enormous mouth. I saw its two rows of teeth, curved and white; its steamy breath blinded me. I felt it bite, I felt it pulling off the damaged wing. I was so frightened I felt no pain. I was falling into a deeper trance, as though I were dropping off to sleep. I could see its crumpled green skin, its maw palpitating as it digested, and how it half closed its eyes as it swallowed that mouthful of me. I would resign myself to my destiny, then. Better that way. Feeling sad, perhaps. Waiting for it to finish eating me. Then, once I'd been eaten, I could see through its insides, through its soul, through its bulging eyes—everything was green—that my family was coming back.

They entered the hut, as apprehensive as before. I wasn't there anymore! Saying: Where could he have gone? They went over to the corner where the buzz-buzz bug had been, they looked, they searched. Gone! They sighed with relief, as though they'd been rescued from some great danger. They might have smiled; they were pleased. Thinking: We're free of that shameful thing. They'd have nothing to hide from their visitors now. They could now go on with their everyday lives, perhaps.

And that's the end of the story of Gregor-Tasurinchi, over by the Kimariato, the tapir-river.

I asked Tasurinchi, the seripigari, the meaning of what I'd been through in that bad trance. He pondered my question for a while, then made a gesture with his hand as though to chase something invisible away. "Yes, it was a bad trance," he agreed at last, thoughtfully. "Gregor-Tasurinchi! I wonder why. Something bad behind it, doubtless. Being changed into a buzz-buzz bug must be the work of a kamagarini. I can't really tell you for certain. I'd have to go up the pole of my hut and ask the saankarite in the world of clouds. He'd know, I expect. You'd best forget it. Don't talk about it anymore. What's remembered goes on living and can happen again." But I haven't been able to forget and I go on telling about it.

TRANSLATED FROM the Spanish by Helen Lane

(EXCERPT FROM: Mario Vargas Llosa. *The Storyteller*. Trans. Helen Lane. London and New York, Penguin, 1989, pp. 116–122, 202–207.)

RETURNING

Ib Michael

The grasshoppers are thirsty. They called to the rain with high-pitched screams. In Domingo's hut we're making the final preparations. A simple kerosene lamp burns in the narrow room behind the record player. There are deep, dark shadows on the bamboo walls. Tsuanka passes the bottle. I'm sitting on a plank bed made of pieces of *chonta* with Domingo in front of me. Now the jungle-dark- brown-secret is poured in a plastic cup, and Domingo hands it to me. Here, in my thirtieth year, I empty the bitter chalice, anxious to get to the matter at hand. I give the cup to Tsuanka,who fills it again. There is no solemnity in his movements. Domingo drinks his portion, and Tsuanka exchanges some words with the children, who have gathered in a corner. He lifts the bottle toward the flame of the lamp, shakes it a little: the contents are gone, it's totally empty. Then he throws the bottle over to Paki, who catches it and runs from the hut with Domingo's little girl.

Now my journey-companion brings the palm of his hands to his knees, stretches his elbows well, leans on his chin and breathes in — all the way down to his diaphragm. He does that a couple of times, then he gets up, shaking his arms and legs. He looks like somebody who is shaking off water after a shower. I don't try to imitate him. I just relax with my eyes half-closed, make an occasional remark to Tsuanka. I sit and think about someone I'll contact, and I'm opening a channel to a person I feel very close to, someone whose transmissions have often been strong.

Rapidly I lose all sense of time. Finding myself in a little dream state of self-hypnosis, suddenly I hear my voice, which has a strange high sound:

"I have crickets in my blood!"

Then my eyes clap open, and I see the new colors in the room. Tsuanka is speaking to me, saying I should be quiet, I shouldn't speak, and I make a gesture accepting the remark. Domingo has already crawled in behind my eyes. Suddenly he gets up, goes outside with firm steps, and vomits in the night. It became a milky way, I'm thinking. I notice the queasiness myself, but I repress it. I have a strong blockage against throwing up. I've felt this way since childhood.

"Are you going out?" asks Tsuanka. "Come."

But I say no with my head, bend my legs under me and sit down, making myself comfortable on the plank bed. I close my eyes.

(. . . ..)

My temples are filled with the shrill sounds of cicadas. They rush down the inside of my skull. But is it the reality of the forest or is it my own reality? I half-open one eye.

"Tsuanka, is it raining?"

"No, Miguelito! You're escaping from the *arutam*.[1] You're a little rabbit, jumping after the children's shining ball! Now shut your eyes and don't talk so much."

But I can't keep my eyes closed. Only Domingo is together and closed in his own circle. He moves his lips. Is he counting the number of spirits? Or is he talking to a distant relative? I don't dare ask more. Then I begin to see directly through the walls of the hut, into the sparkling, starry background. It is full of big fireflies and green-eyed moths, a cloudless night with no rain to see. The earth shook, strong winds blew, but I ran back to the dwelling where I'm sitting now, crying in a quiet pool.

Then Tsuanka calls with a voice that comes from the mountains.

"KAKARAM! KAKARAM!"

Domingo moans due to the blow, then his breathing becomes methodical as he groans. A tornado fills the room, zips me open, beginning with the "connection between the bones in the skull" all the way down. I'm split wide, like a cracked walnut. It's my resistence that's been broken by the words of power.

I see a free-floating pattern of a snake that's exactly the same color as the one rising from where the trees slide into the sky and Makanshi's thunder. I'm a snake-body finding my balance as I make my way over the forest floor. The scales are gliding on rolls of water-pearls, strong smells flicker like lightning. All sounds are distant. The poison sack in the jaws tightens nicely. The fang bones lie folded back protectively. The sounds are only shadows. They pump through my head with a milk-like, downy distance. The eyes are looking through a gray cataract.

Smells, however, have a whole spectrum all their own. They have color and form and collect in front of the head prism. The nose is a bunch of needles and sneezes in tinkling patterns every time the tongue flicks into the inner caves of smell, transmitting new perceptions and information.

The forest floor is warm, the radiant earth-heat being distributed from the head to the tip of the tail. I am Makanshi, glittering hunter, warrior quick as lightning. It has just rained. The vegetation is inundated, the prism tingles. It is broad daylight for human beings, but it is night. Day and night are only registered through the warmth the earth either gives or takes.

Makanshi is hungry. It feels like a rhythmic contraction increasing speed. Makanshi has few enemies. The worst of them is the snake-eating hawk whose night vision is sharp and whose impact is so quick that it's already too late. There's a scent now. A single clear spectral line is vibrating: the prey! I'm moving fast, head rising. I never hear myself, but I know I'm among the noiseless few. I move through the leaves, but so does the wind. I feel the little pump of the poison sack raising the fangs.

Makanshi is hunting. The prey is near! The tail moves like a whiplash of excitement. A downy structure is emerging, the shape disappearing for the eyes, which means it's so close that the organ of temperature takes over scent as well as sight and finds the warmest blood vessel in the prey.

The impact becomes one with the signal, the fangs hitting the pulse like a double needle, emptying the poison in a piercing shot. Oh, I unhitch my jaws, the orgasm of the body is pressing down the furry ball, tough punch, the beating of the waves from the long muscles. Then comes tiredness, bleeding, blue colors.

Makanshi is satisfied. Makanshi coils himself on the warmest spot to digest. A rotten stump finishes off the light. Then comes the scent that awakens the warrior: a human being. Too big to picture, but I get furious every time. He contracts!

Makanshi that was just resting and sunning himself in the new colors couldn't stand this whiplash break of the prism and went to attack. But Makanshi who was so full moved too late in the upswing, and man was one of the quickest-reacting species alive in the forest . . .

I screamed when the stroke hit me. The snake-scream is terrible, screeching stars in cotton. The whole rainbow went limp and ended up in a place above the jungle canopy.

"Kakaram! Kakaram!"

I'm running toward the lightning. This time I'm not running away. The lightning is ball lightning, a furious jaguar on caterpillars. No. Now it's fighting with Panki the boa. The scales and the fur of the jaguar are sparkling, so I stop, hit by the lightning itself. It is me they are about to flay, not each other. In that instant, I know why, many years ago in the jungle of Lacandón, I received a tooth from a jaguar that I'm still wearing around my neck like an amulet. Two strong guardian spirits are about to flay me in mutual rivalry. The jaguar is crushing, jumping, rolling, tearing. First it splits Panki in thousands of scales that become eyes in the night and float out of reach, then it shakes all my tendons apart and consumes me, skin and hair, as they say. Finally, it picks its teeth with selected palm species and plods into the forest.

I don't know whether I did it right or wrong, whether I got the *arutam* or didn't. I'll ask first thing tomorrow. Exhausted, I fall asleep.

TRANSLATED FROM the Danish by Luis Eduardo Luna

(EXCERPT FROM: *Rejsen Tilbage.* Copenhagen: Gyldendals, 1977, pp. 209, 212–213)

NOTE

1. The soul of a dead warrior that can make one invulnerable and immortal, the primary power one is hunting for in visions.

AERIAL WATERS

Néstor Perlongher

I

Harsh embarcation, irate bard
Ripples or undulates noctilucas
iridescences threading their way
in the ethereal sulphuric weaving:

   trace
   (erasable persistence)
   in the castling of magmas
   in the altar cloth divided into squares

   — of the mind, the room
   to be worn in the house (kitsch art)
   turned mediocrities to dark red crystal
   in the light and ravished canvas corset.

   But all the frill
   of the altar cloth's lacework wove
   less a text than a form, a figure. . .

Boreal or gentle, their fringe
never ceased illuminating the slippery
volleys of the minuet, along the flat stone floor: nail,
detached and impudent, and, scratching its dance steps,
the inane, translucid flying.

Through mirages of living skin
in the wrenching of mucous membranes,
the strumming of the nail
elevated the canticles
to the empty, sublunar ceiling.

Harsh minstrel, burnished mane,
mambo after-taste, modulating, inflicts
intensities on the slime,
                plastic
porosity of thick matter.

In the after-taste a spasm
contorted the spells of impotency
and transmitted to the lacework
the unctuousness of nylon

scratching them
in a delicate precipitation.

II

Twinkling of ebonite, the lilacs of the cross
file away the nail's rough turgidity
or chap the spilling of a rosary
along the edge of the altar cloth.

Fringed convulsions, if the medusa punctures the fish,
the flotation of a canticle, of a pitcher ripples in the
    whirlpooling.

The wave in song to give the consistency of a night veil
to the marshy oil, to steal the childhood of a scandal
from the god of the rain forest, or to grant the levity
of a tour in space to the fleeting iridescences (they tremble).

Patrolling the sidesplitting laughter of the rapid poplar, the
    ceremony
to time bursts it with strass inlays or mobile spangles
that scratch the film turned translucid.

The fleeing of the cormorants
and in their place the gentle seagulls of desire,
the vertigo of all the marrow
chiaroscuroing the wayfarer's journey.

Where do you go when you aren't there?
Where are you when you go out of yourself?

Close by, or suddenly, the hint of music draws near
and warns of trails turned to mud in the dissolution of the
    filàfil
then with a jerk the rigidity of the (shaking) knee is reestab-
    lished
and the beak of the flower in the drum opens the scar of a
    tendril
                    splitting

the valleys of the Mass, the alveoli
of that, because they were Mass, mercury had to be thrown
   on the mallard,
a dexterous mirror hand.

III

Rarified atmosphere, the nebulous
incense of flowers circulating
curves at the foot of the pearl, the spectacles
and the "crystal light," so that the
princess of the waters, first fruits
of the dew of the
night air
in the alveolus of the vibration
it grows taut, is
suspended:

      ah, if it were to curdle, take shape
      in the space full of presences
      the opaline of a rimmel
      that stamped down, twitching upon itself,
      the bucking of the humps, whose

                  "fleeting nature"

(brief vertigo)
      cracks, Niagara of the mother-of-pearl *soutien*
      shredded thread in the nylon mud
      a Nile passes
      the force of a brutal
      current, a movement
      of continued speed:

its Elysian helixes,
air to the simoom, palpating
knottedness, give

the gift.

V

If the liquid divinity were to drown
or boil, in the carnal heat,
its latex beach — not
promontories, but grottos —

granules of blackness
oh noctiluca aflame with passion stiffening
the ring of surf
on the waves of shells and crabs

on the tense and tenuous skin
wharf the precipice in whirlpools
the simulacrum of its frenzy

stamps hollow spaces in the coral avalanche
so that the wing of a wasp tasting dragonflies
might flatter its volcano

VII

The foot, the foot's coming and going, the shove of the floor
in the instep, smooth combination was weaving its braid,
ethereal, with the chorus, the impetus of the chorus, the raft-
ing of voices in elated swarms encircled the lamps with a
multicolor whipping, pink strap tying to the fainting the
temblor of the tucos freed the livid flotation of the wake in
whirlpools of beams of light, so weightless, they dishevelled
the fringe with the slightest touch of an anima, of an aura,
the coiled coiffure crowns white priestesses, limousine of
patent leather that embarked each breath, anxieties, when
iridescent bubbles melt giving off their gas, from grayness
falling like dew with a gulf of incense, a fan of smoke, wave,
margin and aureole of light, crucifix stretched to the ton-
sured tip of members covered with ivy, sculpture of vines
varnishing torsions of the brown thighs, predicted against
the light of the linen in the foot's coming and going, its
rhythm, I rule in the sparkling of the colors, the leaf, femi-
nine, its plant-witchcraft, had a fixity of tide embracing
coastal swamp, in the corpuscles of mist, the Hydra thrust in
the modulated howl of the interrogation, the stumbling, in
the swaying that arched while slipping on the damp laths,
aura slick with the slime of bitter puddles and in its gondola
to rise into the howling, the glandulating of the speeds in the
silt, or perhaps island of crippled neon, amongst whose
cracks in the humors of the transpiration could be glimpsed
the shining of the star, or the purpurins of the dress made of
night that belongs to the goddess desiring to shine.

X

                DIAMOND

Skyscraper's almond-shape whose foundations
through faucets pipes windows like waves corpuscles and
   bathrooms
will reach the great Lake of Beings,
                the Entities

                FIXED ENTITIES
                PREFIXED

Their prefixed wake, their cascade
if Manes plunge
to the ivy, a light
curls the fierce waves

Sea urchins
Living waters

Cartilaginous hoods
for the make-up of the margins

Cellophane sirens
in the holes of the net,
half-body of a naiad
in the technicolor surf
whose flecks of foam scattered
an arc of dust particles
and bubbles, blue arc
                    in time
with pulling of tendons and syncopated catalepsies

fallen on account of pressure

bluish vapor in the rolling flight
in the feverish rocking those rhythmic
                        or mixed puppets
implant their hair in the crystal
of cloud, empty twilight
of quivering iridescence
volumes of shining
sliding their X-shaped crosses
through gardens of mire.

IT WAS THE CRYSTAL
THE THOUSAND CRYSTAL FACETS
THE RHYTHMIC SHINING
THE CELEBRATORY
                HYMNS OF AN
                            ANNUNCIATION
KALEIDOSCOPE
        ENAMELED FRENZY

The Serpent's Step

brief serpents, of evaporated steps
Lezama Lima

1.

The translucent step of the serpent
drools in the instant the echo that stinks
or covers its smell with jade, the way green backstitching
lifts colorations in the tour of uncreated space,
transnatural, its hump in diluted contact
erases almost forgetting the legends of soap
but while hauling the halo countersigns
or ringed fingers resurge that show the step's lucidity.

2.

Streamer of cobras in the Mohave ballet
getting wet in the shade of spiralled Araucaria pines
for marking on the ivy the levity of a step
that is in truth the step of the grass through the air
dampened by the circles of empty eyes in nitrate
windows tributes of macramé scanning the zither's
pupil like verse, its hummingbird in love the cornea
gores simulating on the carpet of moss
in the watery air that dew of the smoke in its
dehiscence.

TRANSLATED FROM the Spanish by Steven F. White

(Nestor Perlongher. *Poemas Completos.* Buenos Aires: Seix
Barral, 1997, pp. 247–252, 255, 257, 260–261, 289.)

THE MOTHER OF THE VOICE IN THE EAR
(excerpt)

Alfonso Domingo

I think I'm prepared for a*yahuasca,* if such a thing were possible. I've been on an almost complete fast for several days. I only ingest water and some fruit. Hunger, which at first was obsessive, now torments me like a gust of wind that then subsides, like a hand with its tongs around my stomach. I don't know if I'm purifying my body with this punishment and the ritual baths, but I look at it in a different way. Tests of the body are nothing compared to the mental ones, which, perhaps on account of that physical weakness, take on an unusual importance. There's also that persistent doubt: What am I doing here? Why am I putting myself through these fasts and such concentration? I never would have suspected that in the middle of the jungle I'd be doing spiritual exercises like these. The only thing missing is the hair shirt. Fortunately, Riwanteri leaves me alone, and just says a few sentences to me through Franky, who acts as a kind of protective veil. Other times, it all makes sense to me, and things fit into place. I don't think it's a coincidence that *ayahuasca* has appeared on my path. It is a fundamental piece in the vegetal puzzle in which I find myself. I hadn't thought about it before. It's the perfect formula, and comes from the same lineage as the magical roots of this world which, for now, fascinates me as much as if I had traveled through time and not space. My curiosity was piqued by Don Julio, and (why not admit it?) certain expectations. The key could be anywhere, the answer to a search deeper than that of the lost city. And, in any case, a journey like this will add a different sort of vertigo to my collection. That's why I've decided to try *ayahuasca.* This very night I will have an encounter with the vine of dreams. With the Mother of the Voice in the Ear. At this point, it's hard to really know where the story is going, or what's in store on this adventure. But in order to go on to a new chapter, you've got to finish the previous one and turn the page.

The Mother of the Voice in the Ear

> There where the mountain ends.
> On the peak, even I can't say where.
> I've wandered there where my head and my
>   heart seem
> lost.
> I've wandered far away.
> *Dream song of the Papago Indians*

I

From the travel notebook of Alvaro Fonseca

Riwanteri sits down, facing North. It seems like he's both focused and absent. At his feet lie various receptacles and a clay vessel containing the brew. In the center of the circle, a small fire gives off a blue, sweet smoke, the result of the combustion of wood and a slightly aromatic plant. The smoke serves two purposes, both of which are protective: it keeps away the inevitable mosquitos and serves as a magic envelopment against bad spirits, those dark inhabitants of the night and the mind that are best sent into exile at a time like this. The lighting, which comes from some torches lit in the corners of the dwelling and in the fire in the middle, is tenuous and warm. It contrasts with the blue and white smoke in a series of colors that rescues faces from the shadows and weakly illuminates the communal dwelling where the session is being celebrated. The dwelling is elliptical and has four entrances, one at each of the cardinal points. The roof is conical, and the entire construction corresponds to the Yacaruna spiritual universe in which the world is ordered in nine levels of consciousness and knowledge.

The shaman, after picking up one of the burning sticks, ritually envelops himself in smoke. When he has immunized and protected himself, he proceeds to carry out the same operation with all those who are present. He goes in circles around the Indians, Franky, and, finally, it's my turn. I notice that warm breath, that vegetal heat caressing my cheeks and back. I can't avoid it. A dark uneasiness invades me. I feel as if I were wrapped in something that I don't control and that mitigates my curiosity to know the plant of power. Something could go wrong and could completely ruin the trip. I'm already on the magical toboggan, but I can't help thinking that fear, like an anchor, has fixed me to one place on the ground.

Everything is set and we wait, sitting in silence, in the center of the dwelling. Riwanteri has taken his place and initiates a small meditation that lasts a few minutes. Right away, he begins to distribute the dark brown, thick and harsh potion (exactly the way it tastes as it slides down my throat on its way to my stomach) to each person present. The concentrated taste of root syrup strikes me as something unmistakable and super strong. It had already seemed this way to me earlier when I contemplated the decoction being prepared throughout the day over a low fire in a pot where they put the mixture of macerated vines and leaves while they sang ritual songs. Its smell is unusual and distinct, and I wouldn't say that it is very agreeable. Now it has become a heat that expands through my center as if it were propagating itself in my veins and circulatory system starting from my stomach. I hear the music of the drums around this bonfire where a good part of the village is gathered. There's also the sound of flutes and some sort of maracas in a rhythm that slowly envelops me. For a few minutes, once my eyes are closed and I'm lying against a tree trunk, I feel a certain warmth ascend through my body while I hear the ceremonial songs and animal chants directed by the shaman, who begins to move with a surprising energy given his age. One chant slowly increases in volume and rhythm and suddenly a strange laxness invades my extremities, an odd feeling of bodily disorder bordering on dizziness, as if I were under the effects of drunkenness. The only thing missing is nausea and just the thought of it makes a ball strike the roof of my mouth from my stomach and struggle to get out. More than nausea, it's the kick of a trapped horse in pain. As a kind of reflex action, I repress the urge to vomit and open my eyes. What I see makes me forget momentarily my twisted stomach. From the darkness of the night, a series of geometric shapes comes spinning toward me. They're like circular labyrinths that become strange spirals as they spin. I close my eyes in order to distinguish the hallucinatory shapes more clearly. The figures are of different sizes and are located capriciously throughout my field of vision.

In the shadows, I can make out brilliant points of colors aligned in a precise, geometric pattern. What I observe is a mixture of puzzle and kaleidoscope, as if a filter had been interposed to disperse colors and volumes in luminescent radiations. It all resembles a billboard of giant dimensions seen up close, where I discern that the colors aren't pure the way they appear to be when seen from a distance, but rather that they are dispersed in a varying gamut of minuscule points. Up close, they remind me of the eyes of the children in this village, little points like the heads of spermatozoids that populate my vision suspended in a color of dark blue silk. They give off a luminous aura that carries me to a world in which curves, lines and shapes rule, a place from which, for some time now, I haven't left.

It's the geometric country.

II

I contemplate the figures from within. I'm in the eighth wonder, in perfect psychedelia. Music explodes in shapes and colors. Each drum is a focus of energy that reaches me in precise, curved waves. And, nevertheless, in spite of the pleasant sensation that the geometric country produces in me, there's something that fastens me to its forms and evolutions. It's as if I couldn't leave so easily and I'd have to cross some barrier.

Then I discover it. The shapes suddenly order themselves and before me, in a three dimensional colored background, the abstract figure of a monster emerges. It's the monster of the geometric country. And I don't know how to overcome it, because I'm sure that for me to go on, I'll have to defeat it. Fear, which has been crouching down all this time, peers at me with its wolf-like ears.

I'm trying to find a way out when a harsh and bitter taste in my throat takes me by surprise. The ball bouncing around in my stomach attacks again and this time I don't have the strength to keep on holding it in, enveloping it. I vomit. Between spasms, I throw up part of the brew. With the nausea subsiding, I look at the liquid that I've spilled on the ground and I see the ironic smile of a figure that looks like me. Right away, I know what that figure represents. It's the face of fear, the face of the monster of the geometric country that remains outside and liberates me from its clouded chains. Instantly, I feel free. The impression is reinforced by the decision that I've just made. I gather all my worries, my obsessions, my black ballast. I place them in formation, lining them up perfectly, and I order them to give a casualty report. One by one, they sound off, just as I had felt them after the funeral ceremony. When they finish, I give an order: "Break ranks and go to hell!" And they leave, while I laugh at how easy it is. They disappear, go up in smoke and then a blues song enters my mind that I decide to call "Explorer's Blues." I'm as happy as a child. That's the feeling: I walk through a place filled with flowers, colors, wonders, and everything is a ball with which I play, simultaneously inside and outside of it, while the music I feel within me falls in kernels and I realize at last I've learned to understand it. A thrilling sense of happiness, pleasure and plenitude inundates me. The music embraces me and rises through my skin. It seems like I have a hundred ears. I mount these songs, ride them like horses. My arms and my body seem ethereal and float lightly and I wonder if I can levitate, if I can elevate myself in the air in order to move through it and fly, one of my old dreams. But then other dreams come, ones inhabited by the Yacarunas and other indigenous tribes that I don't know and that pass, evanescent, beside me. I discover Eskimos, and peoples from Siberia, India, Asia, Africa, Europe, people of all races and colors, united by a common link: knowing that they are members of a single people on the earth.

The people who dream.

III

A vibration with the heartbeat of the world: that's what dream means. Dreaming: to beat with the original impulse of creation.

I now see that two vital moments exist for the orb. One is sunrise, when the light begins to awaken the colors and the souls of diurnal creatures. It is an inspiring moment, filled with sap, blood and breath. At the same time, somewhere, right at the antipodes, there's an expiring at sunset, in a perfect systole-diastole sort of equilibrium. These are the two poles of the "heart of the world." At both ends, everything remains momentarily suspended, for just the amount of time that it takes for it to breathe once. It is the hour in which one can feel the earth as something living and beating. Each day, the world repeats the circular breathing that reaches every corner of the planet. As a precise and eternal mechanism, it breathes, forcing spirit into all creatures. If dawn awakens everything that is diurnal, when night arrives so do the nocturnal beings, the inhabitants of its hidden face.

IV

I don't move at all, but I'm surrounded and perfumed by vertigo as if I were inside a centrifuge where it is not the anguish of circular velocity that reigns, but pleasure and absolute beatitude. With joy, I feel my whole being spin, ready at any moment to break apart and fly off in pieces. Little by little, my body, which is flying inside an eagle over a clean and distant canyon, lands in a swirling of leaves and trees.

I appear to be in possession of all my organs and, nevertheless, I'm certain that I'm not in my own body. I think about the astral journey and I try to see myself from some place. I'm unable to do so for the simple reason that I'm no longer in the same place. And I'd swear that I haven't moved at all from the ceremonial dwelling of the village, sitting in front of the fire. But what village? There's no trace of humans anywhere. I want to stand up. It's not possible that all this has happened and that they've just abandoned me. For a moment I think about Temeni and César when they went into the jungle after drinking *ayahuasca*. Has the same thing happened to me? Then I realize that my body weighs nothing and that everything I can see is illuminated with a spectral clarity, as if there were a full moon.

The landscape is absolutely unreal, desolate. I already know what I miss: I'm not surrounded by jungle. The gigantic trees have disappeared, and before my eyes stretches a desert panorama. There's hardly any vegetation and the rocks and the earth have a strange light, which is the result of the mixture of lunar illumination and an odd interior phosphorescence. The mineral from which these luminescent radiations emanate crosses the earth as well as the veined and stratified rocks that resemble brush strokes planted randomly. In their order, nevertheless, I notice a purpose: it seems like they are signalling the stars. I really don't understand what's going on, but I'm not worried about it. I know that I'm here for some reason. For a moment, a suspicion makes its way into my brain. I've traveled to another era. It's as if I had entered the archives of time, in which every event is written, and as if I had been allowed to glimpse an ancestral seal engraved in my genes, something hidden and remote.

The secret of the ancient gaze.

V

Once there was a time when humanity was not alone on the earth, a time when we were companions of lightning and rain, water and fire. A new, burning, vigorous blood used to run through our veins. Our eyes had a calm, tender light. The secret of strength could be found on our foreheads. This strength was remote and powerful, as constant as the wind that chisels shapes on rocks, a cyclical and animated energy that was always distinct in terms of its uniformity, like the waves of an infinite sea that is never sad.

There was an era, once, when the moon used to speak and the sun brought everyone a new day like a newly-made wonder. At night, you could read the sky, and the stars were more than just lit and distant points.

At that time, humanity considered itself not an owner, but yet another creature, and it participated in the profound and intimate order of things. In that age, humanity could see the invisible thread that united it with other creatures and could pronounce the secret name of trees and plants, the one that should only be proclaimed in their company and their presence in order to feel their tenuous heartbeat, the green, subtle and vital breath that pushes them off the earth and lifts them to greater heights.

The Mother of the Voice in the Ear has taken me to that remote epoch, lost in the night of time, when humanity possessed that special gift in its gaze and on its skin. The human gaze knew, knew the stones and rocks, each mineral and its virtues, merely by passing eyes and mind along their edges; by walking over them, by touching them with hands and caressing their surface. It knew about colors and tones, shadows and shinings.

At that time, humanity could call the animals and distinguish in the night their sounds and their songs, their fears of death, their struggles and dialogues. Life was not something absurd and incomprehensible. We knew the instruction manual of the world. Original sin meant losing that gaze.

VI

I've walked through that remote landscape with the certainty that something is going to happen. In the rocks that surround me, near a blue river that flows peacefully, an emptied space attracts me with its black shadow among the shining of fantastic minerals. The cave is enormous and has strange, enigmatic, arcane and hieroglyphic drawings on its walls similar to some of the designs from the country of geometry. It was as if the grotto were an entrance road to that country through which I passed at the beginning, and on account of some strange mechanism had left to reach an outer world anchored in another time. The light from a fire that I discover in the back guides me in my journey toward the interior of the cavity. I advance among stalactites and stalagmites of various muted colors. My gaze has a strange sensor and I receive infrared rays that change the perception of the colors, which is why I see the light of the distant bonfire as white, but I can make out hot and cold rocks, and I receive a warmth that comes from the ground and wraps itself around my body, giving me a sense of wellbeing.

The thrill of discovering something increases while I go closer to the small fire. Now I can see a man crouching down, striking flint against another rock resembling iron ore that has been sharpened and polished as a weapon. It's as if he's in a drunken stupor. At his feet there is straw, dry leaves, branches and bigger pieces of wood. As he moves and strikes iron against flint, numerous sparks fall and ignite the straw and firewood that he's gathered in many places. There are already two, three, four fires. With their light, I now see the gleam of several pairs of eyes in the dark background of the cave. It's a whole tribe. And they just witnessed amidst cries and guttural sounds of admiration and surprise a ceremony of incalculable consequences. They would no longer have to lie in wait for lightning to strike the savanna to make flames, or keep vigilant watch over the fire so that it never went out. They'll be able to create it whenever they want. It's no longer a gift from the gods. They themselves can bring it from the void when they need it. All they require is iron ore and flint. The man still strikes the stones together frenetically, producing sparks and more sparks amidst the leaping and the dancing of the rest of the tribe, but he doesn't notice, as I do, the evil gaze of another mature man who observes him with hatred.

The flames of the small fires begin to obsess me and suddenly I find myself staring at them. What I see next is the ceremonial dwelling where we began the *ayahuasca* session and where I've returned after these visions. The music, which has accompanied me at all times, now has an intimate character. No one is singing now. There's only the sound of a drum and a strange, other-worldly flute whose notes I can climb somewhere. I've opened my eyes and I glance incredulously around the room. I see the indigenous people in different places. Some have disappeared, while others still struggle with inner demons. But the majority is peaceful, happy and relaxed, just like me. Some are pale or the color of green wax. I can see how their faces change when I look at them. I see the waves of circular energy in space and I realize that I'm slowly coming down. For some time, everything seems unreal to me, and during those strange minutes I can't articulate anything. I stare at the others like an idiot without being able to answer Franky who asks me how it went. Then I think I've fallen into a deep sleep.

VII

After the first session, I can't say that I'm the same. Something fundamental has changed inside me, but it's still too soon to be able to write something with a minimum amount of analytical perspective. I'll limit myself to registering what happened in that state that I can't define or qualify either as dream or hallucination. Everything was much more real than that, but it unfolded on planes on which I never had moved before and which were both as new as they were fascinating to me.

Besides, what happened suddenly brings forth new ideas in my head that I write down with no sort of selective process. Perhaps they were sleeping in my mind or come from my reading or old conversations, and sometimes they tempt me with their airs of transcendence — like the one that plans to summarize my thought and state. The sentence is perhaps pretentious, like a quotation taken out of context, but remains, such as this one:

The sense is what's sensed.

VIII

So, there's no turning back. One can't, one shouldn't remain in the attics of memory, precisely because of what that lost paradise meant to us. Memory is an important piece of luggage that helps us to confront what awaits us when we awake from our dreams: that world of difficult light.

After that first night, I'm considered a "human being" by the Yacarunas. *Ayahuasca* has given me the gift of the first vision, which for them is sufficient. I can't write now about everything I've thought about over the last few days after having participated in several more sessions. I've wanted to obtain in those trances some clue about the lost city, but, each time, I realize more and more that it's just an excuse to continue diving into my inner self. *Ayahuasca* is wise and powerful and has taken me to another lost city, another territory, another time.

It has taken me to the most important moment of my childhood.

TRANSLATED FROM the Spanish by Steven F. White

(EXCERPT FROM: Alfonso Domingo. *La madre de la voz en el oído.* Madrid: Editorial Fundamentos, 1991, pp. 157–167.)

LAST RIVER
(and other poems)

Steven F. White

LAST RIVER

At the century's edge, standing alone,
I hear my many souls leaking away.
Soon I'll be an empty shape, skin and bone,
with no escape and no excuse to stay.

Somewhere the Web site and the spider meet.
Cannibal-gods and cyber-energy
converge with the extinct and obsolete
and each second opens eternity.

Spears compute air as they curve in the skies
before meeting their dream of flesh and blood.
Space shuttles conjure Stone Age flames and rise
with humans above the last river's flood.

To be a canoe and not be afraid
to ride heaven's current in the river.
To carry no more than my ghost to trade
for a future no one can deliver.

The river is a horizontal tree
to navigate by hammock as I sleep.
The tree is an upright river of me
since memory's cortex is rough and steep.

There's no end to what the water's lifting,
no limit to all there is to forget.
I'm unmoored, detached, and now I'm drifting
into darkening eddies of sunset.

The clear juice of night's fruit tattoos my skin
with zigzag patterns of the universe.
Is my body free of time and toxin,
or is it the spoiled road from bad to worse?

I have drunk from the geometric muse,
woman of water, air, fire, vine and leaf,
mythic being, forbidding to refuse,

when she sings me the heart of all belief.
Are both plants eyes she left by accident
like green beads lost from a necklace of light?
Or were they a present from the gods sent
so one can enter the portals of night?

I vomit streams of iridescent snakes
into obsidian waters of fear.
A twisting, mating ball of life awakes,
glowing, only to sink then disappear.

Living in the times, learning in a place,
where politics divides and culture binds,
where the sacred is an evolving space
not meant to house the fixed ecstatic minds.

I am cubic feet per second flowing,
psychic volume always moving east.
I will be the sediment of knowing,
deposited, carried and then released.

There is a kind of truth that will remain
somehow related to a settling face,
enigma too beautiful to explain,
too impossibly real to leave no trace.

But the particles have foreign voices.
They speak a mixture of every tongue.
This liquid journey provides new choices
and currents for all the symmetries sung.

I hear the darts of illness whistle past.
I hear the plants give up their oxygen.
I hear the first drop of rain and the last.
I hear the falling forests cut by men.

We vanish from the televised empire:
nothing in money, something in the earth,
our waste and wreckage piled ever higher
so that our children know what we are worth.

Once upon a time was there harmony?
Did our eyes once watch the world in wonder?
Was it every merrily, merrily?
Or were we lost in nightmares and thunder?

I see tiny hands in the whirlpool's teeth.
Among giant rocks, the ghost-children moan,
picked apart by scaly creatures beneath
the falls and glyphs of Father Sun on stone.

In the House of Waters, I am singing,
drowning in light from the blood-red baby,
whose mother entered me with him, bringing
in her arms the potion of ancestry.

In twists and turns of umbilical vine,
in the blood-rivers of generations,
I make all possible predicates mine,
consuming my son of transformations.

The rapids are where the river flowers.
As a shiver rips the body she kissed,
I abandon a life measured in hours,
and wonder how death could ever exist.

I'm one river then two when I divide:
part vessel waterfalling with my scars,
part feather floating free of me to ride
other currents rising toward the stars.

Through star-engendered archipelagos,
where pairs of red suns watch me like reptiles,
I snake toward a mouth beyond milk floes
and can taste the photons as my son smiles.

How could I drown in the creator's form
as the perfect chaos is perfected
within a still pool's undersurface-storm
if my song gives shape to what's reflected?

In crossing between as mobile frontier,
as that river of diamonds and scrolls,
in the trance of here-is-there-there-is-here,
I can carry the conductor of souls.

MARIRI

Like a rising tide, like emptying cities,
in the viscous possible, in the formless,
or the way a liquid whispers at the height of its column
before emerging with a sound independent from air,
awakened, vibrating, turning into whirlpool

with the same spiral as the shapes approaching
or receding or unseen,
and the smell of snakes that arrive on earth
then writhe from time's throat, infinitely still.

The whole thing so quick, so living,
and yet embedded, like a tree in the neophyte's lungs,
the swallowed smoke among branches, perhaps,
calling like the blue voice of the cure,
at peace, everywhere, and then
releasing the white vipers of extraction.
Where is it from anyway? How did it get in?
The constant battles, the fear of loss, the power,
like the serpent that can steal it all from a rival's chest
or the colored cords that the Queen in her necklace of thorns
pours into the kneeling healers' upturned mouths.

Which is why, in the numinous, opening, to know,
then, like the spirits of plants, within,
like the bee's stinger or sharp pathogens
or everything my sick flesh cannot understand,
in legions, in fears barely surfacing,
and human struggles, waves,
dark actions suddenly revealed
like vegetal darts and their breathing targets,
equatorial, for me as I go searching,
like without a weapon among the armed.

So, what is it made of, this harmony of rainbows
that there is between daybreak and space, like wet lips at work?
That thunder already rumbling
which spreads, sowing its victims with animal shrapnel,
but when the white phlegm instead
rises from its secret place, uncoiling itself to wage war.

Inside the circle protected by circuits of color
once the great plants begin to speak
extending their generous vines and leaves,
into the material, into the longing for answers,
into oneness, ablaze in the reign of their song.

BLOOD OF THE GODS

In the hiss of rain striking the Amazon,
I hear the gods praying
because they are hungry
and I am a morsel to be believed.
"You'll get some nice bites
unless you tuck your pants in your socks,"
warns the guide, who carries an anti-ophidia syringe
strapped beneath his shirt.

That's when I recognize the snaking body
of the vine of the soul, *Banisteriopsis caapi,*
vanishing in the jungle,
disappearing in the sky.
A machete flashes, opens
the infinity of my own helixes,
and in the porous cross-section
I see the tunnel where I will be sucked
into the carnivorous flower of a god
who's searching for sustenance in belief.
I remember I will see myself drinking *ayahuasca*
and traversing the dark landscape of a scream
on legs of lightning until I reach a clearing
littered with scraps of ancestors
and generations yet to be born.
I'm no more than a raw dream of being
reborn in the rain forests of the night,
and I drink this bitter, bitter blood of the gods
so that I can circulate in their veins.

THE HUMMINGBIRD

Kiss these flowers, drink their colors,
in the garden where I'm sleeping.
They're like whirlpools, all these flowers,
their throats of gold, yours of ruby.

Give me the force, give me the light
to be the message of your wings.
Sketch above me with your long beak.
Let your design of healing fall.

Mark my body with my singing
so you'll know me when I flourish.
Your eyes are now a field of eyes
in the garden's flow of flowers.

Can I call you when I need you?
Will you help me when I'm frightened?
Drink my colors, they're like whirlpools.
Kiss this flower, my open mouth.

SEPULTURA TONDURI

(based on a painting by Pablo Amaringo)

The being covered with steel scales on fire
chants something that sounds like your death.
Perhaps this bloodsong is already entering
your red chambers, and no one knows
what it knows, or if a heart could resist such music,
or if the snake around its arm, or if the violet
flares from its head, or if that melody
permeating air like air, night like night, and you like you,
or if soldiers ripped your dreams from bed
and marched them ever farther from dawn.

Who will help you now to perfect the art of living?
Your dense colors part like a beaded curtain
and that last waft of you comes before the molten one
who invokes the serpent to be your coffin
and the great tortoise shell overturned as the table
    for your wake
with mushrooms as candles and firefly-flames
so there is light for the pigs to dig your grave
and the shroud-ripper bird to shriek goodbye.
But even as reptilian walls squeeze you into darkness,
your only ally keeps beating against the power of the song.

Painting by Pablo Amaringo: *Vision 46: Sepultura Tonduri,* from
Ayahuasca Visions. Collection of Steven F. White.

RIO NAPO

Dale Pendell

Give me words, my jaguar wife:
words of the forest, Napo, Rio Napo —
land of water, watered land.
Napo, Rio Napo, slipping through the fingers,
      quicksilver down a rain-soaked log.

I came for words, you gave me water,
the river wide and stretching,
      rushing, a waterfall around me
      washing my ears.
You gave me boa, giant boa —
      intestines hollow, ribs hanging
      like stalactites in a limestone cave.

I saw a forest intricate and spanning,
insect vectors stringing like lianas,
and everywhere the drip, the hanging roots,
the ants, and insect hum and trill.
Pheromones, alkaloids, perfume and fungus,
Napo, Rio Napo:
      I am a healer, but my own child is sick.

I saw a steel boot, spiked and jointed,
crushing the forest like truck tires over moss.
Napo, Rio Napo,
      land of the spirit vine.
      falling water, and a drum-like song.
Give me words, my jaguar wife.
      I am a healer, but my own child is sick.

I saw a cornfield, a open house high on poles,
a clean house, with kettles, one shotgun,
      and a firepit.
Give me words, their land is taken
by a lawyer from Quito,
      they had no papers.

      Papers? It is a very wet place.
      I got the land from my grandmother.
      Here is our Chagra, where we grow corn,
      here, our bananas and plantain. There we fish.
      These are our medicines. All
      of that land we return to forest,
      and that part, we never cut.

Give me words. What are papers?
This is our home and all we have.
Napo, Rio Napo
flood your banks, my jaguar wife,
your teeth are sharp, your eyes are red,
your hollow skull glows purple in the night.
      I am a healer, but my own child is sick.

      Jatún Sacha, Ecuador

BIBLIOGRAPHY

Abreu, Regina. "A doutrina do Santo Daime," in *Sinais dos tempos: Diversidade religiosa no Brasil,* ed. by Leilah Landim. Rio de Janeiro: ISER, 1990, pp. 253–263.

Agurell, S., Bo Holmstedt and Jan-Erik Lindgren. "Alkaloid Content of *Banisteriopsis rusbyana," American Journal of Pharmacy* 140 (1968): pp. 148–151.

Airaksinen, M. M. and I. Kari. "ß-carbolines, psychoactive compounds in the mammalian body," *Medical Biology* 59 (1981): pp. 21–34.

Allen, J. R. F. & B. Holmstedt. "The simple ß-carboline alkaloids," *Phytochemistry* 19 (1980):pp. 1573–1582.

Alegre, G. *Tashorintsi, tradición oral matsigenka.* Lima: Centro Amazónico de Antropología y Aplicación Práctica, 1979.

Andritzky, Walter. "Sociopsychotherapeutic Functions of Ayahuasca Healing in Amazonia," *Journal of Psychoactive Drugs* 21.1 (January-March, 1989): pp. 77–89.

___. "Ethnopsychologische Betrachtung des Heilrituals mit Ayahuasca *(Banisteriopsis caapi)* unter besonderer Berücksichtigung der Piros (Ostperu)," *Anthropos* 84 (1989): pp. 177–201.

Arévalo, Guillermo. "El ayahuasca y el curandero Shipibo-Conibo del Ucayali (Perú)," *América Indígena* 46.1 (1989): pp. 147–161.

Artaud, Antonin. *The Theater and Its Double,* trans. Mary C. Richards. New York: Grove Press, 1959.

Ayala Flores, Franklin and Walter H. Lewis. "Drinking the South American Hallucinogenic Ayahuasca," *Economic Botany* 32 (1978): pp. 154–156.

Baer, Gerhard. "Eine Ayahuasca-Sitzung unter den Piro (Ostperu)," *Bulletin de la Societé Suisse des Américanistes* 33 (1969): pp. 5–8.

___. *Die Religion Der Matsigenka. Ost-Peru. Monographie zu Kultur und Religion eines Indianervolkes des Oberen Amazonas.* Basel: Wepf & Co. A G Verlag, 1984.

___. *Cosmología y shamanismo de los matsiguenga: Perú Oriental.* Quito, Ecuador: Ediciones Abya-Yala, 1994.

Barbira Freedman, Françoise. *Ethnicity and Boundary Maintenance Among Peruvian Forest Quechua.* Ph.D. dissertation. University of Cambridge, 1979.

Barker, S. A. J. A. Monti, and S. T. Christian. "Metabolism of the hallucinogen N,N-dimethyltryptamine in rat brain homogenates," *Biochemical Pharmacology* 29 (1980): pp. 1049–1057

___. "N,N-dimethyltryptamine: An endogenous hallucinogen," *International Review of Neurobiology* 22 (1981): pp. 823–110.

Barreiro, José. *The Indian Chronicles.* Houston: Arte Público Press, 1993.

Barriales, Joaquín. *Matsigenka.* Madrid: Secretariado de Misiones Dominicanas, 1977.

Bellier, Irène. "Los Cantos de Yajé Mai Huna (Amazonía Peruana)," *América Indígena* 46.1 (1986): pp. 129–141.

Benjamin, Walter. *Understanding Brecht.* London: New Left Books, 1973.

Berger, P. L., and T. Luckmann. *The Social Construction of Reality.* New York: Anchor, 1966.

Bertrand-Rousseau, Pierrette. "De cómo los Shipibo y otras tribus aprendieron a hacer los dibujos (típicos) y a adornarse," *Amazonía Peruana* 5.9 (1983): pp. 79–85.

Bianchi, Antonio & Giorgio Samorini. "Plants in association with ayahuasca," *Jahrbuch für Ethnomedizin* (Yearbook of Ethnomedicine) 2 (1993): pp. 21–42.

Bidou, Patrice. "Le Travail du Chamane. Essai sur la personne du chamane dans une societé amazonienne, les Tatuyo du Pirá-paraná, Vaupés, Colombie," *L'Homme* 33.1 (1983): pp. 3–43.

___. "Le Chemin du Soleil. Mythologie de la création des Indiens Tatuyo du Pira-Paraná, Amazonie colombienne," *L'Homme* 25.1 (1985): pp. 83–103.

Bidou, Patrice and Michel Perrin. *Lenguaje y palabras chamanísticas.* Quito: Abya-Yala/MLAL, 1988.

Bonilla, Victor Daniel. *Siervos de Dios y amos de indios: el estado y la misión capuchina en el Putumayo.* Bogotá: Ediciones Tercer Mundo, 1968.

Bristol, Melvin Lee. *Sibundoy Ethnobotany.* Ph.D. dissertation. Harvard University. Cambridge, Massachusetts, 1965.

___. "The Psychotropic Banisteriopsis Among the Sibundoy of Colombia," *Botanical Museum Leaflets.* Harvard University. 21.5 (1966): pp. 113–140.

Brown, Diana. *Umbanda: Religion and Politics in Urban Brazil.* New York: Columbia University Press, 1994.

Brown, Michael F. "From the Heron's Bones: Three Aguaruna Hallucinogens and Their Uses," in *The Nature and Status of Ethnobotany,* ed. by Richard Ford. Anthropological Papers No. 67. (1978) Museum of Anthropology, University of Michigan, Ann Arbor, 1978, pp. 119–136.

___. *Tsewa's Gift: Magic and Meaning in an Amazonian Society.* Washington, D.C.: Smithsonian Institution Press, 1985.

___. "Ropes of Sand: Order and Imagery in Aguaruna Dreams," in *Dreaming: Anthropological and Psychological Interpretations,* ed. by Barbara Tedlock. Cambridge: Cambridge University Press, 1987, pp. 154–170.

Buckholtz, Neil S., & W. O. Boggan. "Effects of tetrahydro-ß-carbolines on monoamine oxidase and serotonin uptake in mouse brain," *Biochemical Pharmacology* 25 (1976): pp. 2319–2321.

___. "Monoamine oxidase inhibition in brain and liver produced by B-carbolines: structure-activity relationships and substrate specificity," *Biochemical Pharmacology* 26 (1977):pp. 1991–1996.

Burroughs, William S. and Allen Ginsberg. *The Yagé Letters.* San Francisco, California: City Lights Books, 1963.

Burga Freitas, Arturo. *Ayahuasca: mitos y leyendas del Amazonas y relatos.* Buenos Aires: Editorial Tor, 1939.

Calavia Sáez, Oscar. *O nome e o tempo dos Yaminawa: Etnologia e história dos Yaminawa do Alto Acre.* Ph.D. dissertation. FFLCH, Universidade de São Paulo, 1995.

Calvo, César. *Las tres mitades de Ino Moxo y otros brujos de la Amazonía.* Iquitos, Perú: Proceso Editores, 1981. English translation *The Three Halves of Ino Moxo: Teachings of the Wizard of the Upper Amazon* by Kenneth A. Symington. Rochester, Vermont: Inner Traditions International, 1995.

Callaway, Jace C. "A proposed mechanism for the visions of dream sleep," *Medical Hypotheses* 26 (1988): pp. 119–124.

Callaway, J.C., M.M. Airaksinen, D. J. McKenna, G. S. Brito, & C. S. Grob. "Platelet Serotonin Uptake Sites Increased in Drinkers of Ayahuasca," *Psychopharmacology* 116 (1994): pp. 385–387.

Callaway, Jace. C., L. P. Raymon, W. L. Hearn, D. J. McKenna, C. S. Grob, G. S. Brito, D. C. Mash. "Quantitation of N,N-dimethyltryptamine and harmala alkaloids in human plasma after oral dosing with Ayahuasca," *Journal of Analytical Toxicology* 20 (1996): pp. 492–497.

Callaway, J.C., D.J. McKenna, C.S. Grob, G.S. Brito, L.P. Raymon, R.E. Poland, E.N.Andrade, E.O. Andrade, D.C. Mash. "Pharmacology of Hoasca Alkaloids in Healthy Humans," *Journal of Analytical Toxicology,* 20 (1996): pp. 492–497.

Callaway, J.C., D.J. McKenna, C.S. Grob, G.S. Brito, L.P. Raymon, R.E. Poland, E.N.Andrade, E.O. Andrade, D.C. Mash. "Pharmacokinetics of Hoasca Alkaloids in Healthy Humans," *Journal of Ethnopharmacology* 65 (1999): pp. 243–256.

Cardona Cruz, Germán. *El yajé y otros cuentos.* Cali, Colombia: Luna Nueva, 1990.

Carneiro, Robert L. "The Amahuaca and the Spirit World," *Ethnology* 3.1 (1964): pp. 6–11.

___. "Hunting and Hunting Magic among the Amahuaca," *Ethnology* 9.4 (1970): p. 339.

___. "Chimera of the Upper Amazon," in *The Don Juan Papers: Further Castaneda Controversies,* ed. by Richard De Mille. Santa Barbara: Ross-Erikson Publishers, 1980, pp. 94–98.

Carr, D. "Minds in Museums and Libraries: the Cognitive Management of Cultural Institutions," *Teachers College Record* 93.1 (1991): pp. 6–27.

Castoldi, Alberto. *El texto drogado: dos siglos de droga y literatura.* Madrid: Anaya & Mario Muchnik, 1997.

Castro, Ignacio and Jorge Alemán. "Fin de un viaje," *Archipiélago* 28 (primavera 1997): pp. 67–72.

Centro Espírita Beneficente União Do Vegetal. *União do Vegetal—Hoasca. Fundamentos e Objetivos.* Brasília: Centro de Memória e Documentação, Sede Geral Brasília, 1989.

Chaumeil, Jean Pierre. *Voir, savoir, pouvoir. Le chamanisme chez les Yagua du Nord-Est péruvien.* Paris: Éditions de L'École des Hautes Études en Sciences Sociales, 1983.

___. "Réseau chamaniques contemporains et relations interethniques dans le haut Amazone (Pérou)," in *Otra América en Construcción. Medicinas Tradicionales. Religiones Populares,* ed. by Carlos Ernesto Pinzón and Rosa Suárez. Bogotá: Instituto Colombiano de Antropología, 1991, pp. 9–21.

Chernela, Janet M. "Death, Memory, and Language: New Approaches to History in Lowland South American Anthropology," *Latin American Research Review* 33.1 (1998): pp. 167–192.

Chevalier, Jacques M. *Civilization and the Stolen Gift: Capital, Kin, and Cult in Eastern Peru.* Toronto: University of Toronto Press, 1982.

Chiappe, Mario, Moisés Lemly, and Luis Millones. *Alucinógenos y shamanismo en el Perú contemporáneo.* Lima: Ediciones del Virrey, 1985.

Chumap Lucía, Aurelio and Manuel García-Rendueles. *"Duik múun..": universo mítico de los Aguaruna.* (Published in two separate volumes). Lima: Centro Amazónico de Antropología y Aplicación Práctica, 1979.

Cipoletti, M. S. *Aipe coca.* Quito: Abya-Yala, 1988.

Cipoletti, M. S. and E. J. Langdon, eds. *La muerte y el más allá en las culturas indígenas latinoamericanas.* Quito: Abya-Yala, 1992.

Colby, G. and C. Dennett. *Thy Will Be Done.* Chicago: Harper Collins, 1996.

Commissão Pro-Indio do Acre. *Shenipabu Miyui: História dos Antigos.* Rio Branco, Brasil, 1995.

Cooper, John M. "Estimulantes e narcóticos," in *Suma etnológica brasileira.* Vol. 1 (Etnobiologia), ed. by Berta G. Ribeiro. Petrópolis: Vozes, 1986. pp. 101–118

Couto, Fernando de la Rocque. *Santos e xamãs. Estudos do uso ritualizado da ayahuasca por caboclos da Amazônia, e, em particular, no que concerne sua utilização s ócio-terapêutica na doutrina do Santo Daime Dissertação de Mestrado.* Universidade de Brasília. Departamento de Antropologia (DAN). Programa de pós-graduação. 22.06.1989.

Crites, Stephen. "The Narrative Quality of Experience," *Journal of the American Academy of Religion* 39.3 (1971): pp. 291–311.

d'Ans, André Marcel. *La verdadera biblia de los Cashinahua: Mitos, leyendas y tradiciones de la selva peruana.* Lima: Mosca Azul, 1975.

Davis, Harold and Betty Elkins de Snell. *Kenkitsatagantsi matsigenka: cuentos folklóricos de los Machiguenga.* Yarinacocha, Perú: Instituto Lingüístico de Verano, 1976.

Davis, Wade. "Hallucinogenic Plants and Their Use in Traditional Societies," in *Applying Cultural Anthropology: An Introductory Reader,* ed. by Aaron Podolefsky and Peter J. Brown. Mountain View, California: Mayfield, 1994, pp. 226–229.

___. *One River: Explorations and Discoveries in the Amazon Rain Forest.* New York: Simon & Schuster, 1996.

Davis, Wade E. and James A. Yost. "The Ethnobotany of the Waorani of Eastern Ecuador," *Botanical Museum Leaflets.* Harvard University, 3 (1983).

De Corredor, Blanca and William Torres C. *Chamanismo: un arte del saber.* Bogotá: Anaconda, 1989.

De Friedemann, Nina S. and Jaime Arocha. *Herederos del jaguar y la anaconda.* Bogotá: Carlos Valencia, 1982.

Deleuze, Gilles. "Dos cuestiones sobre el uso de la droga," *Archipiélago* 28 (primavera 1997): pp. 73–83.

___. *Logique de la sensation I.* Paris: Editions de la Différence, 1981.

___. *Lógica del sentido.* Trans. Miguel Morey. Barcelona: Paidós, 1989.

Deleuze, Gilles and Felix Guattari. *Mil mesetas: capitalismo y esquizofrenia.* Trans. José Vázquez Pérez. Valencia: Pre-Textos, 1988.

Deltgen, Florian. "Culture, Drug, and Personality: a Preliminary Report about the Results of a Field Research Among the Yebasama Indians of Rio Piraparana in the Colombian Comisaría del Vaupés," *Ethnomedicine* (Hamburg) 5.1/2 (1978): pp 57–81.

Descola, Philippe. *La Nature Domestique. Symbolisme et Praxis dans l'Écologie des Achuar.* Paris: Éditions de la Maison des Sciences de l'Homme, 1986. English edition: *In the Society of Nature. A Native Ecology in Amazonia.* Cambridge: Cambridge University Press, 1996.

___. *The Spears of Twilight: Life and Death in the Amazon Jungle.* Trans. Janet Lloyd. New York: The New Press/HarperCollins, 1996.

Dobkin de Ríos, Marlene. *Visionary Vine: Hallucinogenic Healing in the Peruvian Amazon.* San Francisco: Sharp Publishing Co., 1972.

___. "Curing with ayahuasca in an urban slum," in *Hallucinogens and Shamanism,* ed. by Michael J. Harner. London: Oxford University Press, 1973.

___. *Hallucinogens: Cross-Cultural Perspectives.* Albuquerque: University of New Mexico Press, 1984.

___. "Drug Tourism in the Amazon," *Yearbook for Ethnomedicine and the Study of Consciousness* 3 (1994): pp. 307–314.

Dobkin de Ríos, Marlene and Michael Winkelman. "Shamanism and Altered States of Consciousness," *Journal of Psychoactive Drugs: A Multidisciplinary Forum* 21.1 (January-March 1989): pp. 1–7.

Domingo, Alfonso. *La madre de la voz en el oído.* Madrid: Editorial Fundamentos, 1991.

Don, N. S., McDonough, B. E., Moura, G., Warren, C. A., Kawanishi, K., Tomita, H., Tachibana, Y., Bohlke, M., & Farnsworth, N. R. "Effects of "Ayahuasca" on the human EEG," *Journal of Phytomedicine* 5.2 (1998): pp. 87–96.

Dwyer, Jane Powell. *The Cashinahua of Eastern Peru.* Providence, Rhode Island: Haffenreffer Museum of Anthropology (Brown University), 1975.

Ecorasa. *Ecorasa: autobiografía de un secoya.* Quito: Cicame, 1990.

Eliade, Mircea. *Shamanism: Archaic Techniques of Ecstasy.* Princeton: Princeton University Press, 1964.

Fericgla, Josep M. "Theory and Applications of Ayahuasca-Generated Imagery," *Eleusis* 5 (August 1996): pp. 3–18.

___. *Los jíbaros, cazadores de sueños.* Barcelona: Integral, 1994.

Fernandes Leite Da Luz, Pedro. *Estudo comparativo dos complexos ritual e simbólico associados ao uso da Banisteriopsis caapi e espécies congêneres em tribos de língua Pano, Arawak, Tukano e Maku do noroeste amazônico.* Masters dissertation. National Museum, Universidade Federal de Rio de Janeiro, 1996.

Fernandez, J.W. "*Tabernanthae iboga:* Narcotic ecstasis and the work of the ancestors," in *Flesh of the Gods: The Ritual Use of Hallucinogens,* ed. by Peter T. Furst. New York: Praeger, 1972. pp. 237–260.

Friedemann, Nina S. de and Jaime Arocha. *Herederos del jaguar y la anaconda.* Bogotá: Carlos Valencia, 1982.

Fróes, Vera. *Santo Daime. Cultura Amazônica. História do Povo Juramidam.* Manaus: Suframa, 1983.

Furst, Peter T. *Flesh of the Gods: The Ritual Use of Hallucinogens.* New York: Praeger, 1972.

___. *Hallucinogens and Culture.* Novato, California: Chandler & Sharp, 1976.

Furuya, Yoshiaki. "Umbandização dos Cultos Populares na Amazônia: A Integração ao Brasil?" in *Possessão e Procissão. Religiosidade Popular no Brasil,* ed. by Hirochika Nakamaki and Américo Pellegrini Filho. Osaka: National Museum of Ethnology, 1994.

Gandre, Hipoleto and Juan Echevarría. *Cool Tobacco, Sweet Coca.* London: Themis, 1996.

Gebhart Sayer, Angelika. *The Cosmos Encoiled Indian Art of the Peruvian Amazon.* New York: Center for Inter-American Relations, 1984.

___. "The Geometric Designs of the Shipibo-Conibo in Ritual Context," *Journal of Latin American Lore* 11.2 (1985): pp. 143–175.

___. "Una terapia estética. Los diseños visionarios del ayahuasca entre los Shipibo-Conibo," *América Indígena* 46.1 (1986): pp. 189–218.

___. *Die Spitze des Bewusstseins. Untersuchungen zu Weltbild und Kunst der Shipibo-Conibo.* Hohenschäftlarn: Klaus Renner Verlag, 1987.

Goldman, Irving. *The Cubeo: Indians of the Northwest Amazon.* Urbana: University of Illinois Press, 1963.

Gow, Peter. "River people: shamanism and history in Western Amazonia," in *Shamanism, History and the State,* ed. by N. Thomas and C. Humphrey. Ann Arbor: University of Michigan Press, 1994, pp. 90–113.

Grob, Charles S., D.J. McKenna, J.C.Callaway, G.S. Brito, E.S. Neves, G. Oberlender, O.L. Saide, E. Labigalini, C. Tacla, C.T. Miranda, R.J. Strassman, K.B. Boone. "Human Pharmacology of Hoasca, a Plant Hallucinogen Used in Ritual Context in Brazil," *Journal of Nervous & Mental Disorder* 184 (1996): pp. 86–94.

Groisman, Alberto. "Muerte y renacimiento: concepciones acerca de la espiritualidad de la muerte en la doctrina del Santo Daime," in *La muerte y el más allá en las culturas indígenas latinoamericanas,* ed. by M. S. Cipoletti and E. J. Langdon. Quito: Abya-Yala/MLAL, 1992. pp. 91–111.

___. *"Eu Venho da Floresta": Un estudo sobre o contexto simbólico do uso do Santo Daime.* Florianópolis: Editora da UFSC, 1991.

___. "Messias, Milênio e Salvação: Motivação e engajamento na Doutrina do Santo Daime," in *Religiosidad y Resistencia Indígenas: Hacia el Fin del Milenio,* ed. by Alicia Barabas. Quito: Ediciones Abya-Yala, 1994.

Groisman, Alberto & Ari B. Sell. "Healing power: cultural-neurophenomenological therapy of Santo Daime," *Yearbook Cross-Cultural Medicine* 6 (1995): pp. 241–255.

Halifax, Joan. *Shaman: The Wounded Healer.* New York: Crossroad, 1982.

Harner, Michael J. *The Jívaro.* New York: Doubleday, 1972.

___. "The Sound of Rushing Water," in *Hallucinogens and Shamanism,* ed. by Michael J. Harner. New York: Oxford University Press, 1973. pp. 15–27

___. *The Way of the Shaman.* New York: Bantam, 1982.

Hashimoto, Y. & K. Kawanishi. "New organic bases from Amazonian *Banisteriopsis caapi.*" Phytochemistry 14 (1975): pp. 1633–1635.

Henman, Anthony Richard. "Uso del Ayahuasca en un contexto autoritario: el caso de la União do Vegetal en Brasil," *América Indígena* 46.1 (1986): pp. 219–234.

Hofmann, Albert. "Natural Science and the Mystical World View," in *Entheogens and the Future of Religion,* ed. by Robert Forte. San Francisco: Council on Spiritual Practices, 1997, pp. 48–55.

Hugh-Jones, Christine. *From the Milk River: Spatial and Temporal Processes in Northwest Amazonia.* Cambridge: Cambridge University Press, 1979.

Hugh-Jones, Stephen. *The Palm and the Pleiades: Initiation and Cosmology in Northwest Amazonia.* Cambridge: Cambridge University Press, 1979.

Illius, Bruno. *Ani Shinan: Schamanismus bei den Shipibo-Conibo (Ost-Peru).* Tübingen: Verlag S & F, 1987.

Jackson, Jean E. *The Fish People: Linguistic Exogamy and Tukanoan Identity in Northwest Amazonia.* Cambridge: Cambridge University Press, 1983.

Juncosa, José E. *Tsachila: los clásicos de la etnografía sobre los Colorados,* (1905–1950). Quito: Abya-Yala, 1988.

Kapferer, Bruce. *A Celebration of Demons: Exorcism and the Aesthetics of Healing in Sri Lanka.* Bloomington: Indiana University Press, 1983.

Karsten, Rafael. *Blood Revenge, War, and Victory Feasts Among the Jibaro Indians of Eastern Ecuador.* Smithsonian Institution. Bureau of American Ethnology. Bulletin 79. Washington: Government Printing Office, 1923.

___. *The Civilization of the South-American Indians. With Special Reference to Magic and Religion.* London: Kegan Paul, 1926.

___. *The Head-Hunters of Western Amazonas.* Helsinki: Societas Scientiarum Fennica. Commentationes Humanarum Litterarum VII. 1. 1935.

___. *Studies in the Religion of the South-American Indians East of the Andes.* Edited by Arne Runenberg & Michael Webster. Helsinki: Societas Scientiarum Fennica. Commentationes Humanarum Litterarum XXIX. 1.1964.

Katz, Fred and Marlene Dobkin de Ríos. "Hallucinogenic Music: An Analysis of the Role of Whistling in Peruvian Ayahuasca Healing Sessions," *Journal of American Folklore* 84 (1971): pp. 320–327.

Kensinger, Kenneth M. "Banisteriopsis Usage Among the Peruvian Cashinahua," in *Hallucinogens and Shamanism,* ed. by Michael J. Harner. Oxford: Oxford University Press, 1973.

___. "Studying the Cashinahua," in *The Cashinahua of Eastern Peru.* ed. by Jane Powell Dwyer. Providence: Haffenreffer Museum of Anthropology (Brown University), 1975. pp. 9–86.

Labate, Beatriz Caiuby & Sena Araújo, Wladimyr, eds. *O Uso Ritual da Ayahuasca.* Campinas: Editora Mercado de Letras, 2000.

Lagarriga, Isabel, Jacques Galinier and Michel Perrin, eds. *Chamanismo en Latinoamérica.* México: Plaza y Valdés, 1995.

Lamb, F. Bruce. *Wizard of the Upper Amazon: The Story of Manuel Córdova-Ríos.* Boston: Houghton Mifflin, 1974. rpt. Berkeley: North Atlantic Books, 1990.

___. *Río Tigre and Beyond: The Amazon Jungle Medicine of Manuel Córdova-Ríos.* Berkeley: North Atlantic Books, 1985.

Langdon, E. Jean. "Yagé among the Siona: Cultural Patterns in Visions," in *Spirits, Shamans and Stars,* ed. by David Brownman and Ronald A. Schwartz. The Hague: Mouton, 1979.

___. "The Siona Hallucinogenic Ritual: Its Meaning and Power," in *Understanding Religion and Culture: Anthropological and Theological Perspectives,* ed. by John H. Morgan. Washington, D.C.: University Press of America, 1979.

___. "A Cultura Siona e a Experiência Alucinogênica," in *Arte Gráfica Indígena,* ed. by Lux Vidal. São Paulo: Editor Nobel, 1992.

___. "Dau: Shamanic Power in Siona Religion and Medicine," in *Portals of Power: South American Shamanism,* ed. by E. Jean Matteson Langdon and Gerhard Baer. New Mexico: University of New Mexico Press, 1992.

Langdon, E. Jean Matteson and Gerhard Baer, eds. *Portals of Power: Shamanism in South America.* Albuquerque: University of New Mexico Press, 1992.

Lewin, Louis. Banisteria *Caapi, ein neues Rauschgift und Heilmittel.* Berlin: Verlag von George Stilke, 1929.

___. *Phantastica.* Linden: Volksverlag, 1980. Reprint from 1929.

Liwszyc, G.E., Vuori, E., Räsänen, I., Issakainen, J. "Daime— a ritual herbal potion," *Journal of Ethnopharmacology* 36 (1992): pp. 91–92.

Luna, Luis Eduardo. "The Concept of Plants as Teacher Among Four Mestizo Shamans of Iquitos, Northeast Peru," *Journal of Ethnopharmacology* 11 (1984): pp. 135–156.

___. "The healing practices of a Peruvian shaman," *Journal of Ethnopharmacology* 11 (1984):pp. 123–133.

___. *Vegetalismo: Shamanism among the Mestizo Population of the Peruvian Amazon.* (Acta Universitatis Stockholmensis, Stockholm Studies in Comparative Religion No. 27). Stockholm: Almquist and Wiksell International, 1986.

___. "Bibliografía sobre el ayahuasca," *América Indígena* 46.1 (1986): pp. 235–245.

___. "Icaros: Magic Melodies among the Mestizo Shamans of the Peruvian Amazon," in *Portals of Power: Shamanism in South America,* ed. by E. Jean Matteson Langdon and Gerhard Baer. Albuquerque: University of New Mexico Press, 1992, pp. 231–253.

___. *A Barquinha.* Una Nueva Religión en Río Branco, Amazonía Brasileña. *Acta Americana* 3:2:137–151. Stockholm, 1995.

___. "Schamanismus in Amazonien, Ayahuasca, Anthropomorphismus und die natürliche Welt," in *Schamanische Wissenschaften. Ökologie, Naturwissenschaft und Kunst,* ed. by Franz-Theo Gottwald and Christian Rätsch. Munich: Eugen Diederichs Verlag, 1998, pp. 187–204.

___. "Die schamanische Kraft der Pflanzen: Pflanzen als Lehrer am Amazonas," in *Shamanen, zwischen Mythos und Moderne,* ed. by Alexandra Rosenbohm. Leipzig: Militzke Verlag, 1999, pp. 82–89.

Luna, Luis Eduardo and Pablo Amaringo. *Ayahuasca Visions: The Religious Iconography of a Peruvian Shaman.* Berkeley: North Atlantic Books, 1991.

Mabit, Jacques. "Ayahuasca Hallucinations Among Healers in the Peruvian Amazon." *Document de Travail.* Lima: Instituto Francés de Estudios Andinos, 1988.

Mabit, Jacques, R. Giove & J. Vega. "Takiwasi: the use of Amazonian shamanism to rehabilitate drug addicts," *Yearbook Cross-Cultural Medicine* 6 (1995): pp. 257–285.

MacRae, Edward. *Guiado pela lua: xamanismo e uso ritual da ayahuasca no culto do Santo Daime.* São Paulo: Brasiliense, 1992.

___. "A importância dos fatores socioculturais na determinação da política oficial sobre o uso ritual da ayahuasca," in *Drogas e cidadania,* ed. by Cassio de A. Leite. São Paulo: Brasiliense, 1994. pp. 31–45.

Matthiessen, Peter. *At Play in the Fields of the Lord.* New York: Random House, 1965.

McDowell, John Holmes. *Sayings of the Ancestors: the Spiritual Life of the Sibundoy Indians.* Lexington: The University Press of Kentucky, 1989.

___. *So Wise Were Our Elders: Mythic Narratives of the Kamsá.* Lexington: The University Press of Kentucky, 1994.

McKenna, Dennis and N. Towers. "On the Comparative Ethnopharmacology of Malpighiaceous and Myristicaceous Hallucinogens," *Journal of Psychoactive Drugs* 17.1 (1985): pp. 35–39.

McKenna, Dennis J., G. H. Neils Towers, and F. Abbott. "Monoamine Oxidase Inhibitors in South American Hallucinogenic Plants: Tryptamine and Beta-Carboline Constituents of Ayahuasca," *Journal of Ethnopharmacology* (1984): pp. 10195–10223.

McKenna, Dennis J., Luis Eduardo Luna and G. H. Neils Towers. "Ingredientes biodinámicos en las plantas que se mezclan al ayahuasca: una farmacopea tradicional no investigada," *América Indígena* 46.1 (1986): pp. 73–99.

McKenna, Dennis, Luis Eduardo Luna, and G. H. Neils Towers. "Biodynamic constituents in ayahuasca admixture plants." In *Ethnobotany—The Evolution of a Discipline,* ed. by Richard Evans Schultes and Siri von Reis. Portland, Oregon: Timber Press. 1995, pp. 349–361.

McKenna, Dennis, C.S. Grob, and J.C. Callaway. "The scientific investigation of Ayahuasca: a review of past and current research," *Heffter Review of Psychedelic research* 1 (1998): pp. 65–77.

McKenna, Terence. *The Archaic Revival: Speculations on Psychedelic Mushrooms, the Amazon, Virtual Reality, UFOs, Evolution, Shamanism, the Rebirth of the Goddess and the End of History.* San Francisco: Harper, 1992.

___. *True Hallucinations.* San Francisco: HarperSan Francisco, 1993.

McKenna, Terence and McKenna, Dennis. *The Invisible Landscape: Mind, Hallucinogens and the I Ching.* New York: The Seabury Press, 1975.

Melo, Alfredo Gregório de. *O cruzeirinho (Hinário).* Rio de Janeiro: Editora Beija-Flor (Centro Eclético de Fluente Luz Universal Raimundo Irineu Serra), 1992.

Merwin, W. S. *Travels.* New York: Knopf, 1994.

Metzner, Ralph, ed. *Ayahuasca: Hallucinogens, Consciousness, and the Spirit of Nature.* New York: Thunder's Mouth Press, 1999.

Meyer, Bernhard H. *Beiträge zur Ethnographie der Conibo und Shipibo (Ostperu)*. Ph.D. dissertation, 1974, University of Zurich, Switzerland.

Michael, Ib. *Rejsen tilbage*. Copenhagen: Gyldendals, 1977.

Michaux, Henri. "Volver en sí: conciencia asolada de sí," *Archipiélago* 28 (primavera 1997): pp. 14–18.

Milanez, Wánia. *Oaska. O Evangelho da Rosa*. Campinas: Sama Editora, 1993.

Monod, Jean. "Os Piaroa e o invisível," in *Os alucinógenos e o mundo simbólico: O uso dos alucinógenos entre os índios da América do Sul*. ed. by Vera Penteado Coelho. São Paulo: Editora Pedagógica e Universitária/EDUSP, 1976. pp. 7–27.

Monteiro da Silva, Clodomir. "La cuestión de la realidad en la Amazonía: Un análisis a partir del estudio de la doctrina del Santo Daime," *Amazonía Peruana* 6.11 (1985): pp. 87–106.

___. *O Palacio de Juramidan. Santo Daime: um ritual de transcendencia e despoluição*. Dissertação de mestrado. Recife, Pernambuco. Março 1983.

___. "La Cuestión de la Realidad en la Amazonía: Un Análisis a Partir del Estudio de la Doctrina del Santo Daime," *Amazonía Peruana* 6.11 (1985): pp. 87–106.

Moore, Sally Falk and Barbara Myerhoff, eds. *Secular Ritual*. Amsterdam: Van Gorcum, Assen, 1977.

Morton, C.V. "Notes on yagé, a drug plant of southeastern Colombia," *Journal of the Washington Academy of Science* 21 (1930): p. 485.

Mota de Melo, Sebastião. *O Justiceiro (Hinário)*. Rio de Janeiro: Editora Beija-Flor (Centro Eclético da Fluente Luz Universal Sebastião Mota de Melo), 1992.

Nakamaki, Hiochika. "Quem Não Toma o Chá Não Tem Alucinações: Epidemiologia de Religiões Alucinógenas no Brasil," in *Possessão e Procissão. Religiosidade Popular no Brasil*, ed. by Hirochika Nakamaki and Américo Pellegrini Filho. Osaka: National Museum of Ethnology, 1994.

Naranjo, Claudio. *The Healing Journey: New Approaches to Consciousness*. New York: Pantheon, 1973.

___. "Ayahuasca Imagery and the Therapeutic Property of the Harmala Alkaloids," *Journal of Mental Imagery* 11.2 (1987): pp. 131–136.

Naranjo, Plutarco. *Ayahuasca: religión y medicina*. Quito: Editorial Universitaria, 1970.

___. *Ayahuasca: etnomedicina y mitología*. Quito: Libri Mundi, 1983.

Narby, Jeremy. *Le Serpent Cosmique: l'ADN et les origines du savoir*. Paris: Terra Magna, 1995. English translation by the author with Jon Christensen. *The Cosmic Serpent: DNA and the Origins of Knowledge*. New York: Tarcher/Putnam, 1998.

Niño, Hugo. *Primitivos relatos contados otra vez: héroes y mitos amazónicos*. Bogotá: Editorial Andes/Instituto Colombiano de Cultura, 1977.

Ocaña, Enrique. *El Dioniso moderno y la farmacia utópica*. Barcelona: Anagrama, 1993.

___. "Topografía del mal viaje: Prolegómenos a una crítica de la conciencia psiquedélica," *Archipiélago* 28 (primavera 1997): pp. 77–83.

Ott, Jonathan. *Ayahuasca Analogues: Pangaean Entheogens*. Kennewick, Washington: Natural Products Co., 1994.

___. "Ayahuasca and ayahuasca analogues: pangaen entheogens for the new millennium," *Jahrbuch für Ethnomedizin* (Yearbook of Ethnomedicine) 3 (1994): pp. 285–293.

___. "Ayahuasca: Ethnobotany, Phytochemistry and Human Pharmacology," *Integration* 5 (1995): pp. 73–97.

___. *Pharmacotheon: Entheogenic Drugs, Their Plant Sources and History*. Kennewick, Washington: Natural Products Co., 1996.

Payaguaje, Fernando. *El bebedor de yajé*. Shushufindi—Río Aguarico, Ecuador: Vicariato Apostólico de Aguarico, 1990.

Peláez, María Cristina. *No Mundo se Cura Tudo: Interpretações sobre a "Cura Espiritual" no Santo Daime*. Dissertação de Mestrado apresentada no PPGAS-UFSC, Florianópolis, 1994.

Pendell, Dale. *Pharmako/Poeia: Plant Powers, Poisons, and Herbcraft*. San Francisco: Mercury House, 1995.

Perlongher, Néstor. *Aguas aéreas*. Buenos Aires: Ultimo Reino, 1991.

___. "O desaparecimento da homosexualidade," *SaudeLoucura* (São Paulo, HUCITEC/USP) 3 (1991): pp. 39–45.

___. "Droga e êxtase," *SaudeLoucura* (São Paulo, HUCITEC/USP) 3 (1991): pp. 77–90.

___. *Poemas completos (1980–1992)*. Buenos Aires: Seix Barral, 1997.

Pike, Kenneth. *Language in Relation to a Unified Theory of the Structure of Human Behavior*. Vol. 1. Glendale, Calif.: Summer Institute of Linguistics, 1954.

Polari de Alverga, Alex. *Inventário de cicatrizes*. Rio de Janeiro: Comitê Brasileiro pela Anistia / Teatro Ruth Escobar, 1978.

___. *Camarim de Prisioneiro*. São Paulo: Global, 1980.

___. *O livro das mirações: viagem ao Santo Daime*. Rio de Janeiro: Rocco, 1984.

___. *O guia da floresta*. Rio de Janeiro: Record, 1992.

___. *Forest of Visions: Ayahuasca, Amazonian Spirituality, and the Santo Daime Tradition*. Rochester, Vermont: Inner Traditions, 1999.

Prance, Ghillean T. "Notes on the Use of Plant Hallucinogens in Amazonian Brazil," *Economic Botany* 14 (1970): p. 37.

Ramírez De Jara, María Clemencia & Pinzón, Carlos Ernesto. "Los Hijos del Bejuco Solar y la Campana Celeste. El Yajé en la Cultura Popular Urbana," *América Indígena* 46.1 (1986): pp. 163–188.

Ramos, Alcida Rita. *Memórias Sanumá: espaço e tempo em uma sociedade yanomami*. São Paulo: Marco Zero, 1990.

Rätsch, Christian. *Enzyklopädie der psychoaktiven Pflanzen*. Aarau, Switzerland: AT Verlag, 1998.

Reichel-Dolmatoff, Gerardo. "Notas etnográficas sobre los indios del Chocó," *Revista Colombiana de Antropología,* 9 (1960), pp 75–158.

___. "El Contexto Cultural de un Alucinógeno Aborigen: Banisteriopsis Caapi," *Revista de la Academia Colombiana de Ciencias Exactas, Físicas y Naturales.* 13.51 (diciembre 1969).

___. "Notes on the cultural extent of the use of yagé (Banisteriopsis caapi) among the Indians of Vaupés, Colombia," *Economic Botany* 24 .1 (1970): pp. 32–34.

___. *Amazonian Cosmos: The Sexual and Religious Symbolism of the Tukano Indians.* Chicago: University of Chicago Press, 1971.

___. "The Cultural Context of an Aboriginal Hallucinogen: Banisteriopsis caapi," in *Flesh of the Gods: The Ritual Use of Hallucinogens,* ed. by Peter T. Furst. New York: Praeger Publishers, 1972. pp. 84–113.

___. *The Shaman and the Jaguar: A Study of Narcotic Drugs among the Indians of Colombia.* Philadelphia: Temple University Press, 1975.

___. *Beyond the Milky Way: Hallucinatory Imagery of the Tukano Indians.* (Latin American Center Publications, UCLA Latin American Studies vol. 42). Los Angeles: University of California Press, 1978.

___. *Yurupari: Studies of an Amazonian Foundation Myth.* Cambridge, Massachusetts: Harvard University Press, 1996.

___. *Desana Texts and Contexts.* Wien-Föhrenau: Engelbert Stiglmayr, editor. Acta Ethnologica et Linguistica Nr. 62, 1989.

Renard-Casevitz, France Marie. "Fragmento de una lección de Daniel, shamán matsiguenga," *Amazonía Indígena* (México) 4.8 (1984): pp. 4–6.

___. *Le banquet masque: une mythologie de l'etranger chez les indiens Matsiguenga.* Paris: Lierre & Coudrier, 1991.

Rivier, L. & J. Lindgren. "Ayahuasca, the South American hallucinogenic drink: Ethnobotanical and chemical investigations," *Economic Botany* 29 (1972): pp. 101–129.

Robinson, S. *Hacia una comprensión del chamanismo Kofan.* Quito: Editorial Abya-Yala, 1966.

Roe, Peter G. "Marginal Men: Male Artists among the Shipibo Indians of Peru," *Anthropologica* 21 (1979): pp. 189–221.

___. "Art and Residence among the Shipibo Indians: A Study in Microacculturation," *American Anthropologist* 82 (1980): pp. 42–71.

___. *The Cosmic Zygote: Cosmology in the Amazon Basin.* New Brunswick, New Jersey: Rutgers University Press, 1982.

___. "Ethnoaesthetics and Design Grammars: Shipibo Perceptions of Cognate Styles." Paper presented at the 31st Annual Meeting of the American Anthropological Association, Washington, D.C., 1982(b).

___. "Mythic Substitution and the Stars: Aspects of Shipibo and Quechua Ethnoastronomy Compared." Paper presented at the First International Conference on Ethnoastronomy. Smithsonian Institution, Washington, D.C., 1983.

Rothenberg, Jerome. *Technicians of the Sacred.* Berkeley: University of California Press, 1985.

Sánchez-Parga, José. *Textos textiles en la tradición cultural andina.* Quito: Instituto Andino de Artes Populares del Convenio Andrés Bello (IADAP), 1995.

Schultes, Richard Evans. "The identity of the Malpighiaceous narcotics of South America. *Harvard Botanical Museum Leaflets* 18 (1957):pp. 1–56.

___. "Ethnotoxicological significance of additives to New World hallucinogens," *Plant Science Bulletin* 18 (1972): pp. 34–41

___. *Where the Gods Reign: Plants and Peoples of the Colombian Amazon.* Oracle, Arizona: Synergetic Press, 1988.

___. "Richard Spruce, the Man," in *Richard Spruce (1817–1893): Botanist and Explorer.* ed. by M. R. D. Seaward and S. M. D. Fitzgerald. London: The Royal Botanic Gardens, Kew, 1996, pp. 16–25.

Schultes, Richard Evans and Albert Hofmann. *The Botany and Chemistry of Hallucinogens.* Spring, Illinois: Charles C. Thomas, Publishers, 1980.

___. *Plants of the Gods: Origins of Hallucinogenic Use.* New York: McGraw-Hill, 1979. rpt. Rochester, Vermont: Healing Arts Press, 1992.

Schultes, Richard Evans and Robert F. Raffauf. *Vine of the Soul: Medicine Men, Their Plants and Rituals in the Colombian Amazon.* Oracle, Arizona: Synergetic Press, 1992.

Schwartz, Marcy. "Is There an Aesthetic in This Hybrid? Literary Absences in García Canclini's Globalization of Culture," Paper presented at the 1997 Modern Language Association Convention, Toronto, Canada.

Seaward, M. R. D. and S. M. D. Fitzgerald, eds. *Richard Spruce (1817–1893): Botanist and Explorer.* London: The Royal Botanic Gardens, Kew, 1996.

Sena Araujo, Wladimyr. *Navegando Sobre as Ondas do Daime: História, Cosmologia e Ritual da Barquinha.* Campinas: Editora da Unicamp, 1999.

Serra, Raimundo Irineu. *O Cruzeiro (Hinário).* Rio de Janeiro: Editora Beija-Flor (Centro Eclético de Fluente Luz Universal Sebastião Mota de Melo), 1991.

Siskind, Janet. *To Hunt in the Morning.* New York: Oxford University Press, 1973.

Soares, Luiz Eduardo. "O Santo Daime no contexto da nova consciência religiosa," in *Sinais dos tempos: Diversidade religiosa no Brasil,* ed. by Leilah Landim. Rio de Janeiro: ISER, 1990, pp. 265–274.

Spruce, Richard. "On Some Remarkable Narcotics of the Amazon Valley and Orinoco. Ocean Highways," *The Geographical Review* 55.1 (1873): pp. 184–193.

Steiner, George. *After Babel: Aspects of Language and Translation.* London: Oxford University Press, 1975.

Strassman, R. J. & C. R. Qualls. "Dose-response study of N,N-dimethyltryptamine in humans I: Neuroendocrine, autonomic, and cardiovascular effects," *Arch. Gen. Psychiatry* 51 (1994):pp. 85–97.

Strassman, R.J., C.R. Qualls, E.H. Uhlenhuth, & R. Kellner. "Dose-response study of N, N-dimethyltryptamine in humans II. Subjective effects and preliminary results of a new rating scale," *Arch. Gen. Psychiatry* 51 (1994): 98–108.

Szara, S. "Dimethyltryptamine: its metabolism in man; the relation of its psychotic effect to the serotonin metabolism," *Experientia* 12 (1956): pp. 411–441.

Tastevin, Constantin. "Le Haut Tarauac," *La Geographie* 45 (1926): pp.158–175.

Taussig, Michael. *Shamanism, Colonialism, and the Wild Man: A Study in Terror and Healing.* Chicago: University of Chicago Press, 1987.

Taylor, D. "The making of the hallucinogenic drink from *Banisteriopsis caapi* in northern Peru," In *Ethnopharmacological Search for Psychoactive Drugs,* ed. by D.H. Efron, B. Holmstedt, and N.S. Kline. U.S. Public Health Service Publication No. 1645. Washington, D.S., 1967.

Tedlock, Dennis, ed. and trans. *Popol Vuh.* New York: Simon & Schuster, 1985.

Torres C., William. *Yagé: Nomadismo del pensamiento.* Unpublished manuscript.

Townsley, Graham. "Song Paths: The Ways and Means of Yaminahua Shamanic Knowledge," *L'Homme* 33. 126–128 (1993): pp. 449–468.

Turner, Victor and Edith Turner. *Image and Pilgrimage in Christian Culture: Anthropological Perspectives.* New York: Columbia University Press, 1978.

Vargas Llosa, Mario. *El hablador.* Barcelona: Seix Barral, 1987. English translation *The Storyteller* by Helen Lane. New York: Farrar, Straus & Giroux, 1989.

Vickers, William T. "The Jesuits and the SIL: External Policies for Ecuador's Tucanoans through Three Centuries," in *Is God an American?: An Anthropological Perspective on the Missionary Work of the Summer Institute of Linguistics.* ed. by Soren Hvakof and Peter Aaby. Copenhagen: IWGIA, 1981, pp. 51–61.

___. *Los sionas y secoyas, su adaptación al ambiente amazónico.* Quito: Abya-Yala, 1989.

Villafranca-Saravia, Mario. "Ayahuasca, o lo que hay al final," in *Narradores de Junín,* ed. by Isabel Córdova Rosas. Huancayo, Perú: Departamento de Publicaciones de la UNCP, 1979, pp. 53–59.

Villavicencio, M. *Geografía de la República del Ecuador.* New York: Craighead, 1858.

Weil, Andrew T. *The Marriage of the Sun and Moon: A Quest for Unity in Consciousness.* Houghton-Mifflin, Boston, 1980.

Wheeler, Alvaro. *Ganteya bain: el pueblo siona del río Putumayo, Colombia.* Bogotá: Instituto Lingüístico de Verano, 1987.

Whitten, Norman E. *Sacha Runa: Ethnicity and Adaptation of Ecuadorian Jungle Quichua.* Urbana: University of Illinois Press, 1976.

___. *Sicuanga Runa: The Other Side of Development in Amazonian Ecuador.* Urbana and Chicago: University of Illinois Press, 1985.

___. *Sacha Runa: etnicidad y adaptación de los Quichua hablantes de la Amazonía ecuatoriana.* Quito: Abya-Yala, 1987.

Wilbert, Johannes. "Tobacco and Shamanistic Ecstasy among the Warao Indians of Venezuela," in *Flesh of the Gods: The Ritual Use of Hallucinogens,* ed. by Peter T. Furst. New York: Praeger, 1972, pp. 55–83.

___. "Eschatology in a Participatory Universe: Destinies of the Soul among the Warao Indians of Venezuela," in *Death and the Afterlife in Pre-Columbian America,* ed. by Elizabeth P. Benson. Washington, D. C.: Dumbarton Oaks Research Library and Collections, 1975, pp. 163–189.

___. "To Become a Maker of Canoes: An Essay in Warao *Enculturation,*" in *Enculturation in Latin America: An Anthology,* ed. by Johannes Wilbert. Los Angeles: UCLA Latin American Center, University of California, 1976.

Williams, Raymond. *Politics and Letters: Interviews with New Left Review.* London: New Left Books.

___. *Modern Tragedy.* Stanford: Stanford University Press, 1966

Winkelman, Michael. "Psychointegrator Plants: Their Roles in Human Culture, Consciousness and Health," *Yearbook of Cross-Cultural Medicine and Psychotherapy* (Berlin) (1995): pp. 9–53.

Wittgenstein, Ludwig. "Remarks on Frazer's Golden Bough," translated by A.C..Miles and Rush Rhees. *Human World* 3 (May, 1971): pp. 28–41.

Wolfes, O. & K. Rumpf. "Über die Gewinnung von Harmin aus einer südamerikanische Liane," *Archive für Pharmakologie* 266 (1928), pp. 188ff.

Wordsworth, William. *The Prelude: 1799, 1805, 1850.* Ed. Jonathan Wordsworth. New York: Norton, 1979.

APPENDIX
Selected Works in Their Original Languages

Hinos De Raimundo Irineu Serra

Estrela D´Água

Vou chamar a estrela d'água
Para vir me iluminar
Para vir me iluminar
Para vir me iluminar

Dai-me força e dai-me amor
Dai-me força e dai-me amor

Dá licença eu entrar
Dá licença eu entrar
Nas profundezas do mar
Nas profundezas do mar

Foi Meu Pai quem me mandou
Foi Meu Pai quem me mandou
Conhecer todos primores
Conhecer todos primores

Dai-me força e dai-me amor
Dai-me força e dai-me amor

A Minha mãe que me ensinou
A Minha Mãe que me ensinou
Conhecer todos primores
Conhecer todos primores
Com amor no coração
Para cantar com os meus irmãos
Para cantar com os meus irmãos
Para cantar com os meus irmãos

A Terra Aonde Estou

A terra aonde estou
Ninguém acreditou
Dai-me amor, dai-me amor
Dai-me o pão do Criador

A Minha Mãe que me ensinou
Quem me deu todo primor
Dai-me amor, dai-me amor
Dai-me o pão do Criador
A riqueza todos tem
Mas ninguém quer acreditar
Dai-me amor, dai-me amor
Livrai-me de todo mal

Eu Balanço

Eu balanço, eu balanço
Eu balanço tudo enquanto há

Eu chamo o sol

Chamo a lua
E chamo estrela
Para todos vir me acompanhar

Eu balanço, eu balanço
Eu balanço tudo enquanto há

Eu chamo o vento
Chamo a terra
E chamo o mar
Para todos vir me acompanhar

Eu balanço, eu balanço
Eu balanço tudo enquanto há

Chamo o cipó
Chamo a folha
E chamo a água
Para unir e vir me amostrar

Eu balanço, eu balanço
Eu balanço tudo enquanto há

Tenho prazer
Tenho força
E tenho tudo
Porque Deus Eterno é quem me dá

Passarinho

Passarinho está cantando
Discorrendo o A.B.C.
E eu discorro a tua vida
Para todo mundo ver
Passarinho está cantando
Canta na mata deserta
Dizendo para o caçador
Você atira e não acerta

Passarinho verde canta
Bem pertinho para tu ver
Sou Passarinho e tenho dono
E o meu dono tem poder

Passarinho verde canta
Com alegria e com amor
Sou Passarinho e canto certo
E com certeza aqui estou

As Estrelas

As estrelas já chegaram
Para dizer o nome seu
Sou eu, sou eu, sou eu
Sou eu um filho de Deus

As estrelas me levaram
Para correr o mundo inteiro
Para eu conhecer esta verdade
Para poder ser verdadeiro

Eu subi serra de espinhos
Pisando em pontas agudas
As estrelas me disseram
No mundo se cura tudo

As estrelas me disseram
Ouve muito e fala pouco
Para eu poder compreender
E conversar com meus caboclos

Os caboclos já chegaram
De braços nus e pés no chão
Eles trazem remédios bons
Para curar os cristãos

Jardineiro

Minha Mãe, minha Rainha
Foi Ela quem me entregou
Para mim ser jardineiro
No Jardim de Belas Flores

No Jardim de Belas Flores
Tem tudo que eu procurar
Tem primor e tem beleza
Tem tudo que Deus me dá

Todo mundo recebe
As flores que vem de lá
Mas ninguém presta atenção
Ninguém sabe aproveitar

Para zelar este jardim
Precisa muita atenção
Que as flores são muito finas
Não podem cair no chão

O Jardim de Belas Flores
Precisa sempre aguar
Com as preces e os carinhos
Do Nosso Pai Universal

Ia Guiado Pela Lua

Ia guiado pela lua
E as estrelas de uma banda
Quando eu cheguei em cima de um monte
Eu escutei um grande estrondo

Esse estrondo que eu ouvi
Foi Deus do Céu foi quem ralhou
Dizendo para todos nós
Que tem Poder Superior

Eu estava passeando
Na praia do mar
Escutei uma voz
Mandaram me buscar

Aí eu botei os olhos
Aí vem uma canoa
Feita de ouro e prata
E uma Senhora na proa

Quando Ela chegou
Mandou eu embarcar
Ela disse para min:
-Nós vamos viajar

-Nós vamos viajar
Para um ponto destinado
Deus e Virgem Mãe
Quem vai ao nosso lado

Quando nós chegamos
Nas campinas desta flor
Esta é a riqueza
Do Nosso Pai Criador

Sou Filho Desta Verdade

Sou filho desta verdade
E neste mundo estou aqui
Dou conselho e dou conselho
Para aqueles que me ouvir

O saber de todo mundo
É um saber universal
Aqui tem muita ciência
Que é preciso estudar

Estudo fino, estudo fino
Que é preciso conhecer
Para ser bom professor
Apresentar o seu saber

Encostado A Minha Mãe

Encostado a Minha Mãe
E Meu Papai lá no astral
Para sempre eu quero estar
Para sempre eu quero estar

Minha Flor, Minha Esperança
Minha Rosa do Jardim
Para sempre eu quero estar
Com Minha Mãe juntinho à mim

Eu moro nesta casa
Que Minha Mãe me entregou
Eu estando junto com Ela
Sempre dando o seu valor

Fazendo algumas curas
Que Minha Mãe me ordenou
De brilhantes pedras finas
Para sempre aqui estou

Flor Das Águas

Flor das águas
Da onde vens, para onde vais
Vou fazer minha limpeza
No coração está Meu Pai

A morada do Meu Pai
É no coração do mundo
Aonde existe todo amor
E tem um segredo profundo

Este segredo profundo
Está em toda humanidade
Se todos se conhecerem
Aqui dentro da verdade

Pisei Na Terra Fria

Pisei na terra fria
Nela eu senti calor
Ela é quem me dá o pão
A Minha Mãe que nos criou

A Minha Mãe que nos criou
E me dá todos ensinos
A matéria eu entrego à Ela
E o Meu Espírito ao Divino

Do sangue das minhas veias
Eu fiz minha assinatura
O Meu Espírito eu entrego a Deus
E o meu corpo à sepultura

Meu corpo na sepultura
Desprezado no relento
Alguém fala em meu nome
Alguma vez em pensamento

Hinos De Sebastião Mota De Melo

Eu Subi Meu Pensamento

Eu subi meu pensamento
Dentro de um grande jardim
Levantei a minha voz
Oh! Minha Mãe, rogai por mim

Eu limpei a mentalidade
Vi uma roda girando
Dentro desta grande luz
Meu Pai está me olhando

Oh! Meu Pai que está no céu
Este poder Ele nos dá
Ele nos deu este grande Mestre
Aqui na terra para nos ensinar

Vamos seguir meus irmãos
Não devemos demorar
Ouça o estrondo da terra
E o gemido do mar

Eu olhando para o céu
Vi uma estrela correndo
Ela veio me rodeando
Eu senti meu corpo esmorecendo

Quando Tu Estiver Doente

Quando tu estiver doente
Que o Daime for tomar
Te lembra do Ser Divino
Que tu tomou para te curar

Te lembrando do Ser Divino
O universo estremeceu

A floresta se embalou
Porque tudo aqui é meu

Eu já te entreguei
Agora vou realizar
Se fizeres como eu te mando
Nunca hás de fracassar

Tu já viste o meu brilho
E já sabes quem eu sou
Agora eu te convido
Para ires aonde estou

Te Lembras Do Teu Mestre

Te lembras do teu Mestre
Te lembras do amor
Te lembras da firmeza
E da palavra que jurou

Sai para o invisível
Anda no astral
Entra na casa santa
Do nosso Pai universal

Segue o teu caminho
Deixa quem quiser falar
Que a força do teu Mestre
É quem te pode derribar

Não sabem o que estão dizendo
E nem sabe o que diz
Eu estando com o meu Mestre
Eu me acho mais feliz

Meu Mestre a Vós eu peço
Pelo nome do Senhor
Aumentai a minha luz
Dai-me força e dai-me amor

Meu Filho Eu Te Amo

Meu filho e te amo
Dentro do meu coração
Meu Pai eu te honro
Com meu joelho no chão

Meu filho eu sou o Homem
Que outro homem não vê
Meu filho eu te mando
Vai cumprir o teu dever

Meu filho eu sou teu Pai
Que foi com quem tu falou
Recebe a tua luz
Para ter o teu valor

Cumpre o teu dever
Faz a tua obrigação
Não escutas e nem te importas
Com conversa de irmão

Recebe com amor
Com atenção e com carinho
Que estas são as flores
Que eu mando para teu jardim

No Sol, Na Lua, Na Terra, No Mar

No sol, na lua
Na terra e no mar
Procurei esta verdade
E eu sei aonde está

No sol, na lua
Na terra e no mar
Esta verdade é pura
Estou aqui para apresentar

No sol, na lua
Na terra e no mar
Quem quiser que procure
E veja o Mestre aonde está

No sol, na lua
Na terra e no mar
Desceu nesta verdade
Deus do céu para ensinar
No sol, na lua
Na terra e no mar
Eu chamo as estrelas
E todas vêm me acompanhar

Eu Não Sou Deus

Eu não sou Deus
Mas tenho uma esperança
Eu não sou Deus
Mas sou sua semelhança

Deus é fogo.
Deus é água. Deus é tudo
Eu convido os meus irmãos
Para começar nossos estudos

Eu não sou Deus
Mas tenho uma esperança
Eu não sou Deus
Mas sou sua semelhança

Deus no céu.
Deus na terra, Deus no mar
Eu convido os meus irmãos
Para ficar em seu lugar.

Hinos De Alfredo Gregório De Melo

Ligaçao Divina

Por esta ligação Divina
Por estes fios de amor
Podemos estar mais perto
Do Nosso Pai Criador

Chuva que cai sobre a Terra
Chuva vinda do astral
Podemos ficar mais perto
Do Nosso Pai Universal

O trovão é uma força
É o poder da palavra
Onde Deus fala mais perto
A toda humanidade

O sol com vosso brilho
A toda mata resplandece
Por onde as bençãos divinas
Sobre a humanidade desce

A lua nas alturas
Consagrada em Vossa calma
Na mais perfeita harmonia
Nos dá força em nossa alma

As estrelas pequeninas
Sua luz incandescente
Como disse o Nosso Mestre
Só Deus Onipotente

Estes seres reunidos
São a força criadora
Que brilha neste Jardim
Da Nossa Mãe Protetora

Meditação

Quando eu olho para a Natureza
Meu coração se conforma
Em ver tanta criatura
E cada um vivendo de sua forma

Sempre olho para o firmamento
E vejo um grande poder
E eu sou pequeno aqui na terra
Peço força para compreender

Sempre olho para a humanidade
A multidão me desperta
Em ver tanta criatura
E todos ter que seguir na rota certa

Eu vejo todos animais
Cada um compõe seu lugar
Que aqui neste Jardim
De tudo tem que habitar

Eu olho para a floresta
Vejo tanta imensidão
Que para se ver é preciso
Se ter Deus no coração

Eu vejo todos os insetos
Cada um com seu destino
Com isto a vida nos prova
Que existe um Criador Divino

Tudo existe na terra e no mar
E nesta luz que nos cobre
O mistério deste segredo
Meditando é que se descobre

Tudo, tudo dá para se ver
Até aonde a vista alcança
Aqui neste jardim de Amor
Da Rainha da Esperança

E dai-me firmeza e amor
Concentrado, em harmonia
Considero este reinado
O Jardim da Virgem Maria

Hinos De Daniel Pereira De Matos
Os Anjos Varredor

I

Baixou doze anjos celestes
Deus Jesus quem os mandou
Em amor a nossa missão
São os anjos varredores.

II

Baixou doze anjos celestes
Todos são anjos varredores
Vêm varrer os maus pensamentos
E nos afirmar no santo amor

III

Baixou anjos celestes
Com vassouras de luz nas mãos
Para varrer os maus pensamentos
E nos limpar o coração

IV

Anjos de Deus meu Salvador
Com vossas vassouras de luz
Nos varrei os maus pensamentos
E nos alimpai para Jesus

V

Jesus por nós morreu na cruz
Com todo amor sem dar um gemido
Para nós dar a salvação
E a vida eterna dos remidos

VI

Nos varreis anjos celestes
Com vossas vassouras de luz
E nos limpe o pensamento
Para sempre adorar Jesus

VII

Damos mil graças a Deus
E a Virgem da Conceição
Pela limpeza recebida
Da alma ao coração

VIII

Todos malignos pensamentos
Vêm do maldito atentador
Só Deus e Nossa Senhora
É quem nos salva desse horror

IX

Salvemos os anjos de Deus
Os celestes varredor
Eles nos varre e nos limpa
E nos segue a Deus Salvador

X

São João fez sobre a terra
Caminhos para o Salvador
Jesus veio plainou e nos deu
E ainda nos manda os varredores

Flores Naturais

As flores naturais
São plantas de Jesus
Ele é o jardineiro
Eterno de luz

As flores naturais
São plantas de Jesus
E todos os mundos
São jardins de luz

As flores do céu
Todas são maravilhas
Falam e passeiam
Com a Virgem Maria.

Dos jardins da terra
Sublime de ver
Por bosques e montanha
Mil flores nascer

Por lindas campinas
Por prados e terreiros
E por todos lugares
Deus é o jardineiro

E no jardim do mar
Lá todo alumia
As flores são luz
Do rosário de Maria

Meus irmãos seguimos
Nesta romaria
Louvando a Deus Jesus
E a Virgem Maria

Salve Rainha

Valsa da Rainha do Mar

Vou cantar uma valsa
Dos mistérios do mar
Como toda alegria
Vamos brincar

Com as lindas sereias
E as ninfas do mar
As lindas Princesas
Todas vêm dançar
Nesta linda noite
Que estamos a brincar
Vêm as lindas fadas
E a Rainha do Mar

Todas com alegria
Vêm nos visitar
Trazendo flores mimosas

Para nos ofertar
As flores são mistérios
Do jardim do mar
São plantas de luzes
Dos mistérios do mar

Estes lindos mistérios
Vêm nos afirmar
Nas luzes sublimes
Da Rainha do Mar.

Hino De Francisca Campos Do Nascimento

Hino da santissima trindade e a virgem da caridade

Oh Virgem mãe da caridade
Vós me curai com o vosso santo amor
Curais a mim e todos meus irmaos
Com a luz do vosso divino amor

Oh Virgem mãe da caridade
Vós me curais com o vosso santo amor
Vós curais meu corpo e minha alma
Pra Jesus Cristo Salvador

Oh Virgem mãe da caridade
Mãe do nosso Salvador
Vós curais aos inocentes
Que estão doentes por causa dos pecadores

Oh Virgem mãe da caridade
Só vós é quem pode nos valer
É quem pode curar as nossas almas
E dos pecados pode nos defender

Eu vós peço oh mãe da caridade
Para que vós venha nos socorrer
Nos valei na hora da morte
Do Demônio venha nos defender

Coro

Salve O Divino Pai Eterno
Salve Jesus Cristo Salvador
Salve O Divino Espirito Santo
Que nos irradia com a luz do amor.

Luis Eduardo Luna

Poemas En Domingo: Diez Poemas De Tarde

Barcarola Número 1

En las perdidas aguas,
río abajo,
apenas naufragando
entre la sed vegetal.
Vi, y escuché,
y el murmullo aquél de los insectos,
y el motor del agua en el río,

y las conversaciones del negro,
en el negro atardecer,
y aquellas cuerdas,
rotas entre madera,
y la voz destemplada,
en un pequeño grito.
Y selva y selva.
Ni siquiera recuerdo,
cómo empezó aquel día,
y cómo,
en una confusión de voces,
y de gritos,
y de saltos,
y de no sé qué ordenanzas,
vinimos todos a subir,
a treinta kilómetros por hora,
en una colina azul,
y desde allí,
por la enmarañada selva,
ver el río,
y en el río,
el reflejo de las aguas,
y en las aguas, el reflejo del tiempo,
y en el tiempo,
el reflejo de unos aconteceres.
Arena tiene a veces el recuerdo.
Y su cuerpo,
entre la arena negra del río,
y en el río
aquella barca tenaz que fue cruzando
tantas cosas.

Extraperlo Número 2

Era el calor del verano,
en el verano eterno.
Enfrente, oscura cara de concha de tortuga.
Careidón, supongo.
En el cuadrado, una mesa,
el jugo verde, el amarillo mango,
la blancura infinita de unas manos.
Y sólo la sonrisa,
la incongruencia,
y a través del obstáculo,
de la glacialidad,
de la monotonía,
ver surgir un resquicio
por donde, tenue,
se va a filtrar la melancolía.
Era trópico y sol.
En el aire
sólo flotaba el polvo.
Y alguna huella olor a pino,
que se quedó perdida por traviesa.
Y ya no podía,
Distinguir las caras.
El viejo aquél,
con más de quinientos años
hablando de los Estados Unidos,
y de las torres de Manhatttan,
y de los veleros en la Costa Azul.

Y por las noches,
las aventuras de Laín entre los mambos,
y la orquesta de fieltro
que nos vino a encerrar en cualquier carpa.
Oh sí.
Y tiene un hijo,
que no sabe inglés.
Y aquel fue nuestro primer día,
con su rostro de galápago,
mirándome,
y sonriéndome.
Y su mujer,
apenas si podía ser
un poco bella.
Era polvo amarillo
el que estaba lloviendo
la tarde.

El Buscón. Número 3

Cuando le vi venir,
atado al fardo,
No pude prevenir una sonrisa.
Era delgado,
apenas,
apenas torre cotejando el cielo.
Y no pude imaginar aquel tesoro
en el último rincón de su escafandra.
Pasaron algunas horas
en que apenas pregunté.
Parecía
de algún modo poseído del Insecto.
Aquel Insecto que a las doce cantaba,
y que nunca se atrevió a presentarse,
quizás por no tener corbata.
Entonces era un prisma,
el lugar al que marchamos,
succionando cocacolas,
masticando bollitos amarillos
de maíz.
Varios centímetros de ancho tenía aquella curva,
y el golpe era ancho en su base,
y era de caucho rojo con motitas.
Y me empezó a hablar,
y cuántas cosas dijo
que apenas entendí,
y cuántas cosas quedaron aserradas,
martilladas,
golpeadas en el minuto aquel,
en el instante aquel en que me dijo:
Yo soy Tarsisio,
el de las grandes muelas.

Nigromancia. Número 4

Se pasó trabajando muchos años,
esperando a que todo esto le volviera,
y su fruto,
a tropezones hecho,
y sus manos,
cargadas de tantas ampollas,

de tantos esfuerzos,
de tantos pensamientos,
esperaban todos los días
el milagro.
Y vestido en lana,
acunado en las regiones más oscuras,
obstinado y firme,
el milagro no venía,
porque nunca supo si existía,
si lo había imaginado
o era el fruto del tiempo
y del verano.
Y así pasó los años,
recolectando piedras,
construyendo castillos
que envejecieron con él.
Y nunca supo si era al otro lado
donde se amontonaban las piedras,
si cada figura era copiada
en un espejo inmortal,
por detrás de las pirámides.
Mas él,
quizás lo supo,
y sin decirme nada,
me dejó en la ignorancia,
recolectando piedras.
En el verano,
cuando lleguen las lluvias,
ir a nadar con el recuerdo
del nigromante antiguo
que se murió de viejo
recolectando anuncios.

Atlanta. Número 5

Sumergido en el agua,
el resplandor de los tallos le atraía,
y fue cavando una viga
para acercarse a ellos,
y en el azul profundo descubrió las alas
blancas y hermosas de las algas,
y el dulce ritmo de las cigarras
haciendo el amor.
De cuatro en cuatro,
hacia la enorme torre,
cruzada enormemente por negros meteoritos,
vio subir los insectos,
milimétricamente alineados
hacia el azul.
Y el cielo tenía la color rosada,
y era pálida el agua,
y entre las tibias olas descubrió figuras
con sólo dos dimensiones,
discurseando leves,
agitando los brazos,
 y él allí,
con los ojos fijos,
mirando todo aquello,
a la orilla del lago.
En el último fondo,
cerca de un río,

o en el río,
el lento batir,
la perfecta sucesión de movimientos,
las alas blancas,
nuevamente apareciendo,
llorando en el aire,
y en el agua,
mostrando y descubriendo,
en su pausado giro,
el barco de la ilusión,
en el ancho río,
dentro del
agua.

Autogiro. Número 6

Veloz recorrí el mundo
desde aquel autogiro,
cerca de una cañada,
en una tarde verde,
al pie de una casa,
bordeando una selva,
vadeando un río,
escribiendo en las hojas secas
de un plátano maduro.
Entre las ortigas,
se dormían,
intactas,
las manzanas,
los melocotones,
los duraznos. . .
Y yo estaba,
encima de una rampa
de cuatro brazos
contemplando el mundo
desde arriba.
Y mirando esto,
inconformista,
decidí mirar las cosas
desde abajo.
Y vi la sucesión de raíces,
en el polen malva
de la tierra,
y el licor seminal de los almendros,
recorriendo las piedras,
y la faja de colores
que no había imaginado.
En el autogiro blanco,
en la noche malva de la tierra,
vi el mundo desde abajo,
y me lancé a la deriva,
en la marea de doncellosos olores.
Es suave el tacto de los dedos de los árboles,
pendiendo como racimos,
hacia abajo,
en el pudín violeta
de la tierra.

Desabrido. Número 7

En el bar,
a muy pocos metros del polvo,

el indio Apolinar cruzaba los callos de los pies
bajo la mesa.
Con su único ojo, pequeño y brillante,
describía el espíritu de los árboles.
Y aquellas manotas de corteza de árbol,
tallaban en el aire la figura
de Oguara y de Yagé,
de Yoco y de Chagró,
y el ojo tuerto.
Y el aguardiente que se bebía
en el soplo de un trago.
Y apenas respondía,
y su voz de planta vieja
recorría la selva dando saltos,
bajo la luna llena.
Y en su casa,
durmiendo en el cuadrado de una manta,
tronchado como un lirio,
vela en silencio la noche
el indiecito nieto.
Y a la luz de la hoguera,
entre tanta mano oscura,
Yagé, como una diosa,
bailando desnuda.

Interioridad. Número 8

Aquello fue en los peñascos,
en un crepusculario de un mes que no me acuerdo.
La casa había quedado sola,
y en el silencio de fruta y nieve,
el tableteo del bambú
sobre la cama.
En la enramada,
ya casi maduras,
amarillas de sol y de pájaros,
esperaban las badeas entre miríadas de insectos.
Agua golpeaba las peñas,
en un descender de alturas.
En el remanso verde,
rodeado de peces,
en el zambullir del agua
y remolinos de arena,
creció el mensaje
como un libro abierto.
Y era rojo el destello de su cubierta dura,
y suaves sus palabras entre la hierba muerta.
Tirando el pan a lo lejos
tan cerca de la selva,
fui de nuevo impulsado
hacia el misterio.
No muy lejos de allí,
entre las piedras blancas,
carne rosada y bermeja
se cepillaba los dientes.
El gato montés dormía,
con la cola entre las manos.
Sólo se oía el silencio
del bambú sobre la cama.

Mandrágora. Número 9

Fue la noche de las chicharras,
la primera vez.
La luz era un atisbo,
en la punta de un cirio.
En la madera jugosa,
con caras de rata,
me espiaban los espíritus,
vigilaban mis ojos fatigados,
y miraban la llama encabritada,
equilibrando las sombras.
Y vino la oscuridad,
y aquel inmenso espacio,
ya tornado concreto,
negro y duro alrededor del cuerpo,
se condensó en agudeza,
en sensibilidad despierta,
y el ronco temor,
el amplio grito,
el dorado crispar al borde de las sábanas,
perforó paredes,
se precipitó afuera
y en el asombro enorme,
por encima de toda convergencia de sueños,
paso a paso,
con solemnidad de muerto,
rondó de largo a largo mis pasillos,
y tocó a mi puerta con sus húmedos dedos.
La luz era un recuerdo
demasiado lejano.
Y el día,
un ignoto rincón del universo.
Al sobrepasar los siglos
crecientes espirales
y llegar a la sexta morada de los dioses,
en un sudario blanco,
henchido de relojes,
rodeado de ratas,
en la noche sin velas,
reposa un hombre antiguo
que se quedó velando
en la cama
un desvelo.

La noche del eclipse. Número diez y último

Vino el aviso en el periódico,
entre las doce y las siete,
la noche del veintitrés de marzo,
de mil novecientes treinta y nueve.
A las cuatro salieron las sombras de sus cuevas,
y bailaron hasta tarde.
Entre los cinco puñales de los antiguos Mesías,
atentos escuchamos tanta música.
De la profunda maleza fueron saliendo muertos,
en lenta procesión desesperada.
Mas todo allí siguió como hasta entonces,
incluso Karman hizo un brindis
por los no nacidos.
Allí vinieron todos, antiguos y remotos,
y prestaron sus dones,
y en un acuerdo enorme,
en la armonía perfecta,
ocupamos el sitio de hermano Nostradamus,
de Rosacruz, de Anselmo,
del amigo Plotino y del cercano Ulises.
Y fue curioso observar
aquellos otros verdes,
aquellos otros golondrinos,
todos tan parecidos,
en los cientos de círculos de la lejana historia,
con distintos ropajes,
con la misma mirada,
en el feroz momento del eclipse.
Vinieron a relucir las lenguas,
y todos los acertijos,
y con más o menos fortuna
comparamos las obras
con las del viejo Júpiter,
aburrido de esperar por tantos siglos
la noche del eclipse.
Hubo ronda de vino,
y néctar con galletas.
Y a la hora del juicio,
que fue toda una farsa,
nos reimos de aquellos
que tomaron en serio
nuestro esperpento.
Ya casi al amanecer,
cuando avanzantes y agudos
llegaban los papagayos,
se disolvió la tropa,
casi a fuerza de palos.
Cuando el azul se vino,
a instaurar sus poderes,
con sus chillidos de pájaros
y el zumbar de los insectos,
entre rendijas de piedra,
en sus oscuros ojos,
aún se reían
los muertos.

Domingo 27 de febrero de 1972.

Néstor Perlongher

(Selecciones de *Aguas aéreas*. Buenos Aires: Último Reino, 1991.)

Recio El Embarque, airado aedo
riza u ondula noctilucas
iridiscencias enhebrando
en el etéreo sulfilar:

> un trazo
> (deleble persistencia)
> en el enroque de los magmas
> en el cuadriculado del mantel

> —mental, la sala
> de entrecasa (arte kitsch)
> compostelaba medianías
> en el corset de voile, leve y violado.

Pero los voladitos
de los encajes del mantel urdían
más que un texto una forma, una figura. .

.

Boreal o suave, sus caireles
no dejaban de iluminar los resbalosos
voleos del minué, por las baldosas: uña
desprendida y procaz, arañando sus pases
el inane, traslúcido volar.

Por espejismos de piel viva
en el tirón de las mucosas
los rasgueos de la uña
elevaban las cántigas
al cielorraso hueco, sublunar.

◆

Recio el cantor, bruñidas las guedejas,
dejo de mambo inflige al modular
intensidades en el cieno,
                              plástica
porosidad de la materia espesa.

En el dejo un espasmo
contorsionaba los ligámenes
y transmitía a los encajes
la untuosidad del nylon

rayándolos
en una delicada precipitación.

II

Titilar de ebonita, las lilas de la cruz
liman del clavo la turgencia áspera
o paspan el derrame del rosario
por la puntilla del mantel.

Acaireladas convulsiones, si la medusa pincha al pez, tremola
en el remolineo la flotación de un cántico, de un cántaro.

Cantarolan por darle al óleo cenagoso
la consistencia de un velo de noche, por hurtarle
al dios de la floresta la niñez de un escándalo
u otorgarle a la red de iridiscencias pasajeras (tiemblan)
la levedad de un giro en el espacio.

Patrulla el desternillar del álamo veloz la ceremonia
al tiempo que lo desboca con incrustes de strass o lentejuela
    móvil
que rayan la película devenida traslúcida.

La huída de los cormoranes
y en su lugar las mansas gaviotas del deseo,
el vértigo de los meollos
asombrillando el pajarear.

¿Adónde se sale cuando no se está?
¿Adónde se está cuando se sale?

Al lado, o de repente, la musiquilla se aproxima
y avisa que las huellas se hacen barro en la disolución del
    filafil,
entonces de un tirón se restablece la rigidez de la rodilla
    (trémula)
y el pico de la flor abre en el témpano la cicatriz de un
    pámpano

                              rajando
los valles de la misa, los alvéolos
de eso que por ser misa hubo de echarle azogue al ánade,
una mano de espejo a la destreza.

III

Enrarecida atmósfera, el incienso
nebulosa de flores repartiendo
curva al pie de la perla el espejuelo
y la "luz de cristal" , para que emerja
—princesa de las aguas—la primicia
del roce del
sereno
en el alvéolo de la vibración
se tensa, se
suspende:

                    ah si cuajase
                    en el espacio pleno de presencias
                    la opalina de un rimmel
                    que estampase, crispando sobre sí
                    el corcoveo de las gibas, cuya
                                   "fugacidad"

(vértigo corto)

                    casca, niagara lo nacarado del soutien
                    — desmenuzados hilos en el barro de nylon
                    pasa un Nilo
                    la fuerza de una bruta
                    corriente, un movimiento
                    de continuada velocidad:

sus hélices elíseas
aire al simún, palpando
nudosidades dan

el don.

V

Si la divinidad liquida ahógase
o bulle, en el calor carnal,
su playa látex –antes
que promontorios, grutas —

gránulos de negrura
oh noctiluca enardecida yergue
en la onda de conchas y cangrejos
el anillo de espuma

en la piel tensa y tenue
muelle el despeñadero en remolinos
el simulacro de su frenesí

huecos estampa en el alud coral
para que halague su volcán el ala
de un camoatí libélulas libando.

VII

El pie, el vaivén del pie, el empellón del piso en el empeine, lisa combinación urdía su trenza, etérea, con el coro, el ímpetu del coro, el embalse de voces en elevado enjambre circuía las lámparas de una verberación multicolor, rosada correa la que atando al desmayo el temblor de los tucos liberaba la lívida flotación de la estela en remolinos de haces, tan livianos, despeinaban el fleco con el roce de un ánima, de un aura, el rodete corona sacerdotisas blancas, limousine de charol que embarcaba los hálitos, las ansias, al derretir grisú las pompas irisadas, de rosar la grisura con un golfo de incienso, un abanico de *humo, ola, orla y aureola de la luz,* crucifijo estirado hasta el tonseo de miembros enyedrados, escultura de lianas barnizando torsiones de los muslos morenos, adivinados al trasluz del lino en el vaivén del pie, su ritmo, rijo en el rutilar de los colores, tenía una fijeza de marea abrazando el pantano costanero, la hoja, femenina, su brujería vegetal, hincaba en los corpúsculos de bruma la hidra, el aullido modulado de la interrogación, en el traspié, en el cimbreo que se arqueaba al resbalar en los listones húmedos, aura mojada por la lama de charcos agrios y en su góndola remontar el aullido, el glanduleo de las velocidades en el légamo, o acaso isla de neón tullido entre cuyas hendiduras podía vislumbrarse, en los humores de la transpiración, el brillo de la estrella, o eran las purpurinas del vestido de noche de la diosa deseándose brillar.

X

DIAMANTE

Rascacielo almendror cuyos cimientos
por caños cañerías ventanolas corpúsculos y baños
van a dar al gran Lago de los Seres,
                                       los Entes

          ENTES FIJOS
          PREFIJOS

Prefijada su estela, su cascada
si manes a la hiedra

zambullen, una luz
riza las torvas ondas

Erizos
Aguas vivas

Caperuzas cartilaginosas
para los maquilleos de las orlas

Sirenas de celofán
en los agujeros de la red,
medio cuerpo de náyade
en el tecnicolor de espumas
cuyas salpicaduras esparcían
un arco de partículas de polvos
y burbujas, arco azul
                    al compás
de tironeos de tendón y sincopadas catalepsias

caídas de la presión

vaho azuloso en el rodar al vuelo
en el vaivén febril estos títeres rítmicos
                              o mixtos
implantan su cabellera en el cristal
de nube, crepúsculo vacío
de temblorosa iridiscencia
volúmenes de brillo
deslizando sus aspas
por jardines de limo.

ERA EL CRISTAL
LAS MIL FACETAS DEL CRISTAL
LOS BRILLOS RITMICOS
LOS HIMNOS
          CELEBRATORIOS DE UNA
                    ANUNCIACION

CALEIDOSCOPIO
          FRENESI ESMALTADO

NOTES ON CONTRIBUTORS

Pablo Amaringo Shuña was born in Tamanco, in the Peruvian Amazon, in a family with a long shamanic tradition. His father, grandfather, and other relatives were *vegetalistas,* shamans deriving their knowledge from power plants. Don Pablo himself was a practicing *ayahuasquero* for many years. A man with many gifts, he is a self-taught artist, specializing in Amazonian landscapes and visionary art derived from his experience with ayahuasca. In 1988, together with Luis Eduardo Luna, he founded the *Usko-Ayar Amazonian School of Painting,* an institution dedicated to the artistic rendering of Amazonian nature and environmental education. His work as well as that of his students has been exhibited worldwide. During the Earth Summit in 1992, he received the Global 500 award of the United Nations for his outstanding contribution to the preservation of the environment. He is co-author with Luis Eduardo Luna of *Ayahuasca Visions: The Religious Iconography of a Peruvian Shaman,* a book depicting 49 paintings and a large body of information on mestizo cosmography.

Jimmy Aroca, was born in Chile, and is currently studying Political Science at Helsinki University. He is an amateur cartographer, a philatelist, and is interested in Geography, History and Culture.

Françoise Barbira Freedman was born and raised in France before studying Anthropology at Cambridge, England. She has had close ties with the Jakwash Lamista of Peruvian Amazonia ever since her doctoral fieldwork in the late '70s. Her current pilot project of *Yaku Mamay,* near Iquitos, Peru, aims at applying the knowledge of women's shamanic plants to health. Mother of four children, she teaches Medical Anthropology at Cambridge University and also coordinates Birthlight, a charitable trust to promote the enjoyable experience of pregnancy, birth and babies.

Mengatue Caiga is a shaman, now in his 70s, of the Huaorani tribe in Ecuador.

Oscar Calavia Sáez was born in Logroño, Spain in 1959. He studied History and Anthropology at the Complutense University in Madrid, received a Master's Degree in Social Anthropology from the University of Campinas in Brazil as well as a Ph.D. in Anthropology from the University of São Paulo. Since 1986, he has been a resident of Brazil and is currently a Professor of Anthropology at the Federal University of Santa Catarina. His published books include *Fantasmas falados: mito, historia e escatologia no Brasil* and *Deus e o diabo em terras católicas: Brasil-Espanha* as well as the forthcoming *O nome e o tempo dos Yaminawa* and *Os caminhos de Santiago e outros ensaios sobre paganismo.*

César Calvo was born in Iquitos, Peru in 1940. He studied Literature, Psychology and Law at the University of San Marcos in Lima. Winner of the first prize in the "Young Poet of Peru" competition in 1960, he was awarded the National Poetry Prize of Peru in 1970. His books of poetry include *Ausencia y retardos, El cetro de los jóvenes,* and *Pedestal para nadie.* His novel *Las tres mitades de Ino Moxo y otros brujos de la Amazonía* was translated into English by Kenneth A. Symington and published as *The Three Halves of Ino Moxo: Teachings of the Wizard of the Upper Amazon.*

Francisca Campos do Nascimento was born in 1934 in a rubber settlement in the State of Acre, Brazil. Seriously ill, her body covered with ulcers, she went to see Daniel Pereira de Matos in 1957, who treated her with *Santo Daime.* After a seven-year process she was cured, and promised to dedicate her life to works of charity. For 34 years, she was the main medium in the religious ceremonies carried out at the *Centro Espírita y Culto de Oração, Casa de Jesus, Fonte de Luz,* in Rio Branco, Brazil under the direction of Mestre Daniel Pereira de Matos, and, then, after his death, of the religious leaders Antônio Geraldo and Manuel Hipólito Araújo. In 1990, she decided to create her own religious center, *Centro Espírita e Obra de Caridade Príncipe Espadarte Reino da Paz,* one of the religious centers of the doctrinal line best known as *Barquinha* (the boat). She lives in Rio Branco with her husband, surrounded by their many children and grandchildren.

Jean-Pierre Chaumeil, anthropologist, is a research director at the Centre National de la Recherche Scientifique (CNRS, France), and subdirector of the Equipe de Recherche en Ethnologie Amérindienne (Research Team on

Amerindian Ethnology), also of CNRS. Since 1971, he has conducted fieldwork numerous times among the Yagua of the Peruvian Amazon, and has written several books about them, including *Ñihamwo* (Lima, 1987) and *Guía etnográfica de la Alta Amazonia I* (Yagua chapter, Quito-Lima, 1994). In 1982, he defended his doctoral dissertation at the Ecole des Hautes Études en Sciences Sociales (EHESS, Paris) on Yagua shamanism *(Voir, savoir, pouvoir, le chamanisme chez les yagua du nord-est péruvien,* Paris, 1983. Spanish edition Lima, 1998). He is also a co- editor of *Chamanismes et religions universalistes,* Paris, 1999.

Arlindo Daureano Estevão (Daso) is a member of the Cashinahua, a Pano indigenous group of the Peruvian and Brazilian Amazon. He lives in the village of Cana Recreio, Purus River, Brazil.

Wade Davis holds degrees in Anthropology and Biology and received his Ph.D. in Ethnobotany from Harvard University, under the direction of Richard Evans Schultes. Mostly through the Harvard Botanical Museum, he spent over three years in the Amazon and the Andes engaged in ethnobotanical research while making some 6000 botanical collections. His later work took him to Haiti, Borneo, Tibet and the high Arctic. He is the author of seven books in addition to *One River: Explorations and Discoveries in the Amazon Rain Forest,* including *The Serpent and the Rainbow,* an account of his exploration of the Vodoun religion and Haitian culture, *Shadows in the Sun,* and *Passage of Darkness.* A native of British Columbia, he divides his time between Vancouver and Washington, D.C.

Philippe Descola was born in Paris in 1949. He obtained a master's degree in Philosophy before studying Anthropology under the supervision of Claude Lévi-Strauss. In 1983, he received his doctorate from the École Pratique des Hautes Etudes. He has lectured at the universities of Cambridge, Oslo, Vienna, São Paulo, Quito, and Oxford, among others. He is the author of *In the Society of Nature: A Native Ecology in Amazonia* as well as *The Spears of Twilight: Life and Death in the Amazon Jungle.* He also has edited several books, including *Dictionnaire de l'anthropologie et de l'ethnologie* and *Nature and Society: Anthropological Perspectives.* He is presently a professor of Anthropology at the École de Hautes Etudes en Sciences Sociales in Paris.

Alfonso Domingo was born in Turégano, Spain in 1955. He has degrees in Information Sciences and Political Science, specializing in Iberoamerican Studies. He lives in Madrid but travels a great deal (to Lebanon, Libya, El Salvador, Panama, the Sahara, the Amazonian rain forest and elsewhere) due to his work as a maker of documentary films for Spanish television. He is the author of *La madre de la voz en el oído,* a novel that won Madrid's prestigious "Feria del Libro" prize in 1991.

Angelika Gebhart Sayer is a social anthropologist and a native of Germany. She has done fieldwork among the Yanomamo in Venezuela, the Xinguanos in Brazil, and the Shipibo-Conibo in Peru, focusing on ethnic healing systems, religion and art. Her dissertation *Die Spitze des Bewusstseins. Untersuchungen zu Weltbild und Kunst der Shipibo-Conibo* was published in Germany in 1987. She is now living in Boulder, Colorado, running a Center for Yoga and Ayurveda.

Allen Ginsberg (1926–1997), perhaps the United States' most well-known poet, was one of the original members of the Beat movement in the 1950s and a catalyst of the San Francisco Poetry Renaissance with his landmark, iconoclastic poem *Howl.* Other books by Ginsberg include the epistolary novel he wrote in conjunction with William S. Burroughs *The Yagé Letters* as well as *Kaddish and Other Poems: 1958–1960, Planet News: 1961–1967, The Fall of America: Poems of These States 1965–1971, Mind Breaths: Poems 1972–1977, Plutonian Ode: Poems 1977–1980, White Shroud: Poems 1980–1985,* and *Collected Poems 1947–1980.*

Michael Harner, Ph.D., is the founder and president of the Foundation for Shamanic Studies in Mill Valley, California, an organization devoted to the study, preservation, and teaching of shamanism worldwide. He was initiated into shamanism while doing anthropological fieldwork in the Upper Amazon in the early 1960s and subsequently pioneered the current revival of shamanism and shamanic healing in the West. He actively teaches practical shamanism and shamanic healing internationally and directs cross-cultural and field research for the Foundation for Shamanic Studies, as well as being its general director. The Foundation, which is a nonprofit incorporated educational and charitable institution, has an international faculty of thirty persons, and field associates and staff of thirty-five. He is former professor and chairman of the Graduate Faculty Department of Anthropology at the New School of Social Research, and has taught at the University of California at Berkeley, where he received his doctoral degree, and at Columbia and Yale, as well as having served as co-chairman of the Anthropology Section of the New York Academy of

Sciences. Besides in the Upper Amazon, where he started his research in 1956, he has done fieldwork in Mexico, western North America, the Canadian Arctic, and Samiland (Lapland). His books include: *The Jívaro: People of the Sacred Waterfalls, Hallucinogens and Shamanism, The Way of the Shaman,* and a book in preparation, *The Shaman's Ladder.*

Isabela Hartz was born in 1958 in Rio de Janeiro. She has been involved with *Santo Daime (ayahuasca)* since 1981, living for several years in Céu do Mapiá, the spiritual center of the doctrinal line created by Sebastião Mota de Melo, founder of CEFLURIS. She has done numerous exhibitions in Brazil and has worked as a fashion designer. She has created the cover art for over one hundred books. She is now living in Florianópolis, southern Brazil.

Kathleen Harrison has a B.A. in Art and an M.A. in Ethnobotany. She has accumulated years of fieldwork experience in indigenous cultures, including those of the Amazon Basin of Peru and Ecuador, Guatemala, Belize, Thailand and especially among the Indians of Mexico. The focus of her work is the study of medicinal and visionary plants and the rituals, artforms, stories and beliefs that accompany them. For fifteen years, she has managed Botanical Dimensions, a small non-profit organization that supports fieldwork and education regarding the cultural uses, mythologies and preservation of healing and shamanic plants. Kathleen lives in Northern California, where she teaches and writes on various aspects of ethnobotany and ritual, as well as perception and illustration of the natural world.

Raimundo Irineu Serra was born in São Vicente de Ferré, Maranhão, in the Brazilian Northeast, in 1892. In 1912, he moved to the western Amazon area where he worked on rubber plantations, and as an officer in the commission created by the federal government to establish the limits of Brazil's Acre state in relation to Bolivia and Peru. He learned the use of *ayahuasca* in the region of Cobija, in Bolivia, from a Peruvian practitioner. In 1930, he initiated his public work with *ayahuasca* (which he called *Santo Daime)* in Vila Ivonete, a district of Rio Branco, capital of Acre State. In the forties, he created the *Centro de Iluminação Cristã Universal* (CICLU) in the rural area of Rio Branco, a religious center that continues its activities to this day. Mestre Irineu, as he is called by his followers, died in 1971.

Elsje Maria Lagrou has been a Lecturer in Social and Cultural Anthropology at the Federal University of Santa Catarina (Brazil) since 1993. She has a degree in Contemporary History from the Catholic University of Louvain (Leuven, Belgium), where she wrote on the writer Etty Hillesum (1914–1943). She holds a Master's degree in Anthropology from the Federal University of Santa Catarina (Brazil) for her dissertation *Uma etnografia da cultura Kaxinawa: entre a cobra e o Inca.* She received a Ph.D. in Social Anthropology from the University of St. Andrews (Scotland) and also from the University of São Paulo (Brazil) with the thesis *Cashinahua cosmovision, a perspectival approach to identity and alterity* (the Portuguese version is entitled *Caminhos, Duplos e Corpos. Uma abordagem perspectivista da identidade e alteridade entre os Kaxinawa).* She has published articles in specialized journals on Amerindian Ethnology, Cashinahua worldview and social organization, Ritual, Shamanism, Anthropology of Art and Aesthetics, and Mythology.

F. Bruce Lamb was born in Colorado in 1913, and died in Santa Fe, New Mexico, in 1993. He held a Ph.D. from the University of Michigan and traveled widely in North, South and Central America, as well as in Africa and Asia, holding many posts and consultancies in the field of forest engineering and tropical forestry. His *Mahogany of Tropical America* has been called a major contribution in his field. His fieldwork with indigenous populations began with the Apiaca Indians in Mato Grosso, Brazil, during World War II. He is the author of *Wizard of the Upper Amazon: The Story of Manuel Córdoba-Ríos* and *Rio Tigre and Beyond: The Amazon Jungle Medicine of Manuel Córdoba-Ríos.*

E. Jean Matteson Langdon began her initiation to the shamanic world of southern Colombia in 1970 with a study among the Sibundoy Indians. At the suggestion of Scott Robinson, she then journeyed to the Amazon Basin to conduct three years of study with the Siona Indians, gathering more than one hundred native texts told to her about the shamanic experience. She has made several return trips to the Siona, and, since 1983, has worked in Brazil at the Federal University of Santa Catarina, where she has conducted research on Indian Health Policy and the incorporation of native health knowledge in health service programs. Her publications on shamanism include *Portals of Power: South American Shamanism* (1992) and *Xamanismo no Brasil: novas perspectivas* (1996). She also edited a book on death in South American Indian cultures, which was published in Ecuador in 1991.

Luis Eduardo Luna, born in Florencia, in the Colombian Amazon region, is co-editor with Steven F. White of the *Ayahuasca Reader.* He received his Ph.D. from the Institute of Comparative Religion at Stockholm University. A Guggenheim Fellow and Fellow of the Linnean Society of London, he is also the author of *Vegetalismo: Shamanism among the Mestizo Population of the Peruvian Amazon* and, with Pablo Amaringo, *Ayahuasca Visions: The Religious Iconog-*

raphy of a Peruvian Shaman, a project that grew from their work to establish the internationally-recognized *USKO-AYAR Amazonian School of Painting* in Pucallpa, Peru. From 1994–1998 he was a Professor in Anthropology at the Universidade Federal de Santa Catarina in Florianópolis, Brazil. He is currently a Senior Lecturer in Spanish at the Swedish School of Economics in Helsinki, and, since 1986, an Associate of the Botanical Museum of Harvard University.

Peter Matthiessen, born in New York City in 1927, has been nominated for the National Book Award in both fiction, for *At Play in the Fields of the Lord* (made into a film by Hector Babenco), and nonfiction, for the travel books *The Tree Where Man Was Born* and *The Snow Leopard.* Since graduating from Yale University in 1950, he has maintained an active life, travelling in South America, New Guinea, Nepal, Africa, Australia, Siberia, the Caribbean and elsewhere, all places that form the background of his diverse published works. His writing demonstrates an engagement with a number of causes, including the incarceration of Native American Leonard Peltier in *In the Spirit of Crazy Horse,* vanishing species in the pioneering work *Wildlife in America,* the problems of the commercial fishermen of Long Island's South Fork in *Men's Lives* as well as a book on Chicano activist César Chávez. He is also the author of *The Cloud Forest: A Chronicle of the South American Wilderness.*

Dennis J. McKenna was born in 1950 and has pursued the interdisciplinary study of ethnomedicine and plant hallucinogens for the last twenty years. He received his doctorate in 1984 from the University of British Columbia and subsequently obtained a fellowship at the National Institute of Mental Health, where he conducted research that he continued at Stanford University in the Department of Neurology. He has worked for Shaman Pharmaceuticals and the Aveda Corporation, and currently does scientific consulting for clients in the herbal, nutritional, and pharmaceutical industries. He co-edited (with his brother Terence) *The Invisible Landscape: Mind, Hallucinogens and the I Ching* and has published articles in *Journal of Ethnopharmacology, European Journal of Pharmacology, Brain Research, Journal of Neuroscience, Journal of Neurochemistry,* and elsewhere. He lives in Minnesota's St. Croix Valley with his wife Sheila and daughter Caitlin.

Alfredo Gregório de Melo, one of Sebastião Mota's sons, was selected by his father to be his spiritual successor and the person who would be in charge of continuing his work. As early as the 1970s, he undertook responsibility of the management and administration of CEFLURIS *(Centro Eclético de Fluente Luz Universal Raimundo Irineu Serra.)* Now, at age 50, he is not only a spiritual leader of CEFLURIS, but is also developing an ecological project in the Valley of the Juruá River, in the same place where his father, Padrinho Sebastião Mota, was born.

W. S. Merwin was born in New York City in 1927 and is considered one of the most important contemporary poets of the United States. His books of poetry include *A Mask for Janus* (1952), *The Dancing Bears* (1954), *Green with Beasts* (1956), *The Drunk in the Furnace* (1960), *The Moving Target* (1963), *The Lice* (1967), *The Carrier of Ladder*s (1970), for which he received the Pulitzer Prize, *Writings to an Unfinished Accompaniment* (1973), *The Compass Flower* (1977), *Opening the Hand* (1983), *The Rain in the Trees* (1988), and *Travels* (1994). He is also a highly-accomplished translator of numerous Spanish classics such as *The Poem of the Cid* and *Lazarillo de Tormes* as well as poetry by Jean Follain, Osip Mandelstam, Roberto Juarroz and Muso Soseki. He has received many fellowships, including Rockefeller, Guggenheim, Academy of American Poets, and National Endowment for the Arts. He currently lives in Hawaii and, in 1987, was the recipient of the Governor's Award for Literature there.

Ib Michael, born in Denmark in 1945, has studied Meso-American Indian Languages and Cultures at Copenhagen University and has traveled to Mexico, Guatemala, and Honduras to study Mayan and Aztec ruins, monuments and scriptures. He translated the *Popol vuh,* the sacred book of the Quiché-Maya, into Danish. He has published poetry, novels and documentaries. In South America, he lived in the Peruvian and Ecuadorian Amazon among several indigenous groups, including the Shuar, Aguaruna and Ashaninca, with whom he participated in *ayahuasca* ceremonies on several occasions. He incorporated these experiences in his novels and travel writing. He also has spent time in Southeast Asia, China and Tibet, and has travelled by boat to Polynesia and Easter Island. His work has been translated into several languages. Farrar, Straus & Giroux recently published his novel *Prince.*

Jonathon S. Miller-Weisberger was born in Berkeley, California in 1970 and has lived for over twenty years in Ecuador, where, since 1990, he has been collaborating with five different indigenous groups on cultural heritage-strengthening projects and rain forest conservation. He is currently working toward a "new" ethnobotany, which he sees as a crucial link between the people and the forest, reviving vanishing plant lore among indigenous youth in hopes that this will inspire the wisdom to preserve traditional values and the rain forest itself.

Sebastião Mota de Melo was born in 1920 on a rubber plantation on the banks of the Juruá River, in the State of Amazonas, Brazil. He served as a Kardecist medium for many years, establishing himself with his family in 1959 in the outlying areas of Rio Branco, Acre. In 1965, he met Raimundo Irineu Serra (1892–1971) and soon became one of the leading figures of the *Centro de Iluminação Cristã Universal* (CICLU), a religious center created by Irineu Serra. In 1974, with approximately one hundred followers, he separated himself from the CICLU, establishing an independent religious center. In 1983, his community moved to a remote place on the banks of the Igarapé do Mapiá, a branch of the Purus River, which is known as the spiritual center CEFLURIS *(Centro Eclético de Fluente Luz Universal Raimundo Irineu Serra),* a religious doctrinal line using *Santo Daime (ayahuasca),* with thousands of members throughout Brazil, as well as in Europe, Latin America, the United States and Japan.

Hugo Niño was born in Bogotá, Colombia in 1947 and has taught Literature at the Universidad Pedagógica Nacional and Anthropology at the Escuela de Pedagogía Artística de Colcultura. He has published articles on Anthropology, Linguistics and Literature in journals such as *Teorema, Gaceta Colcultura, Eco,* and *Revista de la Universidad Nacional.* He is the author of the book *Primitivos Relatos Contados Otra Vez,* that won the Casa de las Américas award in 1976, and of *Los Mitos del Sol,* published in 1994.

Alfredo Payaguaje is a member of the Secoya tribe from the community of San Pablo de Kantesiaya on the Aguarico River in Ecuador's northernmost Amazonian province. Since he is from a long lineage of respected healers, he always has had a great interest in his family's heritage. Before his grandfather, Don Fernando Payaguaje passed on, he made several recordings of his grandfather's advice, wisdom and experiences, which he later transcribed, translated into Spanish (with the help of a friend who was a Capuchin priest), and published as *El bebedor de yajé.* He recently co-authored a bilingual education booklet on Secoya Ethnobotany, now being used by his village school.

Fernando Payaguaje was a highly-respected contemporary traditional Secoya healer and spiritual leader, who died late in his 90s in 1993. *El bebedor de yajé* (The Yajé Drinker) is an autobiographical account of his life and experiences as a shaman.

Dale Pendell is writing a poetic history of the plant allies. The first volume, *Pharmako/Poeia: Plant Powers, Poisons and Herbcraft,* was published by Mercury House. The middle book, *Pharmako/Gnosis: Plant Teachers and the Poison Path,* will appear shortly.

Hilario Peña is a well known Ingano shaman originally from Puerto Limón, a village south of Mocoa, now living in Guayuyaco, in the Colombian Amazon.

Daniel Pereira de Matos, Mestre Daniel to his followers, was born in Maranhão in 1904 in the Brazilian Northeast and died in 1958. Little is known about his life. According to Francinete Oliveira dos Santos, with whom he lived for a year and had a son, at the age of seven he somehow came under the care of the Brazilian Navy. Since he was the son of slaves, no official record of his birth exists in the Navy's archives. In 1942, during the Acre Revolution, he arrived in Rio Branco in the Brazilian Amazon as an officer on a frigate, and decided to stay in Acre after the revolution ended. He worked there on rubber plantations, and also as a barber and carpenter. In 1943 or 1944, he met Raimundo Irineu Serra, with whom he drank *Santo Daime (ayahuasca)* several times. He experienced a vision with *Santo Daime* in 1945 in which he was urged to create a religious group based on his own doctrine, now known as *Barquinha* (the boat). This group currently has at least four independent centres in Vila Ivonete, a district of Rio Branco.

Néstor Perlongher was born in Avellaneda, Argentina in 1949 and died in São Paulo, Brazil in 1992. He received a degree in Sociology in 1982, moved to Brazil and studied Social Anthropology at the University of Campinas, where he later taught. One of Latin America's outstanding poets, his books include *Austria-Hungría* (1980), *Alambres* (1987), *Hule* (1989), *Aguas aéreas* (1990), *El chorreo de las iluminaciones* (1992) and *Poemas completos* (1997). He also published the studies *El fantasma del SIDA* (1988) and *La prostitución masculina* (1993).

Alex Polari de Alverga, poet, writer and lecturer, has published three books on *ayahuasca* and *Santo Daime: O Livro das Mirações* (1984), *O Guia da Floresta* (1992) and *O Evangelho de Sebastião Mota* (1999). He founded the community Céu da Montanha, one of the first centers of Santo Daime outside the Amazon region. Polari de Alverga is currently one of the leading members of CEFLURIS *(Centro Eclético de Fluente Luz Universal Raimundo Irineu Serra.)* He lives in the community of Céu do Mapiá, where he is carrying out social, environmental and spiritual work.

Alberto Prohaño is a renowned Yagua shaman and has been the leader of the community Edén de la Frontera (río Marichín, Peruvian Amazon, near the Colombian border) for over thirty years. He is originally from the Yacarité region (Atacuari River, left tributary of the Amazon). He belongs to a line of at least three generations of shamans. His fame extends well beyond the limits of his own group and his region. The Yagua tribe (an isolated linguistic family) has approximately 4,000 members, of which nearly 25% are currently living in Colombia, due to recent migrations.

Gerardo Reichel-Dolmatoff (1912–1994), Colombia's pioneering anthropologist and archaeologist, was of Austrian and Russian heritage. Although he was born in Salzburg, he lived in Colombia from 1939 until his death. Author of more than 25 books and 200 articles, his research spanned many disciplines, including anthropology, archaeology, ethnohistory, and history of art. His research on Amerindian ethnoecology, art, iconography, architecture, mythology, ethnobotany, medicine, astronomy, ethics, material culture, philosophy, humanism, science and technology, and his pioneering research on indigenous imagery and use of hallucinogens allowed a holistic understanding of Colombian Amerindian cultures. His research on the archaeology of the early Formative phase in the Caribbean Coast and of chiefdom societies of the Andes, and his syntheses of the prehistory of Colombia created the bases for contemporary Colombian archaeology. His analyses of particular geographic areas by means of archaeology, ethnohistory and ethnography produced methodologies to explain specific regional dynamics (e.g. in the Sierra Nevada), while his transdisciplinary studies of Amazonian Indians enabled him to achieve a fuller interpretation of the normal and altered states of cultural expression among peoples whose cosmology is based on the ritual ingestion of *yajé*.

Scott S. Robinson is Professor of Social Anthropology at the Universidad Metropolitana, Iztapalapa Campus, in Mexico City. He is a co-signer of the Treaty of Barbados (1971) and has produced documentary films and videos. He also has published articles on the complex issues regarding hydropower dam resettlement. Currently, he is engaged in research on appropriate models for introducing digital technologies in traditional societies.

Richard Spruce, one of the greatest botanists of all times, was born at Ganthorpe, in Yorkshire, England, in 1817. Besides doing intensive fieldwork in his native country and in the Pyrenees, he spent 15 years in the Amazon and in the Andes, where he made extensive collections, identified hundreds of species new to science, wrote thousands of notes and letters on many aspects of the natural world and the cultural use of plants by the indigenous populations, and recorded vocabularies of twenty-one different Amazonian dialects for the first time. His work was fundamental for the understanding of the genus *Hevea* as well as other plants of economic importance. After Spruce's death in 1893, and based on his materials, Alfred Russel Wallace compiled *Notes of a Botanist in the Amazon and the Andes*. Richard Evans Schultes and, later, M.R.D. Seaward, among others, have made the greatest contributions in terms of the dissemination of Spruce's work.

Michael Taussig is a professor of Anthropology at Columbia University and is the author of *The Devil and Commodity Fetishism in South America* and *Shamanism, Colonialism, and the Wild Man: A Study in Terror and Healing*. His most recent book is *Mimesis and Alterity: A Particular History of the Senses*.

Donna Torres is a Miami-based artist whose work explores ideas related to shamanism and shamanic inebriants. Research trips to South America have provided important sources of information for her painting. For fifteen years, she has studied the pre-Columbian culture of San Pedro de Atacama and, more recently, the Mataco in northern Argentina. She has participated in exhibits of visionary art in Mexico, Europe, and the United States, and some of her paintings have been used as cover art for books. She is currently a graduate student in fine arts at Florida International University in Miami, Florida.

William Torres C. is a Colombian anthropologist and serves as the Director of the *Fundación de Investigaciones Chamanistas* of Pasto, Colombia. He has carried out fieldwork among the Kogi and Arhuaco of the Sierra Nevada de Santa Marta, the Guambiano, Camëntsá and Inga of the southern Andean region of Colombia, the Sikuani of the Orinoco, and the Cofán, Muinane, Nukak, Siona, Witoto and Ticuna of the Colombian Amazon. He is the author of *Chamanismo: un arte del saber* and *Yagé: nomadismo del pensamiento*.

Mario Vargas Llosa, born in Arequipa, Peru in 1936, is one of Latin America's most prominent writers. He received a degree in Literature from the University of San Marcos in Lima and a doctorate from the University of Madrid. His numerous novels, which have been translated into more than twenty languages, include *The Green House, Conversation in the Cathedral, Aunt Julia and the Scriptwriter, The War of the End of the World, The Storyteller, The Real Life of*

Alejandro Mayta, and *In Praise of the Stepmother.* He is also the author of the critical study *La utopía arcaica: José María Arguedas y las ficciones del indigenismo.* In 1995 he was awarded the Jerusalem Prize. He now lives in London.

Mario Villafranca Saravia is a Peruvian short-story writer whose work was anthologized by Isabel Córdova Rosas in *Narradores de Junín.*

Steven F. White, born in Abingdon, Pennsylviania in 1955, is co-editor with Luis Eduardo Luna of the *Ayahuasca Reader.* He received a B.A. in English from Williams College as well as M.A. and Ph.D. degrees in Spanish from the University of Oregon. He has lived and worked in many Latin American countries, an opportunity that enabled him to edit bilingual anthologies of poetry from Nicaragua, Chile and Brazil. He also translated, with Greg Simon, Federico García Lorca's *Poet in New York.* He is the author of the critical study *Modern Nicaraguan Poetry: Dialogues with France and the United States.* Recent books of his poetry include *From the Country of Thunder, Paisagem com uma vela e abelhas assirias* (Florianópolis, Brazil) and *Fuego que engendra fuego* (Madrid). He has been teaching at St. Lawrence University since 1987, and is one of the co-founders of its Caribbean and Latin American Studies program.

Estanislao Yaiguaje was the son of the last great Siona shaman, Leonides Yaiguaje, who was famous throughout the Putumayo region. He attended the mission school as a child and was the only Siona who agreed to reproduce his drawings on paper. He commented that the colors in the designs do not capture the beauty of the colors seen in the visions. Each design represents the designs seen on the "other side" and which permeate the scenes that one is seeing — appearing on the clothing, benches, walls, and other spaces in the heavenly realms.

Ricardo Yaiguaje (1900–1985) was the son of one of the last great Siona master-shamans on the Putumayo River. Because of his father, he had the most experience in shamanic training among other men his age. While most of them were attending the mission school, his father kept him in the village to pursue his apprenticeship. In spite of his training with his father and other shamans in the region, he never attained the full status of master-shaman due to a series of misfortunes, which, according to Ricardo, were caused by other shamans who were jealous of his potential power as a shaman.

Co-editors Luis Eduardo Luna and Steven F. White at the exhibit "Visions that the Plants Gave Us," The Richard F. Brush Art Gallery, St. Lawrence University. Photograph © Matthew C. Siber.

GENERAL INDEX

---

* *We have included the scientific names in parentheses for plants that are well-known in botanical literature. In cases of doubt, we have left only the vernacular names.*

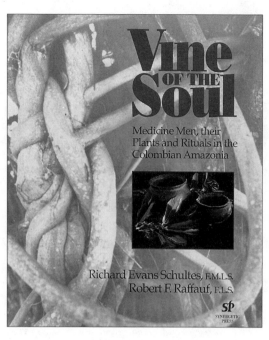

VINE OF THE SOUL
Medicine Men, their Plants and Rituals in the Colombian Amazonia

Richard Evans Schultes,
Director of the Botanical Museum (Emeritus), Harvard University
& *Robert Raffauf,* Professor of Pharmacognosy &
Medicinal Chemistry (Emeritus), Northeastern University

A companion volume to Schultes' classic *Where the Gods Reign,* this collaboration has created an exceptional photographic essay continuing his detailed descriptions of the Amazon Indians' use of medicinal and other sacred plant substances. Through over 160 documentary photographs taken mostly during the '40s and '50s and their commentaries, the reader is guided by these legendary scientists on a journey where healing with plants is the norm and where ritual and magic play an essential role in everyday life.

In addition to being a must book on the shelf for anyone interested in adventure, *Vine of the Soul* provides scientific, medical, environmental, and anthropological communities with up-to-date analysis of the chemistry and medicinal properties of Amazon flora (such as *ayahuasca,* "the vine of the soul"). Schultes and Raffauf offer us a feast of impressions and facts that will help to achieve, in Sir Ghillean Prance's words, "the ethnobotanical conservation of a rich heritage which is in great danger of disappearing forever."

> *"Quite simply a masterpiece . . .* Vine of the Soul *deserves to be read by everyone interested in rain forests, indigenous peoples, shamanism, hallucinogens, ethnomedicine, and conservation."*
> Mark Plotkin, President, Amazon Conservation Team (ACT)

> *"This latest collaboration brings together an extraordinary amount of information on the ethnobotany and phytochemistry of the plants used by the people of this region, and presents it in a way that is fascinating and inspiring to read."*
> Michael J. Balick, NY Botanical Garden, from the Epilogue

> *"We have here a wonderful integration of ethnobotany, chemistry and photography to produce a book that will long be an important historic record of one of the threatened cultures of the world. I hope that readers learning about* ayahuasca, *the "vine of the soul," and other psychoactive drugs discussed here will have their concern heightened for the future fate of the Amazon Indians and their societies."*
> Sir Ghillean T. Prance, Royal Botanical Garden, Kew, from the Foreword

Paperback, 288 pages • $22.95

> *"Who knows what plants of potential medical or other value, quite apart from their scientific interest, have already gone the way of the dodo?"*
> R. Darnley Gibbs (1974)

WHERE THE GODS REIGN
Plants and Peoples of the Colombian Amazon
Richard Evans Schultes
Director of the Botanical Museum (Emeritus), Harvard University
Foreword by **Mark Plotkin,** President of the Amazon Conservation Team (ACT)

This fascinating study in the field of ethnobotany is a complete anthropological overview of the Amazon rain forest ecosystem, containing chapters on the rivers, ethnic groups, cultural activities, rubber and coca plants, drugs and medicines, and others. By focusing on an excellent series of photographs taken by himself during the '40s and '50s accompanied by his own explanatory text, Dr. Schultes documents a unique resource of both biological and human development.

Dr. Schultes, Director Emeritus of the Botanical Museum of Harvard University, is the recipient of numbereous awards for his half century of contributions to science and ethnobotany, including the World Wildlife Fund Gold Medal and the Cross of Boyaca from the Republic of Colombia. *Where the Gods Reign* offers an irresistible opportunity to journey the mysterious Colombian Amazon with a most remarkable scientist and eloquent guide.

> *"Richard Schultes is a true ethnobotanist, the incarnation and almost the inventor of this discipline . . .* Where the Gods Reign *is a picture book, . . . of great beauty and tranquility . . . full of fascinating information."*
> Sir John Hemming, *Times Literary Supplement.*

> *"The numerous photographs are at once spectacular, beautiful, fascinating, and of excellent quality . . . It is likely that only Professor Schultes has had or ever will have the resources to produce such . . . a remarkable book."*
> Willard Van Adsall, *Journal of Ethnobiology*

Paperback, 312 pages • $20.00

WHITE GOLD
The Diary of a Rubber Cutter in Brazil
John C. Yungjohann; edited by Ghillean T. Prance

The crisis of the rain forest began a century ago when it was discovered to be a source of rubber. This brought commercial interests into collision with this complex ecology — its plants, its animals and its peoples. At the height of the rubber boom in the early years of this century, a young American, John Yungjohan, struggled for survival as a rubber cutter. The diaries he kept have recently come to light and have been edited by Professor Sir Ghillean Prance, former Director of the Royal Botanical Gardens at Kew, England, currently Director of Science for the Eden Project. Sir Ghillean Prance, a leading expert on the rain forest, enhances the text with his own contemporary photographs and identifies the fungi, plants and animals which are mentioned in the pages of the diaries.

> *"Readers of this journal will find this first hand account fascinating and will appreciate the efforts of a work weary rubber cutter to not only survive the experience but to write about it."*
> Willard Van Adsall, *Journal of Ethnobiology*

> *"It is thoroughly pleasing, easy reading, and would make a good supplement to a high school or college course that deals with economic plants or the Amazon . . . Plan on reading it in one sitting."*
> George K. Rogers, *Missouri Botanical Garden*

Paperback, 104 pages • $7.95

Books can be ordered on our web site at
www.synergeticpress.com, or through your local bookstore.

SYNERGETIC PRESS PUBLISHING
A Division of Global Ecotechnics Corporation
7 Silver Hills Road, Santa Fe, New Mexico 87505
TEL.: (505) 424-0237 • FAX: (505) 424-3336